D0221373

FLORIDA STATE
UNIVERSITY LIBRARIES

JUN 0 7 2001

TALLAHASSEE, FLORIDA

# Industrial Policy in Europe

What is the future for Europe's industries? What policies will be effective in promoting industrial growth?

After a decade or more of deregulation and the retreat of the state there is a growing consensus that government can make a positive contribution to industrial growth. This volume explores both the theoretical basis for industrial policy in Europe and practical proposals for making industrial development happen.

The volume is divided into five parts:

- the rationale for industrial policy and the argument for making it local and participative;
- creating meaningful local and regional economies: making localised learning a reality;
- nurturing small firms;
- creating adequate access to venture capital, especially for new small firms;
- creating the infrastructure and environment for a dynamic, diffuse economy.

The contributors include some of Europe's leading industrial economists, and they approach the subject on a micro, macro and meso level.

**Keith Cowling** is Professor of Economics at the University of Warwick. He is the editor, author or joint author of thirteen earlier books, and has published extensively on industrial economics in leading economics journals.

# Industrial development policy
Series editors: Patrizio Bianchi, Keith Cowling
and Roger Sugden

Europe is currently at a crucial stage in its economic, social and political development. This series addresses the challenges to European economic policy. It will explore the design of industrial economic strategies enabling European industries and regions to flourish and prosper as we begin the twenty-first century.

**Competitiveness, Subsidiarity and Industrial Policy**
*Edited by Pat Devine, Yannis Katsoulacos and Roger Sugden*

**Europe's Economic Challenge**
Analyses of Industrial Strategy and Agenda for the 1990s
*Edited by Patrizio Bianchi, Keith Cowling and Roger Sugden*

**The Impact of Privatisation**
Ownership and corporate performance in the UK
*Stephen Martin and David Parker*

**Economics of Structural and Technological Change**
*Edited by Gilberto Antonelli and Nicola De Liso*

**Industrial Policies and Economic Integration**
Learning from European Experiences
*Patrizio Bianchi*

**Latecomers in the Global Economy**
*Edited by Michael Storper, Stavros B. Thomadakis and Lena J. Tsipouri*

**Privatisation in the European Union**
Theory and Policy Perspectives
*Edited by David Parker*

# Industrial Policy in Europe

Theoretical perspectives and practical proposals

**Edited by Keith Cowling**

London and New York

HD
3816
.E823
I53
1999

First published 1999 by Routledge
11 New Fetter Lane, London EC4P 4EE

Simultaneously published in the USA and Canada
by Routledge
29 West 35th Street, New York, NY 10001

© 1999 Editorial matter and selection Keith Cowling; individual
chapters © their authors

*Routledge is an imprint of the Taylor & Francis Group*

Typeset in Times by The Florence Group, Stoodleigh, Devon
Printed and bound in Great Britain by St Edmundsbury Press,
Bury St Edmunds, Suffolk

All rights reserved. No part of this book may be reprinted or
reproduced or utilised in any form or by any electronic, mechan-
ical, or other means, now known or hereafter invented, including
photocopying and recording, or in any information storage or
retrieval system, without permission in writing from the publishers.

*British Library Cataloguing in Publication Data*
A catalogue record for this book is available from the British
Library

*Library of Congress Cataloging in Publication Data*
Industrial policy in Europe : theoretical perspectives and practical
proposals / edited by Keith Cowling.
p. c. — (Routledge series on industrial development policy)
'This book was fashioned out of papers presented at the Warwick
Conference of the European Network on Industrial Policy (EUNIP) in
December 1997'—Introd.
Includes bibliographical references and index.
1. Industrial policy—Europe—Congresses. 2. Small business—
Government policy—Europe—Congresses. 3. International business
enterprises—Government policy—Europe—Congresses. 4. Europe—
Economic conditions—1945- —Regional disparities—Congresses.
I. Cowling, Keith. II. Warwick Conference of the European Network
on Industrial Policy (1997 : University of Warwick) III. European
Network on Industrial Policy. IV. Series.
HD3616.E823I53  1999–02–20 338.94—dc21

98–37406

CIP
ISBN 0–415–20493–3 (hbk)
ISBN 0–415–20494–1 (pbk)

# Contents

# Figures

# Tables

# Contributors

**Philip Arestis**, University of East London

**Bjørn T. Asheim**, University of Oslo

**David Bailey**, University of Birmingham

**Gian Luca Baldoni,** University of Bologna

**Silvano Bertini,** University of Bologna

**Jonathan Cave**, University of Warwick

**Keith Cowling**, University of Warwick

**Marc Cowling**, University of Warwick

**Jacques De Bandt**, CNRS Université de Nice Sophia Antipolis

**Richard T. Harrison**, University of Ulster

**George Harte,** University of Edinburgh

**Cormac K. Hollingsworth**, Tokyo-Mitsubishi International plc

**Grazia Ietto-Gillies**, South Bank University, London

**Simon Lee**, University of Hull

**Richard Marriott**, Altain Financial Group

**Colin M. Mason**, University of Southampton

**Gordon Murray**, University of Warwick

**Christine Oughton**, University of Birmingham

**Gavin C. Reid**, University of St Andrews

**Malcolm Sawyer**, University of Leeds

**Hans Schenk**, Tilburg University

**Roger Sugden**, University of Birmingham

**Gerry Sweeney**, SICA Innovation Consultants Ltd

**Peter Totterdill**, The Nottingham Trent University

**Johan Willner**, Åbo Akademi University

# Acknowledgements

Early versions of the chapters in this volume were presented in a Workshop (at the University of Warwick) supported by the Commission of the European Community's Human Capital and Mobility Programme. We should like to acknowledge the support we have received under the Euroconference Contract Number ERBCHECCT93014 and Network Contract Number ERBCHRXCT940454.

# Part I

# Overview and redirection

# 1 Introduction

*Keith Cowling*

This book was fashioned out of papers presented at the Warwick Conference of the European Network on Industrial Policy (EUNIP) in December 1997 which focused on Practical Proposals for Industrial Policy in Europe. This particular meeting was the culmination of the first phase of EUNIP covering activities over the period since the launch of the project at a workshop at the University of Birmingham in September 1993. This first phase of the activity of EUNIP was funded largely by the European Union Human Capital Mobility Programme and included a PhD research programme as well as a series of workshops and conferences across Europe. EUNIP is continuing as a largely self-financed network which will sponsor an annual conference, the first being held in October 1998 at Universidad de Barcelona.

Over the first phase of EUNIP much was achieved in terms of creating an active and stimulating network of researchers concerned with industrial policy issues. The final meeting of the first phase sought to concentrate on *practical* proposals for industrial policy in Europe as a means of maximising the impact of the work of the network in evolving a particular approach to policy-making which we see as both new and exciting, but also particularly appropriate at this stage of Europe's development. We are endeavouring to descend from the ivory tower we have been occupying in order, hopefully, to capture the attention and interest of policy-makers for ideas which may appear sometimes rather divorced from the practical world of politics within which they have to operate. Undoubtedly this transition in our work will not be unproblematic, but at least we have seriously sought to achieve it, specifically in response to the constructive assessments of policy-makers made at our conference at the Royal Institute of International Affairs, Chatham House, London in June 1997.

Given that the general approach to policy-making by the network has evolved continuously over the past several years it seems useful to try and crystallise out the present stage in our thinking, whilst recognising that different individuals within the network will give particular emphasis to particular aspects of our collective approach. Undoubtedly the view presented here will represent a more accurate description of Keith Cowling's view on policy than that of other members of the network, but I hope that the views of others is fully encapsulated at least in the major features of the approach as identified below. This description of our approach also provides a framework for grouping the papers included in this volume (and indeed for their initial selection) and will indicate the lacunae which remain.

In practice so-called free market systems are planned: the strategic decisions of the dominant corporations give rise to their corporate strategies, the broad plans which are the crucial determinants of the activities with which they are associated. Moreover, strategic decision-making in these firms is concentrated in the hands of an elite. Quite who does and who does not control a firm has been the subject of intense debate, but a consensus view is that control rests with a subset of those having an interest in a firm's activities, and certainly does not rest with the firm's workforce. A systemic consequence of this situation is that free markets suffer from inherent difficulties. As systems they are necessarily plagued by strategic failures, defined as reasons for the strategic decision-making process in an economy preventing the attainment of a socially desirable outcome. It is precisely because free market systems concentrate strategic decision-making in the hands of a few that development paths based upon a dominant role for transnational corporations are inherently problematic. For example, it can be argued that transnationals manage international trade to suit their own strategic objectives, thereby throwing in doubt the extent to which 'free trade' is in truth free. Given that it is estimated that transnationals are responsible for approximately 75 per cent of the world's exports, important queries have to be raised about the implications of a 'free trade' system. The 'free' in free trade protects the negative freedom of strategic decision-makers from government intervention but emasculates the positive freedom of others to determine their own economic development. Free trade could mean that a firm is free to organise production activity across Europe in ways which enable it to divide and rule labour and governments, transfer price so as to minimise tax liabilities, whilst at the same time maintaining monopoly power in final product markets. The outcomes may not be desirable for the societies in which these firms do or do not operate, but in a world where transnationals are free to trade as they wish, it is left to an élite to decide the transnationals' strategies.

Thus, at the heart of free market systems, we may expect strategic failures which result in a stream of deficiencies. It would therefore seem essential to explore the possibility of creating development paths which avoid such failures. The obvious response is to tackle the source of failures head-on: to look for ways of appropriately involving more and more people affected by strategic decisions in the process of making these decisions, to design ways of democratising strategic decision-making. Obviously, this would be a long-term project requiring multi-dimensional change. In part this would need to be sought within the hierarchical structures of the big corporations, and Europe's social chapter could be seen as a tentative first step in this direction. Monitoring the activities of these firms would also be essential. Another

dimension of policy would need to be the nurturing of an alternative structure of production characterised by symmetric, horizontal relationships rather
than the asymmetric, hierarchical relations seen within the dominant mode of
production today: some form of small firm production.

Clearly, the presence of small firms is no guarantee of socially optimal
outcomes, but intuitively there is a sense in which democratic strategic decision-making appears more feasible if an economy comprises smaller firms.
Moreover, in recognising this it is notable that much recent literature has
focused on allegedly successful groupings of small firms, especially with
respect to innovation in the industrial districts of Italy. The idea of groupings of small firms is appealing because it is often argued that technology
requires production on a large scale to minimise cost and it is notable that
in some significant cases small firms have been able to cooperate to achieve
these economies without there having to be concentration of production in
one large, hierarchical organisation.

With these sorts of observations in mind it would seem constructive to
consider the possibility of creating webs of small firms, a large group of
production units which taken individually are quite small but which taken
as a group constitutes a production process on a large scale. The aim would
be for the units to cooperate by providing mutual support in a process which
also promotes the emergence of new and rival production units; the process
would be based on a culture in which the emphasis is on all people, individually and collectively, evolving and trusting in their ability to find
successful development paths, emphasising the development of every person
to realise his or her full potential. In contrast, the concentration of decision-making, within the existing system, channels people into particular
roles, excluding the majority from the most important decisions.

It is important to recognise that to be critical of the existing transna-
tionalism of the major corporations is not necessarily to advocate a narrow,
national or intra-national approach to policy-making. We would see the
development of multinational webs of small firms as part of an alternative
development path where people, and thus economies and societies, are able
to realise their full potential. Instead of internationalising production by hierarchical control and the concentration of decision-making, as transnational
corporations have done, the suggestions we are making would provide an
alternative process which would be non-hierarchical and would foster a
diffusion of decision-making: a bottom-up, multinational process of evolution. To say that a policy for encouraging small firms already exists is not
sufficient. It has to be clear that a policy exists which is appropriate to the
rapid evolution of suitable webs within which small firms can flourish by
retaining a relative anatomy. Anything less is simply giving a small-firm
label to a policy which at best serves the large firms by supplying a dependent periphery, a small-firm fringe.

We would argue that it is crucial in Europe that initiatives be pursued simultaneously at local, regional, national and pan-European levels to

develop webs, multinational webs and democratic strategic decision-making structures and processes more generally. The focus must always be on locality because community control over production is sought: without community control efficiency cannot, in general, be achieved. But to be effective community control must extend outwards to determining the shape of the national economy and the European economy, otherwise actors with a pan-European perspective and competence will undermine community autonomy. The transnationality, or potential transnationality, of the major corporations enables them to pit community against community in the pursuit of their ends. The thrust of strategy must be to create a Europe of the regions, a multinational European Union, to create a Europe of diversity and local autonomy, but within a collective vision for the whole continent. The enormous problems of eastern Europe, the persistent long-term unemployment in many parts of western Europe, the insecurity felt by more and more people throughout Europe, suggests to many that there must be a better way. The book attempts to offer a small contribution to its construction. Inevitably, not all the issues identified are tackled in this volume, but we have sought, within the framework of analysis we have outlined, to offer practical proposals for a way forward.

Within the approach to policy-making advocated above we present the papers in more or less coherent groups. Part I of the volume, 'Overview and redirection', provides this short introduction plus a paper demonstrating that targeting is an intrinsic feature of virtually all industrial policies (Cowling, Oughton and Sugden, Chapter 2), the real issue being the selection processes underpinning the chosen targets. Part II, 'Creating meaningful local and regional economies', groups five papers relating to dimensions of policy-making which we have identified as particularly crucial elements of any sort of industrial policy as we seek to root the development path of the economy within the community. The topics covered include sustainable regional development (Sweeney, Chapter 3), innovation and endogenous regional development (Asheim, Chapter 4), innovation in work organisation (Totterdill, Chapter 5), the case for a politically independent federal England (Lee, Chapter 6) and finally a case study of bottom-up regional policy-making (Bertini and Baldoni, Chapter 7). Part III, 'Nurturing small firm economies', relates very closely to issues of local and regional policy-making and this is reflected within the papers of both sections. Nurturing the economic development of the locality or region, we have argued, is closely related to the nurturing of a small firm economy. The papers comprise a broad-based paper on the creation of an entrepreneurial society (Marc Cowling, Chapter 8), a second on practical networking issues (De Bandt, Chapter 9), another on making small firms work (Reid, Chapter 10) and finally one identifying the creation of a small-firm economy as the creative answer to merger policy failure (Schenk, Chapter 11). Part IV on 'Venture capital' is again closely linked to the previous section, since finance is so often a crucial element in the success or failure of small firms: the two papers in this section provide an assessment of UK experience in the development of informal venture capital markets, and the lessons for Europe (Mason and Harrison, Chapter 12) and some practical guidance on policy initiatives for promoting early stage venture capital funds (Murray and Marriott, Chapter 13). Finally, Part V, 'Creating the infrastructure and economic environment for a dynamic, diffuse economy', offers a collection of papers dealing first with the internet as a potentially important enabling technology for a diffuse economy (Cave, Chapter 14), second, with the potential efficiency of a public enterprise infrastructure (Willner, Chapter 15), third, with various contributions on regulating the activities of the transnationals which would appear to be a crucial requirement for establishing and maintaining a small-firm economy of any significant autonomy (Bailey, Hart and Sugden, Chapter 16; Ietto-Gillies, Chapter 17; and Hollingsworth, Chapter 18), and a final contribution on an appropriate and complementary macroeconomic policy (Arestis and Sawyer, Chapter 19). To provide further, quick insight into all the papers included in the volume we allow the authors to speak for themselves: their abstracts follow.

## Chapter 2: A reorientation of industrial policy?
## Horizontal policies and targeting, by Keith Cowling, Christine Oughton and Roger Sugden

Recent industrial policy debate argues that there has been a reorientation of industrial policy away from sectoral measures towards horizontal policies. This paper assesses the extent and the basis of this shift and argues that popular perception of recent industrial policies is based on a false dichotomy between horizontal and sectoral initiatives. A review of British and European Union experience indicates a shift more apparent than real, both in terms of the emphasis on horizontal policies and the extent to which those policies actually constitute explicit targeting. Hence, the paper challenges conventional wisdom and sets out a more complex analysis which illustrates that targeting is an intrinsic characteristic of virtually all industrial policies. It follows that more rigorous discussion of industrial policy requires detailed analysis of the selection processes underlying industrial policy measures. Our analysis reveals that the much discredited approach of 'picking winners' represents only one particular kind of sectoral policy. While picking winners is unlikely to provide the basis for a successful industrial policy the same cannot be said of all sectoral policies: other types of industrial strategy based on targeting resources may significantly enhance industrial performance and economic well-being.

## Chapter 3: Sustainable regional development: new dimensions in policy formulation, by Gerry Sweeney

Sustainable development is a complex concept, embracing mutually reinforcing economic, socio-cultural and environmental development. Policy to promote sustainable development has not only to address these three dimensions but also to take account of a number of other phenomena. The environment is socially constituted. Its exploitation and conservation are dependent on the attitudes and values of society at large and of the local communities which live within a particular environment. Man's management of it is limited by its autonomous dynamism and fulfilled within the paradox that the global is managed locally. The environment is a local phenomenon as are the social communities on whose entrepreneurial and innovative dynamism national economies depend. Economic development and the technical progress which drives development is a local phenomenon, springing from the social capital of particular localities and it depends as much on organisational as on technological innovation. Technical progress has in fact been impeded in recent decades by a lack of organisational innovation, in government as well as in industry and business. There may now be a beginning of change. There is an emerging trend towards self-governance as local communities begin to take control of their own destiny and to undertake public functions, indicating not only an erosion of the determinist role of government but also the possible start of the organisational innovation on which a new wave of progress depends. A model is presented of the interactions between government policies and instruments on the one hand and the social capital of communities on the other. The factors which should guide government partnership with communities in stimulating new modes of self-governance and those which should influence policy-making are described. The model and key factors demonstrate how sustainable development might be achieved.

## Chapter 4: The territorial challenge to innovation and endogenous regional development, by Bjørn T. Asheim

The combined effect of understanding industrialisation as a territorial process (that is, the importance of agglomeration and 'non-economic' factors for economic development) and innovation as a social process (that is, an institutional and cultural embedded interactive learning process) has dramatically changed the basis for launching industrial and technology policies towards small and medium-sized enterprises (SMEs) with the intention of promoting endogenous regional development. While innovative, non-high-tech SMEs (for example, in industrial districts) previously were looked upon as dynamic but fragile exceptions from the modern high-tech-based path of industrialisation (for example, Silicon Valley) due to the threats of globalisation, this new understanding looks at innovative and competitive SMEs as a result of successful regionalisation strategies, that is, as an alternative way of achieving global competitiveness. This regionalisation strategy is based on: (a) learning as a localised process (arguing for the importance of historical trajectories and 'disembodied knowledge'); (b) innovation as an interactive learning process (involving a critique of the linear model of innovation and pointing to the importance of cooperation in promoting competitiveness); and (c) agglomeration as the most efficient basis for interactive learning (arguing for the importance of 'untraded interdependencies' and bottom-up, interactive regional innovation systems). Based on these theoretical propositions and empirical analyses of innovative activity of SMEs in industrial districts in the Third Italy and Norway, the paper concludes with a short discussion of implications for industrial and technology policies towards SMEs in networks in the context of a globalised, post-Fordist 'learning economy'.

## Chapter 5: Europe's advantage? Work organisation, innovation and employment, by Peter Totterdill

New ways of working, and new types of work, could transform Europe in the twenty-first century. There is now a clear opportunity to enhance the competitiveness of European businesses, to increase the performance of public services, and to raise both quality of life in the workplace and cooperation between social actors. At the same time new forms of work organisation can offer an important resource in the crucial struggle against unemployment in Europe. But the urgent task is to raise awareness as widely as possible of the need for innovation, and for a change from models based on cost-cutting and the reduction of deskilling of labour.

This paper is the product of active collaboration between some of the leading European organisations involved in the enhancement of working life and competitiveness. The European Work and Technology Consortium was originally created to prepare a Medium Term Plan for Collaborative Action at the request of Directorate-General V of the European Commission. Informed by the outcomes of this Plan, the partners are now actively engaged in collaborative research, development and dissemination in the field. Building on past achievements in each member state, the Consortium will provide an important vehicle for exchanging experience, promoting innovation and resourcing change throughout the EU.

The aim of the paper is to share a broad vision of how these goals can be achieved through partnership and cooperation at local, national and transnational levels. In particular it seeks to explain:

- why work organisation is an important issue for policy-makers, social partners, enterprises and other interests;
- how change can be successfully promoted;
- why the Consortium is a necessary part of the European picture.

The paper is also an invitation to social and economic partners, to industrial experts and to researchers who wish to join the debate and to collaborate with the Consortium in the transformation of work in Europe.

### Chapter 6:  The competitive disadvantage of England, by Simon Lee

This chapter contends that England suffers from a competitive political and economic disadvantage relative to the other constituent nations of the United Kingdom. This disadvantage has left England with parallel deficits in the public resources, institutions and policies with which attempts have been and are being made to improve the economic performance of the English regions. These deficits in turn reflect a more important wider deficit in England's national and regional identity. Because Englishness has been defined in terms of the institutions of the central British state, the English regions have been actively discouraged from developing their own distinctive identities. With the British Empire dismantled externally, there is no longer any justification for a domestic political settlement and the outmoded British identity that seeks to perpetuate it, nor indeed for the centralisation of political power in London and the maintenance of an industrial policy which promotes the interests of the City of London, the property market and the defence sector to the detriment of other sources of innovation, employment and economic growth in England. The conclusion drawn is that a politically independent federal England might offer a more effective constitutional framework for industrial policies to remedy England's competitive disadvantage.

### Chapter 7:  The activation of bottom-up methodologies in a newly opened regional economy: an experience in the Oeste region of Santa Catarina, Brazil, by Silvano Bertini and Gian Luca Baldoni

This contribution is a case study describing a project of regional policy realised according to a bottom-up approach, inspired by the Italian experience, in a marginal region of Brazil, a country that only in the last decade opened its economy to the Mercosur countries and to international competition. The project followed the typical approach for developing bottom-up policies: diagnosis, definition of objectives, definition of projects, local concertation and construction of consensus, and definition of criteria of intervention. The experts, in the definition of the strategy of the intervention, realised that the crucial factors for success were not only the projects themselves, but the establishment of an institutional network that could give continuity to the policy action and let local policy-makers monitor and adjust the projects in process, in order to respond to real needs of local beneficiaries.

## Chapter 8: The entrepreneurial society in practice, by Marc Cowling

The aim of this paper is to put forward a positive agenda for promoting an 'entrepreneurial society'. To achieve this, we consider how public policy towards entrepreneurship has evolved in the UK and then compare this with a number of other countries in the light of their experiences. At all times we keep one basic question in mind: Is there a role for government in terms of promoting and sustaining entrepreneurial activity? We conclude that there is no overall strategy *vis-à-vis* the development of a vibrant and dynamic entrepreneurial sector in the UK and that this has restricted the level of economic development. However, we do find clear evidence that the devolution of policy-making has led to increasingly innovative and flexible responses at the regional level.

## Chapter 9: Industrial policy in Europe: practical issues of networking and co-operation, by Jacques De Bandt

Typical cases of organisational failures are explored, in which potentially innovative SMEs don't have access to the required complementary competencies they lack. A bottom-up local industrial policy would consist of the creation of conditions and support systems enabling SMEs to compensate for existing organisational failures. Technological intermediation systems and specialised informational service provisions do not meet such requirements. The alternative solution is through the organisation of networking partnerships within specific competence blocs. Practical issues relate to the identification of partners and the organisation of cooperation. One particular issue is the level of complexity at which cooperative interactions among the actors can indeed be organised.

## Chapter 10: Making small firms work: policy dimensions and the Scottish context, by Gavin C. Reid

The basic framework of the discussion revolves around two samples of Scottish small firms for the periods 1985–8 and 1994–7. It is shown that both samples were drawn during similar (prosperous) phases of the macroeconomic cycle. Further evidence is advanced which indicates that grant and subsidy regimes have not been major determinants of survival and performance. However, the performance of small firms is shown to be better in the second sample period than in the first. If macroeconomic effects are neutral and grant/subsidy regimes are insignificant, then reasons for performance differences, it is argued, must lie elsewhere. A plausible source of this is the institutional framework. To this end, the evolution of institutional design for stimulating enterprise is documented and dated, and it is shown that the two sample periods fell within two distinct policy regimes. The first involved sectoral indicative planning, under the umbrella of the Scottish Development Agency (SDA), up until 1988. The second involved decentralised enterprise stimulation, under Scottish Enterprise (SE), from 1988 onwards. It is therefore suggested that at least part of the superior performance of small firms in the second sample period may be attributable to the new institutional framework, especially as modified by the Business Birth Rate Strategy.

## Chapter 11: Industrial policy implications of competition policy failure in mergers, by Hans Schenk

Most studies of merger results have not been able to find any positive effects of mergers and acquisitions on firm performance. Since economic systems which favour mergers therefore run a risk of jeopardising the real competitiveness of their firms *vis-à-vis* economic systems which favour investments in wealth-creating projects, this paper argues that a general policy presumption against mergers would be warranted. It is suggested that this would imply that a full efficiency test should be part of competition policies. However, since this will meet with substantial resistance, it is suggested for practical reasons that a restructuring and reorientation of industrial policies should compensate for the half-heartedness of current merger control policies. In particular, it is suggested that both the making and execution of industrial policies should be decentralised towards the lowest possible institutional level. Policies should focus on maximising *de novo* entry and increasing the chances for survival of SMEs by developing a virtual stock exchange on the internet with regional service and admissions counters.

## Chapter 12:  Public policy and the development of the informal venture capital market, by Colin M. Mason and Richard T. Harrison

The role of risk capital in facilitating entrepreneurship has recently emerged as a central issue in the debate on job creation in Europe, and the European Commission has introduced various measures to increase the number of early-stage venture capital funds. These developments have largely ignored the importance of the informal venture capital market, and none of the measures that the Commission has announced to increase the availability of risk capital have been targeted at this part of the financing spectrum.

However, the informal venture capital market plays a crucial role in the entrepreneurial process, both as the main source of start-up and early-stage venture capital and through the 'hands-on' involvement of investors, most of whom are themselves successful entrepreneurs. In the context of a growing recognition of the importance of the informal venture capital market in the Commission and some member states, this chapter considers how best to stimulate the informal venture capital market. It does so by providing a critical evaluation of the experience of the UK, which has taken the lead in Europe in measures to encourage informal venture capital activity. The main elements of UK policy are tax incentives and support for business angel networks. The chapter concludes that these measures have had a positive effect in stimulating the informal venture capital market in the UK but that there are shortcomings in their design and implementation. In the light of the UK's experience the chapter identifies the need for modifications to existing initiatives and proposes a range of additional measures which, it is argued, when taken together will result in a significant increase in informal venture capital activity over the medium term and, in turn, additional entrepreneurial activity.

## Chapter 13:  The liability of small-scale investment: a simulation model of the performance of an early stage, technology-focused, venture capital fund, by Gordon Murray and Richard Marriott

This paper initially identifies a major and contemporary policy concern, namely the disinclination of European venture capital firms to invest in start-up and early-stage technology-based firms. In both explaining and addressing this capital market failure, the authors seek to identify and model the key parameters which impact on the commercial performance of a specialist, technology focused, early-stage, venture capital fixed-term fund. Using both input (costs) and output (investment performance) data provided by a number of specialist independent venture capital firms, a spreadsheet simulation of a ten-year term fund is developed. Investment outcomes based on a 'decision tree' model are converted into cashflows. These figures are used to generate internal rate of return (IRR) and net present value (NPV) performance calculations for the investment commitments of the venture capital management company/general partner and the institutional investors/private partners in the fund.

The generically defined model allows the user to address both conceptual and pragmatic questions regarding the relationship between fund size, structure and performance. The effect on fund performance of two venture capital related, state support schemes (guarantee and leverage options) is also examined. The paper concludes that scale-related diseconomies are a major barrier to venture capital funds focusing on new technology-based firms. In the absence of a 'star' investment, funds of less than £20 million are particularly risky for the venture capital management company which claims a residual reward based on fund performance. While both state-supported leverage and guarantee schemes can play a valuable role in mitigating the negative consequences of small fund size, the authors argue that equity leverage schemes are more likely to meet the desired outcomes of the state.

## Chapter 14:  Universal service, universal access and the Internet, by Jonathan Cave

The perennial topic of universal access/service policy is receiving renewed attention as a result of the growth of the electronic highway. This reflects the fact that some services available over the Internet are regarded as candidates for universal provision or targeted subsidies and the related observation that competition on the Internet and elsewhere is undercutting provider subsidies for universal access/service: conventional providers face eroding profit margins while universal access/service pay-or-play obligations give Internet competitors a regulatory cost advantage that is strengthened by the non-economic pricing of Internet access and usage. Some view these developments as arguments for subjecting Internet service providers to pay-or-play universal access/service obligations while for others the innate efficiency of alternative providers and the nearly complete solution of the access problem signal the end for policy in this area. This paper develops some of the resulting policy issues. It concentrates on two technological possibilities: internet voice telephony (IVT) and electronic mail (e-mail). Beginning with the arguments for universality, it moves on to describe elements of policy most affected by new technologies: the service bundle; eligible group(s); provider(s); and the payment mechanism(s). After a summary of current developments in the economics of messaging and policy initiatives, it concludes with a discussion of general policy and the specific issues of network standards, interconnection, portability and marginal customers.

## Chapter 15:  Market structure, corporate objectives and cost efficiency, by Johan Willner

Privatisation and deregulation are usually motivated by the view that public ownership is inefficient, in particular under conditions of monopoly. However, while a market with a large number of private entrepreneurial firms can be expected to perform well, it is not certain that a welfare-maximising public monopoly becomes more efficient by being privatised and replaced by an oligopoly. The tendency to privatise is partly based on the view that only reward and punishment matter. However, the analysis suggests that privatisation would under such conditions increase the amount of slack in a managerial firm, if efficiency were affected at all. Budget cuts might reduce the efficiency of a utility that is provided free of charge. An increase in the number of oligopolists is also likely to reduce cost efficiency. The reason why private companies can perform well in practice might actually be the fact that this narrow view of human motivation is flawed. The analysis is therefore amended so as to include intrinsic work motivation as well. Some empirical evidence and practical conclusions are also discussed.

## Chapter 16: Regulating transnationals: free markets and monitoring in Europe, by David Bailey, George Harte and Roger Sugden

This chapter examines the development of the so-called free market economy and the position of transnational firms as central actors therein. It argues that the increasing negative freedom of élite strategic decision-makers within transnationals increases the risks of strategic failure. The chapter highlights two key dimensions of strategic failure at the European level: the divide and rule of government and communities by transnationals; and the intensification of centripetal tendencies. It suggests that just as transnationals are central to the unfolding, negatively free market economy, so too they should be central to the design of an industrial strategy which seeks to democratise decision-making and to tackle systemic failure in the nature of free markets. A proposed first step is the creation of monitoring bodies at different levels of government across Europe. Such bodies could investigate the impact of transnationals on economies, and in doing so network with other community actors. Policy debate could be catalysed and alternative forms of internationalism might be promoted, linking corporate and community bodies in the development of multinational webs.

## Chapter 17: Industrial strategy in the era of transnationals: analysis and policy issues, by Grazia Ietto-Gillies

The paper discusses some elements related to transnational companies and their activities, which are considered relevant in developing a strategy for industrial policy. They range from complementarity between trade and foreign direct investment, to the new configuration of international integration based on activities of transnationals, to issues of diversification of activities by nation-states and by mode of penetration into a market. This is followed by a discussion of advantages of multinationality particularly in relations to other players in the economic system such as uninational companies, consumers, labour and governments. Emphasis is laid on the transnationals' ability to operate across different nation-states, and thus different regulatory regimes, and on the need to shift the focus of analysis from the cost of multinationality to its advantages. A discussion on areas which require further research is followed by some suggestions for an industrial policy framework which stresses the following: countervailing power for other economic players; concentration on the degree of multinationality rather than nationality of ownership; analysis of the impact of profits from foreign investment as well as of the effects of foreign direct investment itself.

## Chapter 18: Multinational enterprise investment and industrial policy, by Cormac K. Hollingsworth

This chapter discusses recent policies attracting MNE investment to Europe, in particular the UK. These policies have involved payments of subsidies to MNEs to encourage their investment in economically depressed areas. The chapter describes a simple model which suggests that development agencies should not be over-reliant on MNEs to encourage economic development. In fact, encouraging MNE investment together with measures to encourage independent locally based development seems the most sensible policy.

## Chapter 19: The macroeconomics of industrial strategy, by Philip Arestis and Malcolm Sawyer

The purpose of this chapter is to explore the macroeconomics of industrial strategy. In particular, it is argued that an industrial strategy can potentially ease the constraints of capacity which lie behind inflationary pressures and the foreign trade position on the achievement of full employment. An implicit assumption behind our approach is that high levels of demand can help to underpin an industrial strategy and its promotion of investment and economic change.

There has been a general separation between macroeconomic analysis and industrial economics. At the academic level, with a few exceptions, macroeconomic analysis has proceeded with little regard to the industrial economics literature. This is not another way of saying that macroeconomics did not have microeconomic foundations. It is rather that the foundations which have been most often used have been those of atomistic competition. It is also the case that there has been a general focus on the operation of labour markets rather than of product markets. For its part, the study of industrial economics has generally ignored macroeconomic considerations.

Our general approach is a post-Keynesian one, which has two particular implications in the context of this chapter. First, the level of aggregate demand is viewed as relevant for the level of economic activity, and also for the rate of investment, which in turn determines the future productive capacity of the economy. Second, the labour market is given little role in the determination of the level of employment (and indeed we would cast doubt on the usefulness of the notion of a labour market).

# 2 A reorientation of industrial policy?

## Horizontal policies and targeting

*Keith Cowling, Christine Oughton and Roger Sugden\**

## Introduction

In the early 1980s discussion of industrial policy was dominated by privatisation and deregulation while open discussion of positive industrial policy (Jacquemin, 1987) slipped quietly off the political and academic agenda.[1] The 1990s saw a return to public debate over the nature of industrial policy with the publication of the Competitiveness White Papers in the UK and Europe. However, it is frequently argued that the new industrial policies, for example, the competitiveness policies of the 1990s, represent a reorientation away from sectoral initiatives towards horizontal industrial policies. Whilst once the fashion was for industrial policies which favoured the targeting of particular sectors, the current trend is to reject such an approach. The targeting of sectors is rejected on the basis that it is impossible to 'pick winners', it being, perhaps, safer to adopt apparently neutral policies which might enable industry more generally to flourish and prosper. For example, Porter (1990, p. 675) expresses popular sentiment:

> policy must shift to much more indirect forms of government assistance designed to support efforts by *any* industry to upgrade its demand conditions, human resources and scientific expertise. Government also has a legitimate and important role in encouraging the development of particular skills or technologies that are important to upgrading in a *substantial number of industries*.

Our aim in this paper is to consider the extent and basis for horizontal policies. We discuss the shift to horizontal measures in the context of British

\* A first draft of this paper was written whilst one of the authors was visiting the University of Wisconsin – Milwaukee (UWM); we would like to acknowledge the support provided under the co-operation agreement between UWM and the University of Birmingham. We would also like to acknowledge the helpful comments and suggestions from participants at the *European Network on Industrial Policy* Warwick Workshop, December 1997.

and European Union experience, pointing out that the shift is nowhere near complete and indeed has not gone as far as some might presume. Moreover, we question the degree to which horizontal policies are non-sectoral, suggesting that actually they are a form of targeting. Once this is recognised, it is our view that possibly more appropriate forms of targeting should be considered. To adopt such an approach would not be a return to the allegedly bad old days of picking winners but it might be a move towards a more efficient and dynamic economy.

## The shift to horizontal policies

Industrial policy measures may be classified into two types of intervention: sectoral and horizontal.[2] Sectoral measures are designed to influence the performance of different industries or sectors within the economy while horizontal measures aim to influence the overall performance of the economy and the competitive framework in which firms operate. Policies directed at education and the science base; support for generic technologies such as information technology; and monopolies, mergers, competition and international trade initiatives: all fall into this latter category, although this does not necessarily preclude their specific use at the industry or sector level.

Every economy is faced with limited resources and indeed the fundamental economic problem is to address the allocation and distribution of *scarce* resources. It is precisely because resources are limited that policies for supporting particular sectors has appeal. There is variation across sectors in terms of impact on economic performance. It might therefore seem instinctively reasonable to concentrate resources in those sectors offering maximum pay-off to an economy. However, the immediate retort to this argument is that in practice it is *impossible* to design a policy for successful targeting, not least because the appropriate sectors *cannot* be identified.

This has been seen as the impossibility of picking winners (Burton, 1983; Schultze, 1983). The presumption is that public policy is essentially designed and implemented by bureaucrats, and nowhere in the world is there a set of bureaucrats with the expertise, knowledge, imagination or entrepreneurial flair that qualifies them to identify appropriate sectors. We have sympathy with this view of bureaucrats and indeed would not ourselves advocate a picking-winners approach.

Pitelis (1993, p. 3) identifies such an approach as a cornerstone of British experience and as one which ended in failure:

> throughout the post World War II period, industrial policy by consecutive British governments was highly interventionist. The main form this intervention has taken, most notably in the 1960s, was a focus on *large size* and on '*picking winners*' ('*national champions*') . . . There is wide consensus now that these policies have been a failure; among others, because of the very nature of the problem of 'picking winners'.

British industrial policy in the 1980s was based on the view that there was a need for microeconomic reform in the form of a sharpening of incentives (Walker and Sharp, 1991) and correction of government failure (Pitelis, 1993). This period was characterised by a withdrawal of support measures, privatisation and, in the case of Britain, a decline in regional expenditures as industrial policy became more centralised. The withdrawal of support was accompanied by an abeyance of industrial policy debate until concern over the relative economic performance of both the UK and European economies sparked renewed interest in sources of competitiveness and the role of the state. The competitiveness papers published in 1994 (DTI, 1994; CEC, 1994) both identify improvements in per capita income (standards of living) as a policy objective. In addition the EU paper has a wider set of policy objectives which include employment creation and raising the investment share. While both the UK and EU White Papers document a number of detailed and specific policy measures, emphasis is placed on the need to create the right *underlying* conditions to allow industry to flourish. Hence, ostensibly the White Papers signal a reorientation from sectoral to horizontal and generic industrial policy.

However, this reorientation would appear to be by no means absolute. Consider, for example, the objective maintained in both the UK and EU White Papers to raise GDP per capita (living standards). This objective could be achieved by a number of routes. One possibility would be to target or diversify resources into high value-added or high growth sectors.[3] Plainly, such an approach would be sectoral by nature but it need not exclude generic policies such as those designed to raise educational standards or encourage the widespread adoption of information technology. Of course, technology policy may be both generic and specific. However, the popular view that the comparative advantage of advanced economies lies in knowledge-intensive industries suggests that technology policy might usefully be directed at those industries rather than at others. A second possibility would be to encourage improvements in productivity across all industries. Such a policy might arguably involve horizontal measures but it is important to recognise that while some industry/firm barriers to growth/improvement may be generic (for example, poor management), other obstacles to improvement are likely to be industry or sector specific, for example, skill shortages in particular sectors and particular localities or regulatory requirements. Hence some elements of sector-specific policy, and in this sense targeting seems inevitable.

Finally, a strong argument for targeting turns on the question of the efficiency of different types of intervention. That is, an efficient industrial policy should ideally target resources in initiatives that are likely to have the highest return. While it may be desirable to aim to catalyse improvement in performance across all industries, the cost of attaining a given level of improvement may vary widely across industries. Indeed, the fact that both potential productivity growth and technological opportunity differ across sectors provides an argument for concentrating resources where they are likely to have most impact. Given that resources are limited, policy should arguably be targeted so that objectives, such as raising productivity growth, are met at minimum cost.[4]

What these examples illustrate is that there is no clear dichotomy between sectoral and horizontal measures even in cases where the objectives of industrial policy are generic rather that sector specific. It is, therefore, important to note that while the *objectives* of industrial policy may have shifted away from the sector-specific support towards more generic support (which may entail a wider range of measures), the instruments and implementation of industrial policy still incorporate significant sectoral elements.

Of course, sectoral policy does not have to be a policy of national champions. A notable general exception is agricultural policy on research, development and innovation. Here, policy has been directed at supplying an atomistic industry with the results of public research. And the outcome has been striking: performance, as measured by labour productivity growth, has been *more than three times better* in this industry than for UK industry as a whole (see van Ark, 1996). The same sort of relative performance is seen in Denmark, France, Germany, The Netherlands, Sweden and the United States; the only exception is Spain.

The persistence of sectoral policy can be seen from an analysis of the data in Tables 2.1 and 2.2. Table 2.1 shows that while there was a decline in overall United Kingdom industrial support in the early 1980s, the decline in sectoral support was by no means complete. Expenditure on the civil aircraft industry increased significantly between 1979 and 1990 and expenditure on shipbuilding remained roughly constant (see Table 2.1). Similarly, it is evident that between 1977–8 and 1983–4 assistance to British Leyland alone outstripped combined assistance on national measures and technology support, although it is important to note that this expenditure arose not out of a positive policy of attempting to 'pick winners' but as a result of a reactive policy designed to salvage a 'loser'. Table 2.1 also illustrates the sector specificity of the UK's technology policy in the 1980s. Finally, it is important to note that significant support was targeted at the export sector between 1978–9 and 1990–1 and that regional measures, which were also significant in this period were often targeted at certain sectors.

Table 2.2 reports European Commission data on state aid to the industrial sector. While there is evidence of a decline in some elements of sectoral support, for example, a fall in the proportion of expenditure going to shipbuilding in the early 1990s, the table reveals that the proportion of state aid spent on 'horizontal objectives' remained constant between 1988–90 and 1990–2 and declined from 45 per cent to 35 per cent between 1990–2 and 1992–4. The proportion going to so-called sectoral aids *increased* from 20 to 25 per cent between 1988–90 and 1990–2 and then declined to 17 per cent in 1992–4. This suggests that there are aspects of the UK's shift to horizontal measures that might be more apparent than real.

A similar picture emerges across Europe. Table 2.3 illustrates that, for the European Community as a whole, the proportion of state aid devoted to horizontal measures declined from 42 per cent in 1988–90 to 29 per cent in 1992–4; sectoral measures declined from 20 to 15 per cent between 1988–90 and 1990–2, but then rose to 17 per cent between 1992 and 1994. Hence, the data provide little evidence of a shift from sectoral to horizontal policy measures; rather, the most marked trend is the increase in regional measures which now account for over half of all EU state aid to industry. Moreover, it is evident that the decline in horizontal measures and the 'U-shaped' movement in sectoral aid, have been accompanied by a trend increase in the proportion of *ad hoc* state aid given to individual enterprises. *Ad hoc* aid to individual enterprises can fall under any of the three categories shown in Tables 2.2 and 2.3 since any of these measures can be used to support individual companies. The proportion of *ad hoc* aid in total aid is shown in Table 2.4, which indicates that there has been a significant increase in aid to single companies and, as the Commission notes, 'a limited number of individual aids of important volume are responsible for a disproportionate part of total aid granted' (CEC, 1997, p. 22). The bulk of this aid is given for the rescue and restructuring of companies and may be used to support ailing companies or national champions. In short, rather than providing evidence of a shift in European industrial policy away from the support of individual companies and/or individual sectors towards a more general set of horizontal policy measures, the data point to the persistence of sectoral measures, an increase in *ad hoc* subsidies and a decline in horizontal initiatives.

Sectoral elements of industrial policy also form a central part of UK science and technology policy. Expenditure on R&D has a heavy sectoral bias; over 50 per cent of the government's R&D budget is spent on two sectors: defence and civil aerospace. At the same time, it is evident that the Technology Foresight exercise and the subsequent Foresight programme are sectorally based policies that have echoes of the (discredited) 'picking winners' approach.

The publication of the Office of Science and Technology (1993) White Paper, *Realising Our Potential: A Strategy for Science, Engineering and Technology*, signalled a shift in Britain's science and technology policy by placing greater emphasis on applied and commercial research (as opposed to basic research) and encouraging closer links between industry and the science base (primarily by permitting greater government and industry control over basic research). The White Paper starts from the observation that while the science base in Britain is strong by international standards its full potential is not realised by industry because of poor links between the industrial sector and the science base. Hence, it follows that policy should be directed at encouraging closer affiliation between industry and public and private research organisations in order to speed up the rate of commercialisation of basic research. This approach may be criticised on a number of grounds. First, no evidence is presented to show that links between

*Table 2.1* UK gross industrial assistance, 1975–90 (£m, current prices)

| | 1975/6 | 1976/7 | 1977/8 | 1978/9 | 1979/80 | 1980/1 | 1981/2 | 1982/3 | 1983/4 | 1984/5 | 1985/6 | 1986/7 | 1987/8 | 1988/9 | 1989/90 | 1990/1 |
|---|---|---|---|---|---|---|---|---|---|---|---|---|---|---|---|---|
| **National assistance** | | | | | | | | | | | | | | | | |
| Investment grants | 65.4 | 26.7 | 6.1 | 2.3 | 1.4 | 0.5 | | | | | | | | | | |
| Special employment measures | 4.0 | 95.0 | 181.0 | 151.0 | 111.0 | 377.0 | 261.0 | 231.0 | 118.0 | 41.0 | 32.0 | 27.0 | 15.0 | 6.0 | | |
| Accelerated projects scheme | | | | | | 3.7 | 10.9 | 6.5 | 0.4 | | | | | | | |
| Selected investment scheme | | 7.8 | 14.8 | 15.3 | 11.2 | 20.5 | 32.8 | 11.9 | 8.2 | 5.0 | 1.9 | | | | | |
| Support for major projects | | | | 3.1 | 11.0 | 0.2 | 1.4 | 4.4 | 7.2 | 11.9 | 10.2 | 10.3 | 3.8 | 2.1 | 1.4 | 1.7 |
| Energy conversion | | | | | 2.1 | 6.7 | 9.3 | 7.0 | | | | | | | | |
| Coal firing scheme | | | | | | | | | | | | | | 1.9 | 1.0 | 0.1 |
| Consultancy initiatives | | | | 0.1 | | | 0.1 | 1.8 | 4.2 | 10.1 | 12.3 | 11.1 | 4.3 | 10.8 | 35.6 | 41.2 |
| **Industrial support** | | | | | | | | | | | | | | | | |
| ICL (R) | 10.0 | | | | | | 200.0 | | | | | | | | | |
| Hotels and tourism (R) | 2.3 | 0.7 | 0.3 | 0.1 | 0.1 | | | | | | | | | | | |
| Mineral exploration grants (R) | 0.2 | 0.1 | 0.1 | 0.2 | 0.5 | 0.7 | 1.4 | 0.7 | 0.5 | 0.6 | 0.7 | | | | | |
| Section 8 loans (R) | 4.5 | 15.7 | 14.0 | 15.0 | | | | | | | | | | | | |
| Section 8 grants | 0.8 | 21.5 | 2.0 | 17.5 | | | | | | | | | | | | |
| Sectoral schemes | 3.2 | 7.1 | 20.4 | 45.2 | 50.2 | 45.8 | 17.1 | 6.8 | 1.6 | 0.6 | 0.1 | | | | | |
| Offshore supplies IRG scheme | 1.1 | 5.4 | 11.7 | 14.3 | 19.8 | 27.9 | 22.2 | 24.1 | 22.6 | 17.7 | 9.1 | 4.1 | 0.3 | | | |
| British Leyland | | | 325.0 | 174.0 | 150.0 | 300.0 | 520.0 | 360.0 | 90.0 | | | | | | | |
| NEB/BTG (R) | | | 27.0 | 39.0 | 70.0 | 49.0 | 39.0 | 37.0 | 8.0 | | | | | | | |
| Private sector scheme | | | | | | | | 10.3 | 14.8 | 4.4 | 2.7 | | | | | |
| Steel castings rationalisation | | | | | | | | | 7.1 | | | | | | | |
| **Technology support** | | | | | | | | | | | | | | | | |
| Microelectronics industry support pr. 1 | | | | | 1.2 | 1.3 | 3.7 | 11.7 | 10.7 | 16.4 | 11.7 | 0.7 | 0.2 | | | |
| Microelectronics industry support pr. 2 | | | | | | | | | | 1.8 | 5.5 | 7.5 | 4.6 | 7.5 | 2.4 | 0.8 |
| Small engineering firms inv. subsidy I | | | | | | | | 10.9 | 8.4 | 3.8 | 2.9 | | | | | |
| Small engineering firms inv. subsidy II | | | | | | | | | | 26.3 | 6.0 | | | | | |
| Flexible manufacturing scheme | | | | | | | | | 15.9 | 4.1 | | | | | | |
| Robot support programme | | | | | | | | | 1.0 | 5.1 | | | | | | |
| Advanced manufacturing technology | | | | | | | | | 1.5 | 8.5 | 10.6 | 13.7 | 5.9 | 4.0 | 3.1 | 0.3 |
| Fibre optics scheme | | | | | | | | | 8.2 | 11.6 | 3.9 | 4.2 | 2.6 | 0.8 | 0.7 | |
| CADTES | | | | | | | | | 6.7 | 11.2 | 3.9 | 0.1 | | | | |
| Innovation linked investment scheme | | | | | | | | | | 0.5 | 0.6 | 0.3 | 0.1 | | | |
| Other | | | 4.2 | 13.2 | 29.8 | 36.4 | 56.2 | 65.8 | 70.0 | 65.2 | 109.3 | 110.7 | 97.6 | 80.1 | 67.4 | 63.4 |

Table 2.1 Continued

| | 1975/6 | 1976/7 | 1977/8 | 1978/9 | 1979/80 | 1980/1 | 1981/2 | 1982/3 | 1983/4 | 1984/5 | 1985/6 | 1986/7 | 1987/8 | 1988/9 | 1989/90 | 1990/1 |
|---|---|---|---|---|---|---|---|---|---|---|---|---|---|---|---|---|
| **Civil aircraft** | | | | | | | | | | | | | | | | |
| Concorde | 68.0 | 46.0 | 48.0 | 42.0 | 23.0 | 36.0 | 35.0 | 13.0 | | | | | | | | |
| Launch aid (R) | | | | | | | | 10.0 | 10.7 | 64.3 | 81.6 | 91.7 | 102.1 | 99.0 | 123.0 | 107.0 |
| **Shipbuilding assistance** | | | | | | | | | | | | | | | | |
| Shipbuilders' relief | 6.2 | 8.0 | 12.8 | 10.8 | 11.0 | 15.8 | 8.8 | 18.3 | 14.0 | 13.5 | 22.7 | 8.4 | 11.0 | 8.7 | 10.3 | 12.1 |
| Section 7 loans (R) | 29.0 | 0.6 | 7.7 | | | | | | | | | | | | | |
| Section 7 grants | 5.3 | 4.0 | 24.0 | 2.5 | 2.4 | | | | | | | | | | | |
| Section 7 equity | 0.5 | 0.3 | 18.0 | | | | | | | | | | | | | |
| Home credit scheme (R) | 182.2 | 145.9 | 134.2 | 205.3 | 148.1 | 225.2 | 298.2 | 181.7 | 157.1 | 130.0 | 240.1 | 28.8 | 77.3 | 204.4 | 140.0 | 213.1 |
| Construction grant scheme | 4.2 | 1.0 | 0.5 | 0.3 | 0.1 | 0.1 | 0.3 | | | | | | | | | |
| Cost escalation scheme (R) | | 13.1 | 2.3 | | 22.6 | 2.0 | 0.7 | | | | | | | | | |
| Refund guarantees (R) | 20.1 | | 12.2 | | | | | | | | | | | | | |
| Intervention fund | 1.4 | 1.4 | 19.3 | 10.8 | 32.0 | 42.0 | 49.0 | 48.0 | 36.2 | 20.1 | 25.9 | 6.6 | 31.6 | 51.4 | 37.7 | 17.4 |
| **Regional policy** | | | | | | | | | | | | | | | | |
| Building grants | 10.9 | 1.5 | | | | | | | | | | | | | | |
| Discretionary grants | 0.1 | | 0.3 | | | | | | | | | | | | | |
| Operational grants | 2.5 | | | | | | | | | | | | | | | |
| Investment grants | 5.5 | 2.4 | 0.6 | 0.6 | 0.1 | 0.5 | 0.2 | 0.1 | | | | | | | | |
| Regional employment premium | 215.1 | 216.8 | | | | | | | | | | | | | | |
| Regional development grant | 324.9 | 407.7 | 393.4 | 416.9 | 330.8 | 490.5 | 616.8 | 689.6 | 438.9 | 410.7 | 319.7 | 196.3 | 118.7 | 75.5 | 41.3 | 18.7 |
| RSA – loans and equity (R) | 41.7 | 21.5 | 9.1 | 6.9 | 1.5 | 0.1 | 0.1 | 0.1 | | | | | | | | |
| – grants | 22.3 | 20.6 | 9.1 | 6.9 | 1.5 | 0.1 | 0.1 | 0.1 | 8.8 | 6.1 | 6.1 | 3.1 | 2.4 | | | |
| SIRG/OSIS | 1.0 | 1.7 | 2.2 | 3.1 | 3.4 | 5.4 | 5.7 | 5.2 | | | | 2.4 | | 1.3 | 0.1 | |
| Exchange risk guarantee scheme (R) | | | | 42.5 | 123.6 | 90.6 | 62.0 | 39.1 | 97.2 | 72.3 | 7.5 | 28.0 | 54.0 | 70.0 | 130.0 | 101.0 |
| Business improvement grant | | | | | | | | | | 0.2 | 8.4 | 14.6 | 18.4 | 15.5 | 11.4 | 2.1 |
| Revised RDG | | | | | | | | | | | 38.6 | 116.4 | 151.9 | 221.8 | 162.6 | 110.9 |
| REG – investment | | | | | | | | | | | | | | 1.1 | 5.9 | 8.6 |
| – innovation | | | | | | | | | | | | | | 0.3 | 2.2 | 4.0 |
| Consultancy initiatives | | | | | | | | | | | | | | 1.0 | 3.2 | 3.7 |

Source: Wren (1996, Table 2).

Notes: NEB = National Enterprise Board, BTG = British Technology Group, RSA = Regional selective assistance, SIRG = Service industry removal grant, OSIS = Office and service industry scheme, REG = Regional enterprise grant, R = Assistance is fully or partially recoverable, in principle.

*Table 2.2* UK state aid to industry, 1988–94: breakdown by sector and function (as % of total)

| Sector/function | 1988–90 | 1990–92 | 1992–94 |
|---|---|---|---|
| Horizontal objectives | 45 | 45 | 35 |
|   R&D | 8 | 7 | 16 |
|   Environment | n/a | 1 | 0 |
|   SME | 12 | 15 | 7 |
|   Trade/export | 15 | 15 | 7 |
|   Economisation of energy | n/a | 0 | 0 |
|   General investment | 9 | 6 | 3 |
|   Other objectives | 1 | 0 | 0 |
| Sectoral aids | 20 | 25 | 17 |
|   Shipbuilding | 7 | 2 | 0 |
|   Other sectors | 13 | 23 | 17 |
| Regional objectives | 34 | 30 | 48 |
| Total | 100 | 100 | 100 |

*Source*: CEC (1992, 1995, 1997).

*Notes*: n/a denotes not available.
Figures may not sum exactly due to rounding.

the science base and industry in Britain are worse than in other countries. Moreover, even if links in the UK could be shown to be worse than those in other leading economies, this does not necessarily imply that it is these links alone that determine the rate of commercialisation; other factors, such as short-termism in the financial system may also be relevant.

Second, the fact that Britain's science base remains strong by international standards, while British industrial performance shows signs of weakness (as UK per capita income has fallen behind that of our main competitors), suggests that it may be unwise to hand industry (whose performance has slipped by international standards) greater control over the science base (Edgerton and Hughes, 1995). That is, the relatively low rate of innovation within British industry may reflect problems within industry or the financial/industry nexus. If this is the case, handing industry greater control

*Table 2.3* State aid to industry in the European Community (EUR-12), 1988–94: breakdown by main objective (as % of total)

| | 1988–90 | 1990–92 | 1992–94 |
|---|---|---|---|
| Horizontal objectives | 42 | 35 | 29 |
| Particular sectors | 20 | 15 | 17 |
| Regional objectives | 38 | 50 | 53 |
| Total | 100 | 100 | 100 |

*Source*: CEC (1992, 1995, 1997).

*Note*: Figures may not sum exactly due to rounding.

*Table 2.4* State aid to industry in the European Community, 1990–4: annual values in constant prices, 1993 (ECU millions)

|  | *1990* | *1991* | *1992* | *1993* | *1994* |
|---|---|---|---|---|---|
| Amounts including *ad hoc* cases | 43,777 | 39,827 | 41,196 | 43,890 | 42,830 |
| Amounts excluding *ad hoc* cases | 40,614 | 34,590 | 34,282 | 31,821 | 27,344 |
| *Ad hoc* cases as a percentage of overall industry aid | 7 | 13 | 17 | 27 | 36 |

*Source*: CEC (1997, table 8).

over research and invention within the science base is unlikely to improve industrial performance. Indeed, it may even have undesirable effects such as distorting the relationship between basic and applied research and encouraging incremental innovation at the expense of major breakthroughs or 'epoch-making innovations'.

Third, the policy proposals that followed from the White Paper, namely the Technology Foresight Programme were grounded in a sectoral policy that aimed to identify and promote new technology across sectors through the establishment of 15 sector panels with members drawn from industry, government and academia. It has been argued (Edgerton and Hughes, 1995) that the policy of establishing sector panels to chart out areas for future research misunderstands the inherent uncertainty surrounding innovative activity. It follows that in practice the policy is likely to result in 'crude technocratic direction' – a return to the old policy of 'picking winners', only this time directed at the science base rather than at industry.

Technology policy is also seen as a cornerstone of the European Union's horizontal approach. Prior to the 1980s the European Union had little to do with technology policy. However, declining market shares for most European producers of technology (for example, by 1982 US firms had captured 80 per cent of the European market for computers (Woolcock, 1984)) prompted the Commission to consult with the 12 leading European technology firms to develop a strategy to regain market share in emerging and high-technology sectors. Peterson (1996, p. 228) notes:

> the Commission–Big 12 alliance was a critical and largely collective actor in lobbying national governments to create the European Strategic Programme for Information Technology (ESPRIT) in 1982 ... Esprit earmarked 750 million ECUs in Community funding to subsidise R&D projects involving firms from at least two member states. The perceived success of ESPRIT's first phase and continued lobbying by 'national champions' in technology intensive industries led European governments to accept that more and larger collaborative R&D programmes

were needed to respond to large scale initiatives already underway in the USA and Japan.

As a consequence, the first Technology Framework Programme was introduced and operated between 1984 and 1987: subsequent Framework Programmes have operated ever since. But the extent to which they are non-sectoral is open to query. Perhaps questions should be raised following Peterson's (1996) comments on the lobbying by national champions. If a focus on picking winners, hence national champions, has been discredited and abandoned, why has the European Union's technology policy apparently been so influenced by national champions? If it has been so influenced, it would appear to be an old policy in new guise; for some, a wolf in sheep's clothing.

## A form of targeting

Less dramatic than the case where an apparently horizontal industrial policy is in fact a targeting of sectors as a result of lobbying by national champions, it can be argued more generally that an industrial policy comprising entirely horizontal measures nevertheless implies targeting in an economy.

In one sense this is not a new argument. For example, Porter (1990, p. 673) observes:

> every nation practices implicit targeting of some kind, whether it will admit it or not. Government programs are inevitably skewed toward some industries and not others.

This should not be underestimated. However, our concern is wider. Consider an economy where there is no active public policy to support industrial development at all; in other words, an economy where everything is left to a pure free market. In such an economy choices *are* made about which sectors to target, about where to allocate scarce resources. It is simply that they are not made directly by governments or public agencies more generally.

In most economies significant parts of economic activity are controlled by large transnational corporations. As the United Nations (1993) observes, these firms are 'central actors' in the world economy. Moreover, they plan their activities, a point recognised in the seminal economics literature on the nature of the firm. For example, Coase (1937) endorses the idea of seeing firms as 'islands of planning'. This is a position often hidden in a modern literature which refers to firms' corporate strategies, rather than to corporate plans. Furthermore, an implication of firms planning their activities is that they choose to operate in particular sectors. They target particular sectors. Or rather, it is not the firms in some abstract sense which make the choices, it is the strategic decision-makers in those firms (Cowling and Sugden, 1998). The strategic decision-makers of large transnational corporations allocate scarce resources to support particular sectors, to develop some sectors and not develop others. In doing this, however, it should be recognised that the 'sectors' they chose to favour and the 'sectors' they chose not to favour are perhaps not the same set of sectors that are conventionally addressed in the economics literature (as mirrored, for example, in the Standard Industrial Classification (SIC)). Rather, firms target activities or markets that may span conventional industrial classifications.

It has been argued by Sharp and Shepherd (1987, p. 129) that: 'a policy of non-intervention is just as much an industrial policy as an interventionist strategy – it is an implicit rather than explicit policy'. In a similar vein, we would argue that a government policy that apparently chooses not to target particular sectors is just as much a policy of targeting as any other – it is an implicit sectoral approach. Knowingly or otherwise, it is a policy which leaves targeting to the strategic decision-makers of large transnational corporations. Likewise, to adopt horizontal industrial policies is nevertheless to endorse the targeting decisions of firms. Furthermore, we would argue that in many countries over recent years, not least Britain, this endorsement of firms' decisions has in practice been given substantial financial backing by the subsidies and inducements offered to inward investors. Resources which governments devote to attract foreign direct investment are resources supporting the targeting decisions of foreign transnational corporations.[5]

Viewed in this way we would question the appropriateness of accepting a targeting policy which was not more open. In targeting particular sectors the decision-makers in transnational corporations are guided by their own objectives. It would be a remarkable coincidence if on all occasions their choices identified the same set of sectors that another, different group of decision-makers would select, based upon their different objectives. Consider, for example, that firms target sectors/industries according to expected profitability – a standard presumption in economics. This strategy is not the same as a strategy based on targeting high value-added sectors – which the Competitiveness White Papers suggest is particularly important to people in Britain – or targeting employment – currently a particular concern for the European Union. Similarly, suppose the people in an economy have preferences for working in some sectors rather than others, or suppose more generally that a community has a set of objectives which would cause it to prefer development of particular sectors. It seems extremely likely that in practice a community would not be indifferent as to which sectors were more prominent, given that sectors undoubtedly vary in terms of the quality of jobs they offer, the value-added that can be obtained, and so on. Yet the likelihood of a set of horizontal policies leading to the successful development of those preferred sectors against others is virtually zero. This is simply because the horizontal policies would leave explicit targeting to firms' strategic decision-makers. And whilst there is controversy over the precise make-up of strategic decision-makers in transnationals, it is widely accepted that they at most comprise a subset of the people in an economy. This is a point expressed graphically by Kay (1997, p. 126), referring to firms from Britain and the US. He suggested that Anglo–US corporate governance resembles 'entrenched authoritarian political systems, such as those which prevailed in Eastern Europe before the fall of the Berlin Wall'. What this implies is that in Britain and the US, at least, most people are excluded from decisions about which sectors to target.

## An alternative approach

Our discussion leads to the conclusion that choice of sectors needs to be returned to the agenda of policy analysis. However it does *not* imply a need for analysis to identify the particular set of sectors to target. Doubting the appropriateness of choice of sector being left to firms' strategic decision-makers does not suggest that the choice should be left to bureaucrats; nor does it suggest that the choice be left to scientists. Picking winners is not the answer. Rather, the issue is one of creating democratic selection processes. Previous research on targeting has focused on which sectors to address. But that misses the point. Our characterisation of choice of sector in a free market system points to an ideal where a selection process involves the broadest possible range of people in an economy identifying the sectors whose development would best serve their objectives.[6] To involve less than the broadest possible range would necessarily imply a selection process serving a subset of the population, and thus merely the objectives of the subset. Only by involving all interests could this inherent problem be avoided. Of course, the feasibility of an inclusive (or, at least, accountable) industrial policy should not be underestimated. Nevertheless, we would argue that analysis needs to focus on designing processes that enable entire communities to identify which sectors should be targeted.

An argument against this approach might be that it is too planned; indeed, that it risks a tendency to centrally plan. However, nothing we have argued points to a centralised process, and strategic planning cannot be avoided: the fact is that all economies involve planning. As for an approach that is centralised, we would argue that one of the lessons of economies that have been 'centrally planned' is that a centralised approach is at best fraught with dangers and at worst unworkable.[7] Hence we would advocate a process for selecting sectors which is diffuse and democratic. This implies that, within a national economy, the selection of key sectors should be undertaken at a local level, and it would be out of these localities, *from* these localities that a national strategy would be formulated. While we recognise that coherence might be required at national and European levels, the attainment of coherence should be subservient to subsidiarity.

Within each of these local selection processes, the need is to identify the objectives of the people in the local economy, and to consider how these objectives might be met by different 'sectors'. Exactly what is meant by the term 'sector' is problematic in this context and indeed it might be more appropriate to refer to production activities rather than production sectors. Within a locality there would be a set of activities which would be identified for development. Bearing in mind our earlier comment that successful firms do not categorise activities in the same dimensions as the categorisation used by mainstream economics, we should not expect the targeted activities for a locality to correspond to the sectors of the Standard Industrial Classification. Moreover, it is highly likely that the needs for development of each targeted activity in a locality might to some extent have common elements across those activities. To that extent, there might be requirements for development which span activities. This illustrates a reason why horizontal versus sectoral policies is a false dichotomy; targeting may imply common elements, hence initiatives applicable across different activities. Furthermore, the likelihood of there being common elements to the targeting of activities is not confined to particular localities. It could well be that different localities have similar needs for developing activities in their economies. This gives rise to the possibility of locally rooted national and indeed multinational industrial policy.

An example of a common need to develop different activities might be knowledge of and access to appropriate generic technologies, such as information technology. If a particular locality wishes to develop, say, its textile activity and its ceramic activity, in both instances it might need initiatives regarding information technology. But of course this is not the same as requiring *any* development in the information technology sector in that locality. It is information technology relevant to the textile and ceramic activity which matters.

In the context of advocating local selection processes it is interesting to note two of the European Union's recent policy initiatives: the Regional Innovation and Technology Transfer programme (RITTS) and the Regional Innovation and Strategy programme (RIS). Both of these initiatives aim to raise growth and living standards in lagging regions within the European Union by stimulating technology transfer and innovation activity. Moreover, both initiatives *require* the involvement of local actors (local government, local development agencies, firms and universities) in the funding (50 per cent matched funding), design and implementation of the regional strategy. In this context, the choice of sectors to support or develop is left to decision-makers within the region. Hence, the RITTS and RIS approach to technology and regional industrial policy may be seen to involve a degree of economic democracy which is in line with our advocated approach to sectoral targeting.

Finally, whilst stressing that the need is to create democratic selection processes and that research should be directed to this end, we would not deny that within such a process other scientific analysis would have an important role. In part this would be an issue of helping those involved in the democratic process to bring structure and coherence to their activities. In part it would be an issue of modelling the impact of development in particular sectors (Cowling, 1990), albeit again acknowledging the lesson that the sectors conventionally addressed in the economics literature do not necessarily represent appropriate categorisations. However, what is vital to emphasise is that these would be supporting roles. Before they can be taken on, there is a bigger challenge facing researchers: to contribute to the design of the entire process.

## Notes

1   Note that the lack of discussion of industrial policy was not matched by an absence of policy action. Throughout this period expenditure on policies to support the industrial sector remained significant so that even by the end of the 1980s total state aid averaged around 2 per cent of GDP in the EUR-12 economies.

2   It should be noted that a recent paper by El-Agraa (1997) rejects the distinction between sectoral and horizontal industrial policy and argues that industrial policy should be defined to include *only* sectoral policies with horizontal measures best defined as public policy. However, this view is not in keeping with either traditional definitions of industrial policy or recent papers that identify a shift from sectoral to horizontal industrial policy (for example, Gönenc, 1994).

3   This approach would be consistent with the often-stated view that Europe's future competitive advantage lies in knowledge-based industries. Also in the UK, Business Link Personal Business Advisers and Innovation and Technology Counsellors are briefed to target firms with growth potential.

4   This explains, at least in part, why most industrial policies have been targeted at manufacturing rather than services.

5   In practice, however, it is extremely difficult to obtain accurate estimates of subsidies offered to attract inward investment because funding is offered in a variety of forms (direct grants, tax breaks, land, infrastructure) and from a variety of agencies (national, regional and local government). However, a recent report on inward investment in Wales has calculated the subsidy to be as much as £42,000 per job created.

6   A recent paper by Oswald (1997) has argued that if the aim of government policy is to improve public well-being then targeting high growth sectors may not be the best strategy because well-being and growth are not strongly correlated. Instead, policy would be best directed at creating employment since happiness and unemployment are strongly (negatively) correlated.

7   'Central planning' is not always unworkable: it depends on the circumstances and objectives. Global transnational corporations may be seen as centrally planned organisations.

## References

Burton, J. (1983). *Picking Losers: The Political Economy of Industrial Policy*, London: IEA.

Coase, R.H. (1937). 'The Nature of the Firm', *Economica*, IV, 386–405.

Commission of the European Communities (1992). *Third Survey on State Aids in the European Community*, Brussels: CEC.

Commission of the European Communities (1994). *Growth, Competitiveness, Employment: The Challenges and Ways Forward into the 21st Century*, White Paper, Brussels: CEC.

Commission of the European Communities (1995). *Fourth Survey from the Commission: on State Aids in the European Union in Manufacturing and Certain other Sectors*, Brussels: CEC.

Commission of the European Communities (1997). *Fifth Survey from the Commission: on State Aid in the European Union in Manufacturing and Certain other Sectors*, Brussels: CEC.

Cowling, K. (1990). 'The Strategic Approach to Economic and Industrial Policy', in Keith Cowling and Roger Sugden (eds), *A New Economic Policy for Britain: Essays on the Development of Industry*, Manchester: Manchester University Press.

Cowling, K. and Sugden, R. (1994). *Beyond Capitalism: Towards a New World Economic Order*, London: Pinter.

Cowling, K. and Sugden, R. (1998). 'The Essence of the Modern Corporation: Markets, Strategic Decision-making and the Theory of the Firm', *Manchester School*, 66, 1: 59–86.

Department of Trade and Industry (1994). *Competitiveness*, White Paper, Cm 2563, London: HMSO.

Department of Trade and Industry (1995). *Competitiveness: Forging Ahead*, White Paper, Cm 2867, London: HMSO.

Edgerton, D. and Hughes, K. (1995). 'British Science Policy in the 1990s: Technocracy and the Market', *Science, Technology and Innovation*, 8, 4: 21–6.

El-Agraa, A.M. (1997). 'UK Competitiveness Policy vs. Japanese Industrial Policy', *Economic Journal*, 107, 444: 1504–17.

Gönenc, R. (1994). 'A New Approach to Industrial Policy', *OECD Observer*, no. 187, 16–19.

Jacquemin, A. (1987). *The New Industrial Organisation*, Oxford: Oxford University Press.

Kay, J. (1997). 'The Stakeholder Corporation', in G. Kelly, D. Kelly and A. Gamble (eds), *Stakeholder Capitalism*, London: Macmillan.

Office of Science and Technology (1993). *Realising Our Potential: A Strategy for Science, Engineering and Technology*, Cm 2250, London: HMSO.

Oswald, A.J. (1997). 'Happiness and Economic Performance', *Economic Journal*, 107, 445: 1815–31.

Peterson, J. (1996). 'Research and Development Policy', in H. Kassim and A. Menon (eds), *The European Union and National Industrial Policy*, London: Routledge.

Pitelis, C. (1993). 'British Industrial Policy in Theoretical and International Perspective', *Judge Institute of Management Discussion Papers*, 1992–3: 19.

Porter, M.E. (1990). *The Competitive Advantage of Nations*, London: Macmillan.

Schultze, C.L. (1983) 'Industrial Policy: a Dissent', *Brooking Review*, 2, 1: 3–12.

Sharp, M. and Shepherd, G. (1987). 'Managing Change in British Industry', in *Employment, Adjustment and Industrialisation*, 5, Geneva: International Labour Office.

United Nations (1993). *World Investment Report 1993: Transnational Corporations and Integrated International Production*, New York: United Nations.

van Ark, B. (1996) 'Sectoral Growth Accounting and Structural Change in Post-war Europe', in B. van Ark and N. Crafts (eds), *Quantitative Aspects of Post-war Economic Growth*, Cambridge: Cambridge University Press.

Walker, W. and Sharp, M. (1991). 'Thatcherism and Technical Advance: Reform Without Progress?', *Political Quarterly*, 62, 2 and 3: 262–337.

Woolcock, S. (1984) 'Information Technology: the Challenge to Europe', *Journal of Common Market Studies*, 22, 4: 315–31.

Wren, C. (1996) 'Gross Expenditure on UK Industrial Assistance: a Research Note', *Scottish Journal of Political Economy*, 43, 1: 113–26.

# Part II

# Creating meaningful local and regional economies

# 3 Sustainable regional development

## New dimensions in policy formulation

*Gerry Sweeney*

## Policy formulation and implementation

Global warming and other and more local aspects of the dynamics of change of the natural and man-made environments are slowly beginning to influence policy. The phrase, 'sustainable development', is on many lips. Since the UN Conference in Rio in 1992, it has been enshrined in international agreements and been put into national programmes with Agenda 21. The change in policy thinking required to achieve sustainability is, however, probably more profound than many realise. Even a moderate prognostication of the future to 2050 and beyond points to hundreds of millions of deaths in degraded areas, and to attempts by the first world to contain the consequences through large scale solutions, for example, relocation and concentration or densification of cities, large-scale dams and $CO_2$ dumping in oceans (Kuntze *et al.*, 1998). Sustainability means much more than environmental sustainability. The present and projected future are an outcome not only of the exploitation of resources and societies for economic ends but also of social attitudes and desires. Similarly, environmental sustainability will be an outcome of economic and social sustainability. If the concept of sustainability is to be the cornerstone of the future, then policy must take account of three dimensions of sustainability: the economic, the socio-cultural and the environmental.

This paper examines some of the issues significant to sustainable development and then draws on a recent research project (INSURED: Instruments for Sustainable Regional Development) to illustrate the principles which need to underlie policy formulation and implementation at EU, national, regional and local levels of government, if sustainability is to be the primary objective.

## Why regional?

The term 'regional' refers to a locale, a geographical space occupied by a community. This is the critical meaning of the term because the locale is the building block of sustainability. The environment is essentially a local phenomenon which may have a wide and global reach through the ways in which the environment has been exploited or through the economic activities located there. As a local phenomenon, it has shaped the local communities existing within it and they have shaped their environmental space, or both community and the environment have been shaped by external agencies exploiting some advantage offered by the resources of the locale. The greatest significance of the locale is economic because innovation and entrepreneurial dynamism are local phenomena. They happen in specific places and therefore the economic development which generates net new economic wealth and net new employment and replaces declining economic activities happens in specific places. Prosperity is the endogenous creation of communities inhabiting a specific locale, where the interaction of policies, socio-cultural characteristics and external developments produces a new wave of entrepreneurial and innovative dynamics which can have global effects.

## The social constitution of the environment

What happens at the local level is therefore critical to global sustainability but the concept of sustainability is made complex by the fact that the environment does not exist outside human society. It is socially constituted (Munton, 1991; Sweeney, 1995) and hence the conceptual understanding of the environment changes from one society to another. It changes as the values possessed by each society undergo transformation. There is no standard definition or measure of what is the environment which is acceptable and understood by all and the Brundtland (1987) concept of 'sustainable development' is equivocal: 'development which meets the needs of the present without compromising the ability of future generations to meet their own needs'.

It leaves open what the environment may mean and how the environment and the resources which it contains are to be both exploited and conserved for the benefit of present and future society. It does intrinsically recognise the social constitution of the environment in that it focuses on development, and therefore on the exploitation of the environment for the benefit of human society. It leaves open the question of conservation as such. What is to be left to future generations and what are their needs?

## Management and exploitation

Although both living eco-systems and the natural physical elements are in a constant process of dynamic change instigated by their own interactions, man's interventions are such that man is effectively manager of the environment, within the paradox that the global is managed locally. The concern for the environment emanates from a slowly rising awareness of this role and also from a realisation that whilst the natural process of dynamic change may take centuries or millenia or much longer to have effect, as in geological time, man's interventions are relatively instantaneous in their impact. A particular natural eco-system or species is destroyed irrecoverably or the natural process of recovery may take centuries. On the other hand, the environment determines its own dynamic cycles of cold and warmth and its own dynamic interventions such as volcanoes. Some species explode in population, others become extinct. Thus whilst man is effectively the manager, the environment is only partially within human control and it therefore sets a conundrum for man and society: how to exploit, conserve and manage within dynamic forces which are beyond control?

Society also holds an ambivalent perception of the environment. First, the environment is all those resources of seascape and landscape, air, water and soil, the living species of flora and fauna and the artefacts, the man-made structures and products which provide the ambience and the biologically diverse eco-system within which human society lives. The environment is personal, the place where we live, work and play and where others live, work and play. Second, the environment is the source of the resources which society has utilised for its survival and benefit and transformed into artefacts, food and energy and which it has husbanded, depleted or degraded in the process of utilisation. We crowd to the mountains whose 'unspoilt' beauty we wish to enjoy along a motorway whose construction destroyed habitats in many places and whose use is locally and globally damaging. Or we decry those marginalised by current economic policies who seek short-term alleviation of the poverty and disintegration of their families and communities through activities which degrade their environment.

## Policy

Whatever the ambivalences, the concept of sustainable development allied to growing concern at threats to life has been influential, provoking campaigns by environmentalists, national and international scientific and political conferences, and also a variety of policies and agreements setting targets and introducing regulations. Commitment to a wider concept of sustainability is more difficult. Part of the conundrum is that human society and its structures and activities are also dynamic, undergoing continuous change, a rise and decline of shifting power from one system to another. However exogenously or endogenously guided or controlled, the value systems of society and the institutions of society have determined how the environment has been depleted and degraded. Policy reflects the values of society or dominant sections of society in guiding and controlling activity. It is intended or portrayed as meeting the demands and needs of society but it may also be a reflection of the values, opportunity-seeking or vested interests of élite groups within society.

Policy can have effects other than its stated objectives. Housing policy has led to ghettoisation, industrial policy has eroded concepts of equitable social justice, transport policy has disintegrated communities, monocultural agricultural policy has marginalised rural communities. Such effects are not socially sustainable but social sustainability has never previously been a consideration of policy formulation. Policy-making tends to be carried out in an arbitrarily independent manner by departments or ministries organised on a sectoral or mission-orientated basis. Nevertheless, industrial policy, for example, is interdependent with a range of other policies – training and education, fiscal, land use, R&D, regional, environmental, local government and so on. Its effectiveness depends on its being complemented and supported by other policies, or it may be rendered ineffective by them. A systemic approach is required, one which recognises that society, the economy and the environment are dynamic interdependent systems. The health of one part is dependent on the health of the other parts. Policies must be mutually reinforcing and complementary rather than unilateral.

Unsurprisingly, given the interplay between policy, society, the economy and the environment, Cairncross (1991) commented that 'Sustainable development is a useful concept but from the point of view of politicians it begs lots of awkward questions.'

Can a new paradigm be created? Can the three dimensions of sustainability be integrated in policy in a systemic manner so that society, the economy and the environment are mutually sustaining?

## Current malaise

Currently there is neither social nor economic sustainability in much of the world and particularly in the dominant American economy and those economies which have adopted the same culture of individualism and mode of corporate capitalism. The rights of the individual and the gaining of individual advantage and profit have become pervasive in these societies. Adam Smith provided a theoretical, even moral, justification for mass production and for individual profit as the motivation driving economic development. There can be other motivations. At its core, economic development is brought about by technical progress, innovation and the diffusion of innovation as best technical practice. In spite of the hype surrounding information and communication technologies, in the last two or more decades there has been little technological change of a kind which leads to increased prosperity and employment. In US manufacturing industries, increases in profitability have been brought about, not by technical change and new firms introducing new products, but by re-engineering, delayering and other techniques of lowering labour costs and on increasing the volume of lower quality goods (Rigby and Webber, 1997). The need of the organisation for short-term profit, whether a producing or investing organisation, dominates. Management is focused on cost reduction and profit maximisation and on personal gain. Since low-income workers are restricted to buying low-priced goods, the emphasis on lower labour costs and lower quality is reinforced.

Information technology (IT) has been adopted within this culture as a means to reinforce cost reduction and the attainment of short-term objectives, to make money rather than to create wealth. Fordism and scientific management and their many variants are no longer appropriate forms of organisation in an information-intensive age demanding quality and customisation. IT has too often been used to reinforce and further formalise the factors which led to success in the past and managements have thereby built in obsolescence. Technical progress is inhibited as the momentum of the past increasingly smothers the right kind of innovation.

This model of economic organisation is being aggressively 'sold' under the banner of free market economics and labour market flexibility and is resulting in increasing social polarisation. Part of society is enjoying a significant increase in income, but a large and growing minority, whether caught in the US 'poverty in work' syndrome or the European unemployment equivalent (OECD, 1994), is suffering a decline in income in real terms. The more prosperous gain as low-skilled services become ever cheaper. The proportion of 'non-virtuous citizens' (Putnam, 1993), that is those who have little concern for the common good, has become relatively large.

The pattern of development currently in progress has been seen before. Braudel (1984), in discussing the *'longues durées'* or long secular cycles, pointed out that dominant economies decline when they switch investment from manufacturing and trade to interest, speculation and rent seeking. Fischer (1997) confirmed Braudel by illustrating that inflation which characterised the decline phase of the *longues durées* led to a situation in which the rich became richer and the poor poorer and the patterns of social behaviour which gave stability and cohesion to society disintegrated.

## Governance

Technical progress and its output in economic and social development are dependent on organisational innovation and change, even more than on technical innovation and change. It is the lack of organisational change which has led to the present malaise, a lack of change in both business and government. Governments have followed the trends in industry and business, creating large hierarchically structured bureaucracies to manage and provide on a mass-delivery basis the infrastructure required by the economy and the welfare systems demanded by society. There is widespread dissatisfaction with the political system and with mass delivery by governmental bureaucracies. As a result, there is a discernable change occurring: '[a] move from decisive government determination of policy and bureaucratic implementation to a more bargained and collaborative approach: in many countries, significant areas of policy are now conducted by partnerships of state, statutory, commercial, voluntary and local groups' (O'Donnell, 1997).

Whilst there is an increasing consultation taking place at national levels, the real changes are taking place at the level of the locality, as was confirmed in the INSURED project. Local communities, even in highly centralised economies, are reaching out to take greater control of their own destinies. Social groups, private non-profit organisations, business firms and individuals have been taking initiatives to address local social and economic problems and issues by creating new forms of organisation. Communities and social groups within communities have organised themselves to undertake what would formerly have been considered public functions, functions of the political and administrative system. Governments have been collaborating, sometimes overtly and sometimes in a quietly pragmatic manner, with the phenomenon: sometimes devolving responsibility to community groups to deal with poverty, unemployment and social exclusion at their local level, entering into partnership with community and other local groups, jointly working with them, supporting them by funding or engaging them to provide public services as more effective vehicles of delivery. There are many different kinds of partnerships and collaborations, between industrial firms, universities, private individuals, government agencies, community groups, local community councils elected outside the political system and so on. The European Commission, in pursuing the principle of subsidiarity, has devised programmes directly accessible by local communities and groups and has thus given them opportunity, as well as reinforcing their capability, to take initiatives and control their own destiny.

The end result is a growing phenomenon of local self-governance which is rooted in the social cohesion of local communities and is engaged to establish consensual collaboration in order to tackle issues of mutual concern or benefit. Leadership is being given by social entrepreneurs and groups concerned to address local social, economic and environmental issues and willing to implement their ideas in innovative actions and to mobilise their community. Some are rebuilding the social cohesion of a marginalised or disintegrating community as the first step to achieving of a vision of the future. There are also the inevitable tensions as politicians and administrations attempt to control the emerging modes of self-governance of local groups or to constrain their activities. The pattern of the social and organisational innovation taking place is a messy one, shaped by the initiators and emerging from, or adapted to, the local objectives and local circumstances of the action undertaken. The many different shapes defy categorisation by bureaucratic norms and procedures. In other words, a diverse mass of social and organisational innovation is quietly taking place but gradually gaining a momentum which might eventually challenge the momentum of the American model.

## Dynamic localities

At the apex of local self-governance systems are the territorial systems of industrialisation which have emerged in Europe since the Second World War. They provide an alternative to the American model of capitalism and culture of individualism, a European and less aggressive model, which is both innovative and socially sustainable. In recent decades, many local economies have generated their own prosperity through their entrepreneurial dynamism and a competitiveness in international markets based on design, quality and technical excellence. They have intensive social and business inter-relationships, described as extended family or quasi-familial, stimulating rapid interchanges of information and intense collaboration between firms and the institutional infrastructure. The entrepreneurs and labour force have a high level of vocational/professional skills and therefore also of the tacit knowledge essential to integrating new technologies into traditional ones and to batch or quasi-customised production of higher-quality goods. They have large populations of small firms, and the large firms, whether owned locally or elsewhere, are disaggregated, relying on the surrounding webs of small firms for innovative design and development and the manufacture of components. The boundaries between firms and between firms and the public and private infrastructure are grey and porous. Information flows freely. The district has the appearance of a single industrial organisation, informal but tightly interlinked by the personal inter-relationships between all its parts.

The intensive sharing of information is reinforced by multiple membership of societies, clubs, associations and committees. Participation in 'civil associations', whether political, industrial, cultural or hobbyist:

> inculcates skills of cooperation as well as a sense of shared responsibility for collective endeavours. Moreover when individuals belong to 'cross-cutting' groups with diverse goals and members, their attitudes will tend to moderate as a result of group inter-action and cross pressures ... Even seemingly self-interested transactions take on a different character when they are embedded in social networks that foster mutual trust.
>
> (Putnam, 1993)

Each sub-system of society is thus opened through a complex maze of trans-disciplinary and trans-institutional cooperation. Each is listening and talking to the others. There are multiple horizontal interchanges of views, needs, ideas, opinions, through which consensus is developed as to future action. The local government and the agencies of central government are embedded in these interchanges and have autonomy of decision making for matters relating to the cultural, social and economic welfare of their communities. There is transparency and easy access to information. Furthermore, 'the shared value system enables internal conflicts of interest to be contained within the spirit of communitarianism embedded in the local population'. The community develops a strongly participative democracy leading to a self-governance which has emerged autonomously from the social cohesion. Local government and the agencies of central government are active partners in the self-governance, each sector carrying out its functions within the consensus. There is a shared republican value system, a commitment to the *res publica* or common good rather than the individualism of the Anglo-American model and its commitment to individual profit. The prosperity generated is therefore diffused throughout all sections of the society.

The value system and the inter-relationships pervade all aspects of life and create cohesion, attachment to place and a pervasive spirit of communitarianism throughout the cultural, social, political and economic sectors or social sub-systems of the community. The skills, value system, entrepreneurial dynamism, inter-relationships and social cohesion form the social capital out of which springs economic and social welfare and eventually environmental welfare. Some dynamic localities are in fact moving autonomously to care of their local environments, tackling problems caused by industrial and agricultural development and conserving and enhancing their natural and man-made environments and resources. Sustainable development in its three dimensions has become part of the shared value system.

At the core of the problem facing governments and policy makers is diversity. Nature makes no one thing the same as another. Environments are not only local but are very diverse. Even more importantly, so also are communities, their cultures and values, economic activities and structures. They differ sharply in their entrepreneurial and innovative capacities. This happens here and that there. The standardised mass delivery which has characterised national and now EU policies has clearly been inequitable and has had unsustainable effects. Can policy at regional, national and EU levels support diversity and localisation and thereby enable local communities to achieve and maintain a sustainable social, economic and environmental development?

## The INSURED project

This project was one attempt to explore the sustainable development concept from a policy viewpoint. What follows is a personal interpretation of the outcomes of the study against the known characteristics of dynamic local economies. A model of the interactions between policy and local communities and economies is presented and the implications for policy formulation and implementation of the key factors identified in the study are discussed. The key factors have been identified by the members of the research team who have also made many conceptual inputs to the study and these also form part of the interpretation and evaluation.[1]

The core of the project were socio-economic analyses of each region, analyses of selected policies from a sustainability viewpoint and case studies of 'innovative actions'. The sustainability analyses were carried out against ten 'dimensions' identified in the first stage of the study (Schleicher-Tappeser, 1997): the environmental, economic, socio-cultural sustainability dimensions; the social, interspatial and intergenerational equity dimensions;

and the systemic dimensions of diversity, subsidiarity, partnership and networking, and participation.

The innovative actions studied had diverse economic, social and technological objectives and included, for example: In Mittel-Hessen, a welfare to work programme which has resulted in a number of independent and commercially viable activities in, for example, the recycling of cars and the repair and recycling of household equipment. In a parish of Styria, a group of young people began a theatre and music festival which has led to rural tourism and farm enterprises. In the mid-west of Ireland, a company is supporting staff to set up their own companies, each independent but part of a virtual business centre based on close collaboration. The Val di Cornia is suffering from a range of water problems and a consortium of local authorities decided to move away from a proposed large dam project to a course of action integrating many different projects aimed at saving and reusing water. A 'wood chain' has been established in the two Appenzell cantons which lie within the larger St Gallen canton, with the objective of linking small farmers who own sections of mountain forest, small wood-processing firms, planners, architects and builders into an interactive network to exploit timber resources greatly under-utilised in the face of cheap imports. These examples illustrate the variety of actions studied, and although unintended there were many parallels between actions in the different regions, enabling comparisons to be made which illustrated a commonality of key factors in spite of differences in administrative structures and domestic policies.

## *Key factors*

These analyses and case studies led to the identification of the key factors which should characterise government policy and local action if there is to be real progress to sustainability. There are in effect three types of key factors:

- those which should underlie policy formulation to support social capital;
- those to support forms of self-governance;
- those factors which characterise the social capital of a dynamic locality and those which appear to give success to local initiatives and actions.

## Social capital

Social capital is central to sustainable development. It is all those factors which enable a local community to embark on a process of endogenous dynamic development. The four major components of social capital are:

- social cohesion: the shared value system, pervading and being reinforced by the intensive social and business inter-relationships between all sectors of the community. Carried out on the basis of trust, these

lead to sharing of information and know-how, collaboration and cooperation within market competition and consensual governance and
government of the community. They are the basis of the participative
democracy;

• entrepreneurial potential: entrepreneurial potential has traditionally been
considered as the propensity to establish a new manufacturing firm, a
propensity existing in a community with a high proportion of small
independent businesses, firms or farms. The study revealed that one
must now also include the propensity to found an innovative local social
or environmental action as well as an action to enhance the economic
and technological capability of chains of production or groups of firms;

• skills: an education and training system which endows a large proportion of young people with the skills through vocational training,
including through an applied third level system, to make and do things,
on the basis of which to develop a career and eventually to found a
productive firm or some social or environmental activity;

• autonomy of decision-making and of information: the autonomy of
strategic decision-making in all parts of the local infrastructure is a key
characteristic and it is interconnected to the intensive information
exchanges of the social inter-relationships. Both lead to a high level of
learning efficiency. A community with strong social cohesion, skills and
entrepreneurial potential and an infrastructure embedded in the cohesion
can take to itself control of its own destiny, that is, assume autonomy of
decision making, in spite of the lack of subsidiarity in the governmental
structure. There are examples of local communities which have done this
but generally centralisation is a major barrier to economic development.

## A model

The dynamic interactions between policy and local communities and
economies are set out in Figure 3.1. The major interactions are between policy
and programmes or instruments of policy and the social capital of local communities and their economies. On the right-hand side, policies or instruments
orientated and modified by the appropriate key factors support and enrich the
social capital of local communities and economies, their skills, value systems,
environmental quality, cohesion and entrepreneurial potential. The wealth of
its social capital enables a community to take control of its own destiny. On
the left-hand side is the dynamic interplay between social capital and policies
and programmes pursued by all levels of government. When guided or formulated by or according to other key factors, governments participate and act
in partnership with local communities and actors and policies support local
social as well as technological innovation. The social capital and government
policy interact to produce many different and complex modes of governance
and self-governance and of delivery of public services. The social capital
is mobilised into entrepreneurial and innovative dynamism and new actors,

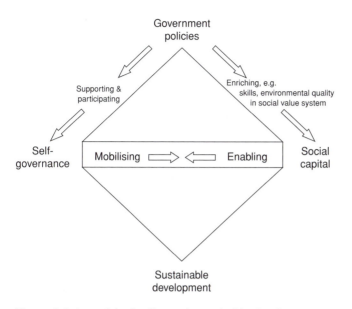

*Figure 3.1* A model of policy and sustainable development

individuals and social groups emerge to lead and found new activities, and enable new forms of governance and of delivery of public policy and functions to emerge. Sustainable development becomes attainable.

The key factors, given in quotes, are discussed below.

## Social cohesion

The study confirmed that 'social cohesion' is the fundamental factor which enables a community to embark on an upward spiral of economic, social and now environmental development. It confirmed the other elements making up the social capital of a dynamic local society and economy. The mode in which these elements contribute to the dynamism was highlighted by other identified factors. They give further guidance to local actors and their communities as to their own strategy formulation and ways of working.

The intensive personal inter-relationships, which in effect produce the social cohesion, are reinforced by the 'joining syndrome', the active participation in community affairs and in civil associations or clubs and societies. The constant interchanges ensure that each part of the economy and society and of the infrastructure is in a continuing process of 'mutual learning, negotiation, moderation and acceptance'. Each section of society, led by the political and administrative system and local technical, social and environmental innovators is thus active in the 'development of a negotiation culture'. The informal process of negotiation provides 'the capacity to develop a shared vision of the future', a common purpose to which each section of the community is committed. Consensus is reached as to actions to be undertaken by local government, government agencies, education and training institutions and innovative groups or organisations such as firms.

'Transdisciplinary cooperation and approaches' develop between each sub-system of society, and this ensures a horizontal partnership in which each has its autonomy but carries out its functional responsibility and tasks in harmony with its partners and the consensus.

That the 'public can participate in the consensual goal setting' is ensured through the informal process, but local government, community groups, environmental groups, large firms, farming, industrial and other associations are active in disseminating information and in stimulating public participation in discussion through newsletters, open public meetings and other means. There is 'transparency and open access to information'. It is an open and complex process of participative democracy resulting in a horizontal mode of self-governance rather than in a structured mode of government from above. Innovative actors, social groups, groups of firms, and public–private partnerships are able to evolve their own modes of self-governance in order to reach interdependent economic, social and environmental objectives.

The social cohesion causes the local society and economy to be an informally structured but unified organisation, able to take its place in the global economy and society. Its ability to do so is reinforced by two factors which characterise dynamic economies. They have a 'local collective capacity for risk absorption and problem solving'. Self-governance is a system which socialises risks across a broad array of public and private organisations and more. The shared value system and cohesion also 'control opportunistic behaviour' which attempts to accrue benefit and advantage to an individual or self-interest group to the disadvantage of wider needs and sections of the community. There is an inherent self-regulating capacity.

## Entrepreneurial dynamism

The central driving force in the creation of new economic wealth and new employment is the 'creation of new activities by entrepreneurs', but social entrepreneurs or innovative actors also play equally central roles in initiatives and organisations established to address technological, industrial, social and welfare issues which they perceive to be critical to the development of their community. Entrepreneurs are the product of their local culture and of the social cohesion and intensive information flows of their community. The propensity to found a new firm or other new activity is therefore found in some places and not in others. The inter-relationships or networks between entrepreneurs and other firms form a self-governing sub-system of society. In places with high entrepreneurial activity, the challenge is to 'maintain the self-governing entrepreneurial dynamism'. In other places, the challenge is to create a 'pervasive entrepreneurial culture' out of which might eventually emerge new economic and social activities, technological and organisational innovation. A pervasive entrepreneurial culture means that each person has the 'capability of taking responsibility for their own destiny' and of being motivated to 'contribute to the welfare of their own community'. The evidence is that not only are people who found activities to address social problems motivated to make a contribution to their own community, but in socially cohesive communities with high entrepreneurial vitality the motivation of entrepreneurs who set up new manufacturing enterprises is to be independent and to contribute to the welfare of their community.

## Skills

New firms are founded around the 'skills' of the entrepreneur and of the workforce in the locality. Self-generated prosperity, through innovation and entrepreneurial dynamism, is correlated with education and training systems in which a large proportion of young people undertake vocational training to a high standard and in which there is an applied technological orientation in the third-level institutions. The education and training systems of regions or countries which have a strong vocational and technological orientation have the social equity objective of endowing 'each person with the ability to reach their optimum level of attainment and fulfilment'. Each is enabled to acquire the skills in making and doing things that are necessary to assuring their own future welfare and to contributing to that of their community. In contrast, academic education systems, such as those of the less-favoured regions of the EU, are individualist and élitist. Skills are weaker and less widespread in the population.

Vocational training has the significance that 'tacit skills' are acquired, the subtle understanding of technology, materials and performance of the final product gained through practice, demonstration and experience. Tacit skills are essential to the integration of new technologies with existing technologies, an integration which leads to innovation and the constant improvement of products and processes. Social skills are also acquired in teamwork, mutual assistance and communication. The continuing need to embrace new technology and the pervasiveness of the environmental dimension inevitably lead to the concept of 'lifelong learning' in which tacit skills in existing and new technologies, in socio-cultural development and in the maintenance of environmental quality are acquired and updated. Tacit skills are as important in environment-orientated innovation as in market-orientated innovation.

National education and training policy has therefore a determining effect on entrepreneurial vitality, the quality of output and diffusion of prosperity and therefore on sustainability. Some dynamic communities have, however, built up their own vocational training systems and thereby been able to embark on an autonomous process of development.

## Autonomy

Autonomy has long been identified as a necessary component of the social capital of a dynamic locality. 'Autonomy of information' is provided by the intensive information exchanges which endow entrepreneurial actors with a high level of 'learning efficiency'. Learning efficiency enables signals of change and new opportunities to be identified early. The local exchanges rapidly diffuse information coming from external sources. Those parts of the local infrastructure and those local agents of national organisations who are embedded in the inter-relationships contribute to the inward flows and learning efficiency. In order for local actors to mobilise the resources to avail themselves of an opportunity or to undertake an innovative action to address social or other problems or issues currently not addressed, there must also be 'autonomy of strategic decision-making in the facilitating infrastructure' which supplies resources and inputs. Autonomy of decison-making by local government, local offices of central government departments and agencies, banks, education and training institutions, unions, associations of entrepreneurs and business, small and large firms, and also of local civil associations, is a *sine qua non* of dynamism and enables each section of the infrastructure to participate actively and to enter into productive partnerships. Subsidiarity in the governmental system, with decision-making at the lowest level, means that a local government has considerable responsibility for the economic, social, cultural and environmental welfare of its community. Local agents of national ministries and agencies can participate proactively in the endogenous development process and respond efficiently and appropriately to local needs. Furthermore, governmental subsidiarity seems to influence private services such as banks to behave in a similarly decentralised manner.

Whilst such autonomy in the infrastructure is generally dependent on national policies and structures, personnel in infrastructural institutions in some local economies because they are embedded in the local value system have assumed a virtual autonomy. They are part of their community, have strong attachment to place and work for the benefit of their community.

## Environmental values

Social cohesion is based on the shared values or culture of a community. The concern for the common good is predominant, but dynamic local economies, their firms and infrastructure also have quality of output of products and services integrated into their value system. This 'quality culture' is now being as it were naturally extended. When a company has a total quality culture, environmental quality is automatically built into all its processes and procedures. A community group takes charge of the quality of its environment when it begins to build or rebuild its 'pride in place', a first step in entering on a process of development. Pride in place restores social cohesion. 'Integrating the environment into the social value system' has become or is becoming a significant element of the strategy of local governments, firms, community groups and other local actors.

The control of 'opportunistic behaviour' referred to earlier becomes even more significant when environmental quality is an integral component of the shared value system. It provides a more effective mechanism than regulatory controls imposed from elsewhere and regulation as such tends to be much more efficient when it is introduced to implement an existing consensus.

## Characteristics of local action

The individuals and groups leading and stimulating the innovative social and economic actions examined in the study exhibited a proactive ability not only to seek out the potential of aids and programmes but also to adapt them to meet particular needs in reaching their own objectives. They have the ability to 'integrate them within their own strategies'. The stated objective of the programme may not have been quite what was done but the local adaptation gave the programme success. They were able to do so because they had developed close inter-relationships with the personnel of the relevant governmental agencies, whether national, regional or local, and engaged themselves in 'building credibility'.

The 'independent standing of local action groups' was a major factor. The ability to achieve a high level of performance by the organisations undertaking the innovative actions was correlated with the independence and autonomy of decision-making of the innovative actors. They had and maintained independent decision-making structures, that is, independent of government or its agencies. They had generated their own funds, enabling them to take independent action, to initiate pilot projects and to enter into negotiation and partnership with state agencies on equal terms. This independence becomes a factor in their credibility.

When an innovative action group has demonstrated its credibility and created a profile of good performance, they become 'attractive to state agencies'. The close inter-relationships with governmental agencies develop into partnerships productive from both the local viewpoint and the governmental viewpoint. Agencies with more local autonomy tend to cooperate closely with such innovative actors and to use them as a means of reaching their own objectives. Innovative groups were engaged to deliver programmes and projects by regional and local public authorities. New concepts of governance and government and of public service are being developed, and through such cooperative actions resources are being put to the point where a successful outcome is virtually assured.

## Factors which characterise policy

Development is a process of dynamic and mutually reinforcing partnership between government which facilitates and provides the means to support the dynamics of development and the innovative actors who drive development and change. Experience of the last decades has demonstrated that governments can, however, only be supportive and facilitating participants, not controlling and directing ones. Communities, economies and the environment are dynamic, in an upward spiral of progressive development or in a downward one. There is no intermediate phase of equilibrium or stability. Centralisation of the infrastructure and especially centralised and top-down formulation and implementation of programmes, whether from EU, national, regional or local government levels, like all exogenous interventions, have negative outcomes whatever the intentions or short-term gains. They break the spiral of growth or prevent it emerging by breaking the social cohesion of a community.

One of the major obstacles to the effectiveness of many policies and programmes is that politicians and administrations are tempted to do something: something which can be seen as addressing a particular problem or offering a hope for the future. Hence, not only do programmes tend to be drawn up in a regulatory or narrowly specified manner, but they often address the wrong target. They are directed at the symptoms rather than at the 'causal factors' or they offer fashionable mechanisms rather than creating a climate conducive to development, and they multiply. Thus one agency was found to have in excess of thirty programmes, most directed to disadvantaged people, and there were other programmes directed to marginalised groups or areas. The core problem was the lack of indigenous development and in particular the absence of a population of small and entrepreneurial firms, primarily because of the lack of skills, a lack endemic to an academic education system. There was also a need for a systemic approach of ensuring the 'complementarity and mutual reinforcement' of one policy area with another rather than an ameliorating approach which shifts the disadvantaged from one form of dependency to another.

Market failure is the predominant justification for government aid and support, but past levels of government intervention and market failure have together created a situation in which firms, innovative actors and social groups are dependent on government support of their strategies of development. Government policies and programmes have intervened in many areas of industrial and technological development, industrial structures and management, employment and education and training, social welfare, housing and health, and so on. Economic, social and other actors have had to enter into partnership with the representatives of government programmes, but as subservient partners to a higher authority determining and prescribing the mode and governance of the government support or action.

Now the role of government is changing as others take the initiative. The creation of new modes of self-governance is a growing phenomenon in

Europe as local groups of firms attempt to meet technological and market change or seize opportunities, as communities attempt to take control of their own destiny or as local groups or individuals mobilise others to respond to the social and environmental problems of their community. The form of governance differs from one to another, evolving to match the character of the action, the functions to be carried out and the objectives. Governments have, albeit sometimes reluctantly, entered into partnership in these forms of governance and used them as a means to implement policy or deliver services. Rather than attempting to control or impose a standard formula, whether on local governments embedded in participative self-governance or on private innovative actions, government policy must now actively seek to create a framework which encourages the 'emergence of new models of governance and self-governance'. This framework should be one of 'cooperative competition' which allows the most effective to flourish and allows an apparently duplicating diversity. Creation of such a framework demands many changes in the value system of those who formulate and implement policy.

## Facilitating

Innovators may be frustrated. Needs may exist but existing programmes may not meet the need, given the degree of detailed specification which makes adaptation very difficult or excludes by setting objectives which are too narrow. If policies and programmes are formulated as 'facilitating instruments', and not prescriptive ones, there is room for diversity and local margins and for innovative development. A programme or policy should have adaptabilty built into it. The essence of organisational and technological innovations is that they are unanticipated. They go off in directions unforeseen by researchers and administrators. Policy should 'facilitate the emergence of unanticipated developments'. As with regulatory approaches, detailed specification of a programme can often inhibit innovative activity and is often directed at the wrong target, causing, for example, the phenomenon of fund chasing. Because the money is there and problems are there, use is made of the programme, however appropriate or inappropriate the programme may be to the local circumstances.

Facilitation also makes the integration of policies more feasible at the point of action since the demarcations of policy are more flexible. They can be made more 'complementary and mutually reinforcing' when integrated in the strategy of a firm or community. Facilitation is an acknowledgement that government is not the dynamic initiator of innovation. Only at the local point of action are policies and programmes integrated and the integration is dependent on the dynamism of the local actors and the quality of government's partnership with local actors.

## Localisation and customisation

Localisation or customisation to local realities is a key aspect of facilitation, expressed as 'recognition of the localisation of communities, the environment and economies'. Communities, economic activities and the environment differ from one locality to another but within each locality there is a tendency to uniqueness and specialisation in one respect or another. Each locality has or needs to develop approaches particular to its own situation and characteristics. This means, therefore, that policies and programmes should 'allow for a variety of development approaches'. Allowing for diversity is a key dimension pervading many of the key factors identified. No one programme can specify the needs of all places if they are to develop endogenously and arrive at a development which is sustainable in all three dimensions.

A critical aspect of development is that entrepreneurs who found new manufacturing firms and social entrepreneurs who found more socially based activities are both local. Or they are people from some other culture who have become integrated in the community which they have entered. They found their activities in their own place and entrepreneurial individuals played a significant role in the initiation and development of the innovative actions studied in the INSURED project. They mobilise the resources of their communities and utilise, as often they must, sources of funding and other aids made available through EU and national programmes. Unfortunately, these have been formulated in some distant place with little knowledge of the actual circumstances and needs of those who attempt to utilise them. Matching the realities of a particular firm or community or innovative development to particular programmes can be difficult. Policies should contain a presence for 'local margins of action', and more.

They should recognise the real boundaries of a community and a local economy. These boundaries are determined by the boundaries of the intensive interchanges and inter-relationships which create the social cohesion. These boundaries may be part of an administrative area or take in parts of two or more administrative areas. The community is the main unit of action and implementation of policy. Including it for administrative convenience in a larger area or dividing it between administrative areas is self-defeating.

A 'local implementation structure embedded in the social inter-relationships' means that there is a local facility to adapt programmes to meet local realities, giving a higher rate of success. The literature demonstrates that the local agents of investing institutions with a high rate of successful investment are those who are well integrated into the social inter-relationships of their communities and adapt, or bend, the proposal to the specification of the programme. Similarly, local agents of state agencies or programmes have a higher rate of success in their 'investments' when they have the same characteristics. An informal customisation is taking place; but having an informal customisation present in the structure for the implementation of policies and programmes runs counter to the inclination often present in bureaucracies to demonstrate accountability through close control and conformity to the rules. Yet, the concept of 'local liaison/animateurs embedded in the local interactive networks' has long been known and indeed practised in some countries. Liaison/animateurs are agents of central or regional governments or agencies whose task is to interact with local industries, entrepreneurs, institutions and social entrepreneurs and groups, alerting them to the potential of government and EU programmes, and enabling them to gain optimum benefit from them. There are also people in state agencies who quietly adopt the same role. Whether formally appointed or informally adopted, it is a quiet undramatic role which fails to capture political imagination and runs counter to a clientelist political culture. Successful formal and informal liaison/animateurs are people who are embedded in the local culture and the local interactive social networks and have a strong attachment to place, usually being native born. They know the innovative actors and actions and they know the local realities.

They play a role in the 'animation and motivation of people' but the prime animateurs are the innovators whom they support. Innovators are those people in the political, administrative, social, industrial or other sub-systems of a community who perceive a new way of doing things: to seize an opportunity, to solve a problem or to help their communities into the future. As the study demonstrated, they create a vision and share it with others in order to motivate them and to engage them to participate in the action. The 'capacity to develop a shared vision' is a significant characteristic of innovators and the social groups which they mobilise. In theory, policies and programmes are in place to assist such people but practice demands a structure of implementation which is local and socially embedded.

Given the role of local innovators, the concept of facilitating should be extended to embrace the giving of 'opportunity for concrete and visible individuals and social groups' and an 'openness to different kinds of actors'. A programme intended for technology transfer to SMEs may be equally useful to community groups developing their own economic strategy. The state system operating at the local level should be able to take the initiative in forming a partnership and thereby not only be open but 'build on existing interests and opportunities'. Entrepreneurial individuals and social groups bring about innovative and progressive change and consciously supporting them brings about a win–win situation, both sides of the governmental/entrepreneurial partnership gain, creating a role model for others but also ensuring an effective utilisation of resources. It is not a situation of picking winners, at which governments are extremely poor, but of supporting actors and actions which have built credibility and are already in the process of winning.

## Partnership

Partnership between government and localities and local innovating individuals or groups is the common element to all new forms of self-governance.

The forms of the partnerships emerging are of a wide variety, a good but informal working relationship with support from the governmental agency or a formal company in which a governmental agency is an active partner. The evidence of this study is that the most productive and creative partnerships are those in which there is 'room and opportunity for equitable interaction' and mutual respect for the 'autonomy of partners' and for 'negotiated responsibilities', negotiation in the context of a shared culture. Imposition of a preconceived form of partnership by the governmental agency as a condition of support has a negative impact. Initiative and innovative development are stifled. 'Allowing evolution of own mode of self-governance' is critical.

Self-governance models and innovative actions, like new products, tend to evolve through a process of 'trial and error development' as they attempt to reach the agreed objective, whether new products, solutions to social problems or improvement of the environment. Governments should be sensitive to the trial and error mode of development: what works may not be what was originally envisaged. In other words, policy should 'enable new forms of self-governance' to emerge. Outcomes may be very diverse but diversity is a significant factor in innovation. Technological alternatives, for example, provide not only flexibility but also open further potential for innovative products and processes. They allow a range of options from which future technological trajectories may emerge. New forms and structures of industrial collaboration, new social initiatives and new institutions may overlap, but they give a diversity which is a strength. They lead to new forms of economic development and new ways of delivering public services. Therefore, whether supporting new forms of self-governance or the development of new technologies or products, there needs to be a recognition that policy should 'support competing and alternative development projects and approaches'.

## Organisational change

The momentum of Fordism is such that it aggressively persists into what is termed the post-Fordist era in spite of its demonstrable lack of the 'capability to integrate social and technical learning and innovation processes' and its consequent lack of efficiency. The new modes of self-governance which are emerging are intuitive responses to integrate learning and innovation processes and develop a capacity to 'cope with complexity and ambiguity'. They have the capability to create a new wave of economic prosperity if they can develop a momentum sufficient to counter the Fordist or scientific management momentum.

When local governments and especially the representatives and agents of central government and its agencies are engaged in interactive and mutually respecting partnerships in the social context of a local community and economy, government has the potential to move into a learning process, itself learning to 'cope with complexity and ambiguity' and developing an ability to meet change through policies which refrain from preordaining what the change must be. For government and each level of government to learn and operate within a framework of transparency and consensus, there must be 'multiple links between different levels', matching the horizontal social cohesion of a locality with inter-relationships between different parts of the the governmental and social and market infrastructure. For the processes of learning and consensus-forming to become efficient in themselves, there must be 'early involvement of several administrative levels'. Learning efficiency is thus enhanced, change is more easily and readily anticipated, consensus is formed and each level can undertake its functions with confidence. Learning and consensus-forming are slow human and social processes but, when action is taken on the basis of consensus, it has the support of all sections and thus attains a high degree of efficiency in execution. It is an iterative process which ensures that democratic participation can be seen to be influencing decision at all levels of government.

Not only does consensus-forming imply that governments are tolerant of multiple forms of self-governance across their territories, but also that they should be proactive in fostering a multiplicity of self-governance structures in the economy, in society and in governmental departments and agencies engaged in policy formulation and implementation. New forms of public–private or private agencies and associations may emerge and evolve to undertake public functions in provision of services. Self-governance is a breaking away from the centralised hierarchical mode of government typical of the Fordist and scientific management culture in which society is viewed as a machine to be manipulated from the centre. Just as social groups engaged in self-governance are dynamic, continuously evolving their structures and inter-relationship patterns, so government must develop an 'ability to change structures' in an organic manner to meet the challenges of organic change in society.

Engaging government in a self-governance and partnership mode of government results in inter- and intra-organisational messiness. Structures become less amenable to being set out in a neat hierarchical organogramme. The temptation of administrators, academics and managers is, however, to tidy up the messiness, but making things neatly structured breaks the horizontal inter-relationships and social cohesion. The objective of government should be to emulate the fuzziness of the structures of dynamic economies. In a dynamic local economy, the boundaries between firms, social groups, local government and other parts of the infrastructure are porous and grey. Each is open to interaction and action with and by the others.

## Time scales

Communities whose cohesion has disintegrated take time to arrive at a consensus and to shape their own modes of self-governance and thus enter on a more progressive spiral of development. Policies which have concepts of some forms of partnership-building as part of their objective must have a built-in 'ability to deal with different time patterns'. It takes communities and associations of whatever kind time to reach consensus and shape an ability to take control of their own destiny. There is much learning, negotiation and moderation to be done. The time taken may differ from place to place. Imposing a three- or four-year time scale may result in an élite group or a centralised bureaucracy capturing the programme to the detriment of the community. Another dimension of differential time patterns is that projects to be supported may take longer or require a longer period for their completion than is specified. Placing too narrow time limits on programmes raises the further issue of continuity. The programme ends, what then? Who is to support a service or infrastructure which has been developed? Communities and groups need 'reassurance of renewal' and of continuity of support when they have embarked on a continuing initiative which may take time to bring to a state of self-support, if ever.

## Policy and industrial policy

Aspects of industrial, technological and innovation and other policies have been touched on and interwoven with aspects of other policies and the knowledge of the factors stimulating economic, social and environmental sustainability and the outcomes of the INSURED study. Industrial policy is a complex of inter-related policies and structures. A prosperous society has at its core a dynamic and innovative manufacturing sector and services feeding new knowledge to the sector. Dynamic manufacturing sectors are localised phenomena, created by the social cohesion and self-governance of the communites or societies of specific places and their individual and collective skills. Skills are a significant factor in innovation and development of products and organisations. Each policy area in a complementary and mutually reinforcing fashion in an ideal situation is engaged in stimulation and support of new and diverse organisational forms of self-governance. The result may appear messy, but creativity and productive efficiency are more surely achieved. Government by being itself consensually cohesive within and between the different levels becomes itself a form of self-governance in which a large variety of organisational forms, private, public and private–public, govern and supply service and support development.

## Note

1   The INSURED project was carried out under the Climate and Environment programme of DG XII of the European Commission in five countries: Austria, Germany, Ireland, Italy and Switzerland, and is supported under the EU Environment and Climate RTD Programme. The study regions are Styria, Mittel-Hessen, Ireland Mid West, Val di Cornia in Tuscany, and St Gallen. Grateful acknowledgement is made to the co-ordinator and partners in this project:

Ruggero Schleicher-Tappeser, EURES, Freiburg, the co-ordinator; Robert Lukesch, ÖAR, Fehring; Filippo Strati, SRS, Florence; Alain Thierstein, SIASR, St Gall, and their colleagues. Responsibility for the model and the interpretation of the key factors made in this paper is the author's.

# References

Braudel, F. (1984). *Civilisation and Capitalism: 15th–18th Century, volume III: The Perspectives of the World*, New York: Harper & Row.

Brundtland, G.H. (Chairman) (1987). *Our Common Future: World Commission on Environment and Development*, London: Oxford University Press.

Cairncross, F. (1991). *Costing the Earth*, London: Business Books and The Economist Books.

Fischer, D.H. (1997). *The Great Wave: Price Revolutions and the Rhythm of History*, London: Oxford University Press.

Kuntze, U., Meyer-Kramer, F. and Walz, R. (1998). 'Innovation and sustainable development – lessons for innovation policies? Introduction and overview', in F. Meyer-Kramer (ed.), *Innovation and Sustainable Development: Lessons for Innovation Policies?*, Heidelberg: Physica-Verlag.

Munton, R. (1991). Personal communication, University College London.

O'Donnell, R. (1997). 'Irish policy in a global context: from state autonomy to social partnership', *European Planning Studies*, 5 (4): 545–58.

OECD (1994). *The OECD Jobs Study: Facts, Analysis, Strategies*, Paris: OECD.

Putnam, R.D. (1993). *Making Democracy Work: Civic Traditions in Modern Italy*, Princeton, NJ: Princeton University Press.

Rigby, D.L. and Webber, M.J. (1997). 'The forms and determinants of technological change in US manufacturing', *Entrepreneurship and Regional Development*, 9 (4): 273–98.

Schleicher-Tappeser, R. (1997). *Sustainable Regional Development: A Comprehensive Approach*, Freiburg: EURES. EURES Discussion Paper, 60.

Sweeney, G.P. (1995). 'The social constitution of the environment', in G. Sweeney (ed.), *Environmental Management and Control*, Dublin: Dublin Institute of Technology, 2 vols.

# 4 The territorial challenge to innovation and endogenous regional development

*Bjørn T. Asheim*

## Introduction

In much of the writings on industrial districts during the last ten to fifteen years the seemingly paradoxical productive role played by traditional, pre-capitalistic socio-cultural structures in competitive, modern local and regional economies has been discussed as well as questioned. Commentators have generally agreed that what made the districts so successful was their combination of functional and territorial integration. The territorial dimension of the socio-cultural structures represented the basic input promoting flexibility and dynamism. However, on the one hand, the continual influence of socio-cultural structures was said to make the districts vulnerable to changes in the global capitalist economy, but on the other hand, much work was put into the evaluation of the adaptability and replicability of the district model to other regions in need of development strategies. The European experience of industrial districts had become a major point of reference in the international debate on regional policy promoting endogeneous development (Asheim, 1994).

In the discussion of transfer of experiences from one region to another it is important to distinguish between specific and general factors explaining the formation and development of regions. The more important the specific factors are, the more difficult it is to transfer experiences from one region to another, as specific socio-cultural factors, which are historically embedded in a particular region, cannot be repeated in another region. However, the main lesson learned from the rapid growth of industrial districts and other specialised areas of production, of seeing industrialisation as basically a territorial process, underlining the importance of agglomeration and non-economic factors (that is, culture, norms and institutions) for the economic performance of regions, represent general aspects, which are much easier to transfer from one region to another.

Another factor contributing to the generalisation of the experiences of industrial districts is the new theoretical understanding of innovation as basically a social process. Compared to the previous dominant linear model of innovation, this implies a more sociological view, in which interactive learning is looked upon as a fundamental aspect of the innovation process, which thus cannot be understood independent of its institutional and cultural contexts (Lundvall, 1992).

What this broader understanding of innovation as a social, non-linear and interactive process meant, was a change in the evaluation of the importance and role played by socio-cultural structures in regional development: from being looked upon as mere reminiscences from precapitalist civil societies (although still productive), to being viewed as necessary prerequisites for regions in order to be innovative and competitive in a post-Fordist global economy. According to Amin and Thrift (1995, p. 8), this forces a re-evaluation of 'the significance of territoriality in economic globalisation'.

Thus, based on modern innovation theory it could be argued that, for example, SMEs in territorial agglomerations can develop their competitive advantage based on innovative activity, which is socially and territorially embedded interactive learning processes. Furthermore, in addition to contributing towards explaining the present success of industrial districts, this broader view on the central importance of innovation in modern learning economies also points at the lack of innovation capacity as a fundamental problem of industrial districts (Asheim 1996), while at the same time expanding the range of branches that could be viewed as innovative from typical high-tech branches of Silicon Valley to traditional, non-R&D-intensive branches of peripheral regions.

Taken together, this theoretical development has dramatically changed the basis for launching an industrial and technology policy towards SMEs with the intention of promoting endogenous regional development. Such a regionalisation strategy can be seen as an alternative to achieving competitiveness in a global economy, a position which is often neglected in the globalisation debate.

## Theoretical foundations of the regionalisation approach

### *Learning as a localised process*

Lundvall and Johnson (1994) use the concept of a 'learning economy' when referring to the ICT- (information, computing and telecommunication) related techno-economic paradigm. They emphasise that 'it is through the combination of widespread ICT-technologies, flexible specialisation and innovation as a crucial means of competition in the new techno-economic paradigm, that the learning economy gets firmly established' (ibid., p. 26). These perspectives of the 'learning economy' are based on the view that *knowledge* is the most fundamental resource in a modern capitalist economy, and *learning* the most important process (Lundvall 1992), thus making the learning capacity of an economy of strategic importance to its innovativeness and competitiveness.

One of the consequences of knowledge-intensive modern economies is that 'the production and use of knowledge is at the core of value-added activities, and innovation is at the core of firms' and nations' strategies for growth' (Archibugi and Michie, 1995, p. 1). Thus, in a 'learning economy', 'technical and organisational change have become increasingly endogenous. Learning processes have been institutionalised and feed-back loops for knowledge accumulation have been built in so that the economy as a whole . . . is "learning by doing" and "learning by using"' (Lundvall and Johnson, 1994, p. 26).

The perspective of 'learning economies' and modern innovation theory emphasises that learning is a localised, and not a placeless, process (Lundvall and Johnson, 1994; Storper, 1995a). This view is supported by Porter (1990, p. 19), who argues that 'competitive advantage is created and sustained through a highly localised process. Differences in national economic structures, values, cultures, institutions, and histories contribute profoundly to competitive success.' Accordingly, Porter emphasises the importance of a national or regional home market as the socio-economic and institutional basis for global competitive advantage (see Lazonick, 1993). This stands in contrast to Reich, who argues that 'the work of nations' is the result of activities that take place *in* the national territory, and not *of* nationally based companies (Reich, 1991; Storper, 1995b). In this context I would argue that Porter's main argument is not based on the importance of the home base as a (national) market, but rather refers to the accumulated localised learning as a result of historical trajectories of innovation and production activity.

This points to the importance of disembodied knowledge, that is, knowledge and know-how which are not embodied in machinery, but are the result of positive externalities of the innovation process. Disembodied knowledge can be both tacit and codified. However, such knowledge is generally based on 'a high level of individual technical capacity, collective technical culture and a well-developed institutional framework . . . [which] are highly immobile in geographical terms' (Castro and Jensen-Butler, 1993, p. 8). Thus, some codified knowledge can be a product of localised rather than placeless learning. This implies that the adaptability of this localised form of codified knowledge is dependent upon, and limited by, contextual, tacit knowledge of, for example, specific industrial districts, and thus can have potentially, favourable impact on their innovativeness and competitiveness (for an example see sub-section on Jæren, Norway, pp. 68–70).

This localised form of codified knowledge can provide an improved basis for 'learning by interacting' (for example, user–producer relationships), which represents a more advanced form of learning than 'learning by doing' and 'learning by using'. 'Learning by interacting' cannot, in order to be fully exploited, be based only on tacit knowledge.

The strict dichotomy normally applied between codified and tacit knowledge can be quite misleading both from a theoretical as well as from a policy point of view. This is especially the case if localised learning is primarily said to be based on tacit knowledge. A claim for the superiority of tacit knowledge on such a ground could lead to a fetishisation of the potentials of local production systems, without discovering the problems such systems could face due to their lack of strategic, goal-orientated actions and strategies, which always has to be based on codified knowledge (for example, formal R&D) (Amin and Cohendet, 1997). The third category of disembodied, codified knowledge represents a concept which would be able to grasp the important basis for endogenous regional development, represented by firms relying on localised learning, but building this localised learning on a strategic use of codified, R&D-based knowledge in addition to tacit knowledge.

Porter, on the one hand, focuses on the importance of 'disembodied knowledge' in promoting innovativeness and competitiveness. Reich, on the other hand, points at 'embodied knowledge' as the most important factor in order to secure a nation's future prosperity, that is, knowledge embodied in production equipment (hardware), which can be operated on the basis of universal, codified knowledge with general, global accessability (software). Reich stresses the role of the quality of the workforce especially, arguing that human capital investments are the most efficient public policy for attracting high-wage and high-value-added activities, demanding high-skill labour, to advanced nations from the 'global webs' of TNCs (Lazonick, 1993; Reich, 1991; Storper, 1995b).

However, Reich's analysis, in contrast to Porter's, partly misses the historical and contemporary insights of the specific importance of *territory* and *non-economic factors* in general for the performance of an economy. Moreover, Reich's policy does not look especially promising from the point of view of keeping advanced, high-cost welfare economies on a high-wage/high-innovation development path, when the contemporary developments in the global economy, such as the rapidly increasing competitive advantage of the Indian soft-ware industry, based on low paid engineers, and the heavy investments in higher technical education in South Korea and Taiwan, are taken into consideration.

### *Innovation as an interactive learning process*

Modern innovation theory has developed as a result of criticism of the traditional dominant linear model of innovation as the main strategy for national R&D policies of being too 'research-based, sequential and technocratic' (Smith 1994, p. 2). This criticism implies another and broader view of innovation as a social as well as a technical process, as a non-linear process and as a process of interactive learning between firms and their environment (Lundvall, 1992; Smith, 1994). This alternative view could be referred to as a bottom-up interactive innovation model (Asheim and Isaksen, 1997), much more adapted to SMEs in networks and the post-Fordist 'learning economy' (Lundvall and Johnson, 1994), and greatly facilitated by geographical proximity and territorial agglomeration.

The emphasis on interactive learning as a fundamental aspect of the process of innovation points to cooperation as an important strategy in order to promote innovation (Asheim, 1996). The rapid economic development in the 'Third Italy', based on territorially agglomerated SMEs in industrial districts, has drawn increased attention towards the importance of cooperation among firms and between firms and local authorities in achieving international competitiveness. Pyke (1994) underlines the close inter-firm cooperation and the existence of a supporting institutional infrastructure at the regional level (for example, centres of real services) as the main factors explaining the success of Emilia-Romagna in the 'Third Italy'. According to Dei Ottati (1994, p. 474):

> this willingness to cooperate is indispensable to the realization of innovation in the industrial district which, due to the division of labour among firms, takes on the characteristics of a collective process. Thus, for the economic dynamism of the district and for the competitiveness of its firms, they must be innovative but, at the same time, these firms cannot be innovative in any other way than by cooperating among themselves.

Thus, if these observations are correct, they represent new 'forces' in the promotion of technological development in capitalist economies, implying a modification of the overall importance of competition between individual capitals. Lazonick argues, referring to Porter's (1990) empirical evidence that 'domestic cooperation rather than domestic competition is the *key* determinant of global competitive advantage. For a domestic industry to attain and sustain global competitive advantage requires continuous innovation, which in turn requires domestic cooperation' (Lazonick, 1993, p. 4).

This perspective emphasises the importance of organisational (social) and institutional innovation to promote cooperation, primarily through the formation of dynamic flexible learning organisations within firms, and between firms in networks as well as in regions. Furthermore, this tendency is strengthened by the hegemonic ICT techno-economic paradigm of the post-Fordist learning economy, which, to a very large extent (and more than previous techno-economic paradigms) is dependent on – and stimulates – organisational innovations in order to exploit its potentials. And the more important organisational innovations are, the more important interactive learning can be considered to be in the promotion of such innovations.

This is, of course, dependent upon contingencies such as the type of industry in question: for example, high-tech industries will continue to be the most dependent on formal R&D, which, due to its basic characteristics, will remain expensive and protected and thus will not promote cooperation. However, in industries with expensive but not especially advanced R&D-based product innovations, such as the automobile industry, more cooperation has been applied in order to share development costs.

Such institutionalisation of a continual organisational learning process involves a redefinition of a firm's relations to its major suppliers based on the recognition that:

> a network based on long-term, trust-based alliances could not only provide flexibility, but also a framework for joint learning and techno- logical and managerial innovation. To be an integral partner in the development of the total product, the supplier must operate in a state of constant learning, and this process is greatly accelerated if carried out in an organisational environment that promotes it.
>
> (Bonaccorsi and Lipparini, 1994, p. 144)

This emphasises that firms of the learning economy are basically 'learning organisations'. They choose organisational modes such as interfirm networking and intrafirm horizontal communication patterns in order to enhance learning capabilities (Lundvall and Johnson, 1994). Lundvall and Johnson (ibid., p. 39) argue that 'the firm's capability to learn reflects the way it is organised. The movement away from tall hierarchies with vertical flows of information towards more flat organisations with horizontal flows of information is one aspect of the learning economy.'

This is in line with Scandinavian experiences, based on the socio-tech- nical approach to organisation theory, which have shown that flat and egalitarian organisations have the best prerequisites of being flexible and learning organisations, and that industrial relations characterised by strong involvement of functional, flexible, central workers is important in order to have a working 'learning organisation'. All experience shows that 'the process of continous improvement through interactive learning and problem- solving, a process that was pioneered by Japanese firms, presupposes a workforce that feels actively committed to the firm' (Morgan, 1995, p. 11).

Brusco (1996, p. 149) – with special reference to the industrial districts of Emilia-Romagna – points to the dominant model of production in the districts 'that was able to be efficient and thus competitive on world markets, in which efficiency and the ability to innovate were achieved through high levels of worker participation and were accompanied by working conditions that were acceptable'. In general, Porter (1990, p. 109) points out that 'labor–manage- ment relationships are particularly significant in many industries because they are so central to the ability of firms to improve and innovate'.

A strong and broad involvement within an organisation will also make it easier to use and diffuse informal or 'tacit', non-R&D based knowledge and intangibles, which in a 'learning economy' has a more central role to play in securing continuous innovation. 'Transactions' with 'tacit' knowledge within and between networking organisations require trust, which is easier to establish and reproduce in flat organisations than in hierarchical ones. Normally, tacit knowledge cannot easily be codified and thus has to be accu- mulated through learning by doing. According to Lipparini and Lorenzoni

(1994, p. 18): 'a high dose of trust serves as substitute for more formalised control systems' (see also Lorenz, 1992; Sabel, 1992). In organisations characterised by an authoritarian management style the attitude of the employees will often be to keep 'the relevant information to themselves' (You and Wilkinson, 1994, p. 270).

The importance of horizontal interfirm cooperation with respect to promoting innovations highlights the qualitative aspects of networking, that is, specifically the governance structure of the networks. Grabher (1993, p. 10) argues that 'loose coupling within networks affords for favourable conditions for interactive learning and innovation. Networks open access to various sources of information and thus offer a considerably broader learning interface than is the case with hierarchical firms.' Through networking the ambition is to create 'strategic advantages over competitors outside the network' (Lipparini and Lorenzoni, 1994, p. 18).

Leborgne and Lipietz (1992) maintain that the more horizontal the ties between the partners in the network are (that is, networks dominated by oblique or horizontal quasi-integration), the more efficient the network as a whole is. This is also emphasised by Håkansson (1992, p. 41), who points out that 'collaboration with customers leads in the first instance to the step-by-step kind of changes (i.e. incremental innovations), while collaboration with partners in the horizontal dimension is more likely to lead to leap-wise changes (i.e. radical innovations)'. Generally, Leborgne and Lipietz (1992, p. 399) argue that 'the upgrading of the partner increases the efficiency of the whole network'.

This reorganisation of networking between firms can be described as a change from the dominance of vertical relations between principal firms and their subcontractors to horizontal relations between principal firms and suppliers. Patchell (1993, p. 797) refers to this as a transformation from production systems to learning systems, which implies a transition from 'a conventional understanding of production systems as fixed flows of goods and services to dynamic systems based on learning'.

### Agglomeration as the context for interactive learning

At the regional level the challenge is to increase the innovative capability of SME-based industrial agglomerations through identifying 'the economic logic by which milieu fosters innovation' (Storper, 1995c, p. 203). Generally, it is important to underline the need for 'enterprise support systems, such as technology centres or service centres, which can help keep networks of firms innovative' (Amin and Thrift, 1995, p. 12). Such innovative support structures could be seen as part of a region's 'untraded interdependencies', that is, 'a structured set of technological externalities which can be a *collective asset* of groups of firms/industries within countries/regions' (Dosi, 1988, p. 226). Accordingly, the main argument for the territorial agglomeration of economic activity in a contemporary capitalist economy is that it provides the best context for an innovation-based learning economy.

These ideas are more or less the same as those which Perroux, another Schumpeter-inspired economist, presented in the early 1950s. Perroux argued that it was possible to talk about 'growth poles' (or 'development poles' at a later stage in his writing) in 'abstract economic spaces' defined as a 'plan' (the vertical relationships of a production system) as well as a 'homogenous aggregate' (the horizontal relationships of a branch), that is, firms which are linked together with an innovative 'key industry' to form an industrial complex. According to Perroux, the growth potential and competitiveness of growth poles can be intensified by territorial agglomeration (Haraldsen, 1994; Perroux, 1970). This perspective on the importance of agglomerations can find support from modern innovation theory originating from the new institutional economics, which argues that 'regional production systems, industrial districts and technological districts are becoming increasingly important' (Lundvall, 1992, p. 3), and from Porter, who emphasises that 'the process of clustering, and the interchange among industries in the cluster, also works best when the industries involved are geographically concentrated' (Porter, 1990, p. 157).

In both conventional and Schumpeterian-based regional economics, agglomeration economies are understood in terms of external economies, normally specified as 'localisation' and 'urbanisation' economies respectively. The idea is used as a *functional* concept describing an intensification of the external economies of a production system by territorial agglomeration. In Marshall's view, external economies are obtained through the geographical concentration of groups of vertically and horizontally linked small firms (that is, 'localisation' economies) (Marshall 1986). In regional economic theory, the achievement of external economies of scale is not conditioned by a territorial agglomeration of industrial complexes such as Perroux's 'growth pole'.

In contrast to regional economic theory, Marshall attaches a more independent role to agglomeration economies. The 'Marshallian' view of the basic structures of industrial districts predates the idea of 'embeddedness' as a key analytical concept in understanding the workings of the districts (Granovetter, 1985). It is precisely embeddedness in broader socio-cultural factors, originating in precapitalist civil societies, that represents the material basis for Marshall's view of agglomeration economies as the specific *territorial* aspect of geographically agglomerated economic activity. This concerns the quality of the social milieu of industrial districts and only indirectly affects the profits of firms. Among such factors, Marshall emphasises, in particular: the 'mutual knowledge and trust' that reduces transaction costs in the local production system; the 'industrial atmosphere' which facilitates the generation of skills and qualifications required by local industry; and the effect of both these aspects in promoting (incremental) innovations and innovation diffusion among SMEs in industrial districts (Asheim, 1992,

1994). By defining agglomeration economies as socially and territorially embedded properties of an area, Marshall abandons 'the pure logic of economic mechanisms and introduces a sociological approach in his analysis' (Dimou, 1994, p. 27). Harrison emphasises that this mode of theorising is fundamentally different from the one found in conventional regional economics or in any other neoclassically based agglomeration theory (Harrison, 1991).

According to the importance modern innovation theory places on interactive learning, it could be argued that the combination of territorially embedded Marshallian agglomeration economies, disembodied knowledge and 'untraded interdependencies' could constitute the material basis for a new form of socially created competitive advantage for regions in the globalised economy. This would represent a strong position against the argument that 'ubiquitification', as an outcome of globalisation and codification processes, in general will 'undermine the competitiveness of firms in high-cost regions and nations' (Maskell, 1997, p. 1). Such an argument is implicitly based on the dominance of a near free-market situation in the global economy, leaving no room for the importance of networks, clusters and agglomerations as the material basis for imperfect competition.

The growing interest in the role of national and regional innovation systems must be understood as a policy instrument aiming at a systematic promotion of localised learning processes in order to secure the innovativeness and competitive advantage of national or regional economies (Freeman, 1995). In this context, it makes sense, analytically as well as politically, to distinguish between different types of regional innovation systems. On the one hand, we find innovation systems that could be called a regionalised national innovation system, that is, parts of the production structure and the institutional infrastructure located in a region but functionally integrated in, or equivalent to, national (or international) innovation systems, which is based on a top-down, linear model of innovation. On the other hand, we can identify innovation systems constituted by the parts of the production structure and institutional set-up that is territorially integrated or embedded within a particular region, and built up by a bottom-up, interactive innovation model (Asheim and Isaksen, 1997).

Thus, it seems as if the most viable alternative for advanced welfare states is a policy of *strong competition* (Storper and Walker, 1989), a form of competition building on innovation and a 'differentiation' strategy on the basis of *localised learning*, in industrial *clusters* and territorial *agglomerations*, supported by interactive, *regional innovation systems*.

# Endogenous development in industrial districts

## *Italian industrial districts*

The European experience of industrial districts has become a major point of reference in the recent international debate on industrial policy promoting endogenous development. The most important general, as well as specific, structural factors of industrial districts (especially in the Third Italy), could be listed as:

- extensive division of labour between firms;
- strong product specialisation;
- effective information network;
- high competence level of the workforce;
- socio-cultural embeddedness;
- existence of public and private support institutions.

Of significant importance is the understanding of industrial districts as a 'social and economic whole', where the success of the districts is as dependent on broader social and institutional aspects as on economic factors in a narrow sense (Pyke and Sengenberger, 1990). Bellandi (1989) emphasises that the economies of the districts originate from the thick local texture of interdependencies between small firms and the local community. Becattini (1990, p. 40) maintains that 'the firms become rooted in the territory, and this result cannot be conceptualised independently of its historical development'.

Thus, the major differentiating factors in play in the Third Italy are not the techno-economic structures as such, but rather the importance of non-economic factors for the economic performance of the regions. This is also in accordance with the new understanding of the social, cultural and institutional context of the learning economy, emphasising the importance of the 'fusion' of the economy with society (Piore and Sabel, 1984).

This formation of innovative capacity and successful fostering of competitive advantage at the regional level has turned many traditional industrial districts, especially in Emilia-Romagna, into *technological districts*, which have been capable of taking on international competition through making dynamic use of new technologies (Cappechi, 1996; Storper, 1992). New demand for a different kind of production and services has created a need for new technological districts, 'directed not at a mass public, or catering for the demands of industry, but oriented towards promoting a better quality of life and environment' (Capecchi, 1996, p. 176). The future challenge in the industrial districts is to do this without endangering the endogenous innovation potential from which they grew in the earlier development phases.

Learning from the Emilia-Romagna model of policy-making it is important to understand that the economic development of the region has not simply been 'the result of a "spontaneous" development but, rather, it has been assisted by a process of institutional building aimed at the creation of an intermediate governance structure capable of establishing a positive enabling environment for firm development' (Bianchi, 1996, p. 204). This points to the relevance of experiences of the third phase of the development of the Emilia-Romagna model, as this is the stage when enterprise support of a more proactive kind has been introduced by agreement amongst SMEs, the regional government and the intermediary agencies.

Furthermore, the creation of networks of supporting institutions, such as service centres are 'not intended merely to supply technical advice that firms cannot find locally. There are a myriad of cases of business centres throughout Europe which, operating on this basis, have failed to change the efficiency of local firms. Rather, the aim should be for a service centre to act as a kind of social catalyst, including groups of firms and institutions, both public and private, to interact and establish virtuous circuits of knowledge diffusion' (ibid., p. 205).

### *A Norwegian industrial district: Jæren*

Although much smaller than industrial districts in the Third Italy, one of the best examples of an industrial district in Norway is Jæren, located south of Stavanger in the south-western part of Norway. Here an organisation called TESA (Technical Cooperation) was established by local industry in 1957, with the aim of supporting technological development among the member firms, which were small and medium-sized, export-orientated firms producing mainly farm machinery. This has, among other things, resulted in the district today being the centre for industrial robot technology in Norway with a competence within industrial electronics/microelectronics which is far above the general level in the country. Furthermore, the use of industrial robots is much more widespread in this region than in the rest of Norway (that is, about one-third of all industrial robots with only 3 per cent of Norway's industrial employment) (Asheim, 1993).

In 1994 TESA had 13 member firms employing more than 2,800 persons and with a turnover of NOK 2.2 billion. The TESA firms have overall a very high export share, with an average of 63 per cent (that is, NOK 1.4 billion in 1992). However, in some firms a far larger share is exported; three firms had an export share of more than 90 per cent in 1992 (Lærdal (medical equipment) 96 per cent, ABB Flexible Automation (painting robots) 96 per cent, and Kverneland (farm machinery) 91 per cent, increasing to 94 per cent in 1993). According to the firms, without the inter-firm technological cooperation within TESA the development of this very strong competitive advantage would not have been possible.

As part of the work to promote the member firms competitive advantage, TESA took active part in the establishment of JÆRTEK (Jæren's technology centre) in 1987. The aim of JÆRTEK is to offer training which prepares workers and pupils in technical schools for the advanced industrial work of tomorrow, and to secure the competence basis for a continued, rapid technological development. To achieve this, the first complete computer-integrated manufacturing (CIM) equipment in Norway was installed in JÆRTEK. Later the CIM concept was diffused to several other member firms, among them Kverneland, which used the investment in CIM to combat the reduced demand for agricultural machinery in Europe through increased productivity and competitiveness. This strategy resulted in a strong increase in turnover in 1994 and 1995, making Kverneland the largest producer of ploughs in Europe.

The best-known firm at Jæren is ABB Flexible Automation, which was called Trallfa Robot before it was bought by ABB in the late 1980s. At that time Trallfa Robot supplied around 50 per cent of the European market for painting robots to the car industry. If ABB had applied their normal restructuring strategy, the robot production at Jæren would have been closed down, and moved to Västerås in Sweden, where handling robots were produced on a much larger scale. Instead, the production capacity at Jæren has been increased from 200 robots in the early 1990s to 600 in 1995, and 1,000 were forecast for 1996. This means that ABB Flexible Automation today covers 70 per cent of the demand for painting robots in the European car industry and 30 per cent in the USA. The workforce has been increased by 80 persons from 1994 to 1996, reaching a total of 230 employed; turnover was around NOK 290 million in 1995, making it the most profitable ABB unit in Norway. In addition, the factory at Jæren has been upgraded to a so-called 'supplying unit' in the ABB corporation, and the production of handling robots has in part been transferred from Västerås to Jæren.

The reasons for the success story of ABB Flexible Automation has partly to do with the informal, tacit knowledge and social qualifications of the workforce (that is, Marshall's 'industrial atmosphere' as a result of strong common values – the Protestant work ethic – and close family ties in the communities that characterise the region), and partly to do with the localised form of codified knowledge constituted by the specific, disembodied knowledge about painting robots at the factory of Jæren, and the general, interactive learning-based knowledge of robot technology in TESA, which represents region-specific 'untraded interdependencies'. These factors were recognised by ABB as being extremely important for the competitive advantage of ABB Flexible Automation (Asheim and Isaksen, 1995).

The close, horizontal interfirm cooperation and interacting learning process, resulting in the development of core technologies (*radical* product and process innovations) existing in this district is almost unique in an international context. The technological cooperation was strongly dependent on the high level of internal resources and competence of the firms, and did not originally involve R&D institutions in the regional 'capital' of Stavanger. However, in later years, regional and national R&D institutions gradually became more closely involved in R&D work (for example, Rogaland

Research in Stavanger, Chr. Michelsens Institute in Bergen, and the Technical University and SINTEF in Trondheim).

It could be argued that there exists a territorially embedded, regional innovation system at Jæren, where TESA, as a 'Business service centre', is at the core of the system, and where the collaborating partners have been extended from the original local firms and technical schools to comprise regional and national R&D institutions. However, the local industry is still governing activities through TESA, which also functions as a secretariat for all industrial robot research in Norway and now is located close to the University College in Stavanger and to Rogaland Research. This embedded regional innovation system has played a key role in securing the competitiveness of the local industry, and will also have an important role to play in the future in promoting the industrial renewal necessary to upgrade some of the more traditional firms in the farm-machinery branch to higher value-added production. The basis for doing so must be said to be excellent against the background of the high technological competence represented by the TESA firms.

## Conclusions

The distinction between the two different types of regional innovation systems, a regionalised, national system and a territorial system respectively, is both important and valid. This is especially the case against the background of alternative, modern theories of innovation, where innovation is looked upon as essentially a social process, and the empirical experiences of endogenous regional development based on agglomerated, networking SMEs, where industrial growth is understood as a territorial process. This perspective favours the kind of policy approaches which are:

(i)   context-sensitive, i.e. adaptable to differences between firms and industrial structures in different regions;
(ii)  production systems-oriented rather than firm-oriented; and
(iii) directed towards the ongoing adjustment capacities of regional economies, rather than once-and-for-all implementations of so-called best practices.

(Storper and Scott, 1995, p. 513)

However, for a regionally embedded innovation system to bring about radical innovations there is often a need to supplement the informal, tacit and disembodied, codified knowledge in this kind of innovation systems with R&D competence and more strategic accomplished basic research and development. In the long run most SMEs cannot rely only on services from territorially embedded innovation systems. Thus, this implies a regional innovation policy which more closely links regionally embedded innovation systems with regionalised and national ones.

# References

Amin, A. and Cohendet, P. (1997) Learning and adaptation in decentralised business networks, paper presented at European Management and Organisations in Transition (EMOT) final conference, Stresa, Italy, September.

Amin, A. and Thrift, N. (1995) Territoriality in the global political economy, *Nordisk Samhällsgeografisk Tidskrift*, no. 20, 3–16.

Archibugi, D. and Michie, J. (1995) Technology and innovation. An introduction, *Cambridge Journal of Economics*, 19, 1–4.

Asheim, B.T. (1992) Flexible specialization, industrial districts and small firms: a critical appraisal, in H. Ernste and V. Meier (eds), *Regional Development and Contemporary Industrial Response: Extending Flexible Specialization*, London: Belhaven Press, 45–63.

Asheim, B.T. (1993) En komparativ analyse av industriregionene Jæren og Gnosjø, in A. Isaksen (ed.), *Spesialiserte produksjonsområder i Norden*, Nordisk Samhällsgeografisk Tidskrift, Uppsala, 109–41.

Asheim, B.T. (1994) Industrial districts, inter-firm co-operation and endogenous technological development: the experience of developed countries, in *Technological Dynamism in Industrial Districts: An Alternative Approach to Industrialization in Developing Countries?* New York and Geneva: UNCTAD, 91–142.

Asheim, B.T. (1996) Industrial districts as 'learning regions': a condition for prosperity? *European Planning Studies*, 4, 4: 379–400.

Asheim, B.T. and Isaksen, A. (1995) Spesialiserte produksjonsområder mellom globalisering og regionalisering, in D. Olberg (ed.), *Endringer i næringslivets organisering*, Oslo: FAFO, 61–97.

Asheim, B.T. and Isaksen, A. (1997) Location, agglomeration and innovation: towards regional innovation systems in Norway, *European Planning Studies*, 5, 3: 299–330.

Becattini, G. (1990) The Marshallian industrial district as a socio-economic notion, in F. Pyke *et al.* (eds), *Industrial Districts and Inter-firm Cooperation in Italy,* Geneva: International Institute for Labour Studies, 37–51.

Bellandi, M. (1989) The industrial district in Marshall, in E. Goodman and J. Bamford (eds), *Small Firms and Industrial Districts in Italy*, London: Routledge, 136–52.

Bianchi, P. (1996) New approaches to industrial policy at the local level, in F. Cossentino *et al.* (eds), *Local and Regional Response to Global Pressure: The Case of Italy and its Industrial Districts*, Research series 103, Geneva: International Institute for Labour Studies, 195–206.

Bonaccorsi, A. and Lipparini, A. (1994) Strategic partnerships in new product development: an Italian case study, *Journal of Product Innovation Management*, 11, 2: 135–46.

Brusco, S. (1996) Global systems and local systems, in F. Cossentino *et al.* (eds), *Local and Regional Response to Global Pressure: The Case of Italy and its Industrial Districts*, Research series 103, Geneva: International Institute for Labour Studies, 145–58.

Cappechi, V. (1996) New technological districts for promoting quality of life and the environment, in F. Cossentino *et al.* (eds), *Local and Regional Response to Global Pressure: The Case of Italy and its Industrial Districts*, Research series 103, Geneva: International Institute for Labour Studies, 175–194.

Castro, E. de and Jensen-Butler, C. (1993) *Flexibility, Routine Behaviour and the Neo-classical Model in the Analysis of Regional Growth*, Department of Political Science, University of Aarhus, Denmark.

Dei Ottati, G. (1994) Cooperation and competition in the industrial district as an organization model, *European Planning Studies*, 2, 4: 463–83.

Dimou, P. (1994) The industrial district: a stage of a diffuse industrialization process. The case of Roanne, *European Planning Studies*, 2, 1: 23–38.

Dosi, G. (1988) The nature of the innovative process, in G. Dosi *et al.* (eds), *Technical Change and Economic Theory,* London: Pinter Publishers, 221–38.

Freeman, C. (1995) The 'national system of innovation' in historical perspective, *Cambridge Journal of Economics*, 19: 5–24.

Grabher, G. (1993) Rediscovering the social in the economics of interfirm relations, in G. Grabher (ed.), *The Embedded Firm: On the Socioeconomics of Industrial Networks,* London: Routledge, 1–31.

Granovetter, M. (1985) Economic action and social structure: the problem of embeddedness, *American Journal of Sociology*, 91, 3: 481–510.

Håkansson, H. (1992) *Corporate Technological Behaviour: Co-operation and Networks,* London: Routledge.

Haraldsen, T. (1994) *Teknologi, økonomi og rom – en teoretisk analyse av relasjoner mellom industrielle og territorielle endringsprosesser,* doctoral dissertation, Department of Social and Economic Geography, Lund University, Lund: Lund University Press.

Harrison, B. (1991) Industrial districts: old wine in new bottles? Working paper 90–35, School of Urban and Public Affairs, Carnegie-Mellon University, Pittsburg.

Lazonick, W. (1993) Industry cluster versus global webs: organizational capabilities in the American economy, *Industrial and Corporate Change*, 2: 1–24.

Leborgne, D. and Lipietz, A. (1992) Conceptual fallacies and open questions on post-Fordism, in M. Storper and A.J. Scott (eds), *Pathways to Industrialization and Regional Development,* London: Routledge, 332–48.

Lipparini, A. and Lorenzoni, G. (1994) Strategic sourcing and organizational boundaries adjustment: a process-based perspective, paper presented at the workshop on 'The changing boundaries of the firm', European Management and Organisations in Transition (EMOT), European Science Foundation, Como, Italy, October.

Lorenz, E. (1992) Trust, community, and cooperation: towards a theory of industrial districts, in M. Storper and A. Scott (eds), *Pathway to Industrialization and Regional Development*, London: Routledge, 195–204.

Lundvall, B.-Å. (1992) Introduction, in B.-Å. Lundvall (ed.), *National Systems of Innovation,* London: Pinter Publishers, 1–19.

Lundvall, B.-Å. and Johnson, B. (1994) The learning economy, *Journal of Industry Studies*, 1, 2: 23–42.

Marshall, A. (1986) *Principles of Economics*, 8th edn, London: Macmillan.

Maskell, P. (1997): Space and industrial competitiveness: the process and consequences of ubiquitification, paper presented at the conference of the IGU commission on the Organisation of Industrial Space, Gothenburg, Sweden, August.

Morgan, K. (1995) Institutions, innovation and regional renewal: the development agency as animateur, paper presented at the Regional Studies Association conference on 'Regional futures: past and present, east and west', Gothenburg, Sweden, May.

Patchell, J. (1993) From production systems to learning systems: lessons from Japan, *Environment and Planning A,* 25: 797–815.

Perroux, F. (1970) Note on the concept of growth poles, in D. McKee *et al.* (eds), *Regional Economics: Theory and Practice*, New York: The Free Press, 93–103.

Piore, M. and Sabel, C. (1984) *The Second Industrial Divide: Possibilities for Prosperity*, New York: Basic Books.

Porter, M. (1990) *The Competitive Advantage of Nations*, London: Macmillan.

Pyke, F. (1994) *Small Firms, Technical Services and Inter-firm Cooperation*, Geneva: International Institute for Labour Studies.

Pyke, F. and Sengenberger, W. (1990) Introduction, in F. Pyke *et al.* (eds), *Industrial Districts and Inter-firm Co-operation in Italy*, Geneva: International Institute for Labour Studies, 1–9.

Reich, R. (1991) *The Work of Nations: Preparing Ourselves for 21st Century Capitalism*, New York: Basic Books.

Sabel, C. (1992) Studied trust: building new forms of cooperation in a volatile economy, in F. Pyke and W. Sengenberger (eds), *Industrial Districts and Local Economic Regeneration*, Geneva: International Institute for Labour Studies, 215–50.

Smith, K. (1994) *New Directions in Research and Technology Policy: Identifying the Key Issues*, STEP Report no. 1, Oslo: STEP Group.

Storper, M. (1992) The limits to globalization: technology districts and international trade, *Economic Geography*, 68, 1: 60–93.

Storper, M. (1995a) Regional technology coalitions: an essential dimension of national technology policy, *Research Policy*, 24: 895–911.

Storper, M. (1995b) Competitiveness policy options: the technology–regions connection, *Growth and Change*, 26, 285–308.

Storper, M. (1995c) The resurgence of regional economies, ten years later: the region as a nexus of untraded interdependencies, *European Urban and Regional Studies*, 2: 191–221.

Storper, M. and Scott, A. (1995) The wealth of regions, *Futures*, 27, 5: 505–26.

Storper, M. and Walker, R. (1989) *The Capitalist Imperative. Territory, Technology, and Industrial Growth*, New York: Basil Blackwell.

You, J.-I. and Wilkinson, F. (1994) Competition and co-operation: toward understanding industrial districts, *Review of Political Economy*, 6: 259–78.

# 5   Europe's advantage?

## Work organisation, innovation and employment

*Peter Totterdill*

## Introduction

New ways of working, and new types of work, could transform Europe in the twenty-first century. There is now a clear opportunity to enhance the competitiveness of European businesses, to increase the performance of public services, and to raise both quality of life in the workplace and co-operation between social actors. At the same time new forms of work organisation can offer an important resource in the crucial struggle against unemployment in Europe. But the urgent task is to raise awareness as widely as possible of the need for innovation, and for a change from models based on cost-cutting and the reduction or deskilling of labour.

This paper is the product of active collaboration between some of the leading European organisations involved in the enhancement of working life and competitiveness. The European Work & Technology Consortium was originally created to prepare a Medium Term Plan for Collaborative Action at the request of Directorate-General V of the European Commission. Informed by the outcomes of this Plan, the partners are now actively engaged in collaborative research, development and dissemination in the field. Building on past achievements in each member state, the Consortium will provide an important vehicle for exchanging experience, promoting innovation and resourcing change throughout the EU.

The aim of the paper is to share a broad vision of how these goals can be achieved through partnership and co-operation at local, national and transnational levels. In particular it seeks to explain:

- why work organisation is an important issue for policy-makers, social partners, enterprises and other interests;
- how change can be successfully promoted;
- why the Consortium is a necessary part of the European picture.

The paper is also an invitation to social and economic partners, to industrial experts and to researchers who wish to join the debate, and to collaborate with the Consortium in the transformation of work in Europe.

# Work organisation and changing patterns of competitiveness in Europe

Changing patterns of competitiveness in global markets, changing expectations of consumers and citizens, and increasing demands for new solutions to growing social and environmental problems all call into question the principles which have underpinned the organisation of work for much of this century.

## *Competitive advantage in the 1990s and beyond*

- Competitiveness must be achieved by means of a strong commitment to innovation, quality, customisation, responsiveness to the market and versatility, rather than by price alone.
- Profitable markets are likely to be segmented and international, involving a large number of specialised customers in several countries. They demand new and sophisticated solutions, reflecting growth in areas such as multimedia and telecommunications, services and environmental protection.
- For manufacturers, segmented markets mean that short production runs and frequent product changes become the norm; Tayloristic approaches are therefore seen to be increasingly unworkable and are replaced by versatile, group-based systems and adapted technology.
- For service providers in both public and private sectors, it is necessary to achieve greater versatility, customisation and high-quality responsiveness while anticipating the wider needs of the market and society.
- Greater emphasis on quality, innovation and versatility enhance the need for continuing vocational education and training, combining technical polyvalency with non-technical skills such as communication, teamwork, problem-solving and planning.
- The future is no longer seen to lie with large, vertically integrated companies; smaller, highly flexible units – either SMEs or loosely attached to parent companies – co-operating with each other will provide much more of the competitive edge for Europe's economy.
- Long-term pressures for increasing levels of innovation demand new forms of communication and co-operation within and between firms, linking them to support services, centres of expertise and research laboratories.

It is by maximising their use of human potential that organisations achieve innovation and change. Throughout many sectors of the European economy there is an increasing recognition of the need for new approaches to management, to the use of skills and to the nature of work itself. In both manufacturing and services, the precondition for effectiveness is to create 'intelligent' organisations, capable of gathering and analysing data from a wide range of sources, of translating this process of analysis into day-to-day practice, and of fostering reflexivity at all levels. The intelligent organisation is therefore defined as one which, informed by strategic research and information, creates new ways of promoting innovation and problem-solving across the whole workforce. Achieving such a vision means changing – and enriching – the way in which people work. As many European managers have come to realise, the task is to raise organisational performance through the enhancement of working life.

Yet organisational change remains constrained by many obstacles. The movement away from traditional ways of working has only just begun in Europe, despite the scale and scope of innovation apparent in other parts of the world. Co-ordinated action is therefore required to smooth the path of change.

## The new European model of work organisation

How can we identify and define the forms of work organisation capable of addressing these challenges? Are emerging European approaches distinct from the well-documented global trends towards 'lean production' or 'Japanisation'?

It can be argued that both Japanese and US models, with their narrow structural emphasis on productivity, are quite distinct from European trends. A tendency towards 'job enlargement rather than job enrichment' appears to characterise, for example, the American automotive industry or Japanese-owned plants in the UK. Workers in such plants are required to be versatile and well trained, but real empowerment and creativity on the shopfloor or in the office is limited.

Existing European tendencies are typically derived from quite different philosophical starting points. Competitiveness is seen as the product of a wider social process, in which education and culture provide the cornerstones of innovation. Critically, the European approach is identified by reflexivity and learning both inside and outside the organisation. Likewise, work is seen as an essential part of human life and an important part of individual identity. By offering real opportunities for creativity and participation to all employees, new approaches to work organisation can fuel learning and innovation. Quality of working life therefore becomes central to the success of the enterprise.

Looking forward, the defining characteristics of a possible European model lie in its attempt to balance four principal elements: the humanisation of work through improved job design and social relations; the widespread scope for innovation throughout the organisation; the design and deployment of technology in ways which maximise workforce potential and environmental protection; and increasing employment to reduce the waste of human resources in the labour market.

There is, of course, no guarantee that this approach will successfully take root on any scale in Europe; indeed, a struggle for dominance is taking place between a range of post-Taylorist alternatives. The Consortium clearly aims to take sides – against the dehumanising aspects and ecological damage which typify some models and for an approach which closes the gap between economic performance, social well-being and environmental sustainability.

The urgent need is to establish a much stronger research base at European level in order to identify the scope of innovative practice in work organisation, the extent of change and the conditions supportive of success. Emerging trends must be evaluated in depth if their impact on efficiency, innovation and employment is to be fully understood. This will be built on the collective research resources of Consortium members.

## Employment and work organisation

Mass unemployment and the resulting patterns of inequality are amongst the most pressing problems which Europe faces. Therefore, new trends in work organisation must inevitably be judged in terms of their impact on employment.

Doubts have certainly been raised about the quantitative impact on jobs of new forms of work organisation. The increased productivity which results from organisational change can often reduce the need for labour. Moreover, the flattening of hierarchical structures can lead to the loss of supervisory and management employment.

While we can make no overall assessment of the quantitative impact on employment, the central argument here is that change based on learning and innovation will help to realise the full value of labour as the new 'wealth of nations', resulting in substantial opportunities for the creation and development of businesses and employment. But without this change, job losses across many industrial sectors could be considerable.

Increased productivity resulting from new forms of work organisation releases resources for the innovation and product development needed to build new economic activity and long-term competitiveness. Displaced staff can often be redeployed into new support functions such as the provision of continuing vocational education and training.

Moreover, the most vulnerable people in the labour market are often the least well trained. For many traditional industrial areas, the low skills base is the legacy of an economy built on Fordist mass production in which jobs were systematically deskilled or automated. In contrast, new forms of work organisation need employees to acquire increasing competence, both technically and in 'core transferable skills' such as planning, problem solving, communication and reflexivity. Acquisition of these skills may offer the individual a more robust position within the labour market, facilitating both horizontal and vertical mobility between firms and even between sectors. This enhancement of jobs and skills could be of particular benefit to women and other groups marginalised within traditionally low-status occupations.

New forms of work organisation can therefore support European employment targets in at least four ways:

1   by enhancing competitive advantage in traditional manufacturing sectors;
2   by enhancing opportunities for new job growth in areas of activity where versatility, innovation and quality are at a premium;
3   by enhancing individual mobility and opportunity in the labour market through the strengthening of non-sector-specific competencies such as problem solving, planning and communication;
4   by enhancing individual, social and economic potential at sectoral and regional levels through the reinforcement of skills, co-operation and networking.

## Problems of dissemination

Despite increasingly well-documented advantages, the spread of new approaches to work organisation and culture remains surprisingly limited in Europe. Inertia, combined with short-term approaches to productivity and investment, inhibit the pace of innovation at several levels:

- At the level of the company, many managers and trade unions fail to understand the nature and potential of work organisation change, or believe that experiences elsewhere cannot be relevant to their own enterprise. This appears to be particularly true of SMEs, where the exposure of management to alternatives is often very limited.
- Access to sources of expertise relating to work organisation and culture remains a serious problem for companies, especially SMEs. New approaches cannot be implemented 'off the shelf', but require a careful process of learning and negotiation. Experts with understanding and experience of these issues are rare or expensive, and companies may be reluctant to embark on a process of major change without appropriate guidance. New technical services and support structures are required to resource companies during the process of transition and beyond.
- Successful change needs to be well resourced with appropriate tools, expertise and understanding. Many organisations lack both the conceptual understanding and the practical tools needed to analyse, to plan and to implement the process of change. Indeed, the internal expertise available to even the largest organisations is insufficient to reflect and to draw on the scope of 'good practice' experience and methods to be found across Europe.
- Organisations often fail to maximise potential gains because their approach to change lacks a cultural dimension. Tayloristic principles are deeply ingrained, and are often reinforced by training and peer-group norms. Renewal of organisational culture requires sustained change over an extended period of time.

- Public policy has often failed to grasp the significance of work organisation for competitiveness and employment, and often lacks the tools to promote innovation and dissemination.

The individual firm is too weak an instrument around which to build change. Innovation is intimately related to the firm's wider social environment, the semi-public sphere which defines access to knowledge, exchange of experience and shared resources. In short, this environment determines firms' ability to overcome internal limitations by developing collective solutions to common problems.

Public policy has a key role to play in changing this environment. Business support organisations, consultants, trainers, employers' associations and trade unions lack detailed knowledge of the nature and potential of new forms of work organisation. While individual cases of innovative practice may develop, few channels exist for the systematic exchange of information and experience. Tools and expertise may be developed within a particular firm or sector but with little opportunity to explore their relevance for other types of organisation. Likewise, experience generated within big companies is rarely disseminated in a format appropriate to SMEs.

The need is to promote opportunities for collective learning about the design and implementation of new approaches to work organisation, building broad communities of expertise at local and sectoral levels and leading to new technical resources to support change. Cultural factors, industrial relations and the co-operation of social partners will clearly be crucial in achieving this goal.

Principal elements in such a programme would include the following:

- Change in the workplace needs to be underpinned by a coherent programme of research designed to identify good practice in system design and implementation. Development programmes are also needed to generate new tools for change and to monitor their use.
- Networking and co-operation between enterprises should play a key role in research and development initiatives, building bridges between academics and practitioners and creating opportunities for the extensive dissemination of outcomes.
- New forms of work organisation are likely to create quite different demands on business support services and this needs to be reflected in local and regional economic development policy initiatives.
- Growing demand for polyvalency and self-efficacy skills in the workplace has far-reaching implications for the content and delivery of training, including the need for further curricular adaptations and innovation in established systems of vocational education.

In short, a range of specialised services, access to continuous networking opportunities and innovative vocational training structures are all required to support new forms of work organisation. Such a support framework should be accessible at local and sectoral levels even to the smallest firms. This, of course, requires clear local, regional, national and European public policy commitments.

## Public policy

How have public policy initiatives sought to influence the emergence of alternative forms of work organisation in Europe?

The first wave of concern about the nature of work occurred during the 1960s, initially in Scandinavia and in other parts of northern Europe, as a result of widespread labour recruitment and retention problems during a sustained period of low unemployment. During the 1970s 'quality of working life' programmes appeared in Denmark, France, Germany, The Netherlands, Norway, Sweden and elsewhere, often generating successful pilot projects but with few examples of the successful outcomes becoming generalised within the wider economy. However, such programmes have played a strategic role in building expertise and in creating a climate conducive to change.

It was not until the 1980s that the full significance of such initiatives began to emerge. Erosion of mass markets and the need for greater flexibility, quality and innovation cast the issue of work organisation in a new light. National programmes in countries such as France, Germany and Sweden began to place more emphasis on the importance of working life in achieving competitive advantage.

But obstacles to the widespread dissemination of new approaches to work organisation are still much in evidence. Targeted intervention by public agencies, industry associations and trade unions is required to address these problems through sustained partnership and co-operation. Such intervention needs to bridge the traditional separation of research and development activities from the mainstream of organisational practice. Moreover, traditional research and development activity exhibited a strong focus on technological promotion, at the expense of organisational needs. This has contributed to enduring losses in productivity and to declining competitiveness.

These gaps underline the need for new forms of action at the local and regional levels. Many localities and regions in Europe have established sophisticated economic development and employment strategies, but most do not embrace work organisation as a policy issue. However, some promising initiatives are beginning to appear. Partnerships between public policy agencies in France and Germany, for example, have created a new generation of institutions designed to promote innovative forms of work organisation at regional level. Likewise, in Sweden universities are collaborating with the National Institute for Working Life to build local programmes for innovation and dissemination.

However, it must also be recognised that the development of a coherent policy framework on any spatial scale faces certain obstacles in terms of perception: unlike other policy priorities, work organisation may seem obscure and intangible. Awareness-raising amongst both policy-makers and social partners is therefore an important first step

## *Policy issues at the European level*

A strategic programme for the development and dissemination of new forms of work organisation would certainly contribute towards the achievement of important European Union targets. The *Growth, Competitiveness, Employment* White Paper cites four overriding objectives:

- to help European firms to adapt to the new conditions of global competition;
- to exploit the competitive advantage associated with the shift towards a knowledge-based economy;
- to promote sustainable industrial development;
- to make supply more responsive to demand.

New forms of work organisation pursue these objectives by helping firms to build new, long-term forms of competitive advantage; these are based on innovation and versatility achieved through the more effective development and deployment of human knowledge and skills. Indeed, the White Paper specifically cites the need to move away from Taylorism as a precondition for the shift towards a knowledge-based 'quality' economy.

This of course raises a number of challenges: the White Paper, for example, points to the need to ensure that education and training systems recognise the growing need for new types of competence associated with emerging patterns of work organisation: 'the ability to learn, to communicate, to work in a group and to assess one's own situation' and 'to learn how to learn throughout one's life'. Indeed, a competitive workforce must be based on the ability to thrive under conditions of uncertainty and unpredictability – conditions characterised by 'the permanent recomposition and redevelopment and know-how'. These needs have since been recognised in the design and implementation of several EU initiatives, notably ADAPT, LEONARDO and SOCRATES.

However, the response to changing conditions cannot be considered solely as a matter of workforce adaptation: the need to restructure organisations themselves must be recognised. According to the Expert Group on Flexibility and Work Organisation:

> Models for the future shaping of company structures and organisational competence have become one of the determining factors for the future competitive strength of European enterprises.
>
> (CEC, 1995, p. 5)

Traditional forms of work organisation are well suited to mass production in a stable environment. But, as this paper has argued, such conditions no longer prevail in the European economy. As the demand for quality, versatility and innovation become increasingly central to the competitiveness of European firms then the need for change becomes imperative.

In addition, the White Paper reaffirms the need to improve existing career opportunities for women. Clearly, this can be done through the creation of new types of job: the growth of the 'caring' professions is specifically cited. EU policy measures, such as the New Opportunities for Women (NOW) programme, have partly focused on the recruitment of women into occupations in which they have traditionally been under-represented. However, new forms of work organisation can also enhance the types of jobs currently undertaken by women through multiskilling, empowerment and job enrichment.

In terms of the 'information society', information and communication technologies (ICTs) may play an important role in helping firms to liberate themselves from traditional patterns of work organisation. However, further study is required to assess the impact of ICTs on company structures and practices, and to formulate appropriate policy responses.

Organisational needs as well as technological innovation should also be established as a clear priority for research and development within the Fifth Framework programme.

### *The case for a European strategy*

To summarise, an EU programme for work organisation can be justified because:

- it would ensure the more effective dissemination of innovations from existing national or regional programmes to enterprises (including SMEs) throughout Europe, especially to those countries without comparable domestic initiatives;
- more effective co-ordination between existing programmes could lead to the pooling of expertise and experience with resulting benefits for quality and for the effective use of resources;
- many aspects of working life remain essentially arduous, monotonous, unhealthy and unstimulating: this calls out for a co-ordinated European programme to ensure that the restructuring of industry takes place through the enhancement, and not the degradation of human labour;
- it would help address the need to create and to sustain employment.

It is therefore clear that a much stronger policy focus on organisational change is required. This is recognised by the DG V Expert Group on Flexibility and Work Organisation, which proposes that:

An action plan for organisational innovation should be set up, in which national and regional programmes for research and development in organisational innovation are combined. This programme should raise awareness of the issue, transfer and diffuse knowledge and experience, promote co-operation between national activities and strengthen European organisational research and development.

(CEC, 1995)

The principal policy problem is twofold:

- how to develop this paradigm further and to provide access to good practice through the development of appropriate models, tools, case studies and evaluative research;
- how to ensure the more effective dissemination of new approaches to work organisation through the provision of appropriate advisory and technical support to companies, especially to SMEs.

## Adding value: the role of the Consortium

In summary, the Consortium believes that there is both the need and potential to build a transnational approach to research, development and dissemination in the field of work organisation. This must be achieved in a way which leads to the maximum possible sharing of information, experience and resources, while valuing the diversity to be found between different member states, localities, sectors, organisations and theoretical frameworks. It must also be achieved through partnership, not just by collaboration between expert institutions but with the active involvement of companies, trade unions and economic development/labour market agencies.

Consequently the aspirations of the Consortium can be summarised in the following terms:

- The European model of work organisation is still emerging, yet it contains characteristics which distinguish it from US and Japanese trends. The task of the Consortium will be to guide and to analyse the further development of the European approach. This approach is one which rejects a narrow focus on productivity, emphasising the centrality of involvement, innovation and creativity at all levels of the workforce. It is also central to Consortium's objectives that innovation in work organisation should offer the real possibility of convergence between improved competitiveness for the firm and enhanced quality of working life for its workforce.
- There is a widely recognised need to establish a sound research base on which the scope, direction and extent of change can be observed and evaluated. This would provide a solid basis for the design and delivery of development and dissemination activities.

- There is particular cause for optimism in the strength and pluralism of European intellectual and cultural traditions; this offers a unique laboratory for innovation. 'Diversity as a learning strategy' is therefore at the heart of the emerging European model of work organisation, and will guide the Consortium's vision and practice.
- At the same time it is essential to look critically and creatively at the dissemination of innovation to organisations across the whole of Europe. The key to this is partnership: creating interlinked 'communities of expertise' involving diverse actors at local, regional, national and transnational levels as well as in key sectors. Every firm or public service organisation should have access to a local or sectoral node capable of offering specialist resources to animate and support the change process.
- Every example of innovation and change – successful and unsuccessful – should be available as a resource for analysis and learning, creating a network culture based on reciprocity, mutual support and collaboration.

How can these aspirations be translated into practical measures? The Plan identified five strategic objectives, and these have been adopted as the principal targets for the continuing partnership.

*Objective 1*: To create a high level of co-ordination at European level between agencies concerned with research, development and dissemination in the field of work organisation.

The purpose of this co-ordination is to ensure the pooling of expertise and experience, thereby minimising duplication of effort whilst advancing the frontiers of good practice. Co-ordination will also provide a strategic point of reference to resource the development of policy in this field.

Objective 1 will be achieved by the creation of a formal Consortium led by the existing partners but also including other local, regional and national bodies. The Consortium would undertake a series of strategic measures to promote the exchange of experience and expertise.

*Objective 2*:  To promote policy measures and expert capacity for the promotion of new forms of work organisation at local/regional level.

While some member states have gained substantial experience and have built large-scale policy frameworks over a number of years, this is not the case elsewhere in the Union. Several countries and regions lack both the appropriate policy frameworks and the institutional structures capable of resourcing change at the level of the enterprise.

The objective is to raise awareness of work organisation amongst policy-makers and to disseminate experience from northern Europe, particularly targeting less-favoured countries and regions. This would be achieved through the creation of local/regional networks of expertise involving universities and research institutes, economic development agencies and the social partners, by undertaking local/regional research and pilot projects, and by linking local/regional networks across the EU.

*Objective 3*: To promote social dialogue on the implications of emerging forms of work organisation.

Work organisation is firmly grounded in industrial relations. Successful change – whether at plant level or in the wider economy – requires a high level of understanding and participation from the social partners. This can only be achieved through informed dialogue both within the enterprise and at a more strategic level in the local, regional and national economy. Exchanges of experience between member states could also provide an important means of raising the quality of this dialogue, and enhancing the role of the social partners as animators and guides of change.

*Objective 4*: To evaluate existing tools and methods of change; to define 'good practice' approaches to work organisation and to promote their dissemination across institutional, sectoral and national boundaries.

Many different approaches to the change process have been developed, but with little systematic analysis or comparison especially at transnational level. Good practices have also been slow to cross boundaries, in part because they have often grown from a specific industrial or organisational base, and require repackaging to reveal their generic qualities. Moreover, drawing on their wide-ranging experience, the partners have identified a number of priority areas in which existing knowledge and practice are underdeveloped.

This Objective has to be understood at two levels: (a) the 'meta level' of change, in other words the model of discourse and action which underpins problem definition, goal setting, system design, implementation and evaluation, including the selection of specific tools to resource individual parts of the process; and (b) the comparative efficacy of specific tools as instruments to achieve definable outputs in fields such as teambuilding, communication, innovation, culture change and performance measurement.

The Objective would be achieved by means of a core programme of research and development co-ordinated by the Consortium.

*Objective 5*: To identify and pilot innovative applications.

At the European level, experience of new forms of work organisation has developed rapidly in some sectors of manufacturing but remains limited elsewhere, including in many service industries.

At local, regional or national levels some sectors may have experienced little innovation even though counterpart organisations in other geographical areas may have changed considerably.

The intention is, first, to identify and assess existing project experiences and findings; second, to build transnational networks which support work organisation change in 'new' situations, whether new to a locality or new to Europe as a whole. This will be achieved through transnational expert teams, who will analyse the scope of potential change, broker the transfer of experience, oversee the implementation of change and evaluate outcomes.

## Current actions

The achievement of the objectives described above will take a number of years. However, support has now been secured from DG V to allow the Consortium to undertake work on the implementation of the Plan, and current activities include the following:

- the creation of a formal Consortium to undertake a programme of research, development and dissemination, leading to active collaboration and co-ordination between leading agencies on a long-term basis;
- undertaking an inventory of existing 'good practice' tools and methods, repacking these tools and methods to make them more universally available, and filling gaps in existing practice;
- exchanging experience through the creation of a European work organisation observatory, based on an electronic case study databank linked to a programme of related network activities involving companies and expert organisations;
- piloting applications in sectors, types of organisation and geographical regions with few precedents or experiences in the field;
- promoting dissemination to firms throughout the EU by building expert capacity and policy structures in localities and regions where these are currently weak or non-existent.

## Conclusion

This paper summarises current thinking and actions in the definition and realisation of a new vision. That vision will not only be drawn into sharper focus during the present phase of collaboration, but will change continuously through experience, experimentation and critical evaluation. It is this open-endedness and receptivity to innovation which constitutes an important source of strength and dynamism for Europe, and which adds excitement to the new initiative.

Fulfilling the aspirations expressed in this paper depends in part on continuing support from the European Union, but also on building and sustaining partnerships with actors and animators at national, regional and local throughout Europe. The Consortium intends to play a key role in building and sustaining these partnerships. Contributions to this process from a wide range of existing and future partners are both welcome and essential.

# References

Andreasen, L.E., Coriat, B., Kaplinsky, R. (eds) (1995) *Europe's Next Step: Organisational Innovation, Competition and Employment*, London: Frank Cass.

Commission of the European Communities (1995) *Social Europe* Supplement 1/95, Brussels: CEC.

European Community (1993) *Growth, Competitiveness, Employment*, White Paper, Brussels: CEC.

European Work and Technology Consortium (1996) *Towards a Medium Term Plan for Collaborative Action at the European Level*, Nottingham: Nottingham Trent University, and Longwy: CERRM.

Fröhlich, D. and Pekruhl, U. (1996) *Direct Participation and Organisational Change: Fashionable but Misunderstood?*, Dublin: European Foundation for the Improvement of Living and Working Conditions.

# 6 The competitive disadvantage of England

*Simon Lee*

## Introduction

This is an opportune moment to be considering the political economy of industrial policy in England for several reasons. First, as part of its wider agenda of constitutional reform for the UK, the Blair government is creating nine Regional Development Agencies (RDAs) for the English regions (DETR, 1997). The introduction of the RDAs from April 1999 will have major implications for industrial policy in England. However, even before the Regional Development Agencies Bill was brought before Parliament, some commentators had already questioned whether such proposals constituted a missed opportunity for both the government and the English regions (for example, Mawson, 1997a). Indeed, campaigners from one English region had issued 'A Declaration for the North' (Campaign for a Northern Assembly, 1997) in the hope of persuading the government to give the north-east (rather than the whole north of England as implied by the Campaign's title) its own referendum on devolution. Any discussion of industrial policy in England must therefore engage with this broader constitutional debate.

Second, the Blair government's adherence for the first two years of office to its Conservative predecessor's planned targets for public expenditure and its own year-long Comprehensive Spending Review (whose results were announced in July 1998) presage a period of austerity in the funding of national programmes supporting industrial policy, innovation and regeneration in the English regions. The combination of this austerity together with the differential approach to devolution in Scotland, Wales and the English regions adopted by the Blair government has raised sensitivities over the dated Barnett Formula for allocating public expenditure between the constituent nations of the UK. In particular, the apparent fiscal disadvantage that England suffers under the Barnett Formula and the fact that the government has chosen to exclude an updating of the formula from its Comprehensive Spending Review have been matters for extensive debate and no little dissent (for example, TC, 1997).

Third, this broader debate about resource allocation has been given added salience in the field of industrial policy because of the sense of grievance expressed by existing enterprise and development agencies in the English regions at their apparently inferior resources for attracting inward investment, especially when compared with those at the disposal of rival organisations in Scotland and Wales. Tempers have run high. Martin O'Neill, the House of Commons Trade and Industry Committee's Scottish chairman, has dismissed the charge from English development agencies of 'gazumping' by the Celtic regions as 'whingeing', attributing their failure to secure more inward investment to their 'rag, tag and bobtail' organisation (*Financial Times*, 19 November 1997). This rag, tag and bobtail organisation depiction in itself raises fundamental questions about the constraints which the centralised British state places upon industrial policy in the English regions in terms of their capacity both to attract inward investment and to incubate small and medium-sized enterprises (SMEs). These questions have been given new salience not only by the ongoing Asian financial crisis, which has raised fears about the future flow of inward investment and turned attention towards the effectiveness of policies to assist indigenous SMEs, but also by the likely implications of the European Union's (EU) Agenda 2000 (EU, 1997) which implies a dramatic reduction – with the potential exception of South Yorkshire and Merseyside – in the level of EU structural funds allocated to the English regions. This 'double whammy' of national austerity and lower supranational support will focus attention in turn on the capacity of development agencies within the English regions to sustain partnerships with and within the private sector to unlock collective external economies of scale in innovation (Oughton and Whittam, 1997).

To address these questions, this chapter analyses recent developments in the discourse about the English regions in order to suggest that there are at least two sources of competitive disadvantage for England arising from the current constitutional and industrial policy settlement. The first source is the deficit in regional institutional capacity which inhibits the English regions in the fierce competition for inward investment projects, when compared to their Scottish, Welsh and Irish neighbours. It is held that these resource and institutional deficits place severe constraints on the capacity to develop an effective regional innovation strategy. A second and parallel source of competitive disadvantage is a fiscal deficit arising from the current but obsolescent Barnett Formula for allocating public expenditure, which penalises the poorer English regions. The source of these twin competitive disadvantages is a third and more important English deficit, namely in England's national and regional identity. Because Englishness has been defined in terms of the institutions of the central British state, the English regions have been actively discouraged from developing their own distinctive identities. This deficit in identity has not been addressed by New Labour's attempts to rebrand the UK as 'Cool Britannia'. To remedy these deficits in institutional resources and identity, it is suggested that, at the very least, the

English regions require democratically elected assemblies as part of a federal constitutional settlement.

## The British state and the English question

Although there has long been a strong regional element of industrial and economic policy in the UK, regional development partnerships and institutions have remained underdeveloped in England (Constitution Unit, 1996a: 30). On its own, the creation of a stronger regional government in England would not in any sense be a sufficient condition for economic and social regeneration; nor is the case for Regional Development Agencies (RDAs) intrinsically or usually in practice associated with the case for democratic regional government. However, citizenship in a democracy implies the right of citizens to develop their own talents to the fullest and the right to identity (Rokkan and Urwin, 1983: 191, cited in Sharpe, 1997: 123). Furthermore, in a multicultural society (such as contemporary England), this right to identity may mean the rejection of a single culture of the state in favour of a political system which acknowledges the right of minorities to institutional structures which recognise their distinctiveness. In the case of those living in the regions of England, neither of these elements of citizenship has been fulfilled. It was neither a concern to nurture talent nor expressions of identity but the needs of regional planning from Whitehall which played a key role in bringing regionalism to the fore in the UK, especially in England, not least in settling the difficult issue of boundaries (Sharpe, 1997: 129).

The debate about the governance and economic performance of the English regions has gathered fresh momentum in recent years. Opinion has remained strongly divided over the likely dividend to economic performance of devolved government for the regions. From the Left, Labour Party policy both in opposition and government has been characterised by a strategic retreat from any short-term commitment to directly elected regional government in England, with the notable exception of an elected strategic authority for London (Labour Party, 1995). Policy has been based on the principle of 'devolution on demand' and the assumption that 'English regions would be artificial constructs', not least because the English 'lack a strong regional identity' (Tindale, 1995: 2–3). From the Right, while the contemporary governance of Britain has had two particularly influential advocates (Major, 1992; Portillo, 1994), one prominent member of the Tory Establishment has described the centralisation of power under the Thatcher and Major governments as 'the Tory Nationalization of Britain' and has written of the greatest damage having been done to local democracy, not least by the centralisation inherent in urban regeneration policy initiatives of the 1980s (Jenkins, 1996: 156–74, 266).

In his analysis of the role of regional structures in different parts of the public sector in Britain, Brian Hogwood (1996: viii) has noted that these structures are 'primarily concerned not with the management of territory but with the delivery of functions, often at a very detailed level'. Thus, there is 'no "regional tier" in England, but a diversity of regions and types of structure' (ibid.: ix). As a consequence, 'there is no systematic use of the word region to describe particular types of geographical arrangements' which 'has practical implications both for British government's own lack of clarity about how it is organised on a regional basis and for the over-simplified assumption in the debate about regional government, particularly within England, that there is a "regional tier"' (ibid.: 8). The patchy, *ad hoc* and often chaotic extension of governmental activity at regional level under the Thatcher and Major governments has therefore led some commentators to conclude that any move to regional governance structures for England would effectively 'need to start from scratch' (Harding *et al.*, 1996: 66). Above all, the English regions would have to be given autonomy from higher levels of national political authority so that they might create their own capacity for independent action. It is this capacity for autonomous action which has been denied to the English regions by Westminster and Whitehall in the past, and which is conspicuous by its absence from the Blair government's current agenda.

The arguments for changes in the governance of the English regions have not become appreciably stronger, or weaker, as a result of recent trends. Part of the problem for advocates of federalist or other alternative constitutional agenda is that 'the link between elected regional government and increased economic innovation and growth remains unproven and unexplored' (ibid.: 75) and therefore neither proposition is wholly convincing. However, this does not mean that there is not a demand for greater regional autonomy nor that regional government structures or other forms of regional administration cannot make a positive contribution to regional economic development (ibid.: 65). There are in fact different, often contradictory, impulses lying behind the recent growth in regional executive capacity and activity under the Thatcher and Major governments and the forms it has taken.

John Tomaney, one of the prime movers of the Campaign for a Northern Assembly and a prominent advocate of regional government, has contended that questions of increased regional expenditure and political decentralization of economic or investment powers cannot be addressed 'without addressing the results of the long cumulative process of the concentration of economic power in the South East and the stark polarity between regions in terms of control over investment' given that 'Economic centralization is fundamental to economic and political power in the UK' (Tomaney, 1995: 205). While locally accountable regional development agencies and localized banks are a necessary element of addressing regional problems, Tomaney insists that they must be part of a wider approach to policy which includes national policies to achieve regional economic devolution across a whole range of policies which may operate to enhance regional inequalities (ibid.: 204–6).

The problem for Tomaney's agenda is that the Labour Party's traditional support for redistribution of income through progressive taxation has been marginalised under Blair's leadership. Furthermore, the exclusion from the Comprehensive Spending Review of a full needs assessment of territorial public expenditure, as part of a modernisation of the Barnett Formula, has meant that the impact of 18 years of Conservative government upon the poorer English regions has been overlooked. Indeed, the fact that several potential candidates for the future elected office of Mayor of London have begun to talk about reclaiming part or all of the fiscal surplus which London delivers to poorer regions of the UK (thereby overlooking the way in which that surplus reflects the politically and financially privileged position of the City of London and the way it has been sustained at the cost of an under-developed regional banking system and articially high cost of capital for manufacturers in the English regions) suggests that accentuating regional structures could lead to a reduced rather than an enhanced emphasis on redistribution and equalisation of territorial expenditure and income.

Peter Roberts (1997) has identified the damage done to the interests of the English regions, not least their quest for a clearer identity and role in the EU, which has resulted from the democratic deficit arising from the absence of a formal tier of elected regional government. Indeed, Roberts has pointed to the largely imperialist light in which Westminster and Whitehall continue to view the English regions, which results in their subservience to the needs of the central British state, fashioning 'the relatively powerless state of localities and regions in a political desert created by excessive central' (ibid.: 255). In this light, the creation of the Government Offices of the Regions (GORs) with their integrated decentralisation of certain Whitehall functions in trade and industry, employment, environment and transport (but not health, agriculture or housing, or delivery of services through Next Steps agencies) can be seen as a movement towards 'a form of direct economic rule and further expenditure control' (ibid.: 261).

The existing English regional democratic deficit has been reinforced by a parallel failure to grant the GORs sufficient autonomy over regional planning and expenditure control, a pattern likely to be repeated in the operation of the RDAs. Furthermore, as Murray Stewart (1997: 144) has suggested, the simultaneous introduction of the Single Regeneration Budget (SRB) has provided a means not only of tightening central Treasury control over both national and regional programmes in England but also of reducing current spending levels and/or resisting bids for additional resources. Thus, SRB funding was planned to decline from £1,447 million to £1,314 million during its first three years of operation – a cut between 1994–5 and 1997–8 of 22 per cent in constant money terms (ibid.: 147–8). Rather than delivering greater regional autonomy over expenditure and policy, the SRB extended a new managerial, competitive and corporatist localism to the English regions (ibid.: 148–9). Stewart has also pointed to the manner in which the pattern of unitary and two-tier arrangements arising from the

1996 local government reorganisation in England has not enhanced the capacity for supra-authority action at the sub-regional or regional levels but has instead reinforced 'affective rather than effective communities, and exaggerated old town and country tensions' (ibid.: 152).

This pattern of fragmentation and rivalry at the sub-regional and local levels has been exacerbated by the Thatcher and Major governments' policies towards the local delivery of business support services in England. There has been great potential not for creative tension but for damaging inter-agency rivalry between the established chambers of commerce, the nascent Business Link network and the Training and Enterprise Councils (TECs). The creation of Business Links has posed a threat to the personal and organisational activities of some of the partners in the Business Link, most notably the chambers of commerce. The chambers have been asked to become a partner in a competitor to their own and members' businesses (Hutchinson *et al.*, 1996: 519). In a manner not dissimilar to Business Links, TECs have 'developed according to their own logic and in response to the existing patterns of business organisation at regional and subregional levels' (Parker and Vickerstaff, 1996: 252). In a similar vein, the strategies and initiatives which have been developed since the late 1960s to promote urban regeneration in the English regions have been variously described as a 'motley pot-pourri' of policies, 'an "alphabet soup" of acronyms' in a mosaic of localities and 'a patchwork quilt of complexity and idiosyncrasy' (Robson, 1988: 143; Robinson and Shaw, 1994: 225; Audit Commission, 1989: 1). A House of Commons Trade and Industry Committee inquiry into regional policy identified a 'bewildering profusion' of economic development bodies in the English regions and dismissed as 'complacent' the DTI's claim that the GORs were helping to coordinate the efforts of other agencies where necessary (House of Commons. TIC, 1995: lii).

In a more recent analysis of the prospects for the English regions, John Mawson has pointed to the role which the RDAs will play in rationalising and reducing the duplication of effort among those agencies and institutions engaged with economic development (Mawson, 1997b: 200). The possibility that the creation of the RDAs may exacerbate rather than reduce the degree of duplication and fragmentation in regional industrial policy has been raised in a series of recent parliamentary select committee inquiries. In its report on the government's proposals for the RDAs, the Select Committee on Environment, Transport and Regional Affairs has pointed to the need to clarify not only the relationship between the RDAs and the GORs in order to avoid the possibility of unnecessary duplication, but also how the government's rhetorical commitment to the principle of subsidiarity will be implemented in practice (House of Commons. ETRC, 1998: xiv–xv).

Echoing Mawson's suggestion that the government's proposed framework for the RDAs might constitute a 'missed opportunity', the Committee further recommended that the RDAs would be more effective in their implementation of regional development strategies if they were to be established as more powerful institutions. This could be achieved by the RDAs taking responsibility for more of the GORs' functions; controlling the training budget for their regions; contracting with the TECs and the Business Links for the delivery of training and business support services; determining applications for Regional Selective Assistance rather than merely advising ministers; assuming responsibility for tourism in their region; and establishing formal relationships with further and higher education institutions in their region (ibid.: xv). These recommendations for stronger RDAs have been repeated in the report of the Select Committee on Education and Employment on the relationship between TECs and the RDAs which has pointed to the fact that the RDAs will not have direct control over all TEC budgets and therefore will have neither a sufficient say in the allocation of training funds nor a direct responsibility for skills (House of Commons. EEC, 1998: ix). Furthermore, the Committee contended that the proposed framework for the RDAs 'could be a recipe for confusion, duplication and frustration for TECs' and that Department for Education and Employment officials' depiction of GORs as being the "focal point between Regional Development Agencies and TECs" is unsustainable' (ibid.: xi).

In defence of its proposals for the RDAs, the Blair government has argued that there is scope (but no necessary guarantee) for it to delegate further functions to the RDAs in the future and indeed to pay grants to the RDAs. It claims that these proposals constitute merely 'the first step in the new regional agenda' in which 'RDAs should be seen as a first step in an evolutionary process which will lead to the English regions being able to choose a greater measure of decentralisation' (HMG, 1998a: v, viii, ix). However, the government has refused to give the RDAs greater control over policy or resources, rejecting the demand for RDAs to have direct control over TEC budgets at the outset (HMG, 1998b). The government's insistence that the RDAs' policies will reflect 'the national policy framework' ('national' here referring to Britain rather than England) and that they will not be given additional powers because of the need 'to be realistic about what we ask them to do' (HMG, 1998a: xi) demonstrates the continuing reluctance of Westminster and Whitehall to decentralise control over policy and resources when decentralising responsibility for the administration of regional industrial policies.

## A deficit in policy: New Labour, new industrial policy?

The political economy of UK industrial policy has tended to embrace a conception of the political which is technocratic, managerialist and functionalist (Lee, 1997a). Too often salvation from the UK's relative economic decline has been found in the idea of a proactive industrial policy, controlled and implemented by an expert technocratic élite insulated from the interference of ideological politicians. A British developmental state or the implementation of a Listian national system of innovation, with its implicit notions of centralised control and manipulation of a set of interacting institutions, have been canvassed as remedies for the UK's decline. The presence of such policies in competitor economies (Freeman, 1987) and their absence from the UK have been identified as the missing link in British economic policy (Cowling and Sugden, 1993). This absence in turn has been attributed to the anti-scientific, anti-industrial culture of the governing élites (Barnett, 1986). However, as David Edgerton (1991a, 1991b) has shown, the British state has consistently implemented its own developmental strategy which has enthusiastically embraced technocratic departments of state, industrial policy and the sustained deployment of expertise in science and technology. Where Britain has diverged from Japan and Germany (those economies much admired by technocratic pragmatists) is that its technocratic departments of state, industrial policy and scientific and technical expertise have been deployed in the military rather than the civil sector. The British developmental state has been guided by an ideology that Edgerton has termed 'liberal militarism' which has sought to defend and extend British economic, industrial and commercial power through the deployment of high-technology weaponry.

Therefore, industrial policy has not been the missing link in British economic policy: on the contrary, it has been an essential continuity in Britain's modern economic and social development. The real problem with this architecture of centralised state institutions and military industrial policy is that it may have been appropriate for building and running the British Empire, but the Empire now exists only in the minds of Eurosceptics. The post-imperial industrial policy legacy is highly inappropriate for the task of regenerating the economies of the English regions, in which one in six adults is reported to possess poor literacy and numeracy skills (*Financial Times*, 11 March 1998). Indeed, the external orientation and centralised control sustained by liberal militarism has denied the English regions the resources and infrastructure to develop their own businesses. Unfortunately, a competitive disadvantage now shared by all the nations and regions of Britain stems from the fact that the Blair government's modernisation programme is being undertaken largely within the parameters of the political economy of Thatcherism, through a process which is hollowing out the notion of stakeholding but doing little to challenge or dismantle the legacy of liberal militarism (Lee, 1997b: 35–140), which sees 60 per cent of the government's R&D expenditure still being devoted to defence and civil aerospace (Oughton, 1997: 487).

Labour's economic and innovation inheritance from its Conservative predecessors is not encouraging. In the 1998 study of international competitiveness produced by the International Institute for Management Development, the UK has fallen from eleventh (1997) to twelfth in the rankings, one place below the Republic of Ireland (*Guardian*, 22 April 1998). Although the UK has been ranked in fourth place (up from seventh in 1997) in the World Economic Forum's 1998 Global Competitiveness Report, the

Forum ranked the UK only twentieth (out of 53) for the quality of its government, including the role of the state in the economy (*Guardian*, 5 June 1998). A dozen years on from the Aldington Committee's conclusion that the UK's poor performance in manufacturing contained 'the seeds of a major political and economic crisis in the foreseeable future' (House of Lords, 1985: 56), surveys of expenditure on innovation in general, and R&D in particular also do not make palatable reading. For example, the Department of Trade and Industry's (DTI) 1997 R&D Scoreboard revealed that the UK maintains the lowest ratio of R&D to sales of any large industrialised economy. In a similar vein, the 1997 CBI/NatWest Innovation Trends Survey revealed that for manufacturing the mean level of expenditure on innovation fell in 1996 to 5.9 per cent of turnover, down from 6.2 per cent in 1995. For non-manufacturing, the mean expenditure on innovation rose only moderately in 1996 to a company average of 11.8 per cent of turnover, up from 10.6 per cent in 1995 (CBI/NatWest, 1997: 14, 21).

Despite this poor performance, in the field of civil industrial policy New Labour is set to continue the trend of declining national government support for innovation that was established with the publication of the Thatcherite White Papers, *Civil Research and Development* (House of Lords, 1987) and *DTI: The Department for Enterprise* (DTI, 1988). Indeed, long before the General Election campaign, Tony Blair laid down the industrial terms of his vision of a young country by stating that 'the days of picking winners are over' (contradicted by the Labour Party's support for Technology Foresight both in opposition and in government). New Labour's industrial policy would not be rooted in ideology, but would instead 'put aside the dogma and divisions of the past' to 'build one nation socially; to work as one nation economically' (Blair, 1996: 117). Unlike its previous four manifestos, Labour's 1997 General Election manifesto (Labour Party, 1997) did not carry even a hint, let alone an explicit mention, of a more proactive industrial policy. The days when, under both Neil Kinnock's and John Smith's leadership (Lee, 1996b), the Labour Party saw a state-owned industrial development bank (Kinnock, 1986: 113; Labour Party, 1990: 15, 1994) as a central prerequisite of an effective corrective to short-termism and under-investment, which would entail 'a full-scale transfer of industrial, financial and political power to the regions' (Labour Party, 1993: 13), appear to have been cast aside as one more disposable and expensive legacy of Old Labour.

While Tony Blair shares with Margaret Thatcher and every postwar British government the belief that an effective modernisation programme can and should be undertaken within the parameters of the centralised British state, New Labour's programme, unlike that of its predecessor, has to be attempted without the windfall dividend of privatisation receipts and North Sea Oil revenues – a fact acknowledged in the Labour Party's pre-Election industrial strategy (Labour Party, 1996). Since taking office, the shape of the coming austerity in national civil industrial policy has become ever clearer, as a consequence of the government's decision not to revise its predecessor's target of a mere 0.4 per cent real annual increase in public expenditure during its first two years of office. The best that was ever achieved under the Thatcher governments was a 1.1 per cent real annual increase at the height of the economic boom in the late 1980s (Dilnot and Johnson, 1997: 14). This has translated, for example, into an increase in the science budget in cash terms of only £11.3 million (from £1,319.1 million in 1996–7 to £1,330.4 million in 1997–8) and a decrease at 1997–8 prices of £25 million (from £1,355.4 million in 1996–7 to £1,330.4 million) (*Official Record*, 29 July 1997: c.223–4). Total expenditure on trade and industry programmes is set to decline from an estimated £3,140 million in 1997–8 to £2,960 million in 1998–9 (Treasury, 1998: 128). The government's Comprehensive Spending Review, with its zero-based budgeting approach to overall, departmental and cross-departmental reviews, leaves little prospect of anything better than steady state funding of national innovation programmes.

Given this context of austerity, it is perhaps hardly surprising that during her first few months at the DTI, Margaret Beckett's rhetoric and actions displayed a continuity with the Major government's competitiveness agenda. There are striking parallels between her attempts and those of her Conservative predecessors, not least Michael Heseltine, to reconcile the need to address widely acknowledged structural weaknesses constraining UK economic performance with the DTI's ever diminishing funding. At her 'Competitiveness UK Business Summit' in July 1997, Beckett's policy agenda, if not her portrayal of the Conservatives' record in office, was one with which Heseltine could have taken little issue. Identifying partnership as the key to competitiveness, Beckett set out her determination to improve the UK's performance on skills and innovation, the latter being identified as one of the UK strengths – together with the potential of the workforce, the science base and the UK's world class firms (DTI, 1997a: 1). The UK's competitiveness would be improved by producing a stable economic framework for growth and addressing the 'underlying drivers of economic success', that is, education, innovation and investment (ibid.: 6). Beckett assured her audience that she wanted partnership to be 'more than warm words', and demonstrated her commitment by duly announcing the creation of a nineteen-member Advisory Group on Competitiveness.

Beckett has subsequently identified the three pillars of the DTI's approach to competitiveness under New Labour as 'strong markets, modern companies and looking to the future' (*DTI Press Release P/97/376*, 11 November 1997). At the same time, in a move strongly reminiscent of Old Labour and the National Economic Development Office's Sector Working Parties, Beckett has created six new business-led working parties to address six key questions, including innovation and the quality and quantity of investment, which the government and its advisers think are critical to improving the UK's economic performance. Critics might regard this measure as nothing more than the creation of one-stop talking shops, given the need for urgent action suggested by the DTI's *A Benchmark for Business*. This benchmarking exercise across seven key sectors has discovered that the UK is still about 10 per cent behind the OECD average for GDP per capita – approximately the same position as it has occupied for the past quarter-century (DTI, 1997b: 5).

In terms of productivity, measured by GDP per hour, the US is 20 per cent ahead of the UK, and France and Germany 25–30 per cent ahead. Furthermore, for every £100 invested per worker in the UK between 1983 and 1993, Germany and the US invested nearly £140, France almost £150 and Japan more than £160 (ibid.: 6). A parallel comparative study by the DTI of five sectors in four countries has found that, although a number of companies in the UK are genuine star performers, with a few notable exceptions they tend to be small and few in number. More alarmingly, the productivity of these leading UK companies tends to be lower than that of their leading continental competitors, suggesting that the body of UK industries has 'as much to contribute in explaining the British productivity gap as the tail' (DTI, 1997c: 38). This is a more disturbing picture of the UK's long tail of underachievers than that recently painted by the pre-Election report from the Commission on Public Policy and British Business (1997).

To redress these disturbing trends, the government intended to deliver its first White Paper on Competitiveness in November 1998. This was originally scheduled for publication in the first half of 1998, but the combination of the negotiations on the Comprehensive Spending Review and Margaret Beckett's replacement as Secretary of State for Trade and Industry by Peter Mandelson caused a postponement of the White Paper's appearance. At the regional level, partnerships have been producing 'up-to-date' strategies for regional competitiveness, in anticipation of the launch of the RDAs. In this latter direction, the government has restored £160 million of EU Structural Funds reserved for the Regional Challenge competition to the GORs in eligible regions and their regional monitoring committees, and has launched a consultation on 13 regional competitiveness indicators drawn up by the DTI (GSO, 1997a, 1997b). The Sector Challenge launched by the Major government has also been subject to an extensive consultation exercise. Laudable though this process of prolonged consultation may be, it does appear that it is a substitute for concrete activity. In short, New Labour's civil industrial policy will be marked by a period of substantial inactivity until the outcome of the Comprehensive Spending Review is known. At the same time, Beckett's desire to be seen to be addressing major long-term structural weaknesses in UK economic performance despite the lack of resources available to her department is resulting, as was the case with her frustrated Tory predecessor, in an output of worthy reports and documents which merely rehearse long-familiar arguments about British decline.

## A deficit in inward investment

A further source of competitive disadvantage for England arises from the relative weakness of its economic development agencies when compared with those in other nations of the UK. This is a weakness not only in the capacity of agencies in the English regions to improve the productivity of indigenous companies, especially SMEs, but also in their capacity to attract inward investment which has become a key source of employment and innovation. The UK remains the second largest recipient of inward investment after the US. The Inward Investment Bureau (IBB) has calculated that the total of 483 inward investment projects it identified for 1996–7 created a total of 46,179 new jobs from an investment of £9.347 billion. In terms of inward investment into the UK, England in general and individual English regions have received a much smaller dividend from the employment generated from inward investment than have other parts of the UK.

Sir George Russell, the chairman of the Northern Development Company (NDC), has accused Scotland and Wales of gazumping the English regions by offering extra grants to attract inward investment projects – grants which the English regions are unable to match. In his evidence to the House of Commons Trade and Industry Select Committee inquiry into the coordination of inward investment, given on behalf of the English regions, Russell contended that poaching had previously occurred, such as Locate in Scotland's £23 million offer to a printed circuit board manufacturer to relocate in Scotland – which exceeded the £12 million on offer from south of the border (House of Commons. TIC, 1997: 4).The NDC may have succeded in attracting some 520 projects totalling £8.8 billion and creating or safeguarding 75,000 jobs since its creation in 1986, but it might have been even more successful had it been able to offer levels of assistance comparable to its Scottish and Welsh competitors. The inequalities facing the north-east have been vividly illustrated by the example of a 1,000 job investment by Acer, a Taiwanese computer manufacturer, which was thought to be heading for a location in Northumberland until a rival bid from Wales virtually doubled the amount of aid on offer overnight. In their defence, Welsh officials have insisted that they have acted within the UK and European Union rules governing such forms of aid.

The inability of the English regions to defend or promote their interests as effectively as other parts of the UK is illustrated by the allocation of £422.84 million of DTI Regional Selective Assistance funding in 1996–7 which saw Scotland (£152.24 million) and Wales (£106.94 million) swallowing around 60 per cent of the funding. By comparison, Yorkshire and Humberside (a region of more than 5 million people) received a paltry £14.4 million. English regions have lacked the resources to be able to offer the £247 million package provided by the Welsh Development Agency to persuade LG to locate its £1.7 billion electronics plant at Newport or the alleged £147 million offered by Locate in Scotland to persuade Hyundai to locate in Fife. During the period 1987–97, Scotland was able to grant £411 million in Regional Selective Assistance (RSA) to UK-owned companies and £554 million to foreign-owned companies. By comparison, Yorkshire and Humberside was able to provide just £126 million in RSA to UK-owned companies and only £37 million to foreign-owned companies (*Financial Times*, 11 June 1998). Paradoxically, in 1995 Scotland's Gross Domestic Product (GDP) per head was 101.5 per cent of the UK average whereas Yorkshire and Humberside's GDP was only 91.2 per cent of the UK average (GSS, 1998). In fact, on this basis no fewer than six English regions were poorer than Scotland and yet their respective resources for developing their regional economies have not reflected these inequalities in income.

David Taylor, a special adviser to John Prescott and head of Enterprise, the Preston-based regeneration company, has suggested that 'The Scottish and Welsh have got away with an awful lot over the years and they know it, and the people that have missed out in all this have been in the English regions. Scotland and Wales have enjoyed a huge advantage' (*Financial Times*, 4 November 1997). As a remedy for the problem, John Siddall, the chief executive of the Yorkshire and Humberside Development Agency, has urged central control of inward investment policy by the Invest in Britain Bureau while a Royal Commission on expenditure allocation has been put forward as an option by Paul Davies, the director of South West Enterprise, who has claimed that his region has been disadvantaged by £600 million on an annual basis when compared to Wales. James Gray, the chief executive of the East of England Investment Agency would prefer a more focused approach to regional assistance, with a concentration on local areas of high unemployment in his region, such as Luton and Lowestoft, while John Finch, the chief executive of the East Midlands Development Company has questioned whether these kind of subsidies are actually needed at all (*Financial Times*, 1 November 1997).

In an attempt to defuse the row between the competing development agencies within the UK, the Blair government confirmed in its Scottish and Welsh White Papers on devolution that a concordat on financial assistance to inward investment projects was being prepared by the DTI in an attempt to secure a settlement which would avoid what the government regards as wasteful competition for inward investment. The concordat will seek to ensure that assistance to inward investment remains within common guide-lines and consultation arrangements governing the whole of the UK (*Official Record*, 20 November 1997: c.281). This move has been given a guarded welcome by the House of Commons Trade and Industry Commitee (House of Commons. TIC, 1997: xvii). On the question of determining the level of Regional Selective Assistance (RSA), once a single site within the UK has been identified for a potential inward investment project, Margaret Beckett reaffirmed that she retained responsibility for allocating RSA within England, while similar responsibilities lie with the respective Secretaries of State for Wales, Scotland and Northern Ireland (*Official Record*, 25 November 1997:

c.515). This statement will in itself do nothing to correct the imbalance in RSA funding resented by the English regions.

The concordat on inward investment may yet not provide the English regions with the more level playing field they are seeking. The central control over inward investment demanded by representatives of some English regions will not be established because the DTI will not be given the power of veto. The DTI appears to have been outmanoeuvred by the Scottish, Welsh and Northern Ireland Offices which were vehemently opposed to the proposal for issues to be resolved solely by DTI ministers and mandarins within the DTI's Industrial Development Unit, as proposed by David Durie, the DTI civil servant in charge of regional policy at the department and endorsed by Margaret Beckett in oral evidence to the Commons Trade and Industry Committee (*Financial Times*, 17 November 1997). The government's proposed solution to placate the Scottish and Welsh Offices is the reconstitution of the Industrial Development Unit to include representatives both from the Scottish, Welsh and Northern Ireland Offices and from the English regions. The government has also pointed to the future role of the RDAs in strengthening the potential for the English regions to attract inward investment (HMG, 1998c: iv). But when, for example, the annual RDA budget for the north-west region will be less than half that of Scottish Enterprise's £475 million, even though the north-west's GDP per capita is lower than Scotland's and its population much larger, this method of resolving English discontent appears to have merely postponed future conflict.

## A deficit in funding

Although regional institutional and industrial policy deficits are major constraints upon the economic performance of England, a more politically explosive source of competitive disadvantage for England arises from the allocation of the public expenditure it receives relative to that allocated to the other nations of the UK under the archaic Barnett Formula – named after Joel Barnett, the Chief Secretary to the Treasury during the Callaghan government of the late 1970s. The Barnett Formula does not determine overall levels of public expenditure in England or the other nations of the UK but shares out, on the basis of population, changes in expenditure plans between these nations. In 1995–6, identifiable general government expenditure per head in England was only 96 per cent of the UK average, compared with 112 per cent of the UK average in Wales, 119 per cent in Scotland and 132 per cent in Northern Ireland (Treasury, 1997a: 84). Attempts to determine whether the Barnett Formula advantages one nation to the detriment of one or more of the others are fraught with difficulty, not least because of the sheer complexity of calculating 'identifiable' and 'non-identifiable' expenditure on a territorial basis (Heald, 1994). However, much of this complexity has been lost on politicians and commentators, who have often approached the expenditure figures with all the detachment of rampant and blinkered nationalists.

When the Treasury conducted its detailed needs assessment of public expenditure in preparation for the Callaghan government's devolution proposals (using data from 1976–7), it concluded that for the services to be devolved expenditure in Scotland needed to be 16 per cent higher than in England and 9 per cent higher in Wales. In practice, expenditure was 22 per cent higher in Scotland and only 6 per cent higher in Wales than in England (Treasury, 1979: para. 6.5). In effect, Scotland received 5 per cent more expenditure per capita than was required under the Barnett Formula. It allocated planned public expenditure on the basis of 10:5:85, with 10 per cent allocated to Scotland (a rounding up from its 9.57 per cent population share), 5 per cent to Wales (a rounding down from its 5.12 per cent population share), and 85 per cent to England (a rounding down from 85.31 per cent). The reasons for this distribution were never made public, the Treasury merely stating:

> No systematic record exists of the reasons for these relationships; and there is no basis on which the pattern for any one year could be presented as being the 'correct' pattern for the foreseeable future. It is not therefore possible to infer from them what future allocations should be or what should be taken into account in their determinations.
>
> (Constitution Unit, 1996b: 65–6)

During their respective tenures, the Thatcher and Major governments steadfastly refused to do anything more than tinker with the Barnett Formula. After the 1992 General Election, the then Chief Secretary to the Treasury, Michael Portillo, recalibrated the Formula to ensure that, in future, changes in Scottish expenditure would be strictly proportional to its 1991 population rather than its 1976 population – the baseline year for calculating the Barnett Formula (ibid.: 66). Thus, under the Formula for calculating the allocation of block grant between the nations of the UK, Scotland receives 10.66 per cent, Wales 6.02 per cent and Northern Ireland 2.87 per cent for every comparable change in the allocation of spending by English departments. Given that Welsh GDP per capita is around only 83 per cent of the UK average, the fact that public expenditure in Wales has been 16 per cent higher than in England is largely defensible. However, for relatively economically and socially disadvantaged regions of England, such as the North-East, Merseyside and Yorkshire and the Humber region, the fact that Scotland has enjoyed identifiable expenditure levels 23 per cent higher than England (identifiable public expenditure per person in England during 1995–6 was £3,743, compared with £4,614 in Scotland) is less defensible when Scotland's GDP is now around 97 per cent of the UK average, compared, for example, to the North-East's 83 per cent.

There is a deeply held grievance among a growing number of English MPs (from both government and opposition parties) that England is severely disadvantaged by the current system of allocating expenditure. Representatives of development agencies in the English regions have laid aside their usual rivalries to unite in their condemnation of the Barnett Formula. John Conlan, the Chairman of Inward, the investment agency for the North-West, has urged the government to address 'serious discrepancies in spending between the English and the Celts' (*Financial Times*, 31 October 1997). His contention is that the 'bizarre mechanism' of the Barnett Formula reflects 'a 20-year-old concept of where the problems in the UK are' which fails to take account of the loss of manufacturing jobs in the North, the North-West and, to a lesser extent, Yorkshire and Humberside during the intervening period. Sir George Russell, the chairman of the Northern Development Company, condemned the formula as 'no longer necessary or just' (*Guardian*, 7 November 1997).

With the authority which emanates from his role as chairman of both Camelot, the National Lottery's administrator, and 3i, the venture capital organisation, George Russell's critique of regional inequalities in the disbursement of government funding has extended to the allocation of funding for tourism, sports, roads, television and indeed the lottery. Thus, the tourist grant aid of 26 pence per capita for England compares very unfavourably with the £5 per capita for Scotland and the £6.40 for Wales; and lottery grants of £28 per capita in Scotland and £32 per capita in Wales appears excessive compared to £13 per capita in the North of England (*Financial Times*, 29 October 1997). This sentiment was echoed by English members of the House of Commons Treasury Select Committee who, during the Committee's inquiry into the Barnett Formula, have described the Formula as 'unfair' (Brian Sedgemoor, Labour Hackney South), demanded a needs assessment for the English regions (Jim Cousins, Labour, Newcastle Central) or a formula based on the Standard Spending Assessments applied to local government in England (Quentin Davies, Conservative, Grantham and Stanford) (House of Commons. TC, 1997). In his evidence to the Committee, Lord Barnett advocated a wholesale review rather than abolition of the formula.

During the tenure of the Major government, the then Scottish Secretary, Ian Lang, had claimed that if public expenditure in Scotland was cut to the same level as the rest of the UK, Scotland would be faced with a deficit of £2,845 million, requiring a 19 pence income tax increase to balance the books (Ian Lang's Dimbleby interview on London Weekend Television, as reported in the *Scotsman*, 13 February 1995, cited in Heald and Geaughan, 1996: 170). The less partisan Institute for Fiscal Studies has more recently calculated that for Scotland to finance all its current services (with relative spending on health and personal social services in Scotland 25 per cent higher than in England in 1993–4) from its own revenues would require a basic rate of income tax of 37 per cent and a higher rate of 58 per cent (Blow, Haull and Smith, cited in Constitution Unit, 1996b: 68). For its part, the Scottish National Party (SNP) has long insisted that Scotland subsidises England rather than vice versa, as critics of the Barnett Formula have suggested. In its 1997 General Election manifesto, the SNP repeated its claim that, on the basis of a 17.9 per cent Scottish share of the UK General Government Borrowing Requirement, a proportionate 8.8 per cent share of privatisation receipts and a 90 per cent share of North Sea oil revenues (based on the 1968 Continental Shelf Jurisdictional Order), Scotland had delivered to England a fiscal balance of £27 billion more than it had received from the Treasury in the period since 1978/9 (SNP, 1997: 18).

Resolving this dispute appears extremely fraught with problems, given the immense difficulty of establishing the basis of 'need' in each nation and region of the UK. Any attempt to redistribute public expenditure from Scotland and/or Wales to the English regions is likely to unleash explosive political forces, especially for the Labour Party, given the preponderance of Scottish and Welsh ministers in key posts, not least the Treasury, and Labour's historical dependence on Scottish and Welsh MPs to compensate for the Conservatives' traditional majority of English MPs. However, it could be argued that one of the central motivations of the whole ideological and electoral thrust of Blair's 'New Labour' towards 'Middle England' is a farsighted recognition of the implications of an independent Scotland for his party's prospects at Westminster.

In its report on the Barnett Formula, the House of Commons Treasury Committee expressed its disappointment that no government studies had been undertaken with regard to the appropriateness of the Formula and how it relates to needs. The Committee concluded that the needs assessment underlying the Barnett Formula should be brought up to date because this would help to demonstrate whether the Formula remains the appropriate method of allocating annual expenditure increases to the four constituent nations of the UK (House of Commons. TC, 1997: viii). However, in its response to the Treasury Committee's report, the government categorically stated that it saw 'no case for reviewing the appropriateness of the Barnett Formula now' (HMG, 1998d: iv). Instead, the government chose merely to restate the position it had set out in its earlier White Papers on Scottish and Welsh devolution which had reaffirmed the existing system. The government will do no more than update the population figures which underlie the operation of the Barnett Formula on an annual basis from 1999 to 2000. The long-overdue, almost posthumous, in-depth analysis of relative spending requirements which should have been undertaken as part of the Comprehensive Spending Review has now effectively been indefinitely postponed. To continue with the Barnett Formula is tantamount to denying both that 18 years of Conservative government ever happened or indeed that Thatcherism had any impact upon the distribution of income and wealth or the pattern of needs among the people of England.

## A supranational deficit?

An additional future competitive disadvantage for the English regions appears likely to emanate from the supranational level. Under the European

Commission's Agenda 2000 proposals, structural funding for the existing 15 member states for the period 2000–2006 will be consolidated at a level of ECU210 billion while about ECU45 billion will be allocated during their pre-accession phase to new member states (EU, 1997: 23, 25). The Commission is determined to ensure both that the overall cost of the EU's structural and cohesion funds is kept below 0.46 per cent of EU GDP both before and after enlargement, and that the population coverage for Objectives 1 and 2 should extend to no more than 35–40 per cent rather than the current 51 per cent of the EU. The implications of these changing priorities in funding appear serious for the whole of the UK, where EU structural funds have helped to fill the vacuum left by declining national funding schemes.

With the possible exception of Merseyside, which may maintain its current Objective 1 status, and South Yorkshire, which is likely to qualify for Objective 1 funding for the first time (having narrowly failed to qualify in 1994) because of the impact upon its GDP per capita resulting from the rationalisation of the coal, steel and engineering industries, all other English regions (together with Northern Ireland and the Highlands of Scotland) are likely to find themselves disadvantaged by the realignment of EU structural funding. During the UK Presidency of the EU, the Blair government appears to have fought a rearguard action in defence of the UK's share of structural funds. Ministers have used meetings with their continental counterparts to press for an allocation of funding based on eligibility criteria other than unemployment. For example, Margaret Beckett called for a balanced assessment of income, employment and development needs (*DTI Press Release P/98/243*, 26 March 1998), while John Prescott reaffirmed that the UK would not accept an 'unfair' allocation of regional aid across Europe as the price of EU enlargement (*DETR Press Notice 369*, 13 May 1998). However, with Germany pressing for a £2 billion rebate from its overall EU contribution, the failure of the UK to resolve this matter during its EU Presidency does not bode well for the English regions. Any substantial loss of EU funding is bound to heighten territorial rivalry for increasingly scarce national industrial policy and regeneration funds. The problem for relatively poor English cities such as Hull or poor counties such as Cornwall is that they might qualify for Objective 1 or 2 status were it not for the richer areas within which they are located or with which they are associated for needs assessment. Cornwall's GDP per capita is around only 69 per cent of the EU average – well inside the 75 per cent threshold – but because it is held to be too small to qualify on its own, when Cornwall is included with Devon (GDP per capita 88 per cent of the EU average), it no longer qualifies (*Financial Times*, 19 November 1997).

## The rebranding of Britain: cool Britannia, frozen England

The notion that England's industrial policy deficit, in terms of its institutions, policies and resources, should be attributed to an absence of a clearly articulated English national identity will be anathema to many contributors to the industrial policy literature, especially those whose conception of the state and the political are technocratic, managerialist, administrative or functional. In his seminal work, *The Competitive Advantage of Nations*, Michael Porter (1990: 6, 13) contended: 'The only meaningful concept of competitiveness at the national level is national productivity' but that certain characteristics of a nation could create and sustain competitive advantage through a highly localised process. This same insight that debates about economic performance, innovation and industrial policy are not a detached and ahistorical technocratic excercise but must instead be located within a broader political and cultural framework was not lost on either Margaret Thatcher or John Major. In both cases, as with every other English prime minister of the twentieth century, their modernisation agenda defined the national identity of the people of England in terms of an unquestionable and unthinking loyalty to the institutions of the centralised British state, that is, the Westminster Parliament as the location of indivisible national sovereignty and the monarchy as the symbol of British national unity.

For Thatcher, the Falklands War could also be used as a reaffirmation of British national identity, the juncture at which Britain 'ceased to be a nation in retreat' and rediscovered a national self-confidence and price which might yet be harnessed to remedy British decline (Thatcher, 1989: 164). But this project was not about shaping England's future by addressing the problems of its domestic economy but rather about re-enacting Britain's past by summoning up memories of imperial conquest and restoring 'the essential and grander identity of the "Imaginary Britain" to the modern subject' (Wright, 1985: 165). In a similar vein, John Major's invocation, on St George's Day in 1993, of George Orwell's wartime essay, *The Lion and the Unicorn*, when he spoke of 'the long shadows falling across the county ground, the warm beer, the invincible green suburbs, dog lovers and pool fillers ... old maids bicycling to Holy Communion through the morning mist' constituted, as Mike Marqusee (1994: 10) has suggested, an attempt to use 'ideological mantras to ward off the demons encroaching ever more menacingly from the crime-ridden, multi-racial, dispossessed inner cities'.

In New Labour's modernisation programme, the association between national identity and economic performance has been forged in terms of Tony Blair's ambition to rebrand Britain as a 'young country', the 'Cool Britannia' much beloved of the merchandisers of youth culture. This is a vision that is exemplified by Blair and Peter Mandelson's enthusiasm for the Millennium Dome. Demos, the London think-tank founded by Geoff Mulgan, now the head of the Prime Minister's No. 10 Policy Unit, has encapsulated the whole Blairite project of national renewal in its pamphlet *Britain TM* (Leonard, 1997). This has portrayed Britain as a corporate trade mark in need of urgent modernisation. Thus British national identity, or rather UK plc (for national identity is equated with the corporate identity of the multinational), is to be 'rebranded' to reflect Britain's or rather London's (for Britain is in reality the metropolis) renaissance as the coolest capital in the world, where the pessimism and introversion of the retreat from Empire is being supplanted by an innovative and style-conscious Britain which 'has a spring in its step and a new mood of confidence' (ibid.: 12).

Rebranding Britain is an inherently and openly acknowledged top-down project. It is to be coordinated by an elite vision group (presumably Mulgan's No. 10 Policy Unit) chaired by the Prime Minister which will agree strategic objectives and by a working party 'from all the agencies – government and business – involved in promoting Britain abroad'. A 'Promoting Britain Unit' based in the Cabinet Office is 'to provide logistical support, systematically measuring performance and track our identity' – because for this project identity can be managed and spun, using logos and branding techniques (ibid.: 11). The 'first priority' must be to cultivate a national consensus ('cultivate' being the operative word for this manufactured project), that 'Achieving greater clarity will require a lead from the top' (we know from whom and in whose interests), and that identity must be professionally managed (ibid.: 63, 64). In reality, this is a project which, under the guise of reinventing the national identity of the whole of Britain, seeks to sustain and enhance the international competitiveness of London's design, advertising and public relations consultancies and the commercial and financial services of the City of London. It is an outward-looking project which does not seek to engage with the world beyond London unless it is on its own terms of incorporation, where the regions of Britain may occasionally produce an innovative talent or product which can be globally marketed behind a manufactured, branded identity.

The problem with this very arrogant project (which during the UK Presidency of the EU has extended to the supranational level: see, for example, Leonard, 1998) is that it ignores its own concession that national identities are not the same as corporate brands. National identities transcend the immediate and the material. Mark Leonard recognises that under Blair 'The state is reforming itself, devolving power to the regions and the localities' and that the link must be made 'between the political and cultural aspects of identity and their economic significance' (Leonard, 1997: 60, 63). What he fails to acknowledge is that very devolution of power reflects a desire in the nations and regions of Britain for the genuine autonomy to be able to escape the constraints of a single identity and a London- and South-East-centric political economy. The political economy of the City of London concerns the highly inflationary impact arising from the prospect of City traders' bonuses topping the £1 billion mark. The political economy of the English regions and other nations of the UK is the political economy not only of artificially inflated interest rates (because of overheating in London and the South-East), but also the 'investment gap' that successive expert inquiries from Macmillan, through Radcliffe, Bolton and Wilson, together with a series of Select Committee reports (House of Lords, 1985, 1991; House of Commons. TIC, 1994) have addressed, with no purposeful action forthcoming from Westminster and Whitehall to remedy a century of relative economic decline (Lee, 1996b). These same arguments about the constraints on innovation have been revisited in four more recent reports (BoE, 1996; CBI, 1997; Enterprise Panel, 1996; House of Lords, 1997) but will remain unresolved as long as those seeking a more proactive civil industrial policy, developmental state, or Listian national innovation system continue to place their technocratic pragmatists' faith in one further administrative reorganisation of the institutions of the centralised British state. To remain wedded to a purely functional, managerial, technocratic or administrative conception of the political is inevitably to confine debate about innovation policy to tinkering and fine tuning but to leave untouched the larger constraints on innovation.

Rather than standing aloof and contenting itself with the discourse concerning practical proposals for future industrial policy in England, the debate about economic development must now engage with the wider, growing and lively political debates concerning the constitution and national identity in England. To this end, the intricate historical relationship between identities and the idea of Britishness have been skilfully woven together by Keith Robbins who has acknowledged that 'the pedigree of even contemporary English institutions can be examined over an almost uniquely lengthy period' (Robbins, 1997: 45). In particular, the pedigree and record of those Whitehall departments charged with supporting innovation and formulating industrial policy should be subjected to the most vigorous of scrutinies. Their failure to deliver a *Mittelstand* in England is in large part a reflection of a constitution and national identity which have been preoccupied with administering a global empire and servicing the commercial interests of the City of London rather than the less heroic but equally important task (for local economic development) of supporting the development of indigenous SMEs. The legacy for industrial policy in the rest of England has been the absence of any structure or pattern of institutions and policies which could legitimately be described as a regional developmental state or system of innovation.

For Stephen Haseler (1996), the form or character of English identity was forged and incubated in a pre-modern, certainly pre-industrial age. It was also exclusive because it was forged by a propertied aristocratic élite preoccupied with building an empire. The role of the populus was to act as onlookers and servants. The defining characteristic of this invented Englishness was the superiority and moral elevation of the Englishman above all other races – a homely, cosy, provincial, somewhat insular Tory Englishness of land, class and race perfectly suited to the task of running an Empire, which in turn provided the widest possible canvas for painting this picture of English superiority and a continuous supply of new races and peoples (ibid.: 36, 63). The problem, as Haseler readily acknowledges, is that this 'frozen Englishness', with its grandiose global imperial focus, has 'degenerated into a reactionary identity and ideology' which continues to aspire 'to punch above its weight' overseas when in fact the body politic's punch-drunkness has prevented it from addressing the more urgent task of domestic economic and constitutional regeneration.

Haseler's thesis (with which the author concurs) is that 'we are now coming to the end of the British story', although Haseler appears to be contemplating the end of the 'island story' without sufficiently acknowledging that there are a few more chapters yet to unfold – not least because the Blair government is presently engaged in its own attempt to rebrand Britishness. The twin pressures of global capitalism and the evolving European Union are forcing the British state to undertake the most profound changes since its very formation (Haseler, 1996: vii). Haseler contends that the UK state was 'essentially a product of Britain's world position and imperial role' whose 'structures, ethos and symbolisms fitted perfectly the needs of the ruling class of a far-flung empire' (ibid.: 159). However, rather than retreating into the reactionary nationalism of 'little Englander' Euroscepticism, which has always diminished and damaged England, Haseler suggests that this transformation should be welcomed and actively embraced as an opportunity to create patterns of self-government and democracy which the centralised British state has refused to countenance. Indeed, Haseler imagines that a release from the UK state may not necessarily ignite the fires of reactionary English nationalism but 'could just as easily light the touch-paper of English regionalism' (ibid.). Haseler's contention is based on a belief that English regional identities are genuine.

National identity in England has degenerated into what Haseler describes as 'contemporary theme-park Englishness – or, "Englishness for export" – the cultural form of the increasingly important heritage industry' (ibid.: 3). This may have helped to boost the competitiveness of the tourist industry and certain sectors of the film industry, for example, Merchant-Ivory productions. However, for those with the ambition to regenerate the regions of England beyond London and the South-East on a more diverse basis than merely a heritage theme-park, especially those who wish to develop an effective policy for business innovation and incubation, traditional notions of Englishness and the subordination of English diversity within the constraints of Britishness will not allow for the development of the institutions at regional and sub-regional level which will provide a degree of certainty sufficient to encourage the private sector to take risks. Indeed, just as the perpetuation of the Little England theme-park Englishness has excluded other, more appropriate notions of English identity, so too has it denied the possibility of regional and local structures which could generate alternative sources of innovation, employment and wealth.

## Conclusion: A federal England?

The Blair government has chosen to frame its modernisation programme within the terms of the political economy of industrial policy laid down by its Conservative predecessors. There has been little evidence of radical innovation in industrial policy. For example, the third section of the Treasury's first pre-Budget report, which was devoted to competition, innovation and investment, outlined a series of practical proposals which could have appeared in any of the Major government's White papers on competitiveness. Thus, the government reiterated its commitment not to pick winners but instead to improve conditions for business; to reform the tax system to create incentives for entrepreneurs to take risks and thereby raise the UK's levels of income and productivity; and to promote public–private partnerships (Treasury, 1997b). Gordon Brown has subsequently promised to devote the 1999 Budget to bridging the productivity gap between UK-based firms and their competitors but it is unlikely that the limited measures announced in the 1998 Budget, including the £50 million University Challenge Fund, or the £240 million venture capital funds created during the UK Presidency of the European Union will even begin to scratch the surface of the 40 per cent productivity gap with the US or the at least 20 per cent gap with Germany identified by a recent report from the management consultants McKinsey, which was discussed at a seminar on competitiveness at No. 11 Downing Street (*Treasury News Release 78/98*, 14 May 1998).

New Labour's conservatism bodes ill for the English regions. What has happened to 18 years of often trenchant criticisms in *Hansard* and select committee reports of the pattern of Conservative industrial policies, from Sir Keith Joseph's 'reading list', through Lord Young's Enterprise initiative to Ian Lang's challenge funding initiatives and competitiveness White Papers? It is self-evident that 18 years of Conservative policies cannot be undone let alone reversed in a matter of a few months. However, it is quite another thing to accept apparently passively the industrial policy legacy of your predecessors and to start to work within its limitations. Perhaps the most worrying aspect of all is that for a government which was not only in opposition for 18 years but also more recently held up as the best-prepared in opposition to govern, New Labour appears to lack its own clear analysis of the causes of UK decline and the remedies thereof.

The essential diversity and pluralism of people living in contemporary England should be welcomed as an asset and bulwark against the homogenisation inspired by global corporate interests. The strength of English society is its very diversity: a diversity which is poorly accommodated within the constraints of the Union state and indivisible parliamentary sovereignty at Westminster. The economies of the English regions are characterised by a huge variety of businesses and sectors, each with its own unique trajectory of development. Such variety has not always been accommodated by a national industrial policy administered from Whitehall or its colonial outposts in the English regions. Innovation is a process which tends towards uncertainty and risk. If entrepreneurs are to be persuaded by business support agencies to take risks and businesses are to be nurtured and incubated through such uncertainty in a long-term partnership, both parties need to know that their efforts will not be undermined by a sudden intervention or change of policy from Whitehall. The constitutional settlement which will ensure the necessary autonomy in regional industrial policy is one that will protect the regions from central interference by giving them a constitutional guarantee of their own independent resources and policy competence. In launching the government's nine new RDAs, John Prescott claimed that the RDAs would address the English regions' desire for control over their own economic destiny by giving them the powers and opportunities to contribute to the prosperity of their own communities; but the fact of the matter is that the establishment of a federal structure of government in England would be the only true guarantee of genuine and lasting autonomy.

Federalism is by no means an alien political tradition to the UK. John Kendle (1997: ix), for example, has contended that the federal idea has been a consistent feature of constitutional debate in the British Isles from the early 1700s to the present day. At the time of the Union of England with Scotland, Kendle points to the preference among many Scots for a more federal structure than an incorporating union which reaffirmed the predominant power of the highly centralised English state (ibid.: 11). In a similar vein, Michael Burgess (1995: 182) has concluded that there is an indigenous British tradition of federalism, a continuity of political and constitutional ideas which arose during the nineteenth century as 'a direct response to real and perceived challenges to the integrity of the state'. Indeed, 'the very nature of the Union – its multi-dimensional character and structure – has guaranteed a secure place for the existence of a British tradition of federalism'. However, as Burgess has readily acknowledged, the genius of the British constitutional system lies in its capacity for 'successfully disguising constitutional questions as mere political issues' (ibid.: 183). Moreover, the British tradition of federalism has been 'the victim of an elaborate constitutional deception', arising partly from the success of the old constutitional system but also from 'genuine public misunderstanding and deliberate élite misrepresentation' of federalism as an inherently centralising project rather than one which respects and protects the integrity of individual nations and regions (ibid.: 184).

During a century of relative economic decline, there have been several flirtations with federalism. John Mawson has cited the example of how the 1918 Labour Party Conference declared the aim of 'separate statutory legislative assemblied for Scotland, Wales and even England with autonomous administration in matters of local concern' (Labour Party, 1918: 70, cited in Mawson, 1997b: 181). More recently, in October 1973, the final report of the Royal Commission on the Constitution contended that a federation of England with Scotland, Wales and Northern Ireland 'would be so unbalanced as to be unworkable' because 'It would be dominated by the overwhelming political importance and wealth of England' (Kendle, 1997: 165). However, the Kilbrandon commissioners did concede that that 'the imbalance would be corrected if England were to be divided into a number of units, each having the status of a federal province' (ibid.). Their majority preference nevertheless was for a system of legislative devolution for Scotland and Wales and 'regional co-ordinating and advisory councils, partly indirectly elected by the local authorities and partly nominated' (ibid.: 167).

Ironically, the federal tradition is not entirely alien even to the Tory tradition. Lord Hailsham's solution to the 'elective dictatorship' of unitary parliamentary sovereignty at Westminster was to contemplate a written, federal constitution for the UK incorporating devolved assemblies for the English regions, Wales, Scotland and Northern Ireland (Hailsham, 1976). If Hailsham's arguments were apposite then after two years of Labour government, they are yet more compelling after two decades of increasing centralisation of political power by the Thatcher and Major governments. A heavy price has been paid for the perpetuation of the outdated; long-standing assumptions, not least those of parliamentary sovereignty vested solely in Westminster, and the idea that the democratic process would not benefit from the introduction of a written constitution. Above all, as Burgess (1995: 188) has concluded, the heaviest price paid for unquestioning loyalty to the structures and identity of the centralised British state is that 'The political economy of the United Kingdom sublocates and stifles economic imagination and development', not least in the English regions beyond London and the South-East. Perhaps the most practical proposal for industrial policy in England, if it is to aspire to the creation of its own *Mittelstand*, is to locate policy within a federal constitution (Hutton, 1996; Mullineux, 1994).

The problem confronting advocates of democratically accountable, federal government for England is the apparent conservatism and indifference of the English electorate to any form of constitutional reform, as illustrated by the pitiful 34 per cent turnout for the May 1998 referendum on instituting an elected mayor and Greater London Assembly for the capital city. A further constraint on elected English regional government is the prospect that the Blair government will abandon any further movement towards elected regional assemblies in favour of a recall of the House of Commons Regional Affairs Committee. The political advantage of this Committee, which might be renamed the English Grand Committee and would be composed purely of MPs from English constituencies, is that it would appear to offer the English their own distinctive political forum while simultaneously maintaining centralised political control of English government at Westminster.

Such a proposal would certainly appeal to the Conservative opposition under William Hague because he has seen such a Committee or the creation of an English Parliament as the means to redress the 'imbalances' arising from New Labour's constitutional agenda (Hague, 1998). Following its failure to return a single MP in Scotland or Wales and the limited prospects for any political recovery, the increasing 'Anglicisation' of Westminster may offer the key to Hague's reinvention of the Conservative Party as a *bona fide* Eurosceptic and Thatcherite English Nationalist Party. The temptation of and electoral advantage in the abandonment of Unionism may be too great for a political party which has traditionally sacrificed any consideration of England's distinctive identity on the altar of Britishness and the Union. It is this possibility of a way back to power for the Tories, and perhaps no other, which may yet persuade those who forlornly hope that Scotland will yet turn away from independence (for example, Tomaney, 1998) to abandon their support for the Union and start imagining a federal English solution to England's competitive disadvantage.

# References

Audit Commission (1989), *Urban Regeneration and Economic Development: The Local Government Dimension*, London: HMSO.

Bank of England (BoE) (1996), *The Financing of Technology-based Small Firms*, London: Bank of England.

Barnett, C. (1986), *The Audit of War: The Illusion and Reality of Britain as a Great Nation*, London: Macmillan.

Blair, T. (1996), *New Britain: My Vision of a Young Country*, London: Fourth Estate.

Bradbury, J. and Mawson, J. (eds) (1997), *British Regionalism and Devolution: The Challenges of State Reform and European Integration*, London: Jessica Kingsley.

Burgess, M. (1995), *The British Tradition of Federalism*, London: Leicester University Press.

Campaign for a Northern Assembly (1997), 'A Declaration for the North', *New Statesman and Society*, 14 November: 4.

Commission on Public Policy and British Business (CPPBB) (1997), *Promoting Prosperity: A Business Agenda for Britain. The Report of the Commission on Public Policy and British Business*, London: Vintage.

Confederation of British Industry (CBI) (1997), *Tech Stars: Breaking the Growth Barriers for Technology-based SMEs*, London: Confederation of British Industry, Small and Medium Enterprise Council.

Confederation of British Industry and National Westminster Bank (1997), *CBI/Natwest Innovation Trends Survey 1996*, London: Confederation of British Industry Technology Group and NatWest Innovation and Growth Unit.

Constitution Unit (1996a), *Regional Government in England*, London: Constitution Unit.

Constitution Unit (1996b), *Scotland's Parliament: Fundamentals for a New Scotland Act*, London: Constitution Unit.

Cowling, K. and Sugden, R. (1993), 'Industrial Strategy: the Missing Link in British Economic Policy', *Oxford Review of Economic Policy*, 9, 3: 83–100.

Department of Trade and Industry (DTI) (1988), *DTI: The Department for Enterprise*, London: Department of Trade and Industry.

Department of Trade and Industry (DTI) (1997a), *Competitiveness UK: Our Partnership with Business*, London: Department of Trade and Industry.

Department of Trade and Industry (DTI) (1997b), *A Benchmark for Business*, London: Department of Trade and Industry.

Department of Trade and Industry (DTI) (1997c), *Differences in Companies'*

*Performance: British Industry's Under-performing Tail*, London: Industry Economics and Statistics Directorate, Department of Trade and Industry.

Department of Transport, Environment and the Regions (DETR) (1997), *Building Partnerships for Prosperity: Sustainable Growth, Competitiveness and Employment in the English Regions*, London: Stationery Office.

Dilnot, A. and Johnson, P. (eds) (1997), *Election Briefing 1997*, London: Institute for Fiscal Studies.

Edgerton, D. (1991a), *England and the Aeroplane: An Essay on a Militant and Technological Nation*, London: Macmillan.

Edgerton, D. (1991b), 'Liberal Militarism and the British State', *New Left Review*, 185: 138–70.

Enterprise Panel (1996), *Growing Success: Helping Companies to Generate Wealth and Create Jobs through Business Incubation*, London: Enterprise Panel.

European Union (EU) (1997), *Agenda 2000: For a Stronger and Wider Union. Bulletin of the European Union Supplement 5/97*, Brussels: European Commission.

Freeman, C. (1987), *Technology Policy and Economic Performance: Lessons from Japan*, London: Frances Pinter.

Government Statistical Service (GSS) (1997a), *Regional Competitiveness Indicators: A Consultation Document*, London: Department of Trade and Industry.

Government Statistical Service (GSS) (1997b), *Regional Competitiveness Indicators: 1995 Manufacturing Labour Productivity and Investment Supplement*, London: Department of Trade and Industry.

Government Statistical Service (GSS) (1998), *Regional Competitiveness Indicators*, London: Department for Trade and Industry.

Hague, W. (1998), 'The Way Forward for the Conservatives in Scotland', *Scotsman*, 24 February.

Hailsham, Q. (1976), 'Elective Dictatorship: The Dimbleby Lecture', *Listener*, 21 October.

Harding, A., Evans, R., Parkinson, M. and Garside, P. (1996), *Regional Government in Britain: An Economic Solution?*, Bristol: Policy Press.

Haseler, S. (1996), *The English Tribe: Identity, Nation and Europe*, London: Macmillan.

Heald, D. (1994), 'Territorial Public Expenditure in the United Kingdom', *Public Administration*, 72: 147–75.

Heald, D. and Geaughan, N. (1996), 'Financing a Scottish Parliament', in S. Tindale (ed.), *The State and the Nations: The Politics of Devolution*, London: Institute for Public Policy Research.

Her Majesty's Government (HMG) (1998a), *Government Response to the First Report of the Environment, Transport and Regional Affairs Committee: Regional Development Agencies*, HC 645, London: Stationery Office.

Her Majesty's Government (HMG) (1998b), *Government Response to the Education and Employment Select Committee's Fourth Report on the Relationship between TECs and the Proposed Regional Development Agencies*, London: Stationery Office.

Her Majesty's Government (HMG) (1998c), *Government Observations on the First Report from the Trade and Industry Committee (Session 1997–98) on Coordination of Inward Investment*, HC 659, London: Stationery Office.

Her Majesty's Government (HMG) (1998d), *The Barnett Formula: The Government's Response to the Treasury Committee's Second report of Session 1997–98, HC 619*, London: Stationery Office.

Hogwood, B. (1996), *Mapping the Regions: Boundaries, Coordination and Government*, Bristol: Policy Press.

House of Commons. Education and Employment Committee (EEC) (1998), *The Relationship between TECs and the Proposed Regional Development Agencies.*

*Fourth Report from the House of Commons Education and Employment Committee*, Session 1997–98, HC 265, London: Stationery Office.

House of Commons. Environment, Transport and Regional Affairs Committee (ETRC) (1997), *Regional Development Agencies. First Report from the House of Commons Environment, Transport and Regional Affairs Committee*, Session 1997–98, HC 415, London: Stationery Office.

House of Commons. Trade and Industry Committee (TIC) (1994), *Competitiveness of UK Manufacturing. Second Report of the House of Commons Trade and Industry Committee*, Session 1993–94, HC41-I, London: HMSO.

House of Commons. Trade and Industry Committee (TIC) (1995), *Regional Policy: Fourth Report from the House of Commons Trade and Industry Committee*, Session 1994–95, HC356-I, London: HMSO.

House of Commons. Trade and Industry Committee (TIC) (1997), *Coordination of Inward Investment. First Report from the House of Commons Trade and Industry Committee*, Session 1997–98, HC 355, London: Stationery Office.

House of Commons. Treasury Committee (TC) (1997), *The Barnett Formula. Second Report from the House of Commons Treasury Committee*, Session 1997–98, HC 341, London: Stationery Office.

House of Lords. Select Committee on Overseas Trade (1985), *Overseas Trade. Report of the House of Commons Select Committee*, Session 1985–85, HL 238-I, London: HMSO.

House of Lords. Select Committee on Science and Technology (1987), *Civil Research and Development. Government Response to the First Report of the House of Lords Select Committee on Science and Technology. Cmnd. 185*, London: HMSO.

House of Lords. Select Committee on Science and Technology (1991), *Innovation in Manufacturing Industry. Report of the House of Lords Select Committee on Science and Technology*, Session 1990–91, HL18-I, London: HMSO.

House of Lords. Select Committee on Science and Technology (1997), *The Innovation–Exploitation Barrier. Third Report from the House of Lords Select Committee on Science and Technology*, Session 1996–97, HL Paper 62, London: Stationery Office.

Hutchinson, J., Foley, P. and Oztel, H. (1996), 'From Clutter to Collaboration: Business Links and the Rationalization of Business Support', *Regional Studies*, 30, 5: 516–22.

Hutton, W. (1995), *The State We're In*, London: Jonathan Cape.

Jenkins, S. (1996), *Accountable to None: The Tory Harmonization of Britain*, Harmondsworth: Penguin.

Kendle, J. (1997), *Federal Britain: A History*, London: Routledge.

Kinnock, N. (1986), *Making our Way: Investing in Britain's Future*, Oxford: Blackwell.

Labour Party (1918), *Report of the Labour Party Conference*, London: Labour Party.

Labour Party (1990), *Looking to the Future*, London: Labour Party.

Labour Party (1993), *Making Britain's Future*, London: Labour Party.

Labour Party (1994), *Winning for Britain: Labour's Strategy for Industrial Success*, London: Labour Party.

Labour Party (1995), *A Choice for England: A Consultation Paper on Labour's Plans for English Regional Government*, London: Labour Party.

Labour Party (1996), *Vision for Growth: A New Industrial Strategy for Britain*, London: Labour Party.

Labour Party (1997), *New Labour: Because Britain Deserves Better*, London: Labour Party.

Lee, S. (1996a), 'The Betrayal of the Entrepreneur and Enterprise in England', paper presented to the 1996 Political Studies Association Annual Conference, Glasgow University.

Lee, S. (1996b), 'Finance for Industry', in J. Michie and J. Grieve Smith (eds), *Creating Industrial Capacity: Towards Full Employment*, Oxford: Oxford University Press.

Lee, S. (1997a), 'Explaining Britain's Relative Economic Decline', in A. Cox, S. Lee and J. Sanderson (eds), *The Political Economy of Modern Britain*, Aldershot: Edward Elgar.

Lee, S. (1997b), 'Competitiveness and the Welfare State in Britain', in M. Mullard and S. Lee (eds), *The Politics of Social Policy In Europe*, Aldershot: Edward Elgar.

Leonard, M. (1997), *Britain TM: Renewing our Identity*, London: Demos.

Leonard, M. (1998), *Making Europe Popular: The Search for European Identity*, London: Demos.

Major, J. (1992), *Trust the People: Keynote Speeches of the 1992 General Election Campaign*, London: Conservative Political Centre.

Marqusee, M. (1994), *Anyone but England: Cricket and the National Malaise*, London: Verso.

Mawson, J. (1997a), 'New Labour and the English Regions: A Missed Opportunity', *Local Economy*, November: 194–202.

Mawson, J. (1997b), 'The English Regional Debate: Towards Regional Governance or Government', in J. Bradbury and J. Mawson (eds), *British Regionalism and Devolution: The Challenges of State Reform and European Integration*, London: Jessica Kingsley.

Mawson, J. and Spencer, K. (1997), 'The Origins and Operation of the Government Offices for the English Regions', in J. Bradbury and J. Mawson (eds), *British Regionalism and Devolution: The Challenges of State Reform and European Integration*, London: Jessica Kingsley.

Mullineux, A. (1994), *Small and Medium-sized Enterprise Financing in the UK: Lesson from Germany*, London: Anglo-German Foundation.

Oughton, C. (1997), 'Competitiveness Policy in the 1990s', *Economic Journal*, 107: 1486–1503.

Oughton, C. and Whittam, G. (1997), 'Competition and Cooperation in the Small Firm Sector', *Scottish Journal of Political Economy*, 44, 1: 2–30.

Parker, K. and Vickerstaff, S. (1996), 'TECs, LECs, and Small Firms: Differences in Provision and Performance', *Environment and Planning C: Government and Policy*, 14: 251–67.

Porter, M. (1990), *The Competitive Advantage of Nations*, London: Macmillan.

Portillo, M. (1994), *Clear Blue Water: A Compendium of Speeches and Interviews given by the Rt Hon. Michael Portillo MP*, London: Conservative Way Forward.

Robbins, K. (1997), *Great Britain: Identities, Institutions and the Idea of Britishness*, London: Longman.

Roberts, P. (1997), 'Whitehall et la Désert Anglais: Managing and Representing the UK Regions in Europe', in J. Bradbury and J. Mawson (eds), *British Regionalism and Devolution: The Challenges of State Reform and European Integration*, London: Jessica Kingsley.

Robinson, F. and Shaw, K. (1994), 'Urban Policy under the Conservatives: In Search of the Big Idea?', *Local Economy*, 9, 3: 224–35.

Robson, B. (1988), *Those Inner Cities*, Oxford: Oxford University Press.

Rokkan, S. and Urwin, D. (1983), *Economy, Territory and Identity*, London: Sage.

Scottish National Party (SNP) (1997), *Win the Best for Scotland: The SNP General Election Budget 1997*, Edinburgh: Scottish National Party.

Sharpe, L.J. (1997), 'British Regionalism and the Link with Regional Planning: A Perspective on England', in J. Bradbury and J. Mawson (eds), *British Regionalism and Devolution: The Challenges of State Reform and European Integration*, London: Jessica Kingsley.

Stewart, M. (1997), 'The Shifting Institutional Framework of the English Regions: The Role of the Conservative Party', in J. Bradbury and J. Mawson (eds), *British Regionalism and Devolution: The Challenges of State Reform and European Integration*, London: Jessica Kingsley.

Thatcher, M. (1989), *The Revival of Britain: Speeches on Home and European Affairs 1975–1988*, London: Aurum Press.

Tindale, S. (1995), *Devolution on Demand: Options for the English Regions and London*, London: Institute for Public Policy Research.

Tindale, S. (ed.) (1996), *The State and the Nations: The Politics of Devolution*, London: Institute for Public Policy Research.

Tomaney, J. (1995), 'Regional Government and Local Economic Development: The Realities of Economic Power in the UK', *Regional Studies*, 29, 2: 202–7.

Tomaney, J. (1998), *New Labour and the English Question*, Policy Paper no. 13, Sheffield: Political Economy Research Centre.

Treasury (1979), *Needs Assessment Study: Report*, London: HMSO.

Treasury (1997a), *Public Expenditure: Statistical Analyses 1997–98*, Cm 3601, London: Stationery Office.

Treasury (1997b), *Pre-Budget Report*, London: Stationery Office.

Treasury (1998), *New Ambitions for Britain: Financial Statement and Budget Report*, HC 620, London: Stationery Office.

Wright, P. (1985), *On Living in an Old Country: The National Past in Contemporary Britain*, London: Verso.

# 7 The activation of bottom-up methodologies in a newly opened regional economy

## An experience in the Oeste region of Santa Catarina, Brazil

*Silvano Bertini and Gian Luca Baldoni\**

## Introduction

The case study here presented is the synthesis of a project of policy assistance carried out in 1996 by Nomisma in collaboration with Pires & Asociados (a consulting company located in Florianopolis) in the Oeste region of the State of Santa Catarina, southern Brazil. The project was not financed by international organisations, but by local administrations, business associations and development banks, all belonging to a regional development forum and promoted by the Forum de Desenvolvimento Catarinense.

The process of opening national economies to external trade is often treated at the macroeconomic level simply as a problem of structural adjustment. However, it is especially at the micro level that economic actors are constrained to change their behaviour and to reorganise themselves in order to face the competitive challenge of an open economy. Many authors and politicians are emphasising the Italian model of spontaneous response from the bottom to the open market, but practical attempts to define policy strategies and concrete actions inspired to imitate this experience are not often cited or realised. This case study represents a practical attempt to reinforce the institutional capacity to activate bottom-up responses to a competitive context.

## The project's approach

Increasingly, countries all over the world are interested in reproducing the development experience of central and northern Italian regions, particularly

\* The case study presented here was carried out in 1996 by the two authors and with relevant contributions from Paola Giannelli and Riccardo Deserti, who also work for Nomisma, the analysis and policies for the agricultural sector. Special thanks to Paola Papini for revising the text and the English form.

that of Emilia-Romagna, which is traditionally one of the most successful. The interest is motivated by the bottom-up model's capacity for inspiring self-generating enterpreneurship, employment, growth and competitiveness in those regions which employ it. This capacity is essential to fostering regional development performance, especially in a phase of opening national economies, a process which renders regions and countries able to self-propogate the process of economic growth and does not make them dependent on foreign or public investment. There is a great interest, especially from the countries involved in creating custom unions and in processes of economic integration, in learning and updating practical methodologies for developing bottom-up policies, in order to mobilise local forces, promote spontaneous enterpreneurship and innovation capabilities.

The fact is that, despite some excessively emphatic illustrations, the development model of central northern Italy is not clearly transferable as a policy model for other national or regional governments. The Italian phenomenon happened spontaneously and emerged as the result of the combination of market dynamics, macroeconomic evolution, institutional and policy environment and social responses at the local level to external pressures over time. In this sense, it presents some transferable and some untransferable elements.

Among the untransferable elements we can include social institutions existing in these Italian regions, deriving from their own history and traditions, characterised by self-government of local communities, self-organisation of economic groups (various groups of artisans, for instance) since the Middle Ages, and centrality of the family, especially in the countryside.

If these elements are crucial for understanding the Italian experience, there are also some lessons we can extract and utilise to elaborate a general and repeatable methodology and try to apply it in other contexts. To be synthetic, we can extract three main lessons from the experience of regions like Emilia-Romagna:

1   The foremost lesson is the necessity to create communication channels between the private and the public sector. This is essential to adjust policy interventions on process in order to respond to the real needs of firms over time; it is problematical for a policy intervention to be perfectly designed and effective from the beginning, but it is possible to improve its effectiveness in progress: removing obstacles, mistakes, misunderstandings.

2   The second lesson is that small or micro enterprises must be linked, through some sort of intermediary vehicle, to essential development factors such as credit system, local administration, export services, innovation centres, and so on. It is difficult for small entrepreneurs to communicate directly with these subjects, especially when the latter are public bureaucratic institutions or big international and managerial companies.

3   Finally, small firms need to be linked together, in order to become relevant actors in political, social and business terms. This does not mean co-operation in generic terms, but recognising the opportunity to achieve common goals by joining together for specific purposes.

Looking to the Italian experience, it can be seen that Italian firms did not co-operate directly together as much as is often described, but they often associated in organisations that were able to represent their interests at the local and the national levels. At the local level, these associations of entrepreneurs influenced local decisions in planning adequate infrastructure for SMEs; promoted consortia for export, for credit guarantee schemes, for innovation and for technical training; supported SMEs in using national or regional facilities for investment, and so on. At the local level there was a sort of continuous dialogue between entrepreneur associations, local administrations, local bankers, local technical schools and universities.

Conceptualising such schemes of institutional relationships, in recent years the Italian government has promoted the institution of the *patti territoriali* (territorial agreements); these are boards organised at the local level, in which administrators and representatives of other local forces and institutions jointly decide the priorities for local policy, develop projects and obtain a state subsidy for their implementation.

The basis of such intervention is the principle of multiplicity of interests and scopes in a local community. Local intervention should take into account a mix of interests: the public interest (welfare, industrial development, low unemployment) and various private interests (profit, economic survival, employment for various economic and social groups; sometimes even humanitarian or cultural purposes). These interests should be respected and combined, in order to valorise each individual contribution to the project in a complementary way.

The role of promoting these various economic and social interests is played by intermediate actors: associations, trade unions, social foundations, administrations. Each of these intermediate actors is legitimized by its own base of representativeness and consensus. This ensures the existence of communication channels between the final beneficiaries of policy projects and policy-makers and a sort of automatic control over the effectiveness of public policies.

The crucial advantage of this system of relationships is that the automatic control makes it possible to adjust the projects in progress according to their capacity to respond to the needs of beneficiaries. This feature is important because normally policy-makers have a range of objectives and a system of values that are quite different from those of entrepreneurs. That is why projects are often rejected by entrepreneurs or fail to reach their established objectives. A mechanism of control over policy projects can make them more flexible and can work to adjust them progressively in order to improve their effectiveness and efficiency. Of course, if the mechanisms of spontaneous adjustment are accompanied by procedures of technical monitoring and evaluation, this capacity of adjustment can be further improved, which is also very useful for this approach. Flexibility and capacity of adjustment while the projects are in progress are two basic conditions for the success of projects.

Another crucial variable for succeeding with this approach is the motivation and the capacity of policy-makers and project managers. If they work in a system of relationships and indirect control as described above, they are induced to be efficient. The support from specific training is crucial in improving their ability to reach the objectives of the projects, but it must not be forgotten that it is this mechanism of control which ensures their motivation and care for the success of projects.

The approach followed in this project was based on five criteria:

- extensive involvement and concertation with institutional, economic and social organisations;
- reinforcing relationships between all these actors;
- starting from a diagnosis of needs, problems, strengths and weaknesses of the local productive system;
- building consensus on priorities and projects;
- introducing mechanisms and procedures for project adjustment in progress.

## The regional context

The Oeste region is located about 600 km west from the coast and from the capital of Santa Catarina, Florianopolis. The region has a population of 350,000 (the state population is about 5 million), most of whom are Italian and German immigrants. The main city, Chapecò, has about 200,000 people. The rest of the population is spread throughout the countryside, in rural villages and small cities. The two biggest cities each have about 10,000 inhabitants.

Almost 50 per cent of the population are engaged in agriculture and livestock breeding. The traditions imported from Europe, along with the favourable climate and the natural environment, make these activities quite productive. When Brazil was a closed economy, this region worked almost single-handedly to provide pigs, turkey and chicken meat for the whole nation. Some big Brazilian groups working in the food sector located their big meat processing plants around Chapecò; large local co-operatives, with the aim of establishing a market for local small breeders did the same. Eventually, in this area five of the biggest Brazilian meat processing plants were concentrated; they are highly capital-intensive, highly productive, and organised according to strict Fordist methods. This situation made the Oeste region quite rich: static and conservative, but rich. The process of market opening and integration into Mercosur changed the scenario quite rapidly.

The process of market opening in the Mercosur area has proceeded quite rapidly in recent years, especially when we consider that countries like Brazil and Argentina were practically closed until the late 1980s. In Brazil, this new context is activating economic, institutional and political reactions. Some are progressive, others regressive or conservative; but whatever they may be, they provoke strong institutional excitement and activism. Apart from problems of macroeconomic adjustment and stabilisation, it is at the local or regional level that enterprises, institutions and local levels of government are inspired to change their behaviour, approaches and methods. In a general context of uncertainty, resistance and lack of experience, it is possible to give some concrete examples of this process.

At the level of the state of Santa Catarina, a *Forum de Desenvolvimento Economico Catarinense* (Forum for Santa Catarina Economic Development) has been promoted. It is composed of one representative of the government, representatives of the various development banks and institutions, important entrepreneurs' associations, municipalities' associations, some representatives of the private sector and experts. The role of this Forum is simply consultative, not executive. In particular it has a mandate to discuss and indicate policy strategies to the government, whose capabilities in this new context are still limited, due to lack of experience and the difficulties of establishing strategies and adopting methodologies according to a bottom-up approach. It must also be considered that the leading parties are often orientated to protect all those sectors and social components that are most exposed to the effects of opening and structural adjustment. The creation of this Forum is the first step to emerge from the need to improve governance and reinforce the linkages and the communication channels between the public and the private sectors. No less important was the fact that the *Forum Catarinense* promoted the formation of regional fora within the state. One of the first of these was the *Forum Regional de Desenvolvimento de l'Oeste de Santa Catarina*.

The *Forum Regional de Desenvolvimento de l'Oeste de Santa Catarina* was promoted by the Association of Municipalities of the Region (AMOSC). AMOSC plays a central role in regional planning and policy in the Oeste region; in fact, there is no intermediate level of administration between the state (Santa Catarina) and the municipalities; there are no provinces or counties or districts or regions. This may not be a problem for medium and large cities, but small cities and villages can have problems of resource availability, co-ordination of actions for territorial planning, political voice and representativeness at the state level. The institutionalisation of AMOSC indicates a real need for co-ordination at the regional level. At the same time, the promotion of the Forum indicates the need for local concertation for economic and social policies.

## Problems emerging in the open market

In the new context, many problems and anxieties emerged:

1     The opening of the market made it clear that in the agricultural sector there was the need for improved quality and productivity; the large local meat processing companies were already starting to diversify their suppliers, even looking outside the region for the best quality and prices available. Many peasants were marginal, unspecialised producers and risked being uncompetitive, unable to reach quality standards and unable to diversify customers and products. There was the real risk of a social crisis and of an exodus from the countryside, initally toward Chapecò and later towards the coast or the big Brazilian towns. The prospect of big foreign investment in the auto sector in the coastal cities (Blumenau, Joinville), might persuade many people to emigrate.

2     These risks were reinforced by the fact that there were few alternatives to the dominant sector in the region; all the other activities, with few exceptions, are almost entirely orientated to the local market. The job losses in agriculture, together with the weakness of the industrial sector, would lead to increased unemployment that would be a determining factor for emigration.

3     Both development banks and development institutions are state-controlled and very bureaucratic. They are not accustomed to interacting democratically and flexibly with the private sector. Development banks had little interest and political advantage to help local small and micro firms; development institutions for SMEs were used to elaborate complex strategic plans: very impressive for politicians, but in practice hardly effective and too rigid.

4     The administrative context, excluding the City of Chapecò, is extremely fragmented into little municipalities and is often characterised by reciprocal rivalry and lack of communication. This rendered local initiatives ineffective, uncoordinated and full of duplications.

5     The level of infrastructure development was still low, at the local level and at the external connections level, concerning both transport and public utilities (water and energy, in particular).

6     Associations of SMEs and micro firms are also very fragmented at the local level, lacking co-ordination and any ability to influence either state policy or the development of the capacity to provide services.

In the light of these problems (some clearly perceived, others not completely), there emerged the need for a public strategy impacting both the economic and social perspectives of the region.

## The spontaneous local response

The first step of the local institutional response was to overcome the administrative fragmentation. As stated above, an association of the region's municipalities (AMOSC) was created in order to fill the gap between the state and the municipality levels of government and administration. The association had a voluntary character and two main functions:

- to centralise and harmonise some administrative functions of the municipalities, such as accounting, database, and so on;
- to promote and co-ordinate common planning activities in the fields of infrastructure development, public utilities, health and social services, environment protection, and so on.

An association on a voluntary and democratic basis can certainly have problems in maintaining an internal consensus. One of the reasons is that most people often require their representatives to concentrate resources and lobbying at the very local level, and to avoid the 'time losses' necessary for regional co-ordination; another reason is the internal political equilibrium within the association. In fact, a small group of municipalities, which considered they were being discriminated against by the majority, and especially by the bigger town of Chapecò, left AMOSC and founded another association called AMERIOS, with the consensus of their voters. This division clearly weakened the capacity for co-ordination in the region.

The second step was the creation of the *Forum Regional de Desenvolvimento de l'Oeste de Santa Catarina*. This event was very important, since it recognised a role for local development in the private sector and non-institutional organisations, in other words, for improving regional governance. The Forum was inspired by AMOSC, but AMERIOS also agreed to participate. Besides these two associations of local municipalities, all the institutions working for development (SEBRAE, SENAI, SENAC), the development banks (BESC, BRDE), the main entrepreneurs' association (FIESC), the association of peasants (CEPAGRI), and minor entrepreneurs' associations participated. Such a spontaneous initiative must be considered very positive, demonstrating a great awareness of the aim of activating collaborative actions for collective advantage. Of course, as was admitted, there was a need for know-how and experience in establishing policy objectives and managing projects in a perspective of stimulating growth from the bottom up.

Within this Forum it was decided to start a pilot project to foster regional economic development and to involve a foreign consulting company to help organise it.

## The realisation of the project

To identify the needs and priorities of the region, the experts realised an analysis of the economic situation of the region mainly by means of field research based on a large number of interviews of entrepreneurs, representatives of institutions and associations, majors and policy-makers. This analysis aimed to evaluate both the competitive position of the region as a whole in the South American context and the level of integration of the local economic system, the impact of the institutional environment. Attention was focused on relationships among firms and between firms and institutions, on firms' dynamics and strategies of growth, as well as on the emerging sectors in the region. The support activities planned by the public administration in each municipality were also analysed, along with the relation between the local and national or federal institutions.

The results of the analysis were summarised in a detailed preliminary report that, in a second on-the-ground mission, was widely discussed within the regional Forum and also presented to the Catarinense Forum. These discussions represented an essential step in ensuring the involvement and the consensus of the local actors in the definition of the priorities for future actions. Finally, a general agreement was reached on four priorities:

- valorisation and promotion of high-quality food products in some emerging sectors other than the traditional local production, in order to diversify agricultural activity and stabilise the position of minor producers;
- improvement of the conditions of SMEs' access to the credit funds offered by local private and public financial institutions;
- reorganisation on a regional and more integrated base of the entrepreneurial associations;
- improvement of the analytical base of the economic system of the region.

Within the executive board of the local Forum, the experts proposed some possible projects to be implemented in the area, and started to assess the political feasibility of the proposals. In line with the priorities listed above, the following projects were presented:

- a consortium of farmers for the valorisation, quality improvement and commercialisation of a typical agricultural product of the region, the 'bean of Oeste';
- a credit guarantee co-operative for SMEs;
- an exchange relationship between local associations and an Italian SME association;
- an economic observatory for the region, managed by the local university.

One of the first problems that emerged during the discussion with the executives of the Forum was the main actors' lack of awareness of the general goal of the intervention proposed. This would carry a serious risk of failure in the implementation phase of the projects. As a consequence, it was decided to send out a third mission, but this time from Brazil to Italy. A group of entrepreneurs and representatives of local institutions organised, in collaboration with Pires & Asociados, a visit to some institutions and examples of enterprise collaboration in Emilia-Romagna, where they had the opportunity to see the actual working of the proposed projects. The mission took place two months after the presentation of the preliminary report; visits were made to a credit guarantee co-operative, various valorisation and promotion consortia, a local technical school and two local associations of small enterprises.

During the mission of the Brazilian representatives, the intervention projects were discussed in more detail. The final proposals, encompassing both the analysis of the priorities and the intervention projects, were finally presented in the last mission to Brazil. They were presented at operational meetings within the *Forum Catarinense*, in another open seminar, and in a big public seminar in Florianopolis (*Seminario Catarinense de Desenvolvimento*).

It must be noted that the central feature of the methodology used in this project was the search for consensus among the main local actors. The analysis and the presentation of the results, as well as the Brazilian representatives' mission to Italy, were used as an instrument to foster the cohesion and involvement of the fragmented local actors. In other words, the methodology was designed to help local administrators consider the problems and the possible solutions on a regional scale, which was the main goal of the Forum itself, as well as to foster the 'environmental' conditions needed to implement single projects.

For each project, there were established: objectives, beneficiaries, expected results, management organisation, other organisations involved, phases of development, way of working, duration, human and technical resources, costs, sources of finance.

It appeared that, apart from the immediate concrete needs of intervention projects, there was a need to improve the institutional framework and capabilities, in order to give continuity to the intervention. The precondition for implementing projects was, indeed, a preliminary intervention on the structure, the internal rules and the competencies of the Forum.

The Forum had two main problems:

- it was strongly affected by problems of political equilibrium and representativeness;
- it developed a bureaucratic, dirigistic structure as a consequence of previous institutional experience; the various fields of action were organised into departments, making the whole organisation rigid and hierarchical.

It was decided that the Forum could be the co-ordinator of development policies in the Oeste region, but that it needed reorganisation. The proposal to reorganise was inspired by the methodology of *patti territoriali* presently applied in Italy to the neediest regions, and consisting of a network of local actors co-ordinating their different aims and competencies towards the specific aims of local development and employment policy.

The proposal to re-organise the Forum was articulated in the following points:

1   to keep a democratic structure and a general assembly open to all the actors potentially involved in the Forum; the assembly should be a crucial meeting-point for participation and consensus and should elect the president, express opinions about Forum activity, indicate problems and objectives, but not make decisions;

2   the executive board to be composed of the president and representatives of five groups of actors: entrepreneurs' associations, local municipalities, development institutions, development banks, knowledge institutions (universities or other training institutions). The number of places for each group to be established according to the principle of ensuring a balance between the entrepreneurial, social and institutional components. Each group to nominate its representatives according to its own rules, by election or direct indication, and within the limits of the places reserved. Trade unions also expressed a desire to participate;

3   the executive board to decide strategies and actions according to the opinions and the indications expressed by the general assembly and to specific technical consultancies; it would also nominate an executive responsible for the implementation of the Forum's strategy;

4   all the departments should be abolished; the Forum should work on a project-by-project basis and according to result-orientated mechanisms, and be separated into two main areas of intervention: economic development and social development;

5   all the projects that the executive board decides to implement require a feasibility study, in which there should be indicated: beneficiaries, expected results, institutions involved, costs, financial sources, timing;

6   the executive responsible to nominate the project managers and control the successful execution of the projects;

7   the projects should be evaluated by experts, in order to adjust, to reinforce or even cancel them. Also the opinions of beneficiaries, expressed within the assembly, could influence such decisions;

8   the decisions about project adjustment, reinforcement or cancellation should be taken by the executive board on the basis of technical evaluations, indications of the assembly and eventual reports of the executive responsible.

## Advantages and risks

This institutional scheme for regional policy-making can be quite suitable for the region in the perspective of reinforcing bottom-up practices in the new open context. It presents the following advantages:

•   it favours the consolidation of the economic and associative democracy;

- it implies the combination of different interests and favours joint efforts and the use of complementary competencies;
- it institutionalises the method of social concertation for relevant decisions for local policy;
- it reduces the fragmentation, especially of municipalities and micro firms' organisations, thereby reducing useless duplication and rivalries and increasing the level of co-ordination;
- it promotes the creation of a think-tank for the whole region, able to collect and mobilise resources and to establish what to do and how;
- it induces all local subjects to operate in a network and to participate in the local debate (including the local university, normally little involved in practical local questions);
- it reduces the level of bureaucracy and accelerates the decision-making process;
- it introduces result-orientated mechanisms;
- it increases flexibility in the management of public policy projects and in development institutions (top-down, bottom-up, feed-back, monitoring, evaluation and adjustment);
- it stimulates the dynamism of project managers and gives space for answers to new needs and for new projects.

Of course, there are some risks. The main risk is related to the excess of individualism (also between institutions and their managers), which can lead to the disaffection of some members of the Forum if the final decisions do not completely agree with their ideas, or better, with their interests. It must be made clear that the collective rules of the Forum are to be respected in all cases, otherwise a new fragmentation can arise. This is also why it could be opportune to establish more rigid rules and to concentrate more resources within the Forum. The risk of internal instability is quite obvious in an institutional framework that is strongly dependent on voluntary adherence, yet it was decided not to introduce stronger rules. Some centrifugal movement already exists; some local municipalities are preparing development plans without the co-ordination of the Forum and, what is worse, with the assistance of development institutions involved in the Forum itself. Such old institutions are fighting to preserve their role as unique referents for SME policy-making. At present, they are an obstacle to adopting a real top-down, bottom-up approach to fostering regional endogenous development.

A second risk is the disaffection of people and entrepreneurs, under continuous pressures of competition and employment instability, towards public sector initiatives, which are in general considered slow and ineffective. This can force local administrators or representatives of entrepreneurs to assume non-collaborative attitudes. At all events, the new structure of the Forum should inculcate good practice in private–public collaboration and in researching multilateral solutions.

The third risk is linked to human resource competencies and resistance, since many people in the public sector are not used to working on result-orientated projects, subject to evaluation and exposed to private sector reactions. Even specialised policy-makers are not familiar with a top-down, bottom-up approach. This experience confirms that people operating as policy-makers, especially at the local level, represent a crucial bottleneck in implementing policies from the bottom in an open context; and this means that there is an urgent need to train people in this field.

## Conclusion

The final presentation of the project and its approval was in December 1996. After one year all the projects presented have been started and the Forum is elaborating two more projects, in collaboration with Pires & Asociados. In the region there is emerging a dynamic climate of institutional co-operation and the project of regional organisation is considered successful and responding to their needs. All the specific projects indicated have already started and are in the implementation phase; other projects are now in the feasibility phase, and specific initiatives such as missions and participation in fairs and exhibitions have been organised. Of course, it is not enough to express a judgement about real effectiveness; the adoption of the new scheme for elaborating local policy projects should be monitored, but the information presented here indicates that the mobilisation of local forces and institutions which already existed have created a mechanism which will finalise efforts into concrete projects, joint ventures and co-operation.

The main lesson of this experience is that the possibility of activating development processes in an open and competitive context is crucially linked to the motivation of individuals and social groups and to the convergence of their interests and expectations to achieve common general goals and actions for growth. Specific instruments and projects carried out by experts are simply channels to address the various local energies and competences towards concrete results, through the reciprocal co-operation and networking of local institutions and social groups.

## References

AMOSC (1995) *Plano basico de Desenvolvimento Regional. Diagnostico e Propostas de Desenvolvimento integrado*, Chapecò: AMOSC.

Bertini, S. (1994) *SME Systems and Territorial Development in Italy*, Bologna: Laboratorio di Politica Industriale.

Bianchi, P., Miller, L.M., Bertini, S. (1996) *The Italian SME Experience and Possible Lessons for Developing Countries*, Vienna: UNIDO.

Cunha, I.J. (1992) *O salto da industria catarinense. Um exemplo para o Brasil*, Blumenau: Parallelo 27.

EPAGRI (1996) *O Desenvolvimento sustentavel do Oeste Catarinense*, Florianopolis: EPAGRI.

Hirschmann, A.O. (1958) *The Strategy of Economic Development*, New Haven, CT: Yale University Press.

Porter, M.E. (1990) *The Competitive Advantage of Nations*, New York: Free Press.

Sabel, C.H. and Piore, M. (1984) *Second Industrial Divide: Possibilities for Prosperity*, New York: Basic Books.

# Part III

# Nurturing small firm economies

# 8 The entrepreneurial society in practice

*Marc Cowling**

## Introduction

Britain is now facing up to a number of key economic and social challenges which will help determine whether we enter the next century with the foundations in place to create and sustain a fair and prosperous society. The explicit aim of this chapter is to put forward a positive agenda for making Britain a 'country of enterprise' in which all sections of society have the opportunity to display their entrepreneurial talents. By doing so we can help to secure a number of desirable objectives, not least increasing technological advancement, creating the industries of the future, reducing unemployment and regenerating stagnant communities. These aspects are all considered in detail subsequently.

For too long entrepreneurs have been viewed with suspicion by the Left as embodying the 'cult of the individual'. To the Right entrepreneurs have been seen as the prime facilitators of the move away from community-based social and economic responsibility towards a society in which individuals provide only for themselves. Yet we choose not to take on board the misplaced and entrenched dogma of either, and simply define entrepreneurship as having the motivation and dynamism to innovate and make things happen. This is crucial to all enterprises, public or private, large or small, and equally to communities. With this in mind, our emphasis is very much on promoting entrepreneurialism through mutually beneficial collaborations between all sections of the business, public and social community.

In terms of how we set about this task, our approach was as diverse as the constituency we seek to promote. Broadly speaking, we developed five key strands of research. First, we considered the evolution of public policy *vis-à-vis* small businesses and entrepreneurship over the last two decades to give us a historical perspective. We then considered what can loosely

*   The author would like to thank his co-authors of the book *The Entrepreneurial Society* from which this paper draws its inspiration, namely, Bob Gavron, Andrea Westall and Gerry Holtham, and also the support of the Institute for Public Policy Research which funded this project. The views expressed here represent the author alone.

be termed 'the state of small business' as it exists in Britain today in terms of numbers, dynamics of entry and exit, sectoral composition and issues relating to survival and growth. At this stage we interviewed a substantial number of entrepreneurs, politicians, academics and individuals responsible for small firm development in a multitude of public, quasi-public and private sector support agencies. Fourth, we surveyed all existing Training Enterprise Councils (TECs), Business Links (BLs) and Enterprise Agencies (EAs) with a view to building up a picture of exactly what support is currently on offer to entrepreneurs and potential entrepreneurs in Britain. Finally, we collected similar information for Japan, the US, Germany and France.

We now begin the main body of the chapter by initially defining the concept of the entrepreneurial society in terms of what it means to us. Having established this, we then move on to make a case for why we should be interested in promoting entrepreneurship in any case, and questioning whether there is a role for government in facilitating this process. We then provide a critical review of the evolution of public policy in Britain, before questioning whether our experiences are really so different from those of other developed countries. We briefly discuss exactly what we know about the fundamental determinants of entrepreneurial success, defined loosely as those factors which enhance survivability in the first instance, and growth in the second, prior to our more detailed examination of three specific policy fields, namely education, advice, training and counselling, and finance. We propose some specific recommendations which we believe would help promote dynamic and sustainable entrepreneurship and also create a culture in which entrepreneurial activity in whatever form is positively encouraged and facilitated.

## The concept of the entrepreneurial society and its rationale

### *The concept*

In an entrepreneurial society, people with motivation and dynamism bring together resources and individuals to pursue their goals and so create wealth and jobs. The skills to do so are not just the presence of owner-managers but are crucial to the success of all enterprises, public or private. Indeed, entrepreneurship is not necessarily about individualism. Experience shows the benefits of business people working in teams and developing peer networks (Gavron *et al.*, 1998).

### *Why promote entrepreneurship?*

A high rate of business formation and dissolution is characteristic of a dynamic economy. Changing tastes and preferences, new technologies, and changes in demography and geography are all accommodated by the entry and exit of firms.

(USGPO, 1995)

This statement would cause considerable concern amongst UK policy-makers, who tend to hold the view that the turbulence generated by the entry and exit of, essentially, smaller firms represents a waste of resources. Much better to try and 'pick winners' or offer large-scale subsidies to foreign-owned multinationals to temporarily locate production in the UK. To an American the entry and exit of firms is interpreted as a sign of environmental dynamism and as a means of facilitating change and ultimately economic growth. Yet failure does not carry the same stigma in the US as it does in the UK: there, to have tried and failed is seen as being a useful experience should one wish to try again. In this sense US entrepreneurial culture places a much greater emphasis upon the learning-by-doing experience in the belief that people will learn not to make the same mistakes again. By contrast, in the UK you tend to get only one shot. This was as true for access to government schemes in the 1980s as it is true for individuals seeking to obtain start-up funding from financial institutions.

Equally as important to the case for promoting the formation of small, start-up businesses and fostering their development is that new businesses can help create new industries, innovate, provide employment, regenerate stagnant communities and provide individuals with a positive career choice. Leadbetter (1997), for example, explicitly refers to the social entrepreneur who channels resources to resolve community-based social problems. It is this interaction between economic and social aspects of entrepreneurship that allow this sector of the business community to tackle a multiplicity of objectives in a way that supporting larger firms cannot.

### Is there a role for government?

Entrepreneurship is not simply about maximising profit; It is also about having the motivation to innovate and make things happen. Supporting entrepreneurs therefore does not necessarily imply subscribing to the cult of the individual. The net must be cast wider to incorporate networking and mutually beneficial collaborations between the entrepreneurs themselves, advisers and providers of finance. We must ask ourselves about the consequences of entrepreneurial activity, and specifically new business formation. What are the wider benefits which would justify public intervention to support this sector?

- *Increased prosperity*: US evidence shows that healthy rates of new business formation precede high regional economic growth (Reynolds *et al.*, 1994);

- *innovation*: new technology based firms (NTBFs) appear to have a positive and highly disproportionate share of innovations: without doubt they outperform more conventional small firms in terms of survival and employment generation (Westhead et al., 1995; Garnsey, 1995);
- *job creation*: Evidence from Scottish Enterprise (1993) demonstrates that, whilst rising local demand is necessary to tackle unemployment, it will have most effect only if it is associated with the birth of new firms at the local level;
- *structural change*: 50 per cent of employees in the UK work in small firms. This has occurred for a variety of reasons, for example via an increase in subcontracting, technological diffusion, lower minimum efficient scales of production and by consumers becoming more heterogeneous in their tastes.

Essentially there is likely to be an increase in self-employment and numbers of small businesses irrespective of policy. On this the Institute for Employment Research (1996) estimates the increase to be in the region of 500,000 additional self-employed individuals by the year 2000. The question for policy-makers is: How do we nurture and support these people to their benefit and to the benefit of society in general?

## The evolution of public policy

The 1980s heralded the dawning of a new era as far as entrepreneurship and small business was concerned. For a variety of reasons the newly installed conservative government wished to facilitate the shift away from large government, large firms and large unions towards a small firms based economy. Small firms policy in its infancy had two fundamental aims: (a) to increase the number of business starts, and (b) to reduce unemployment. In practical terms the two were inextricably linked.

Policy at this time was explicitly focused on promoting business starts across the board. To this end policy initiatives were nationally imposed and administered by the Department of Employment and subsequently by the Department of Trade and Industry. In terms of focus there were two key concerns: (a) to alleviate perceived financial constraints preventing business inception, and (b) to reduce the income risk of starting a business.

By the early 1990s, however, the pendulum had swung to the other extreme. Now the focus of policy was on promoting so-called 'growth firms', usually defined as '*existing firms with the desire and ability to grow*'. In practice this was taken to mean three-year-old firms with at least ten employees. To this end the nature of support shifted to the provision of advice and counselling in the belief that lack of human capital was fundamental to the lack of business growth. In parallel with this dramatic shift in emphasis, policy-making was also devolved to regional agencies through the Training Enterprise Council (TEC) and Business Link (BL) network.

In short, this shift from the 1980s to the 1990s was thus:

| | | | |
|---|---|---|---|
| 1 | START-UPS | $\Rightarrow$ | EXISTING FIRMS |
| 2 | FINANCE | $\Rightarrow$ | SOFT SUPPORT |
| 3 | NATIONAL | $\Rightarrow$ | REGIONAL |

To some extent this was driven by academic research, although at times misinterpreted by politicians, but also by a desire to cut expenditure on the support infrastructure. It also tends to reflect the belief that localised agencies are better placed to design support programmes which address the particular needs of small businesses in heterogeneous localities. Whilst this devolution of power has resulted in greater local accountability and heterogeneity of provision, an unfortunate situation exists currently in which sub-regions have to bid competitively for public funds to provide business support. Thus in many areas there is no provision of support for start-ups at all. This surely cannot be the right approach.

## Is the UK experience different from other countries?

There are three key facts which underpin any cross-country comparisons. The first is that UK birth rates of new firms are fairly comparable with other European and North American countries. The second point is that our business cessation rates are the highest in the developed world (OECD, 1994). The caveat is that only 17 per cent of start-ups subsequently end up either bankrupt or insolvent. Furthermore, the average outstanding debt to financial institutions is a paltry £200. This information is often misrepresented by academics and politicians alike, who tend to use the word failure, which implies there was no choice in the individual's decision to exit, instead of cessation, which implies a very different thing. For example, voluntary exit is particularly prevalent among founder entrepreneurs who having grown their business to a substantial size then seek to realise their capital gains by selling the business on (Westhead and Wright,1997). The truth is that business cessation is a combination of bankruptcy, insolvency, involuntary exit due perhaps to a lack of demand, voluntary exit due to better outside alternatives, and voluntary exit with realised capital gains. Quite clearly the use of the term failure is a misnomer for many business exits.

The next big question is: Are our policies any different from those in other countries? To explore this issue we briefly outline the nature and focus of start-up support in three developed economies, namely France, the US and Japan.

### *France*

Here we find strong linkages between public and private sector agencies at the local and national level. The focus currently is very much on training and they appear to have had considerable success with pre-start training, virtually doubling the survival rates of those individuals who go on to start a business. However, this is supported by the provision of a well-developed and sophisticated programme of financial support, including both debt and equity financing.

## US

Policy intervention in the US dates back to the 1950s. There is a tremendous diversity at the public and private level in terms of what types of support are offered. Importantly, there is a much stronger role for academia. For example, the Small Business Development Centers (SBDCs) provide pre-start support for potential entrepreneurs via the university network. The results are extremely promising in that one year post start-up the average firm has created 2.6 new jobs at a net cost of only $1,750 per job (Chrisman and Katrishen, 1995). If the UK could parallel this success, in the average year, with our start-up rate, we could generate between 600,000 and 1 million gross new jobs. There is also an unparalleled level and diversity of support for NTBFs in the US. The Small Business Investment Company (SBIC) programme, dating back to 1958, has supported such household names as Intel, Federal Express, Apple and Sun Microsystems.

## Japan

Again small business policy dates back to the 1950s. Here the focus is very much upon human resource development. But in Japan this entails supporting not only the entrepreneurs themselves but managers and workers; in short, on enhancing the human capital and hence efficiency and productivity of the whole firm, not just the owner-manager. This ethos is encapsulated in the Japanese saying that 'a company is only as good as its people'. Yet this emphasis on human resource development is also complemented by a wide range of financing initiatives.

In contrast, UK policy has focused explicitly upon the individual entrepreneur, has been by comparison relatively short in terms of the duration of support offered, has been either money *or* training, and has tended to exclude academia. This is further compounded by the 30-year time delay in recognising the need to incorporate smaller firms into our industrial strategy. In fact, the most prominent current issue on the Labour Party small business agenda is late payment of trade debt. In Japan a Law on the Prevention of Delay in Payment of Subcontracting Charges and Related Matters was enacted as far back as 1956.

## What do we know about the determinants of success?

In terms of moving towards an agenda for policy in the future we must first look at what we know about the determinants of success in the small business sector. Here we present a checklist based upon a review of the small business literature. A fuller account of all the issues raised in this article is given in our book *The Entrepreneurial Society* (Gavron *et al.*, 1998) for those with a more academic interest in such matters.

### Human capital

- Previous small business experience;
- professional/managerial experience;
- marketing skills;
- vocational qualifications;
- size of entrepreneurial start-up team.

### Financial capital

- Balanced mix of debt and equity;
- access to seed capital for NTBFs.

### Other factors

- Niche products;
- appropriate advice;
- exporting.

These sorts of findings indicate not only the breadth of support needed to create a vibrant, sustainable and dynamic small business sector, but also the complementarity between the different strands of support that is required. To this end it is unlikely that a single agency can hope to fulfil these requirements. The lessons from abroad suggest that the support infrastructure must integrate public, quasi-public and private sectors to be effective. In addition there must be a continued devolution of policy-making to take into account the particular needs of different localities. However, this must be co-ordinated on a national level to ensure rapid evaluation and dissemination of 'best practice' or indeed 'worst practice'.

## Education, culture and entrepreneurship

The fact is that a substantial proportion of British people would prefer to pursue an entrepreneurial career path. Blanchflower and Oswald (1998), for example, report that 48 per cent of Britons, given the choice, would choose self-employment over waged employment. This is an enormous number of people who harbour entrepreneurial ambitions, however latent. This begs the question as to why so few go on to do so. Here we argue that the education system's potential contribution could be fundamental not only in supporting people who then go on to become self-employed to be better at it, but in terms of creating a cultural environment conducive to raising awareness of self-employment as a very real career option. The key stumbling block at the moment appears to be the lack of integration of what can loosely be termed 'commercial awareness' into the debate on the national curriculum. This is particularly strange given that the self-employment option has now been included in the Welfare to Work initiative.

---

**MINI ENTERPRISE: BRADFORD & DISTRICT TEC**

- Aim: to develop the curriculum and expand students' experience of the real world of business, whilst raising younger people's awareness of entrepreneurship as a potential outlet for their creative abilities.
- Target group: 9–13-year-olds.
- Based on public and private sector collaboration.

---

This contrasts quite distinctly with the experience in many European states, for example The Netherlands, Germany, Austria, Sweden, Denmark and Switzerland, where entrepreneurial skills and culture are promoted through the education system. Here the system is better placed to advance individuals up the ladder of formal education than into the work arena. However, there are schemes currently existing in the UK which tackle this issue head on, and with a considerable degree of success. The first is *Mini Enterprise* and the second *Young Enterprise*. Both are outlined in the boxes.

---

**YOUNG ENTERPRISE**

- Aim: to give students the chance to set up and run their own companies, improve their business knowledge and develop their wider personal skills.
- Annually, more than 33,000 students from 1,700 schools take part with some 2,500 business starts.
- Funded by private business, central government and TECs.

Both of these schemes were founded on the belief that the best way to encourage and develop a child's sense of business skills is through small projects that integrate practical experience and core teaching elements. Mini Enterprise comprises six core units: company structure, marketing and promotions, finance, personnel, business planning and production. These are delivered by an industry adviser who then supports the children in setting up their own projects. On completion, the children sell their 'output' and receive a certificate of their achievements. The measured benefits of the initiative in terms of skills development include practical business experience, team working, problem solving and negotiation, enhanced communication skills, entrepreneurial skills and planning. As a scheme it is a good example of how public and private sectors can combine to expand the curriculum, raise awareness of entrepreneurship and increase the business skills of students.

In a similar vein Young Enterprise gives students the opportunity to set up and run their own companies. On the ground there are three variants, namely: the Company Programme, Project Business and Team Enterprise. The Company Programme (outlined in the box) allows students to become shareholders and directors of their company. Capital up to a limit of £250 can be raised by the sale of shares for purchases of materials and equipment. Products or services are sold through trade fairs. Project Business provides a series of practical seminars relating to economic and financing issues, whilst Team Enterprise is specifically designed for children with learning difficulties and other special needs.

In terms of measurable outputs, a recent evaluation conducted by Pilat (UK) identified several key benefits of the scheme. First, it improved students' business knowledge. Second, it influenced their career and study paths. Third, it was found to increase future employability and success in university entrance. Fourth, it enhanced their personal skills development.

Thus, on balance, exposure to this type of practical business experience during the school years appears not only to improve work-related skills but engenders a more favourable view of the potential that entrepreneurship offers as an alternative career option. It is crucial, however, not to simply allow these schemes to operate in isolation within the education system. What we must seek to create is a nationally co-ordinated ladder of learning which encompasses cultural change *vis-à-vis* the role of entrepreneurship in society alongside the delivery of the practical skills relevant to an entrepreneurial career path. This would include an element of commercial skills training on teacher training courses to fill the supply-side gaps, the setting up of students' (particularly university students') entrepreneurs' clubs to promote networking.

On the issue of graduate start-ups, for example, student surveys show that around 50 per cent of graduates are likely to become self-employed or start their own business (Westhead, 1997). Thus alongside entrepreneur clubs there must be a more proactive role for industrial liaison officers, linking potential entrepreneurs from the graduate community to the wider business support infrastructure. To summarise the key concepts discussed in this section, before presenting our practical policy recommendations for promoting entrepreneurship through the education system, we simply argue that policy in this area needs to become more imaginative and that the education system needs to come to terms with the fact that many university and school leavers today and in the future will pursue entrepreneurial career paths. To fail to make adequate provision for this is to fail these individuals. Likewise to ignore the latent talents of our younger generation by not providing an outlet for their creative abilities and aspirations is closing the door on a wealth of potential talent.

### Policy recommendations

- Promote projects which develop business skills amongst younger children.
- Include commercial competence in teacher training courses.
- Develop entrepreneur clubs at higher education institutions.
- Promote entrepreneurship as a positive career option.

## The provision of advice, training and counselling

In the previous section we laid the foundations for an entrepreneurial society in terms of setting a positive agenda for promoting cultural change via the education system. Here we advance a little further along the ladder to business start-up by considering exactly what types of practical support are offered to potential entrepreneurs and start-up entrepreneurs in the early stages. The focus is on *soft support*, defined as non-financial support measures. Here we discuss the role of Personal Business Advisers (PBAs), mentoring, business incubators and team-building initiatives, all issues related to enhancing the human capital of entrepreneurs at start-up and in their formative years when they are most vulnerable to failure.

In broad terms, pre-start training and advice have two effects. First, they better prepare entrepreneurs for the rigours of business life. Second, they act as a self-screening mechanism by deterring those most likely to fail. In both cases this type of support bridges an information gap. In the latter case pre-start advice allows potential entrepreneurs to make a better-informed decision as to their suitability for an entrepreneurial career path. In many cases this pre-empts possibly ill-judged business starts which subsequently fail, at great economic and social cost to the individual concerned.

We begin by outlining the nature of the business support infrastructure as it exists today. TECs and Business Links are at the hub of this infrastructure on the ground, although five different departments are involved at the ministerial level of government.

The remit of TECs is to set key priorities and objectives for local business support development and delivery, for which funding is provided in the main by the Department for Education and Employment. However, only 10 per cent of total TEC funding (this part provided by the DTI) is for enterprise. Thus the overwhelming majority of TEC funding and support is for workforce training, not entrepreneurship development programmes. Business Links, as their name suggests, provide the core level of support for enterprise. Their original remit was to provide a 'One Stop Shop' or a single point of access for business support. Later, this was somewhat redefined and resulted in BLs focusing on existing businesses by providing advice and counselling through the PBA network. Somewhat surprisingly, the DTI required that BLs should become self-funding within three years of inception, although this was relaxed last year.

In terms of the PBAs and how they fit into the support infrastructure, it is likely that for any entrepreneur walking through the door of a Business Link the initial contact will be with a PBA whose remit is to provide independent advice to suit the client's needs. As to who they are, they tend to be generalists whose main objective is to identify and prioritise needs before referring clients to specialist advisers. Typically, they will have owned or managed a small business or been a consultant to them. In terms of the approach, it is very hands-on. However, concerns have been expressed about their calibre (Bank of England, 1997) and questions have been raised about the relevance of what are perceived in many cases as outdated business skills to the modern economic environment. In defence of the PBA concept, it is extremely unlikely that the best recruits will be attracted for an average annual salary in the region of £25,000.

So are there tangible benefits associated with pre-start advice and counselling, given that the issue of quality is resolved? Broadly speaking, the answer is yes. In the US and France pre-start advice and training has been shown to have a positive and significant impact on business survival. Interestingly, the US research shows that pre-start advice was more beneficial than post-start advice. This was attributable in the main to its role in screening out unsuitable individuals. In France the results are dramatic and show that survival chances increase by over 60 per cent if individuals receive pre-start advice and training. In the UK schemes such as the MIDAS initiative (see box) also support the rationale for the provision of extensive pre-start support.

---

**MIDAS INITIATIVE: UNIVERSITY OF CENTRAL ENGLAND**

- A programme of training, consultancy support, start-up and incubation for senior managers committed to the creation of team-based starts.
- Focuses on experienced managers, professionals, engineers and

scientists with clearly defined skills who are currently employed but actively considering starting a business.
- Collaboration and funding were secured from three local TECs, Birmingham Council, Midland Bank, Price Waterhouse and Eversheds.
- Between 1995 and 1996, 13 companies were started and generated 100 jobs.

For those not familiar with small business start-ups, the typical start would only generate one additional job over this sort of time scale. Thus the scheme highlights the potential benefits that well-designed and co-ordinated initiatives can achieve in this arena. Equally as important is the collaboration between local government, academia, the small business support infrastructure and the private sector. It also emphasises the advantage that team starts have over individual starts, particularly in terms of coverage of core managerial functions.

### Mentor networks

The simple fact is that aspiring entrepreneurs are more favourably disposed to taking advice from their peers than from men in grey suits. Therefore, the formation of networks of mentors might be a logical place to begin to encourage entrepreneurs to tap into the system of advice and support. In many ways this would be complementary to the role of business angels. Importantly, with such networks of current and retired small business people in place, it would then be relatively painless to extend their role to include the proposed university entrepreneur clubs and school-based initiatives. In many cases this sort of peer networking relationship might naturally evolve into non-executive directorships, which can be an important step towards removing the managerial constraints apparent in start-ups and early-stage firms.

**MEDILINK**

- A region-wide network scheme based in Sheffield with the explicit aim of advancing the interests of the medical technology sector in the area.
- It provides a forum for medical companies, hospitals, universities and business support agencies to exchange information and to work together to generate new business opportunities.
- The evidence suggests that this group has played an important role in promoting innovation and small business development in the sector.

### The business incubator

> Perhaps the ultimate form of support is the incubation unit which provides everything needed to get an enterprise up and running.
>
> (Gavron *et al.*, 1998, p. 88)

In terms of the nature of support provided by business incubators, it ranges from premises and shared secretarial/administrative facilities, through to training and in many cases financial support. What they hope to provide is a fast track for companies to reach the developmental stage where they are capable of generating wealth and employment. The key is creating an environment conducive to high growth which ultimately manifests itself by increasing regional prosperity. In line with this aim, many current initiatives of this type are focused on biotechnology and information/communications based start-ups. Other aims, notably pursued through the EU Business and Innovation Centre network, are directly aimed at encouraging innovative enterprise in regions suffering from structural economic problems. In such areas, schemes focus on diversifying industrial activity and creating new growth industries capable of generating and sustaining skilled employment. Here the emphasis is also on ability to export.

Do business incubators work? Here again there is growing evidence that they do. For example, EU-BICs are directly responsible for the creation of several thousand new and innovative businesses across Europe. More importantly from a policy angle is the fact that start-up survival rates are demonstrably higher as is their employment creation potential. For example EC-BICs achieved start-up survival rates of 88 per cent compared to 50 per cent for a matched sample of unsupported starts. At St Johns Innovation Centre in Cambridge, identical start-up survival figures of 88 per cent were recorded, which exceeded even the figure recorded for high-tech starts in Cambridge as a whole. Further, the 64 companies located there employ a total of 1,000 staff with a combined annual turnover of £50 million.

### Spin-outs

The concept of the business spin-out is embedded in the concepts of efficiency and entrepreneurialism. With reference to the latter, the basic argument is that as firms evolve over time and increase in size there is a requirement for more formalised information systems and managerial structures which allow centralised decision-makers to adopt formalised or routinised responses to external shocks which impact upon the firm. This is characterised by a shift from an entrepreneurial or informal style of management and decision-making towards a more formal, bureaucratic style. The effect of such a shift is that entrepreneurial activity within the firm (often called intrapreneurship) is often quashed. Thus the dynamism and entrepreneurial vision which drove on the firm in the early stages of its life-cycle is often lost as entrepreneurs are replaced by formal managerial functions. Regarding efficiency concerns, basic industrial economic theory tells us that once firms are able to exert some degree of market power then the requirement to be efficient in terms of producing the lowest-cost output possible for a given set of factor inputs is removed. One particular scheme, the Enterprise Factory (EUROSME), tackles these efficiency concerns head on with a new and innovative approach towards industrial regeneration. A brief outline is provided in the box.

---

**ENTERPRISE FACTORY (EUROSME): TYNESIDE TEC**

- Arose out of the concern that Jarrow had the highest rate of male unemployment in the UK.
- Based on two economic postulates:
  1. that large firms need to concentrate on core competencies in order to be globally competitive, and
  2. that spin-outs could create more growth than the same functions within the parent.
- Takes non-core functions out of large firms, develops then and sells them on to regional entrepreneurs or via MBOs (management buy outs).
- The transaction provides investment funds for the next phase of 'cold' spin-outs.

---

This fundamental belief that non-core competencies could be placed on the open market to improve productivity, strengthen competition and increase the birth rate of new firms in the locality is arguably the line that industrial policy-makers should have been adopting since the decline of UK manufacturing in the early 1970s. The evidence to date suggests that the scheme's designers were correct. Case studies of spin-outs show that substantial increases in productivity have been achieved.

Yet the key to the scheme's success is the nature of the support provided to spin-outs. Typically the new spin-outs are micro-businesses with around 3–4 employees. They are located in the Enterprise Factory and provided with central services covering a wide range of managerial and human resource development. Alongside this, advanced market research techniques are used to identify commercial opportunity. On average spin-outs remain in the factory for two years or until they have grown to a stable size of 10–20 employees with sufficient growth potential. They are then sold off to the management team or to local entrepreneurs, thus creating and sustaining wealth within the region.

In this section we have considered issues relating to training, advice and counselling in a wide variety of contexts. As is evident from the case studies of specific initiatives this is an area in which many innovative and diverse approaches have been adopted. What is patently obvious is that the best of these schemes have achieved outstanding success, not only in terms of enhancing survival prospects, but in terms of promoting and accelerating growth and wealth creation. A positive outcome has been the dramatic growth in the capability of supported firms to create and sustain high levels of new job generation. A further desirable outcome has been the endogeneity of growth within the region in which the scheme was initiated. Surely organic growth in this context is more efficient than subsidising foreign direct investment from multinationals with no more than a passing allegiance to the regions in which they temporarily locate.

### *Policy recommendations*

- Ensure that there is a basic level of pre-start advice provision available to all potential entrepreneurs across Britain.
- Promote networks of mentors throughout the UK from the ranks of the 4 million existing small business owner-managers and the thousands of retired business people.
- Encourage the formation of private sector entrepreneurs' clubs.
- Increase the level of support for business incubators with appropriate provision for innovation depending upon specific local circumstance.

## Finance

Finance is perhaps the most contentious issue for small businesses. Survey after survey tells us that small businesses are unhappy with providers of debt and equity finance for a variety of reasons. At the academic level the issue is just as hotly debated. On the one hand, we have the credit rationing lobby and, on the other, the no-rationing lobby. Indeed, the roll-call of entrants into the academic debate reads like a who's who of finance. So it is perhaps best to begin with a few relatively uncontentious stylised facts about small business financing:

1   High-technology start-ups in particular and high-tech small businesses more generally are consistently identified as the most constrained small businesses in terms of their ability to access either debt or equity finance in the UK.

2   The overwhelming majority (over 80 per cent) of small business loans in excess of £15,000 involve the posting of assets (collateral) to a value which exceeds the total loan value, often by a factor of two or three times.

3   Around 10 per cent to 20 per cent of small businesses who apply for bank funds are refused. Further, a substantial number who are successful do not receive the full amount they requested.

4   The cost of bank debt very rarely exceeds 3 percentage points over base rates.
5   Only 5 per cent of total UK formal venture capital goes to seed or early stage investment.

In terms of how potential entrepreneurs perceive finance constraints, Blanchflower and Oswald (1998) report that of the 15 per cent of employees who had seriously considered starting their own business, some 51 per cent had not done so due to capital constraints. I guess the big issue for us here (at least initially) is not whether the finance gap is real, but the fact that if potential entrepreneurs believe it is and are prevented from advancing their ideas further then we are losing a potentially valuable economic resource. Even at the post-start stage, undercapitalisation is widely cited as a major contributory factor in failure.

At the heart of the debate is the relationship between risk assessment and information. Clearly, there are difficulties in determining start-up businesses' chances of survival and hence ability to repay loans. This is presumably why the incidence of collateral is so high. Yet the imposition of collateral requirements obviates the need for banks to monitor or properly evaluate loan decisions. This is where the pubic sector has an important role to play: First, by increasing the quality and volume of information flows between banks and potential borrowers banks may be better placed to evaluate lending propositions; second, if finance is linked with the provision of advice and training then we are addressing the quality of entrepreneur issue head on. It is perhaps this lack of complementarity between human and financial capital that has characterised the policy arena to date and arguably contributed to the rather intransigent and hostile relationship between banks and entrepreneurs (Middleton *et al.*, 1992). An example of such a mutually beneficial collaboration is provided by the Business Development Loan Fund (see box).

---

**THE BUSINESS DEVELOPMENT LOAN FUND:**
**BUSINESS LINK OLDHAM**

- The Fund aims to assist the start-up and growth of small businesses, co-operatives and community enterprises in the locality.
- Joint venture between Oldham Council and three banks.
- Grants are matched by a low interest, unsecured loan from one of the banks.
- Applicants are assessed by a panel of local authority and bank representatives and must demonstrate the viability and job generation potential of the business.
- Successful candidates are offered free advice, counselling and support on a continued basis.

In such cases the involvement of the TECs or Business Link has altered the risk profile of the entrepreneurs as perceived by the banks. This has resulted in lower-cost finance, and more generally greater availability of loan packages. These sorts of outcomes have the potential to generate positive and long-term benefits to both firms, banks and also local communities. Indeed, one of the centrepiece schemes dealing with the perceived gap in the financing of small businesses, the Loan Guarantee Scheme, has now begun ten pilot projects incorporating TEC and BL advice into the loan package. We await the results of the evaluation with anticipation.

Regarding equity finance, once again it is the difficulty in assessing the viability of proposals, particularly high-tech, which is the greatest obstacle for start-ups. On this the costs of 'due diligence' make it unprofitable to make investments below £100,000. Consequently venture capitalists tend to favour MBOs and MBIs. A further issue is the high internal rates of return (IRRs) demanded by venture capitalists for high-risk start-up proposals. Here the long lead times associated with high-tech R&D militate against investing in this type of firm. In addition, the venture capitalists' lack of technical skills often represents a significant barrier to funding. Wrapped up in all of this is the widely held perception that high-tech small businesses are the most risky. Research suggests that this is quite clearly untrue (Westhead *et al.*, 1995).

In terms of an agenda for resolving this impasse, perhaps the most promising line is through the promotion of informal venture capital investments via networks of business angel networks (BANs). On this, Harrison and Mason (1996) identify three characteristics of business angels which are fundamental to promoting equity investment to the small business sector. These are: they invest in precisely those areas where institutional providers are reluctant to venture; they are geographically dispersed and favour localised investment; and they bring with their investments expertise in the form of commercial skills and business contacts.

Business angel networks have been the most prevalent means of stimulating informal equity investments in smaller firms. As a rule they are not-for-profit organisations, often funded through public or quasi-public agencies (TECs and BLs). Most commonly they provide 'matching' services for business angels and small firms seeking investment. Of the 37 BANs existing in the UK in 1995, 24 were public sector or not-for-profit. Typically these were found in the least-profitable areas of the small business sector and were often very localised, offering relatively small amounts of equity. On balance, however, the dramatic growth in business angel activity has not really generated funds on the desired scale, nor has it promoted huge increases in numbers of investments in small businesses. The evidence for this is quite strong. For example, the five DTI Informal Investment Demonstration Projects only made 64 investments totalling £3.6 million in three years. Even the largest single fund of its type, the Midland Enterprise Fund, has only completed 95 investments since 1994, although a high proportion, 38 per cent, has gone to start-up and early-stage development.

So why is there such a disappointing lack of activity in the sector? The business angels put it down to a lack of viable investment opportunities. In terms of how this issue might be addressed there are several strands of enquiry which deserve consideration. The first would be to initiate an Equity Guarantee Scheme (EGS) along the lines of SOFARIS in France or BTU in Germany, where the government acts as a guarantor for a specified percentage of the total business angel investment in return for either a fee income or a small stake in the business. This type of scheme appears to have been successful in Europe by reducing the perceived risk associated with equity investment in smaller firms. An EGS might have several positive outcomes: for example, it might increase the number of active business angels; increase the number of investments that business angels make; increase the flow of investment from existing venture capital funds; reduce the risks associated with investing in start-ups and high-tech firms; reduce smaller firms' reliance on debt finance. Other areas in which public intervention might prove to be beneficial is in the setting up of a national database of business angels and small businesses looking for equity funds. This could be administered through the existing network of TECs and BLs. The main advantage of such a network would be to remove the informational problems which often prevent the supply side (the business angels) from ever meeting the demand side (the firms looking for investment).

### *Policy recommendations*

- Promote the creation of strategic partnerships between public and private sector support agencies and providers of debt and equity finance.
- Establish a national database for business angels and investment opportunities.
- Pilot an Equity Guarantee Scheme.
- Promote finance packages which involve an element of advice and training to enhance survival prospects, thus increasing the flow of funds to firms and reducing the requirement for collateralised lending.

## Conclusion

We have put forward a positive agenda for promoting an entrepreneurial society in which individuals and groups of people with the desire to create or innovate have the ability and support to do so. This we believe underpins our ability to address many of the economic and social problems we currently face. The creation of a dynamic and sustainable entrepreneurial base, embedded in a society which is broadly supportive in a cultural sense of entrepreneurial activity, is fundamental to this. In this chapter we have critically reviewed the state of entrepreneurship in Britain and considered whether current public policy is effective in terms of addressing the primary concerns of entrepreneurs. In many cases we found that policy was innovative, diverse and flexible. Yet the overwhelming evidence suggests that the approach has been unco-ordinated and consequently has resulted in rather disparate coverage across geographical regions and industrial sectors. We argue, first, that policy can do more. As entrepreneurs must embrace change so must policy-makers. There is also a clear need to maintain a coherent and global strategy for the development of the small business sector *per se*. Only by setting goals and objectives and then integrating these into an overall industrial and social strategy can we begin to formulate anything like this. As banks have allowed natural and beneficial alliances to evolve with other key players in the business support infrastructure so must policy-makers.

## References

Bank of England. Business Finance Division (1997) *Quarterly Report on Small Business Statistics*, London: Bank of England.

Blanchflower, D.G. and Oswald, A.J (1998) What Makes an Entrepreneur? *Journal of Labour Economics*, vol. 16, no. 1, pp. 29–60.

Chrisman, J.J. and Katrishen, F. (1995) The Economic Impact of Small Business Development Center Counseling Activities in the United States: 1990–1991, *Journal of Business Venturing*, vol. 9, pp. 271–80.

Garnsey, E. (1995) High Technology Renewal and the UK Investment Problem, *Journal of General Management*, vol. 20, no. 4.

Gavron, R., Cowling, M., Holtham, G. and Westall, A. (1998) *The Entrepreneurial Society*. London: Institute for Public Policy Research.

Harrison, R. and Mason, C. (1996) Developing the Informal Venture Capital Market: a Review of the DTI's Informal Investment Demonstration Projects. *Regional Studies*, vol. 30, no. 8, pp. 765–71.

Insitute for Employment Research (IER) (1996) *Labour Market and Skills Trends*. Warwick: Institute for Employment Research.

Leadbetter, C. (1997) *The Rise of the Social Entrepreneur* London: Demos.

Middleton, M., Cowling, M., Samuels, J. and Sugden, R. (1992) Small Firms and Clearing Banks, in N. Dimsdale and M. Prevezer (eds) *Capital Markets and Corporate Governance*. Oxford: Clarendon Press, pp. 141–60.

OECD (1994) *Employment Outlook*. July. Paris: OECD.

Pilat (UK) (1995) *Young Enterprise: The Benefits Evaluated*. Oxford: Young Enterprise.

Reynolds, P., Storey, D. and Westhead, P. (1994) Cross-national Comparisons of the Variation in New Firm Formation Rates. *Regional Studies*, vol. 28, pp. 443–56.

Scottish Enterprise (1993) *The Business Birth Rate Strategy Update*. Glasgow: Scottish Enterprise.

US Government Printing Office (1995) *The State of Small Business: A Report to the President*. Washington, DC: USGPO.

Westhead, P. (1997) *Students in Small Business: An Assessment of the 1994 STEP Student Placement Scheme*. Milton Keynes: Small Business Research Trust.

Westhead, P. and Wright, M. (1997) Novice, Portfolio and Serial Founders: Are they Different? *Journal of Business Venturing*, vol. 13, pp. 173–204.

Westhead, P., Storey, D. and Cowling, M. (1995) An Exploratory Analysis of the Factors Associated with the Survival of Independent High-technology Firms in Great Britain, in F. Chittenden *et al.* (eds) *Small Firms: Partnerships for Growth*. London: Paul Chapman Publishing, pp. 63–99.

# 9 Practical issues of networking and co-operation

*Jacques De Bandt*

## Bottom-up vs top-down

This paper discusses some aspects of a bottom-up approach for the design and implementation of a regional or local technological or innovation policy, as part of a more comprehensive regional or local development strategy, aiming at developing competitive technology and supply bases.

Most local innovation policies are only the local application of top-down policies,[1] defining the different types of support (financial, training, information, technology) which can be supplied to potential innovative firms. Such systems pursue different, more or less complementary, targets:

- the creation of new firms (through different types of incentives, support, transfers);
- support to existing SMEs (through various types of services for specific problems, with some reduction of costs);
- innovation (through incentives, information, means for facilitating access to technology, services).

There are of course exceptions: cases in which real bottom-up technological policies exist (for example, in some industrial districts). In such cases, usually in those places where one single important activity exists, the local actors or producers are requiring from the local authorities some type of specific aid, aiming at developing complementary activities locally. By contrast, in many places local actors or producers don't require such a policy, and nothing happens.

Bottom-up means here not only (a) that policies are defined and implemented at some local level (even if this may be done within a more general framework defined at the national or European level)[2] but also (b) that such local policy is decided on the basis of more or less democratic procedures,[3] and/or (c) in response to specific needs as expressed by local actors.

## Organisational failures

I am considering here, more particularly, the two following cases. The first – in traditional sectors – is one in which local actors or producers have a past (traditions, accumulated know-how, products and markets) but are more or less declining and are too weak (because of size, obsolete technologies or outdated equipment) or have too divergent interests to take the initiative and to design some strategy.[4] The second case – in high-tech sectors – is one in which the actors (SMEs) may also be lacking some of the necessary resources or competencies (which is nearly always the case: some of the competencies or resources have indeed to be developed within the process), but there is the additional difficulty that they don't have access to the complementary competencies which are required.[5]

We have typically in France today and, I would say, to a large extent in Europe overall, a shortage of innovative SMEs. While there is enormous potential for specific applications of existing technologies, particularly in the fields of microelectronics and information technologies, and large numbers of potential innovators, it is hard to come up with the expected innovations, because the required knowledge/competencies are not available through the market.

These are situations which can typically be said to be characterised by some type of organisational failure. In the first case, the SMEs are losing market share and trying to solve their problems, individually, by competing to the death: they don't have the organisational competencies for designing some rules and institutions which would enable them to get out of their vicious circles, to organise some organisational learning process and to solve their problems, or at least part of them. In the second case, the technology providers are (mostly) large (or even very large) firms, whose organisation and competitiveness rest on economies of scale. They cannot, for organisational or cost reasons, respond to specific needs on a small scale, even while they are eager to benefit from the outlets which SMEs are representing. And SMEs cannot afford to pay high prices for the necessary technology transfers: the risks are simply too big.

In both cases, there is thus a gap: supply and demand exist, at least agents with the necessary competencies and others with specific needs to be satisfied. But supply and demand don't meet. This results in corresponding losses of potential value added and profits.

## Technological intermediaries

As concerns technology, the major emphasis is usually (in the top-down policies) on technological intermediaries, that is, on different types of actors helping to transfer information from those who have to those who need the required knowledge/information. Because of the nature of technological knowledge or information, there is no (real) market, supply and demand don't meet, or only exceptionally. In order to meet the unsatisfied organisational requirements, some kind of collective intermediation system is set up. These intermediaries are one way or another aiming at organising transfers or exchange of technology (of technological information or knowledge). In order to do so, they are continuously searching either for potential users of existing knowledge or for providers of knowledge in order to help respond to specific technical questions. They are supposed to act as brokers, having to find out how to make interested parties meet.

This activity consists, in the majority of cases, in helping potential partners to meet and to enter into some kind of contractual agreement for the transfer of some technology. Of course such contracts have different objects: at one extreme, transferring the right to use a well-defined codified technical solution for production purposes; at the other extreme, the decision to co-operate to help solve a specific problem. This means, at one extreme, a 'pure exchange' of a right (the right to use some knowledge); at the other extreme, some form of co-operation, whose content can be only partially defined beforehand.

*A priori* reasoning and empirical observation tend, however, to show that this technological intermediation activity can have and only have poor and rapidly decreasing returns. It is based on the idea that there is a market but that, the market being only poorly transparent or efficient, these intermediaries should and can help facilitate the functioning of market mechanisms.

*A priori* reasoning suffices to convince that the basic hypothesis is simply wrong: there isn't something like a market for technological information or knowledge. Being non-existent, it cannot be improved. This is because technology is in most cases not a product: it is knowledge on the basis of which it may be possible to organise some knowledge production process aimed at solving a problem or meeting a need – and when it is a product (for example, a patent), it is unique and non-reproducible.

What are the intermediaries doing? They are trying to identify what kind of competencies or knowledge exists (where) which can meet some competence requirement (somewhere) within the system. This is fine as far as it goes. It may be quite useful – it is quite useful in all systems – to circulate information about who is doing what, in the hope that, by chance, some correspondence can be organised between some existing competence and some demand for such competence. But taking account of the numbers, the chances of this happening tend to be nil.

While scientific laws are only in the order of $10^2$, technological artefacts are in the order of $10^6$ (and even, if account is taken of the various technological dimensions, in the order of $10^7$). How can one imagine that an intermediary could be able to effectively organise appropriate contacts within this quasi-infinite domain, particularly when this infinite domain is not organised: there is a complete lack of principles that would allow for the organisation of technological knowledge,[6] making the task of intermediaries a sheer impossibility, unless they concentrate on a specific domain and become themselves active players within the interactive knowledge production processes. But this is another job. As a matter of fact, these intermediaries are essentially trying to put potential partners in contact. They are not, or only marginally, entering into the content of the question–response or knowledge production process.

Experience and empirical observation tend to show exactly that: namely (a) that the cases in which they 'produce agreements' are, for most of them, 'obvious cases', in which the agreement would have been reached in any case, even without the intermediaries; (b) that in those cases, while adding only marginal information, the intermediaries are taking charge, at least partially, of the costs (the transaction costs) involved in preparing and making the agreement; (c) that outside the 'obvious cases', these intermediaries are usually unable, except by chance, to organise relevant contacts between supply and demand; (d) that, in any case, the costs of such intermediation systems are very high indeed, out of proportion with the results obtained; (e) that in many places (certainly in France[7]), the reaction to these poor and decreasing returns consists in systematically increasing the numbers of such intermediaries, with the consequence that returns are still lower.

## Informational service activities

A further problem for local industrial policies concerns the service activities. In most of those more or less top-down local policies, some support mechanisms are provided: SMEs can get some kind of subsidies for the partial payment of business services which seem to be required in their innovation process: different types of consulting (marketing, strategy, engineering, design), R&D, training and the like. The question is of course whether such service provisions can solve their problems. This is part of a much wider problem, which concerns the functioning of business services, or what I usually call informational business services.[8]

Such informational services raise two related types of problems in the framework of local industrial policies. The first type concerns the way SMEs support systems are designed and function. Most of those systems are designed for the provision of functionally specialised services (marketing, design, transfer of technology, accountancy, finance) by specialised service providers. Even when those service provisions are *per se* qualitatively good and up to the requirements, those systems are not meeting some more essential requirements, in terms of strategic orientation, comprehensiveness, customisation and continuity. A kind of monitoring function, on a continuous basis, would seem to be required. The second type of problem concerns the interventions of those service providers. In order to be useful, the service has to be thoroughly adapted to the specific problems or needs of the client/customer. In order for this to happen, the client/customer has to be really integrated into the design and production process, which means that the service has to be co-produced and that the client/customer has to participate actively in the production process. More often than not, because of the small size of the client/customer, the service provider tends to consider that he or she perfectly well knows, on the basis of experience, what the (standard) problem of the client/customer is and that a standardised answer or solution can be given to the problem.

One particular problem with informational services, which have to be co-produced, has to do with the fact that in order to be explicit enough about needs (to ask the correct questions or explain adequately the existing problems) and to use correctly the result or to implement adequately the solution, the client/customer must have the necessary competencies. In order to use external competencies he or she needs to have some such competencies. For this reason the usual choice between 'buy' or 'make' is in many cases, and apparently more and more so, replaced by 'buy and make' solutions. This would be difficult to imagine for SMEs, which are precisely characterised by their limited human resources. It would seem obviously necessary to compensate for this by adequate support systems, but taking into account the problem defined above.

We should add here, depending on the degree of bureaucratic complexity of the existing rules and procedures, the necessity to help SMEs to meet existing administrative requirements. As a matter of fact, at least in a country like France, SME entrepreneurs spend a large proportion of their time and effort trying to meet such requirements. But I don't want to expand on that here.

## Networking

The next aspect is networking. One of the central questions is how to bring the required complementary competencies together and to co-operate. But this central question can be subdivided in many sub-questions. The complementary actors and competencies have to be identified. They have to enter some co-operative scheme. They have to negotiate among themselves their rights and obligations, and the rules of the game. They have to manage their co-operation and more particularly the organisational learning processes. They have to manage the knowledge which is exchanged, pooled and produced, and the ownership of such knowledge.[9]

The identification problem brings us back, to a certain extent, to the role of intermediaries. I would suggest: (a) that we find here the same problem of inefficiency as described above and which is related to information asymmetries and adverse selection phenomena; (b) that the databases with information about people looking for partnerships are equally of little help. Of course there are exceptions, again mostly by chance. The hypothesis here is that the information conveyed is too general to be useful.

The only alternative would consist in building and developing specific competence bases (blocs or poles), and in developing, on that basis, a project approach within which networking would appear as one of the organisational procedures. Building the competence basis includes the accumulation of information on the 'sub-system' (set of interrelated activities corresponding to the technical system involved) itself, and thus on the various actors playing some role within this sub-system. Following a project approach means, by definition, that specific goals or targets are selected and defined, and that all activities proceed within this finalised framework.

What this means is the necessity to find the organised support of some actors or institution (for example, an engineering school) within the 'sub-system' in response to the specific needs and requirements of specific projects.

Identifying possible partners is one thing. They have to be convinced to enter some type of co-operative scheme: more than some informal group, it needs to be some type of virtual or real consortium or network or project group, with defined rights and obligations for the partners involved. Again with exceptions,[10] it is hard for SMEs to succeed in bringing together, in a more or less formal framework, the required partners and competencies. As indicated above, those SMEs cannot find the technology providers who would be prepared to transfer the technology because these are not interested in the kind of small-scale application the SMEs are looking for. For the same reason essentially, they cannot set up the required innovative group or consortium.

They thus need some help in order to facilitate the emergence and functioning of networks within which they can solve their problem. The question here is about the kind of organisational set-up which can indeed do this.

For example, within the FUSE Program (of the EU), aiming at diffusing information technologies among SMEs, the organisation consists in setting up local Technology Transfer Nodes (TTN), whose role consists in helping SMEs define their application, find the partners and formalise their project. The EU is financing the TTN and the selected first applications. The intention is now, in order to increase the diffusion for the same amount of financial resources, to put more emphasis on replications, that is, on the duplication of applications already made. This approach seems to be very expensive, requiring substantial resources for rather limited results in terms of technology transfers.[11] I would suggest that this is because the organisational set-up is not really satisfactory, and resembles the usual service provisions rather than networking partnerships. This means that the solution mainly refers to the market (even if part of the payment is subsidised): the solution consists, as in the case of intermediaries, in trying to facilitate the functioning of the market. As a consequence, organisational failures are not compensated for.

I would like to make a parenthesis here. I must admit that the previous remark about service provision is ambiguous. I have insisted above on the fact that the service provision has to be co-produced, meaning by that that the client/consumer must actively participate. This is really to be seen as a co-operative relation, and not as a purely market relation.

While this is of course true, it must be taken into account both (a) the fact that, in a large proportion of cases, the service providers tend not to respect this fundamental requirement, or only marginally, and (b) that what is required, in this case, is not only a bilateral functionally specialised service provision, but a multilateral interactive process. What is needed is a co-operative relation, whose non-market dimensions are important.

## Conditions for networking and co-operation

It may be necessary here to define what I call co-operation, the word being used in (too) many senses. I exclude from co-operation all pure coalitions aiming at promoting common interests to the detriment of some other parties (usually the client or consumer). I exclude all 'contracts' (even long-term contracts) whose object is only to exchange or transfer something: a good, a service, a right to use, an asset (material or non-material). I exclude also all types of division of labour, that is, the distribution of predefined tasks: division of labour *per se* is no co-operation, but actors can co-operate for defining and organising the division of labour. This would thus mean that neither contracts nor enterprises are, as such, co-operative schemes (even if enterprises can be seen as a likely or favourable place for co-operating). Positively, co-operation would mean working together to answer a (new) question or solve a (new) problem, in situations in which answers or solutions are not known beforehand. The probability of finding a relevant answer or solution can be higher or lower.

Let me then come back to the network. I would like to suggest that in order to compensate for the existing organisational failures, three types of conditions seem to be required:

1   creating incentives for co-operation with reference to convergent interests;
2   organising the organisational learning process;
3   managing knowledge and securing intellectual property rights.

The first question is about how to set up the network. As already indicated, SMEs need help in order to meet the requirements for doing so. This is similar, to a large extent, to the organisational content of industrial development strategies, as designed and implemented by MITI in Japan. MITI was helping actors to set up a comprehensive sub-system and organising both roles and relations of actors, but also the development of resources and competencies.

Of course, this similarity raises again the question about what is top-down and what is bottom-up. Clearly top-down was the fact that MITI was taking the initiative (isn't that normal for an 'infant industry'?), referring to collective economic or socio-economic objectives and criteria; also the fact that MITI was mobilising resources and building support institutions. But then, action, risks and responsibility were left to enterprises. Once enterprises decide to play the game, they take over completely.

What then are the conditions for co-operation? For the purpose of a local industrial policy, it is necessary to find out how to bring the complementary actors and competencies to co-operate on the basis of their shared interest in the expected results. As indicated previously, the interests of the technology providers and of the SMEs (or the interests of the various partners whose complementary competencies have to be brought to work together) do not (necessarily) meet. It is thus a requirement not mainly to design incentive mechanisms, but to help organise a comprehensive project group of actors, potentially sharing some common interest in the outcome of the project.

## Complex questions and solutions

The probability of obtaining the expected outcome can vary substantially from one case to the other. There is an important issue here. Because of their differences and besides information asymmetries, the actors do not usually have the same possibility of evaluating the probability of the outcome (a relevant solution or innovation), or necessarily the same representation of what would be a relevant solution and/or the same interest in different kinds (levels) of possible solutions, or the same attitude towards risks. In order to co-operate, they have to come up, not with a 'common denominator' view, but with a compromise common view focusing on a real innovation.

Even if this appears to be possible, I would still suggest that one central issue, which we will find again and again, is the related problem of the level at which the co-operative actors are placing and maintaining their objectives and ambitions. There are strong forces permanently at play which tend to lower the level of ambitions. These forces are of (at least) three different types:

- problems of competencies, that is, the difficulty of facing a complex problem, which one thus tries to simplify;
- problems of costs, that is, the fact that finding the relevant solution will take time and money, which are considered as excessive (taking account of the uncertainties as concerns the outcome). Shortcuts or approximate solutions are looked for;
- problems of interests: some of the actors may have a greater interest in selling their existing solution (product, component, information) than in looking for a more ambitious solution.

The reason why this is a central issue has to do with the fact that, in order to be relevant, the expected outcome is very demanding. This is because we are looking for an unknown answer or solution, which has to satisfy several conditions and requirements. Following Dibiaggio (1998), I would say that what is needed is the production and accumulation of complex knowledge,[12] which means that there is no guarantee that a relevant solution can indeed be found.

The complexity of the knowledge to be produced is related to the complexity of the question or problem at hand, which is multidimensional. The complex knowledge which has to be produced can only be the result of an organisational learning process, including different types of (cognitive) interactions between actors with different but complementary competencies/knowledge/know-how. These interactions can be outlined, in a summarised form, as follows:

- interactions between the scientific and technological competencies: in order to find technologically possible, appropriate or even optimised solutions;
- interactions between the above and the engineering and production people: in order to take account of engineering and technical constraints and possibilities, and to make sure that solutions are feasible;
- interactions between the above and the client/consumer: in order to adapt the solution to the specific requirements or needs (service relation).

## Organisational learning

But there is more to this. In many cases, technology transfers tend to be seen in the reduced sense of transferring a solution and the capability to use this solution. But what is more fundamentally at stake is actually to transfer the technology, in the sense of contributing to the organisation of a cumulative knowledge production or learning process. The dynamics is what really matters. But this means that more fundamental knowledge needs to be produced.

From that standpoint, and linking with what is said above, I would suggest that a 'simpler' solution with a real learning and transfer process is much preferable to a 'better' (more 'complex') solution without such a real transfer and learning process. This suggestion is based on experiences showing that unless technological knowledge is really appropriated and further accumulated (not the least, completed by tacit knowledge), it downgrades progressively (and in some cases, quite fast). The idea of a stock of knowledge, staying there as it has been produced or acquired, autonomously and unaffected, doesn't correspond to any reality.

Once a project group or consortium has been set up, the major problems are those related to the organisational learning processes themselves. At the more theoretical level, this is the type of discussion which is developed by authors such as Nonaka, Egidi, Marengo, and more generally in the literature on design, concurrent design, innovation processes, and the like. At the more practical level, this is the domain of what is actually called 'project management' and/or 'knowledge engineering'.

The question here is about how to organise collective knowledge production processes: both how to be efficient (rapid, cost effective) and, referring to the above discussion, how to stay at the correct level of complexity and ambitions; how to organise the question–response (problem-solving) procedures, including series of iterations, such as to include all of the various above mentioned interactions.

This is typically the place where the danger threatens by way of simplification – simplifying the question or problem at hand – and thus coming up necessarily with a simplified or reduced answer or solution.

Service providers should help client/consumers to have access to higher levels of complexity. This would seem to be the main task of service providers: the client/consumer asks them to bring complementary resources or competencies that will enable the client/consumer to produce the complex knowledge which is required. This is what indirect productivity and non-material investments are about (De Bandt, 1995: 162).

If this is not done – which is more than often the case (service providers being unable or unwilling to enter the demanding organisational learning processes which are required) – other mechanisms or procedures should be implemented in order to compensate for this.

Summarising, what all this means is that a local industrial policy consists in the creation of conditions and support structures to compensate for existing organisational failures and to enable small actors to have access to the required complementary competencies and to co-operate with them. This implies at least three types of actions: (a) to help to organise (within sub-systems, poles, networks) the complementary competencies, in order for them to meet and eventually to co-operate; (b) to help set up project groups or networks, within the framework of specific projects or programmes, in order to launch knowledge creation and innovation processes; (c) to help organise the organisational learning processes at the appropriate level of complexity.

This probably also involves some type of action concerning the management of knowledge: to help actors both to manage knowledge as such (codification, accumulation, maintenance) and to manage intellectual property rights. But this appears to be a more complicated question, which cannot be discussed here.

## Notes

1 Even the EU regional innovation programme, which gives much initiative to local actors, is strongly top-down.

2 For example, in France, the law defines the types of economic competencies or functions which can be exerted at the local level and several policies define the resources which can be made available for different types of actions at the local level. The same exists for example within the European regional innovation programme.

3 This doesn't *per se* guarantee that an appropriate local industrial policy will be designed and decided. Even if the chances are higher (than with technocratic procedures), it may be difficult to come up with such a policy, whose justification may not necessarily be evident to many people and which in any case implies the initiative and perseverance of small numbers of actors.

4 This would for example be typically the case of the pottery sector in my home town, Vallauris (where Picasso was making pottery, from 1947 or 1948). In the case of pottery, cut-throat competition is progressively eliminating the weakest

and reducing the numbers, but at the same time, because of lower quality imposed by lower prices, their collective image is deteriorating and reducing their total market share.

5 Of course, in the other case also, the actors lack access to the complementary resources or competencies which would be required for more ambitious strategies, aiming at developing some activity in the field of new ceramics.

6 We all know for example that descriptors for finding relevant information in databases are only rather poor instruments.

7 This is apparently not only the case in France. Several studies tend to show that in most European countries, transfer of technology systems are growing endlessly, without solving the 'European paradox' (*Green Book on Innovation, Bulletin of the European Union*, Supplement 5/95).

8 I do not want here to go into this discussion. Let me only insist on the fact that informational service markets are inefficient and that important organisational failures exist in this domain. The result is that an enormous gap exists between the expectations of the client/consumer and the services as obtained. I have written several papers on this question (see De Bandt, 1995, 1996, 1997), in order to show both that current theories, based on industrial realities, don't apply correctly (or not at all for most of them) to service or informational realities and that, in particular, market mechanisms don't function efficiently in the case of some or even most informational services.

9 We have of course to take account of the difference between background (or previously accumulated) and so-called foreground (or generated within the co-operative project) intellectual property, the former being usually – but for the tacit part of it – already, in some way or another, protected.

10 I know for example an SME (Europe Technologies), specialising in microelectronics, which is very successful in building up series of networks of partnerships for developing its innovative projects. This is of course due to the specific competencies and expertise they have, but without doubt also to the fact that they are a spin-off from Texas Instruments, through which they have been in contact in the past with many of the relevant players.

11 This is based on partial observations only, and more detailed and systematic evaluations would be required in order to reach stronger conclusions.

12 Dibiaggio (1998) makes a distinction between 'simple' information or data, that is, information which is predefined and whose meaning is thus self-evident, 'problem' information, that is, knowledge or information for answering a new question or solving a new problem, but knowing (on the basis of existing knowledge and experiences) that such an answer or solution can indeed be found, and 'complex' information, that is, the same as above, but in situations in which it is not known beforehand whether a relevant answer or solution can indeed be found.

## References

Cameron, Hugh (1997), *IPR Handling in Collaborative RTD*, Report for the European Commission, draft, July.

Cohendet P. and Llerena P. (1993), 'Apprentissage organisationnel et cohérence: l'importance de la notion de réseau', paper presented to Colloque Les limitations de la rationalité et la constitution du collectif, Cerisy, June.

De Bandt, J. (1995), 'Services aux entreprises: informations, produits, richesses', *Economica*, pp. 28–32, 162–7.

De Bandt, J. (1996), 'Business services: markets and transactions', *Review of Industrial Organization*, vol. 11, no. 1.

De Bandt, J. (1997), 'Can organisational failures be compensated for through bottom-up policies?', paper presented to the International Conference on Industrial Policy for Europe, Chatham House, London, June.

Dibiaggio, L. (1998), *Information, Connaissance, Organisation*, thesis, Université de Nice Sophia Antipolis.

Peat Marwick McLintock (1991), 'The cost of non-Europe for business services', in CCE, *Panorama de l'Industrie Communautaire 1991–1992*, Brussels, CEC.

# 10 Making small firms work

## Policy dimensions and the Scottish context

*Gavin C. Reid*

## Introduction

With the Scotland Bill (1997) provision was made for establishing a Scottish Parliament and an associated Scottish Administration. Thus the most significant constitutional change in the UK for nearly three hundred years was enacted. Many economic powers mentioned in that Bill are subject to 'reservation',[1] with the notable exception that the basic rate of income tax for Scottish taxpayers may be increased or reduced by not more than 3 per cent from that determined by the UK Parliament. Despite this apparently limited scope for economic policy, Scotland continues to be subject to a sophisticated and long-standing regional economic policy framework from the standpoint of the stimulation of enterprise. The concern of this paper is with the impact this framework has on small firms.

The plan of the paper is as follows. I start by briefly establishing the European context, and then by considering small firms in both a UK national and regional (specifically Scottish) context. Two sample periods, 1985–8 and 1994–7, are considered for samples of small firms in Scotland. Then evidence on factors influencing the performance and survival of these small firms is examined. Grant and subsidy schemes are shown to have little influence on either. Evidence is presented suggesting that performance was superior in the second sample period, though both related to similar macroeconomic conditions. The evolution of institutions for stimulating enterprise is considered next, by reference to the Scottish Development Agency (SDA), Scottish Enterprise (SE) and the Business Birth Rate Strategy. The end of the first sample period related to the end of the SDA, and just pre-dated the formation of Scottish Enterprise in 1988. The start of the second sample period just post-dated the Business Birth Rate Strategy, launched in 1993. Thus each sample period related to a distinct policy regime. It is shown that this offers the opportunity of relating performance over each sample period to efficacy of policy regime.

The broad theme of the paper, in terms of industrial policy, is to contrast the use of grant and subsidy regimes with the use of so-called 'incubator institutions' to stimulate enterprise. It will be shown that phases of the macroeconomic cycle were similar over the comparison periods 1985–8 and 1994–7, yet the survival and performance of small firms were considerably superior in the latter period. Statistical analysis suggests this is not due to grant and subsidy regimes. Therefore, the differing institutions for stimulating enterprise over these two periods, essentially pre- and post-SDA, must be considered seriously as possible causes of these performance differences.

## The small firm within the economic fabric

Although large firms tend to receive most attention both in the public eye and indeed in economics itself, small firms are the typical enterprise form and play a major role in the economic fabric of a society in terms of employment creation and innovation. At the start of 1996, according to the latest DTI figures for the UK economy, 99 per cent of businesses in all but one sector (electricity, gas and water supply) were SMEs, defined as enterprises with fewer than 250 employees. These latest estimates take account of very small businesses that do not appear on the official business register.[2] They are estimated using survey data, and whilst they have less reliability for the smallest size class, they help to provide a more complete picture. Of the 3.7 million active businesses in the UK in 1996, over 2.5 million were of size class zero, being sole traders or partners without employees.

The statistical presence of these small firms is just as dominant in Europe. Across all Union member states, SMEs employ 70 million persons, which is 70 per cent of the working population. In 1995, micro-firms (fewer than ten employees) contributed one-third of employment and one-quarter of total turnover. By contrast, big businesses (more than 500 employees) contributed just 29 per cent of jobs and 31 per cent of turnover.

Within Scotland itself, similar patterns prevail. As compared to the UK, the small business sector is somewhat smaller. For example, in 1986 (the first sample period discussed) SMEs in manufactures with fewer than 200 employees had a 26 per cent employment share in Scotland compared to a 30 per cent employment share in the UK; and the corresponding shares of SMEs in manufacturing output for Scotland and the UK were 20 per cent and 23 per cent, respectively.

## Estimates of chances of staying in business

A model of small firm survival is developed in Reid (1993, ch. 9). Profit, net of exit costs ($\pi^*$) is expressed as a function of market ($M$) and financial ($F$) variables, and many other independent variables. Then a long-run requirement for staying in business is that $\pi^* \geq 0$. Although $\pi^*$ is unobserved, violation of this condition *is* observed, so the indicator $S = 1$ for staying in business and $S = 0$ for exiting from business is defined.

The dataset on which this model was applied was a sample of 73 small firms in Scotland. They were analysed by fieldwork methods over the period

1985–8 using two administered questionnaires and a semi-structured inter-view in face-to-face meetings with the owner-manager. The sample was drawn from the case loads of a special type of business incubation unit in Scotland called the Enterprise Trust (see below, pp. 170–176). The typical firm of this sample was a micro-firm with eight full-time employees, sales of £85k (excluding VAT) and assets of £76k in 1985, at which time it was 42 months old.[3] Three years later, about three-quarters of these firms were still in business. This is comparable with figures like 84 per cent for other Enterprise Agencies (the English equivalent of this incubator unit) and 66 per cent for all firms which were VAT registered over the same time period. These last two figures suggest that these latter forms of business incubator units appear to be relatively successful in terms of promoting small business survival.

Table 10.1 reports on a binary probit estimate of the staying in business model, taken from Reid (1993, ch. 9). The following features of the probit are noteworthy: (a) firms in services had better prospects of survival than those in manufactures (*Igp*); (b) extreme product differentiation with marked 'elbow room' (*ElbRoom*) in pricing, and sophisticated advertising forms (*AdvForm*) related negatively to staying in business, probably because such firms produced highly customised or bespoke products; (c) on the other hand, generic advertising (*Adv*) worked in favour of survival, as did size measured by assets (*Passet*); (d) the most powerful negative indicator of staying in busi-ness was the gearing ratio (*Pgear*), typically the owner-manager's bank loan divided by his or her personal financial injection. This presumably was caused by risk exposure and proneness to debt-servicing crises. This first model on which I report here did not consider grant and subsidy influences.

However, in 1994–7, I returned to the problem of analysing factors promoting small business survival, using a larger and more carefully selected sample of 150, again drawn from the case loads of these Scottish incubator units called Enterprise Trusts.[4] They were younger (just 21 months) at the time of initial interview (cf. 42 months for previous sample), and on average employed just three full-time workers (cf. eight full-time workers for previous sample). Most of the owner-managers (78 per cent) had received a grant or subsidy (*Grant*) at the time of launching their firms, and this had had an average value of £4k. This was often in the form of Enterprise Allowance. Other forms included Enterprise Trust grants or interest-free loans and Regional Enterprise grants. Because I only know for some firms what grants or subsidies had been received, I have not classified them. Instead, in estimation, the *Grant* variable is a dummy variable. The respon-dents were also asked whether they found this assistance to be helpful. Most replied affirmatively, their ratings being: crucial (34 per cent), important (17 per cent) and helpful (43 per cent). Naturally, it is of concern to know whether this perceived helpfulness translated into performance.

To answer this, it is helpful to turn to the work of Reid and Smith (1996), which uses statistical cluster analysis to develop a performance ranking of

*Table 10.1* Binary probit model for 1985–8 data

| Variable | Coefficient | t-ratio | Weighted Elasticity |
|---|---|---|---|
| Pgear | −0.71556.10$^{-2}$ | −3.3735*** | −0.16181 |
| Passet | 0.11129.10$^{-4}$ | 1.7327* | 0.11720 |
| AddDebt | 0.10618 | 0.23822 | 0.15358.10$^{-1}$ |
| Adv | 2.4715 | 1.5280† | 0.41776 |
| AdvForm | −1.4921 | −2.0415** | −0.54901 |
| DesComp | −0.14309 | −0.39203 | −0.49855.10$^{-1}$ |
| ProdDes | 0.52472 | 1.2824 | 0.18412 |
| ElbRoom | −0.37973 | −2.2124** | −0.40114 |
| AddCost | −0.16855 | −0.30859 | −0.36360.10$^{-1}$ |
| Igp | −1.3242 | −2.2636** | −0.23596 |
| Constant | 3.0744 | 2.8625 | 0.81277 |

*Notes*:
Likelihood ratio test, $\chi^2 = 31.8384$ ($\chi^2_{0.001}(10) = 29.6$)
Cragg-Uhler $R^2 = 0.42652$
McFadden $R^2 = 0.30836$
Log-likelihood = −25.935
Survival probability = 0.7671
Legend: $t_{0.10} = 1.296$ $^{(†)}$, $t_{0.05} = 1.671$ $^{(*)}$,
$t_{.025} = 2.000$ $^{(**)}$, $t_{0.010} = 2.390$ $^{(***)}$.

*Variables*:
Pgear   = gearing (≡ debt/equity) at time of interview in 1985
Passet  = assets in £000s at 1985 prices at time of interview in 1985
AddDebt = 1 if external finance (debt) used since starting business, 0 if not
Adv     = 1 if firm advertises, 0 if not
AdvForm = 1 for generic advertising, = 2 for rivalrous advertising, = 3 for generic and rivalrous advertising
DesComp = 1 if competition in main market was intense, = 2 if strong, = 3 if generally weak, and = 4 if weak
ProdDes = 1 if main product identical to rivals, = 2 if similar, = 3 if different
ElbRoom = 0 for no 'elbow room' in pricing, = 1 for 1 per cent elbow room, = 2 for 2–3%, = 3 for 4–6%, = 4 for 7–9%, = 5 for 10–15%, = 6 for more than 15%
AddCost = 1 if marginal cost calculable, = 0 if otherwise
Igp     = 1 if firm in manufacturing or construction, = 0 if in services or transport.

these firms based on growth, profitability and labour productivity. It shows that the high-performing firms (7 per cent) had the least access to grants and subsidies (67 per cent), compared to medium (82 per cent) and low-performing (78 per cent) firms. The latter appeared in proportions 33 per cent and 61 per cent. In a binary probit model with a large number of control variables (see Table 10.2), the *Grant* variable was insignificant (t-ratio = 0.461). Important positive influences on staying in business included advertising (*Advert*), access to trade credit (*TrCredit*), allocating time to planning in a week (*TimPlan*), and having previously been financed by a bank loan (*FinBank*). Important negative influences included carrying debt

(*Debt*), using extended purchase commitments (*ExtPur*), and precipitate product and process innovation (*ProdInn, ProcInn*). In a more refined estimation procedure (ordered logit with selection), another grant-related variable (*FinGrnt*), which measured whether firms had previously been financed by a grant or subsidy, was insignificant (Prob. level = 26 per cent). In the selection equation the other grant measure (*Grant*) was also insignificant (Prob. level = 51 per cent). Though this evidence, taken together, is by no means definitive, it is a caution against the presumption that grants and subsidies have been efficacious for new businesses in Scotland.

The survival rate for this 1994–7 sample was 78 per cent, which is very close to the 77 per cent of the 1985–8 sample. In comparing these figures, interpretations must be handled carefully, mainly because the firms in the first sample had progressed further along the early life cycle, being older and larger (by two years and five full-timers) than firms in the second sample. Indeed, as survival rates are known to rise monotonically with age,[5] the 1994–7 sample has to be judged to have superior performance to the 1985–8 sample. The first question to be asked is whether this may be due to a clearly superior macroeconomic environment in the case of the 1994–7 sample, before turning, in the next section, to the possible role of institutional arrangements for enterprise stimulation.

This is an issue which is difficult to resolve definitively, but the evidence points to both 1985–8 and 1994–7 as being favourable phases of the business cycle. For example, over 1985 to 1988 the annual rates of growth in real GDP were 3.8, 4.3, 4.8 and 5.0 per cent in each year. The index of industrial production had annual growth rates of 5.5, 2.4, 4.0 and 4.8 per cent for each year in this time interval and, as a percentage of GDP, fixed capital formation stood as high as 17.0, 16.9, 17.8 and 19.4 per cent, respectively. All of these are cyclically high figures. Thus, in the recession that followed, by 1992 real GDP was actually falling (–0.5 per cent per annum), as was the index of industrial production (–0.4 per cent per annum) and fixed capital formation as a proportion of GDP was lower, at 15.7 per cent. Figures are not yet available in final form for the period 1994–7, but it is clear that again the macroeconomic conditions were good. Recovery began in 1993, largely driven by consumption, but accompanied by rising exports. In 1994 real GDP grew by 4.0 per cent, comparable with performance over 1985–8, and good by European standards. Inflation was less than 3 per cent and unemployment was cyclically low at 9 per cent. One concludes tentatively that in both the sample periods examined, 1985–8 and 1994–7, macroeconomic conditions were good.

If differences in macroeconomic conditions do not explain performance differences of firms between these two time periods, and grant and subsidy regimes appear not to affect performance and business longevity, we may logically seek an explanation for what was happening in the regimes for supporting enterprise over the time periods in question. This takes me into considerations of institutional evolution which are difficult to quantify, but may well be playing a significant role.

*Table 10.2* Binary probit with large set of control variables

| Variable | Coefficient | t-ratio | Weighted elasticity |
|----------|-------------|---------|---------------------|
| Advert | 1.311 | 3.120*** | 0.125 |
| Trcredit | 0.902 | 2.070** | 0.089 |
| Debt | −1.365 | −2.065** | −0.103 |
| Outeq | 3.974 | 0.063 | $0.185.10^{-5}$ |
| Bankloan | −0.467 | −0.500 | −0.028 |
| Grant | 0.489 | 0.461 | 0.073 |
| Gearst | $−0.458.10^{-4}$ | −0.059 | −0.001 |
| Gearnow | $−0.855.10^{-4}$ | −0.142 | −0.003 |
| Extpur | −1.826 | −2.493*** | −0.023 |
| Hirpur | 0.757 | $1.352^{+}$ | −0.025 |
| Leasepur | 5.304 | 0.089 | $0.104.10^{-5}$ |
| Grfixass | $−0.110.10^{-4}$ | −0.851 | −0.031 |
| Netfixas | $0.707.10^{-5}$ | 0.526 | −0.015 |
| Impact | $0.787.10^{-4}$ | 0.518 | 0.002 |
| Sicdum | −0.184 | −0.439 | −0.017 |
| Owncash | $0.248.10^{-4}$ | 0.943 | 0.030 |
| Rapidocc | 0.291 | −1.037 | −0.077 |
| Stkass | −0.017 | −1.831* | −0.027 |
| Othbus | 1.517 | 1.754* | 0.016 |
| Procinn | −0.249 | $−1.348^{+}$ | −0.062 |
| Prodinn | −0.456 | −2.332** | −0.095 |
| Prodgrp | 0.023 | 0.361 | 0.015 |
| Timplan | 0.076 | 1.850* | 0.088 |
| Timdeal | −0.023 | −0.710 | −0.021 |
| Hrswk | $0.748.10^{-3}$ | 0.066 | 0.007 |
| Secschl | −0.026 | −0.131 | −0.021 |
| Runbef | 0.148 | 0.373 | 0.014 |
| Finown | −0.610 | −0.721 | −0.101 |
| Finbank | 2.009 | 1.959* | 0.142 |
| Fingrnt | −0.169 | −0.181 | −0.023 |
| Nprass | 0.006 | 1.210 | −0.008 |
| Constant | 0.491 | 0.323 | 0.087 |

*Notes*:
Likelihood ratio test: $\chi^2 = 51.7 > \chi^2_{0.01}(31) = 50.9$
Cragg-Uhler $R^2 = 0.516$; binomial estimate $= 0.815$
Sample size (n) = 135; % correct predictions = 86%
Critical t-values: $t_{0.10} = 1.289^{+}$, $t_{0.05} = 1.658^{*}$,
$\qquad\qquad t_{0.025} = 1.980^{**}$, $t_{0.010} = 2.358^{***}$

For definitions of variables, see Appendix.

## The evolution of enterprise stimulating institutions

I would argue that the institutions for stimulating enterprise or, more simply, the 'enterprise system', is a public good, in the same way as James Buchanan (1989) once argued that the work ethic is a public good. As such, it is subject to the usual problems of provision by private voluntary action. The provision of this system of enterprise, in terms of its extent and quality, is determined by the design of institutions, of market and non-market forms, which are the delivery mechanisms of enterprise. A proper treatment would be lengthy and complex, but here I want to focus on just three simple examples to display the key issues at stake. They involve three institutional alternatives: an indicative planning system; a mixed indicative planning and market-driven system; and a largely market-driven system. These are considered within the Scottish context and involve the emergence and development of three bureaucratic organisations: the Scottish Development Agency (SDA); the Enterprise Trusts (ETs); and Scottish Enterprise (SE). The first sample period of this paper, 1985–8, relates to the SDA era, and the second sample period, 1994–7, to the SE era.

The SDA was established through a public (rather than private) sector initiative, as embodied in the Scottish Development Agency Act of 1975. Its form had origins in earlier smaller, but relatively successful, institutions for stimulating enterprise, such as the Scottish Council and the Small Industries Council, and also, arguably, in earlier attempts at indicative planning by development boards and corporations. In this sense, the SDA was of an evolutionary institutional design, in that its form bore the unmistakable imprint of earlier institutional forms. By contrast, Enterprise Trusts were established through a private sector initiative, and provide an example of conscious institutional design, with evolutionary features absent. ETs were first established in Scotland in 1982 as part of an initiative by Scottish Business in the Community (ScotBIC, now called SBC). This aimed to foster a partnership between the public and private sector (for example, between corporations and local authorities). Whilst an earlier institution for attending to the needs of small firms had existed in the shape of the Small Industries Council (SICRAS) (for Rural Areas in Scotland), this Council's functions had been taken over by the Small Business Division of the SDA, which then extended its function to urban areas, and greatly modified its form. Again, the SDA's development in this respect was evolutionary. But rather than follow these institutional models, the ETs were designed by ScotBIC as alternatives to what were perceived to be the failures of existing institutions (for example, in terms of remoteness from clients and slowness of response), especially at the local level. We have, therefore, a public initiative leading to an institutional design which was evolutionary; and a private initiative leading to an institutional design which was conscious. The synthesis of these influences is indicated in the centre of Figure 10.1: it is Scottish Enterprise.

Institutionally speaking, the roots of Scottish Enterprise lie in two White Papers of 1988: *Employment for the 1990s*; and *Scottish Enterprise: a new approach to training and enterprise creation*. In terms of policy implementation, this date of 1988 lies at the end of the first sample period, and hence these arrangements cannot have influenced the survival of performance of small firms over 1985–8. The genesis of Scottish enterprise was not entirely institutionally driven, and arose through the efforts of a Falkirk

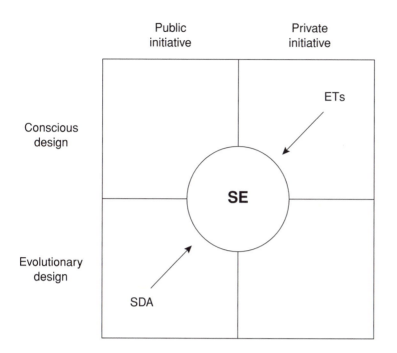

*Figure 10.1* The emergence of Scottish Enterprise

businessman, Bill Hughes.[6] Working outside of conventional channels, he took his scheme to the newspapers directly. He bypassed the SDA without consultation and gained direct access to Downing Street.[7] He was subsequently invited to a meeting at Chequers. There, he met the Secretary of State for Employment,[8] who had already been influenced by the Director of Employment and Training Policy in Massachusetts, who was proselytising for the concept of Private Industry Councils (PICs). These PICs allowed the business community to take an active role in spending training funds of the US Federal Government. Business could play a role in enterprise stimulation, which included the design of training schemes and even extended to influence over school curricula. These PICs were moderately successful in cities like Atlanta, New York and Boston.

A new institutional arrangement was proposed, with two features: (a) it allowed the private sector a greater leadership role than previously, rather than being dominated by the SDA; and (b) it facilitated training at the local level in a way which was felt to be superior to the more centralised management of the old Manpower Services Commission (MSC).

Having set the scene with these three key institutions (SDA, SE, ET), let me now turn to the evolving institutional forms. First, consider the centralised, indicative planning model displayed in schematic form in Figure

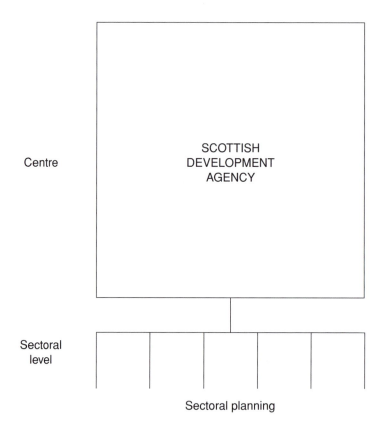

*Figure 10.2* Indicative planning

10.2. At the top (or 'centre') is the Scottish Development Agency (SDA). As a type of indicative planning body, the SDA adopted a strategic sectoral approach. Good sectors for this, in view of their development potential, were thought to be microelectronics, biotechnology, food processing, advanced engineering, textiles and fashion. The centre (the SDA) encouraged exploitation of high value-added niches. It had an institutional advantage in terms of its large scale of involvement.[9] However, it was necessarily remote from local conditions.

Recognition of this in policy circles in the 1980s led to an increased commitment to the development of new (and, especially, small) firms and to the fostering of entrepreneurship. There was thus a transition from an indicative planning orientation to a market orientation. This commitment was still expressed in a sectoral form, with the emphasis being put on targeted activities, such as electronics and offshore engineering. Evolving out of the Small Industries Council [for Rural Areas in Scotland] was the Small Business Division (SBD). The SBD went on to set up various specialist small business advisory services. At the same time the Enterprise Trusts sprang up, under the ScotBIC umbrella, and partially independently of the SBD (though funded 50 per cent by it). The transition of public policy to a market orientation, and the attendant institutional reconfiguration are displayed in Figure 10.3.

The SDA as the centre remained dominant, and the Small Business Division's local offices flourished. This regional involvement by the SBD was 'interlaced' with the activities of the ETs. Unfortunately, the brief of the SBD was unsatisfactory, if not contradictory. It was enjoined to apply commercial criteria to projects, but not to involve itself in projects that might in any case attract private sector support. Lending and equity investment were to be subject to commercial disciplines. Not surprisingly, those projects which were 'selected against' by the private sector ended up on the SBD's doorstep. Loan losses were of high incidence, and over the period 1980–5 the overall rate of return on the SBD's own investments was negative.

The genesis and development of the Enterprise Trusts (ETs) was happier. The Enterprise Trust (ET) movement has quickly proved to be remarkably successful in promoting and supporting the growth of new small firms.

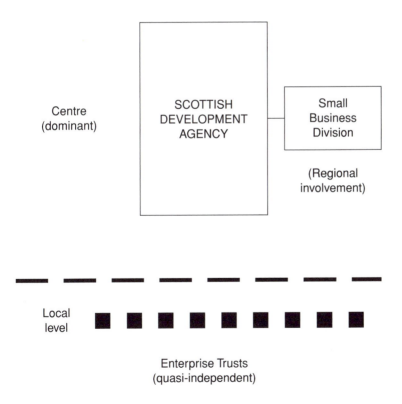

*Figure 10.3* Transition to market orientation

Enterprise Trusts, local examples of which in my locality include GET and NEFET, provide information which is independent, and predominantly free of charge, to any existing or potential small firm. The ET is a small local organisation manned by personnel with some technical expertise and considerable business experience. Since the inauguration of the first ET in Scotland, the Ardrossan–Saltcoats–Stevenson Enterprise Trust (ASSET), in 1982, more than 40 further ETs have been established. To judge by their successful proliferation in such a short space of time, ETs have successfully discovered appropriate niches, as types of small firms themselves. Apart from the funding involvement of the SDA in sponsoring ETs, vertical control (that is, control from above by the SDA) was slight. The ETs were largely 'horizontally' controlled by the mission of ScotBIC (namely, the need for active involvement of industry and commerce in local communities).

By contrast, the role of the SDA, like that of its offshoot, the Small Business Division, was less than happy. Whilst the sectoral strategy had worked in special cases, for example, woollen textiles and oil and gas, it had not worked in electronics and health care, and in general did not work with indigenous high-technology industries. For the successful cases which were regarded as sectoral, it was clear that they could as easily have been interpreted as regional: the Borders for textiles; and Aberdeenshire for oil and gas. Sectoral strategy appears to have been too strongly driven by trends in demand to the neglect of the supply side. A fundamental weakness of the sectoral approach is that it lacks meaning at the company level. Supply-side effects which particularly impinge on companies include skills, property and finance, and these tend to be cross-sectoral in incidence.

To conclude this story, we return to the Hughes Initiative. Borrowing much from the Massachusetts 'growth coalition' idea, Hughes initially proposed a system much more decentralised than even the Enterprise Trust movement. It would have involved some 70 local enterprise units based on small travel-to-work areas. The conception was bold and deliberately intended to be the polar opposite of the indicative planning model. The successful experience of the Enterprise Trusts was drawn upon, but the Trusts were not themselves explicitly involved (indeed, hardly anyone was explicitly involved, including the chief executive of the SDA). Direct contact was made with the Scottish Office and, through the IDS, a White Paper was draw up which started the formal implementation of Scottish Enterprise in 1988. It abandoned the very local travel-to-work areas and aimed to keep intact the Enterprise Trusts at the local level (see bottom of Figure 10.4). A middle or second tier of Local Enterprise Companies was created (see middle of Figure 10.4). An example of this type of institution was Scottish Enterprise Tayside (chaired by William Low). The main aim was to achieve 80 per cent delegation to the regions. Thus the centre would become attenuated, and the regional level predominant. Within each region, local enterprise companies (LECs) were to be created (cf. TECs in England). SDA and Training Agency functions would be combined and then devolved,

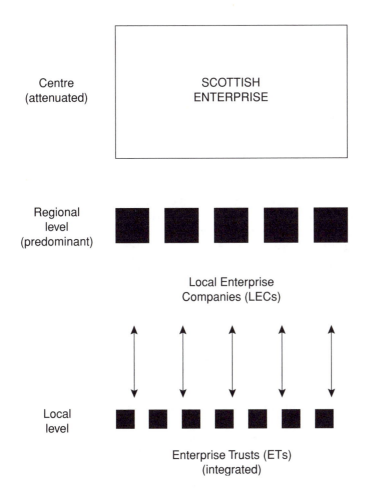

*Figure 10.4* Market-driven institutions

with training occurring at the LEC level. Enterprise Trusts played a significant role in forming the boards of the LECs, often working with the
Chambers of Commerce. They were an umbrella organisation that acted as
a catalyst for Scottish Enterprise. In the new arrangements they were more
fully integrated into the enterprise network than previously (compare Figure
10.4 with Figure 10.3). Technically, the Local Enterprise Companies are
their paymasters, but they remain as strongly coordinated, in a horizontal
sense, as previously. The LECs themselves are partially horizontally coordinated (by the *Handbook* prepared by the IDS), and a main worry at the
inception of Scottish Enterprise was that the LECs might drift out of line
with the *Handbook*'s declared policy. The activities of LECs took place
within broadly defined categories (namely, enterprise, environment, youth

training, adult training, and enterprise and business training) but were deliberately not specified in a detailed sense. They were monitored by a monthly invoice, and received their contracts on the basis of a business plan. This plan was typically quite individual as the LEC was encouraged to make whatever emphasis it wished, as appropriate to its local circumstances. The contractual form was loose, to avoid constraining a LEC in a way which might limit its flexibility to adapt to local conditions.

This new system, as compared to its predecessor, was much more decentralised, more responsive to local needs, and better represented the interests of business. It was especially through the composition of representation on the boards of LECs that this was brought about. Boards had to have two-thirds membership from the private sector and a one-third membership from the public sector. By a clever series of manoeuvres, the form of enterprise stimulation was transformed from an indicative planning system to a market system of regionally based enterprise companies, under which was a further layer of very local Enterprise Trusts.

Building on this decentralised enterprise-stimulating system, SE embarked on its new Business Birth Rate Strategy in 1992, which aimed to bring Scotland up to the UK average so far as new business inception and performance were concerned.[10] After a career spent in Silicon Valley in California, Crawford Beveridge returned to Scotland as chief executive of Scottish Enterprise. He instituted research programmes which enquired into finance, performance in key areas, attitudes to going into business and so on. This work concluded that a key Scottish problem was *conversion*, that is the translating of entrepreneurial interest into action. The strategy was launched in 1993, with action directed towards the financial community (for example, access to loan and equity finance), the education system (in schools and universities), the media (to improve coverage of entrepreneurship and status of entrepreneurs), and business support networks (of which SBC and ETs are a part). By 1995 the numbers of those trying to start a business had doubled;[11] and of those expressing an interest in start-up had increased by a quarter. Over a hundred new initiatives were taken to stimulate entrepreneurship: improved access to stock markets, of women to new starts, of business education within schools, and the creation of a network of Entrepreneurship Centres within five universities along the model of Babson College and driven by the educational philosophy of Professor Bill Bygraves.[12] Thus the second sample period, 1994–7, immediately followed the start of the Business Birth Rate Strategy.

## Conclusion

Neat conclusive results are hard to reach in a policy context, so what is said here is necessarily tentative. The basic framework of the discussion revolved around samples of Scottish small firms for the periods 1985–8 and 1994–7. It was shown that both related to similar (prosperous) phases of the macroeconomic cycle. Further evidence indicated that grant and subsidy regimes appeared not to be major determinants of survival and performance. However, performance was better for the second sample period. The evolution of institutional design for stimulating enterprise was documented and dated, and it was shown that the two sample periods lay in two distinct policy regimes, the first involving sectoral indicative planning and the second involving decentralised enterprise stimulation. It is suggested that at least a part of the superior performance of small firms in the second sample period was attributable to the new institutional framework.

## Notes

1 In a blanket sense, this includes fiscal, economic and monetary policy. More specifically, in an industrial policy context, it includes: wide forms of business association; the regulation of anti-competitive practices and agreements; the abuse of dominant market positions; monopolies and mergers; and intellectual property.
2 These estimates were compiled by the DTI using a variety of sources, of which the main one was the Inter-Departmental Business Register administered by the Office for National Statistics. The published DTI source is the statistical bulletin *Small and Medium Enterprise (SME) Statistics for the UK, 1996.* The statistics of the text were extracted from the DTI Web site (17 July 1997).
3 These are all average figures.
4 Enterprise Trusts were common to both sample periods, thus the effects of this institution are washed out in cross-sample comparisons.
5 See, for example, Reid (1993, ch. 9).
6 From correspondence with Charles Skene, Group Chairman of the Skene Group, it is now evident that he too had an important influence through his 1987 paper to the SCUA Industry Committee on 'Educating Scotsmen and Women for Life in a Competitive Industrial Society'.
7 Gaining a private audience with the prime minister of the day, Margaret Thatcher.
8 Who at that time was Norman Fowler.
9 For example, this was important in encouraging foreign direct investment by large multinational firms through Locate in Scotland (LiS). LiS is one component of the earliest SDA which has survived, by mutation and adaptation, but without its basic function being modified. It has been a highly successful component of the evolving enterprise stimulating institutions, and works by a variety of methods including tracking down prominent overseas business persons who are part of the Scottish diaspora. One of its most conspicuous recent successes has been to attract Cadence Design System to Livingston. The attractive features to Cadence included the Scottish legal system (which has no history of litigious conduct over intellectual property) and the technological expertise of leading Scottish universities (Glasgow, Edinburgh, Strathclyde and Heriot-Watt Universities are involved in a consortium arrangement with Cadence). To paraphrase, the attraction was 'manpower and courts'. System level integration (SLI) will be used to develop systems on a chip (SoC) technology. This is the next generation of microchip, with which an entire computer's circuitry can be reduced to the size of a single chip.
10 See Deakins *et al.* (eds) (1997).
11 *The Business Birth Rate Strategy: Update Scottish Enterprise* (1996).
12 Again the name of Charles Skene enters the picture, as it was he who, through having attended the Babson course, made recommendations to Crawford

Beveridge (Chief Executive, SE) and Sir Donald McKay (Chairman, SE) about introducing the programme in Scotland. I am grateful to Charles Skene for personal communication, in written and oral form, on the genesis of this programme.

## References

Buchanan, J. (1989) 'Economic interdependence and the work ethic', George Mason University, mimeo.

Deakins, D., Jennings, P. and Mason, C. (eds) (1997) *Small Firms: entrepreneurship in the nineties*, London: Paul Chapman.

Reid, G.C. (1993) *Small Business Enterprise: an economic analysis*, London: Routledge.

Reid, G.C. and Smith, J.A. (1996) 'What makes a new business start-up successful?', CRIEFF Discussion Paper no. 9618, Department of Economics, University of St Andrews.

*Scotland Bill* (1997) London: Stationery Office.

**Appendix:   Definition of variables used in Table 10.2**

| | | |
|---|---|---|
| *Advert* | = | 1 if firm advertised, otherwise 0 |
| *Bankloan* | = | 1 if a bank loan was used to launch the business, otherwise 0 |
| *Debt* | = | 1 if business had debt, otherwise 0 |
| *Extpur* | = | 1 if firm had extended purchase commitment, otherwise 0 |
| *Finbank* | = | 1 if firm had previously been financed by a bank loan, otherwise 0 |
| *Fingrnt* | = | 1 if firm had previously been financed by grant/subsidy, otherwise 0 |
| *Finown* | = | 1 if firm had previously been financed by the owner-manager, otherwise 0 |
| *Ftime* | = | number of full-time employees |
| *Gearnow* | = | gearing (e.g. debt/equity) ratio at time of interview |
| *Gearst* | = | gearing ratio at launch of business |
| *Grant* | = | 1 if grant or subsidy was received at launch, otherwise 0 |
| *Grfixass* | = | gross value (£) of fixed assets |
| *Grprof* | = | gross profits (£) for last financial year |
| *Grsales* | = | gross sales (£) for last financial year |
| *Hirpur* | = | 1 if firm had hire purchase commitments, otherwise 0 |
| *Hrswk* | = | number of hours per week devoted to the business |
| *Impact* | = | number of months entrepreneur looked ahead in evaluating impact of decisions |
| *Inbus* | = | number of months firm had been in business |
| *Leasepur* | = | 1 if business had any lease purchase commitments, otherwise 0 |
| *Loan* | = | size of bank loan (£) at launch of business |
| *Netfixas* | = | net value (£) (after depreciation) of fixed assets |
| *Netprof* | = | net profits (£) for last financial year |
| *Nprass* | = | *Netprof ÷ Netfixas* |
| *Othbus* | = | 1 if respondent runs any other business, otherwise 0 |
| *Outeq* | = | 1 if business had any outside equity, otherwise 0 |
| *Owncash* | = | cash (£) put in by inside equity holder(s) at launch |
| *Procinn* | = | 0 (no change), = 1 (slight change), = 2 (significant change), = 3 (important change) in process innovation since starting business |
| *Prodgrp* | = | number of product groups produced |
| *Prodinn* | = | 0 (none), = 1 (1–5), = 2 (6–10), = 3 (11–20), = 4 (> 20) new products since starting business |
| *Ptime* | = | number of part-time employees |
| *Rapidocc* | = | 0 (not at all), = 1 (moderately), = 2 (very) important to rapidly occupy a market niche |
| *Runbef* | = | 1 if entrepreneur had run a business before, otherwise 0 |
| *Secschl* | = | number of years spent at high school |
| *Sicdum* | = | 1 if firm was in manufacturing (01 ≤ SIC ≤ 59) and 0 if it was in services |
| *Stkass* | = | ratio of value of stocks to net fixed assets |
| *Timdeal* | = | proportion of time spent doing deals in a week |
| *Timplan* | = | proportion of time spent planning in a week |
| *Trcredit* | = | 1 if business has trade credit arrangements, otherwise 0 |
| *Wagerate* | = | wage-rate (£) for best-skilled full-time workers per month |

# 11 Industrial policy implications of competition policy failure in mergers

*Hans Schenk*

## The welfare problem of mergers

Investments in mergers and acquisitions frequently consume such large portions of executive time and attention that they should be seen as crucial components of firm behaviour. For example, during 1996 US firms expended no less than $670 billion on mergers and acquisitions, and it is probable that even this amount will have been exceeded during 1997. It is commonly assumed that the only significant economic problem that may arise from mergers is their effect on market power which is usually estimated by their effect on the level of prices. If it is estimated that such an effect will be absent in a particular merger, then the presumption is that this merger will be undertaken in order to generate productive and/or dynamic gains. As a consequence, such a merger will normally be cleared. Many studies, however, have found that merger-active firms do not appear to create superior profitability, productive efficiency or innovativeness in comparison to their own histories and/or to size and industry matched control groups. Sometimes merger-active firms even show relative under-performance in some or all of the respects mentioned.[1] Thus, the welfare losses of mergers and acquisitions may not be captured by their effect on prices but rather by their effect on productive and/or dynamic efficiency.

From a theoretical point of view, it is important to acknowledge that the efficient choice paradigm (March, 1978) does not always apply, that is, that the market mechanism is apparently not efficient enough to prevent firms from systematically adopting strategies that deviate from what one would expect under profit-maximising behaviour.

Such non-efficient behaviour may have significant implications for international competitiveness; for mergers and acquisitions are substantially more prevalent in the European Union and the United States than in Japan. When measured by numbers, and taking into account the sizes of their respective economies, Japanese firms undertake approximately ten times fewer mergers and acquisitions than US, UK and Dutch firms. When measured by value, however, the differences are likely to be much larger still. Table 11.1, which is based on commonly used data from Yamaichi Securities, shows that the

*Table 11.1* US and Japanese mergers compared, 1985–91

| Year | Transaction values ($ billions) | | Index for Japan (US = 100) | |
|------|------|-------|-------|----------|
| | US | Japan | Gross | Adjusted[b] |
| 1985[a] | 146.1 | 0.6 | 0.41 | 0.7 |
| 1986 | 206.1 | 2.5 | 1.21 | 1.9 |
| 1987 | 178.3 | 4.9 | 2.75 | 4.4 |
| 1988 | 238.5 | 9.5 | 3.98 | 6.4 |
| 1989 | 245.4 | 13.9 | 5.66 | 9.1 |
| 1990 | 160.6 | 12.4 | 7.72 | 12.3 |
| 1991 | 98.2 | 0.4 | 0.41 | 0.7 |

*Source*: Adapted and recalculated from OECD (1993).
*Notes*:
[a]  Japanese data are for fiscal years.
[b]  According to the relative levels of GNP.

values of Japanese mergers almost shrink into insignificance when compared to those undertaken by US firms (see last column). When averaged over the seven-year period, Japanese transaction values come to only 5.1 per cent of the American average. Although the series may be biased to a certain extent as it partly coincides with the fourth western merger wave, it seems undisputable that Japan's largest firms have been much less active in the area of mergers and acquisitions than their rivals from the US and the EU (see also Lawrence, 1993). A simple statistic may serve to illustrate this conclusion further. Of the 899 manufacturing firms listed on the Tokyo Stock Exchange in 1964, only 67 firms (that is, 7.5 per cent) had disappeared as a result of merger or acquisition by 1984 (Odagiri, 1992). This contrasts with the US case in which 384 firms out of the 1,000 largest manufacturers of 1950 had disappeared through merger or acquisition by 1972, that is, 38.4 per cent (see Mueller, 1986). For the UK, the comparable figure is 42 per cent (1,265 out of 3,011 firms over the period 1950–77; see Odagiri, 1992). With respect to the 100 largest manufacturers from the US, the EU and Japan, the disposition is as shown in Table 11.2. Top-100 firms disappear as a result of merger and acquisition roughly 3.5 to four times as frequently in the US or the EU than in Japan.

Since it is clear that the interdependence between western economies and the Japanese economy has greatly increased over the last few decades, an important implication may be that the systematic focus of western firms on investments which do not create wealth can only be without consequences for competitiveness if somehow compensated, either 'positively' by superior western performance, or 'negatively' by inferior Japanese performance in other respects, for example, product attractiveness (design, and so on) or services. For example, although Japan's banks may be the largest in terms of assets, Wood (1992) argues that their size is not matched by

*Table 11.2* Disposition of the Triad's largest manufacturers of 1978 with respect to 1993[a]

|  | US | EU | Japan |
|---|---|---|---|
| Liquidated | 0 | 1 | 0 |
| Demerged | 0 | 2 | 0 |
| Surpassed [b] | 21 | 21 | 18 |
| Survived | 58 | 57 | 78 |
| Acquired | 14 | 16 | 4 |
| Other [c] | 7 | 3 | 0 |
| Acquired by another top-100 firm | 12 | 15 | 4 |

*Source*: Calculated from *Fortune International*, various issues.
*Notes*:
[a]   In percentages; with respect to top-100 firms of each respective region.
[b]   Firms which dropped out of the top-100; no further information as to their disposition available.
[c]   Firms which dropped out of the top-100 because of reclassification to another sector (mainly services).

commercial prowess. Since banks are pivotal to the Japanese economy, as they are the country's main engine of credit creation to a far greater extent than in America and the EU, their apparent commercial vulnerability contributes significantly to the fragility of Japan's financial system itself as, indeed, has been evidenced by recent developments.[2]

More generally, if western firms could somehow have realised superior investment quality, then their merger predilections may not be a cause for worry. Looking at the available profitability data, which show superior profitability for the largest US and EU firms in comparison to their Japanese rivals, the largest American and European manufacturers might seem to have succeeded in doing so (see Schenk, 2000). However, such a conclusion would be at odds with the fact that these firms have lost market share at the same time. Out of the total combined worldwide sales of the largest 100 manufacturers from the US, the EU and Japan, the 200 US and EU firms combined had a 1978 share of 87 per cent, and the 100 Japanese firms a share of 13 per cent. The US–EU share had declined to 78 per cent 12 years later. It therefore seems more likely that behind a façade of superior profitability western firms have economised on non-merger types of investment. These firms have not traded in growth for profits, it seems, but value-creating investments for profits in order to free the funds necessary for mergers and acquisitions. Western firms, indeed, appear to have invested relatively less in manufacturing equipment and machinery. On the basis of data on the modernity of plants that have been presented in Maddison (1987), it must be concluded that Japan's manufacturing sector has been able to renew itself much more frequently than has been the case in western economies, implying that recent technological improvements have been embodied at a faster rate in Japanese firms.

Moreover, it is well known that Japanese firms have continued to invest more heavily in R&D than have their western counterparts. Recent calculations made by the Dutch Ministry of Economic Affairs (DMEA, 1995) point out that Japanese firms have invested more than 1.8 per cent of GDP in R&D consecutively since 1985 whereas this figure was only around 1.3 per cent in the EU. When mergers and acquisitions peaked towards the end of the 1980s and the early 1990s these percentages were 2.2 and 1.2 respectively. Whereas investments in R&D amounted to almost 2.2 per cent of GDP in the US on the eve of the late 1980s' mergers and acquisitions boom, this decreased to 1.7 per cent during the early 1990s.

It is therefore likely that at least the cyclical part of the focus of western firms on external growth has created a cyclical relative neglect of investments in process and product improvements allowing Japanese rivals to gain first-mover advantages from new shopfloor technology and new product development, in the end allowing them to eat steadily into the world market shares of their rivals from the US and the EU.

Finally, substantial social costs may also arise as a result of the fact that large firms when on a merger spending spree extend their activities towards small and medium-sized firms as well. It is not rare to find that large firms undertake more than a few of such acquisitions per annum (for example, Unilever undertook 158 acquisitions during 1987–1990, and of these more than three-quarters involved small and medium-sized targets). These are typically the mergers that, according to Ravenscraft and Scherer (1987), fare worst of all – although they do not appear to strengthen the market position of the acquirer when taken as individual cases. As small and medium-sized firms in general are relatively innovative and/or efficient with respect to innovation (see, for example, Acs, 1996; Nooteboom and Vossen, 1995), one implication may well be that some of society's most innovative institutions are simply eliminated from the competitive system as a result of takeover. By having stayed 'alive', these firms might have forced their larger rivals to remain alert. This particular problem may be even more pressing in the EU than in the US. For example, Sharp (1985b) has pointed to the fact that small European firms are under-represented in so-called 'high-tech' sectors. She suggested that one of the likely causes was the relatively high concentration of European R&D within large, established firms. Buigues and Jacquemin (1996) have recently calculated that while 22.7 per cent of small and medium-sized US firms can be classified as 'high-tech', this only applies to 13.3 per cent of this type of firm in Europe. According to *Nature* (4 April 1996), most of the patents in the area of gene technology that have been awarded by the European Patent Agency to Americans were awarded to small and medium-sized firms whereas most of the similar patents awarded to Europeans were awarded to large firms.

## Implications for merger control

Economists who are true believers in the effectiveness of the market system as an error-correction mechanism would rightly ask how it is possible that this system cannot systematically prevent the occurrence of apparently unproductive mergers. For this mechanism is supposed to favour only those firms that maximise profits-cum-productive efficiency and to eliminate either through bankruptcy or through takeover those that do not. While the market mechanism might, perhaps, work as expected in the long run, this need not be the case in the short run if, indeed, firms that belong to the same strategic group economise on post-merger investment. In that case, they will show maintained post-merger profitability performance as lower depreciation allowances imply a smaller deduction from profits. In this scenario, firms would in a manner of speaking trap the system by feeding inaccurate data into it. As long as such behaviours are accepted as normal business practice they may remain unnoticed and therefore go unpunished. Moreover, firms may undertake pre-emptive moves meant to prevent their becoming takeover targets (Schenk, 1996). This implies that the takeover mechanism – which in theory is meant to discipline under-performing managements – would be perverted by the actions of managements themselves. Strictly speaking, therefore, the persistency of unproductive mergers must be an indication of the existence of (some sort of) market power that is strong enough to protect the firms in question from the market mechanism in general and/or takeover in particular.[3]

It would therefore follow that mergers should be tested by using a model that is capable of dealing with those mergers and acquisitions that lead to a decrease in productive (and/or dynamic) efficiency as well. In general, the following situations may arise as a result of merger (see Figure 11.1 in which these have been numbered clockwise):

1 the merger does not affect allocative efficiency nor does it affect productive efficiency;
2 the merger does not affect allocative efficiency but has a positive effect on productive efficiency;
3 the merger does not affect allocative efficiency but has a negative effect on productive efficiency;
4 the merger has a negative effect on both allocative and productive efficiency;
5 the merger has a negative effect on allocative efficiency but a positive effect on productive efficiency;
6 the merger has a negative effect on allocative efficiency but has no effect on productive efficiency.

Recall that Williamson's (1968) trade-off model – which is allowed explicitly in US antitrust cases and implicitly in the EU – was designed to trade

Productive
efficiency

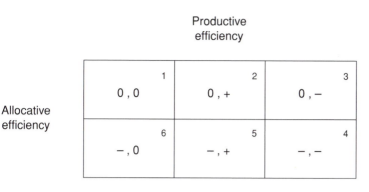

|  | 1 | 2 | 3 |
|---|---|---|---|
| Allocative<br>efficiency | 0 , 0 | 0 , + | 0 , − |
|  | 6 | 5 | 4 |
|  | − , 0 | − , + | − , − |

0 = no effect
+ = positive effect
− = negative effect

*Figure 11.1* Effects of mergers and acquisitions on allocative and productive
efficiency

off potential losses of allocative efficiency against any gains in productive
efficiency. That is, it was especially designed to deal with those mergers
that, from the figure, can be distinguished as type 5 mergers. Thus, it is
evident that this model cannot effectively deal with the most likely outcomes
of merger, that is, type 3 and type 4 mergers.[4] Figure 11.1 also makes clear
that the social desirability of type 1 mergers is dubious, and their private
desirability as well. These are mergers and acquisitions that consume
managerial time but do not create wealth. Type 2 mergers are beneficial
from both a private and a social point of view: they do not affect allocative efficiency (no change in social desirability) and lead to an increase in
productive efficiency (beneficial to the firms in question as well as to society).
Type 3 mergers are undesirable from a private as well as social point of
view, and this applies equally to type 4 and type 6 mergers (type 4 mergers,
of course, being the 'least' desirable).

Thus, it is important to notice that market power cannot only be presumed
when prices are above marginal production costs, or when price–cost margins
are relatively large and/or increasing, but also when improvements in productive efficiency and innovation performance fail to occur after a merger
has been consummated. As has been set out above, this must be a result of
the fact that market power has immobilised the ability of the market system
to punish those firms that have engaged in unproductive expenditures or
investments. Even the fact that improvements in profitability have failed to
materialise could be taken as an indication of some market power being
involved – if it is legitimate to assume that firms are profit-maximising actors,
which is the basic presumption in practically all antitrust and competition
policy statutes. A full efficiency test should therefore be a natural part of

effective merger control regulations. That is, just as it should be possible to allow mergers that improve economic welfare as a result of reductions in costs (as in the US) or increases in innovativeness (as in the EU), it should be possible to stop mergers which do not create wealth. Competition policies that solely allow for an efficiency defence would be at loggerheads with the fact that the mere and persistent occurrence of unproductive mergers is an indication of pre-existing market power or the simultaneous build-up of it.

It is obvious that the burden of proof in matters of productive (and dynamic) efficiency would be on the shoulders of those firms that wish to undertake a merger or acquisition. For it is in their interest to produce a plausible analysis of the gains to be realised. Indeed, it should not be very difficult to come up with a protocol containing the relevant arguments and data if real economies can plausibly be expected. With Dewey (1996), it could even be argued that a test for productive and dynamic effects should replace the usual tests for allocative effects since that would probably reduce the costs of merger control considerably and increase the authorities' grip on the matter.[5] For getting to grips with the allocative effects of a merger is probably much more difficult than getting to grips with its productive and dynamic effects. Relieved from the requirement to assess anything 'so nebulous as "impact on competition"' (Dewey, 1996: 397), the authorities would be able to save on civil servants and economic consultants. Merger investigations would only require a small staff of engineers, accountants and marketing consultants to assess the productive and dynamic efficiency claims laid down by those firms that are seeking to grow by merger or acquisition. Although this would especially apply to the American case, which requires relatively sophisticated analyses, it would also lower the burdens on the EU's assessment officials (and courts) as definitions of the relevant market or assessments of the likelihood of entry, and so on, would no longer be necessary. In order to reduce the burdens of merger control even further, Dewey proposes to limit its applicability to those mergers in which at least one big firm is involved (for example, the largest 500 non-financial US firms). Most notably, this would not exclude any longer the acquisitions of smaller firms by larger ones – thus allowing an assessment of piecemeal build-up of market power – and reduce the necessity to classify mergers as either horizontal, vertical or diagonal.[6] Moreover, the transparency of merger controls would be increased substantially, which would be welcomed both by the firms involved and by those wishing to investigate the decisions taken by the authorities. The chances for opportunistic settlements and regulatory capture – such as are documented for the EU case by Neven *et al.* (1993) – would be significantly reduced.

Of course, many mergers would fail to qualify for vetting – unless one were prepared to adopt an extremely low cutoff figure. Therefore, in relatively small markets it would be possible for quite small firms to gain positions of market dominance. These cases, however, could remain subject to those sections of the law that look to abuse of market dominance, such as article 86 of the Rome Treaty. These sections might even remain applicable to those firms that, after having expanded by means of efficiency-increasing mergers, clearly displayed abuse of market power. Such *ex post* vetting would not need to evade break-up rulings any more since sell-offs, buy-outs and spin-offs have by now become part and parcel of corporate strategies themselves – as evidenced, for example, by such de-mergers as have recently been undertaken by ITT, AT&T, ICI, Baxter International, Sandoz, 3M, Chargeurs, Hanson, Unilever and PepsiCo.

Finally, a rather important advantage of the lean and mean merger control system proposed here would be that it reduces the complexities of the international gearing of merger policies, particularly of those within the Triad. Apart from the jurisdictional questions involved, there is presently much confusion over the interpretations of different merger control procedures and institutional arrangements (see, for example, Waverman *et al.*, 1997). The steadily increasing number of international mergers and acquisitions implies that firms will increasingly have to notify their mergers to different national authorities. Moreover, given the internationalisation of the world economy, it becomes increasingly possible that domestic mergers will have foreign repercussions. Indeed, while the acquisition of Consolidated Gold Fields by Minorco was not challenged by the British and EU authorities, it was terminated by a private antitrust case launched in the US in 1989. Similarly, the acquisition of the Canadian pharmaceutical firm Connaught Labs by France's Mérieux was only conditionally accepted by the US's FTC in 1990 though neither of these firms had production facilities in the US. Also, the recent takeover of McDonnell Douglas by Boeing became the subject of cross-Atlantic confusion as the European Commission decided, for good reasons, to leave its mark on the finalisation of the deal. The transparency of the pertinent discussions would have benefited substantially if an efficiency test had been applied instead of the traditional tests that dominated all these cases. Thus, subjecting all mergers and acquisitions undertaken by the largest 1,500 or so firms from the OECD area to a full efficiency test would seem to be a significant improvement over present arrangements in several respects.

## Industrial policy implications

Though the proposed approach seems straightforward and consistent with empirical research findings at the same time, one should, however, not be overly optimistic with respect to the chances of its actual implementation. For outside the arena of competition policy, more particularly within that of industrial policy, governments – of various persuasions – have displayed a persistent love affair with mergers and corporate bigness, so that the introduction of a really effectual merger control system may well meet up with unjustified but vested instincts. Indeed, in matters of government policy too, love doesn't make the pot boil; on the contrary, it often appears to lead governments in quite inimitable directions (see, for example, Wassenberg, 1999). Thus, despite the available evidence, western governments have traditionally regarded mergers and acquisitions as a panacea for economic problems and more particularly as the outstanding instruments for improving the international competitiveness of domestic firms (see, for example, Adams and Brock, 1988; for confirmation of the permanency of this, see Vernon, 1974). During the 1980s, the Reagan Administration, for example, advocated the promotion of horizontal mergers, arguing that 'because of larger markets, the cost of research and development, new product innovation, marketing, and so forth . . . it takes larger companies to compete successfully' (cited by Adams and Brock, 1988: 2). In Europe, the 1992 Programme not only aspired to reducing internal barriers to trade but also looked forward to what it saw as an inevitable restructuring of European industry, 'one that [would] facilitate the growth of large pan-European firms able to compete on a par with their US or Japanese rivals' (Geroski, 1989: 29). As recently as 1995, the director of industrial policy of the European Commission claimed that mergers and acquisitions were to be regarded as so 'important and beneficial' that they should be welcomed and even encouraged (Marchipont, 1995: 32). Similar positions are and have been taken at the level of the individual member states of the EU. Instead of blaming pro-merger attitudes for industrial policy failures, these policies were merely relabelled, that is, from backing losers to supporting winners (Schenk, 1992), so that it is not surprising that the industrial policy debate has continued until this day.

A particularly telling example of the failed pro-merger policies concerns the European information technology industry (see Kende, 1996). From the mid-1960s through to the late 1970s several of the European computer-producing countries encouraged the creation of a large single producer through merger, based on the premise that scale would lead to effective competition with IBM. The French merged their computer makers into CII, then supported the Unidata venture of CII with Philips and Siemens, as did the Dutch and German governments, and subsequently encouraged its merger with Honeywell-Bull. The German government tried to merge Siemens and AEG (which was later to become a subsidiary of Daimler-Benz before pieces ended up in Sweden's ailing Electrolux) and agreed in 1990 to the takeover of Nixdorf by Siemens. Britain's ICL was formed with government help by a merger of English Electric with Elliott Automation, and a subsequent merger of the newly formed firm with part of Plessey and International Computers and Tabulators (another part of Plessey ended up within Siemens).

It is important to notice that merger predilections are not confined to the days when Servan-Schreiber (1967) published his passionate plea in favour of mergers and consolidations and corporate bigness generally, and the European Commission its Colonna Report (CEC, 1970) in which that plea was endorsed. Although the institutions that were specially founded to support these pleas, such as the IRC in Great Britain (1966) and the NEHEM in The Netherlands (1972), have mostly vanished, the underlying presumptions have survived the ages, as is evidenced by consolidation programmes in the car industry, the steel industry, the aircraft industry, the transport industry (railways, trucking, airlines), the media industry and the telecommunications industry. Indeed, the Cecchini Report (1988) stressed the importance of mergers as the main vehicle through which the estimated welfare gains of further European integration would be realised. As recently as 1996, the Dutch government tried desparately to sell Fokker Aircraft to Korea's Samsung, even after it had become expressly clear that its earlier strategy of consolidating Fokker into Daimler-Benz had failed miserably when the German conglomerate wanted to get rid of its acquired Dutch aircraft manufacturer. Similarly, the US government does not even seem to have contemplated obstructing Boeing's 1997 acquisition of McDonnell Douglas which is likely to create a virtual monopoly in civil aircraft.

Thus, governments have usually accepted the strategic wisdom of those firms which are participating in international competition to such an extent that their policies have become part of the problem. Since introducing a full efficiency test would very probably lead to a substantial transgression upon this strategic wisdom, no matter how beneficial such a measure would ultimately be to the firms themselves, it is very doubtful whether governments would be at all willing to proceed to such a modernism. Therefore, one would be inclined to suggest policy changes that would be perceived as rather less far-reaching. More particularly, it would seem pragmatic to look for constructive instead of regulatory policy alternatives, even if such an approach could not cure the underlying problems fully. In that respect, the following suggestions seem worthwhile.[7]

First, and most fundamentally, governments should dissociate themselves from the efficient choice paradigm which presumes that firms undertake mergers, as any strategic action, solely for reasons of value creation. By implication, they should subsequently refrain from inducing and supporting mergers and acquisitions generally – which, after all, is less far-reaching than proceeding towards a system that sees to the outright prevention of unproductive mergers. Instead, de-mergers and management buy-outs should be advocated as socially beneficial corporate strategies (see Lichtenberg and Siegel, 1990; Thompson *et al.*, 1993; Schenk *et al.*, 1997).

Second, governments should support more seriously than hitherto the entry and survival perspectives of firms that are able to challenge the apparent *modus vivendi* of corporate capitalism. This would imply the development of arrangements that favour the arrival of new firms and the growth of small- and medium-sized enterprises (SMEs).[8] Such policies would no longer require these latter firms to enter into strategic alliances with large firms – which for example is a common requirement in many collaborative R&D programmes – so that at least one means of enforcing locked-in behaviours would be skirted. Adequate financial arrangements would mitigate the tendency among SMEs to succumb to acquisition offers coming from larger firms at a moment when they are incapable of fulfilling their own needs for growth capital. I shall return to the question of financial arrangements below as it is necessary to discuss first the third suggestion that follows from the previous analysis.

Since adequate industrial policies toward SMEs would require the policy authorities to be informed on a large number of firms, which they would be unable to cope with, it follows that these policies should in large part be delegated to policy echelons that are within reach of these firms, that is, to regional and local authorities. Decentralisation of industrial policies is likely to open a full window of opportunities which from a centralised point of view would all seem too minor to be addressed. Regional and local industrial policies can also more easily be fine-tuned to the specific needs in areas that traditionally belong to the sphere of public infrastructure. Regional and local government institutions are likely to be less committed to the interests of a nation's large multinational firms so that they should be able to combine what Porter (1990) has called sophisticated demand with the challenging of SMEs to come up with adequate technologies to tackle all sorts of local problems, ranging from the environment to education. Such problem-orientated technology policies are more likely to contribute to business success than policies which focus on glamorous large-scale collaborative R&D projects (see, for example, Ergas, 1986; Nooteboom, 1994).

A problem that has remained manifest even with western economies running at full speed concerns the supply of finance to SMEs (Hughes and Storey, 1995; McVey, 1998). Increasing concentration in the financial services industry, especially acute during the 1980s and 1990s, has reinforced the orientation of banks toward the wholesale market to the detriment of the retail market (Schenk, 1995). Although it is difficult to estimate the indirect welfare costs of concentration in banking, it has become clear that the infrastructure of the capital market should be geared more to the needs of SMEs than is presently the case. More particularly, the ability to raise equity capital on the stock market should be seen more as a critical component of this infrastructure. Indeed, those new markets that have recently been launched in several European countries (such as the Alternative Investment Market in London; the Nouveau Marché in Paris; the Easdaq in Brussels; and the Neuer Markt in Frankfurt) are explicitly meant to target SMEs. However, these so-called small-cap markets are typically chasing fund managers rather than retail investors (see *The Economist*, 15 March 1997). Since this may have much to do with the fact that the small-cap markets are still tied to, or associated with, the main exchanges, it would be commendable to start establishing independent alternative markets at the regional level. Whereas, at least in Europe, venture capital firms have increasingly left the market for new start-ups,[9] and regular banks traditionally support only firms that can provide collateral, regional stock markets could fill the void that exists especially for high-tech, thus difficult to value, SMEs.[10] The attractive element for investors is that they will not only have the opportunity to spread their risk but also to do this while requiring only relatively small initial investments.

An important recent initiative in this respect has been taken by one of the several institutions that were created years ago to support regional development in The Netherlands, the Gelderland Development Authority (GOM). Assisted by academic experts from Tilburg University and Erasmus University as well as business experts, the GOM is developing a stock market that is entirely set up on the internet. Between eight and ten regional counters are scheduled for The Netherlands, which will assess candidates for quotation and provide guidance as well as information services to both firms and investors. On-line and real-time stock trading as well as pertinent information on registered firms will be available on the internet. Code keys and personal information are to be obtained from the regional counters where identification, clearing, account guarantees, and so on, are settled. Supporting such an initiative would be an innovative challenge for industrial policy authorities and institutions at the regional level which hitherto have either been concentrating their policy efforts on supplying small-scale subsidies, taking small participation in promising ventures, or else have been on the look-out for a purpose. The initiative seems promising as thresholds for quotation on this virtual stock market would be considerably lower than they are at the Amsterdam Stock Exchange, while local intermediary institutions can more easily separate the wheat from the chaff among candidate firms. Traditionally, it has been argued that a major problem for small-scale stock markets is likely to be a lack of liquidity due to small turnovers. Making use of the internet, however, is likely to do away with this problem as there are no limits to expanding the system nationally or internationally. Still, the regional counters would enable the stock exchange to be close to the SME sector.

Making use of the possibilities of the internet would also tend to reduce costs considerably. For example, Poof Products, a toy manufacturer from Michigan with only 45 employees and a turnover of $10 million, was expecting to spend only approximately $100,000 instead of $700,000 as a result of offering $5 million of its shares directly to investors over the internet in 1997 (see *The Economist*, 23 November 1996).[11] By widening the pool of investors, and allocating shares on a first-come, first-served basis, an internet offering can moreover change the typical volatility of initial public offerings (IPOs) by allowing small investors the same chance as large institutional investors of getting in on the ground floor (see Ibbotson and Ritter, 1995; Röell, 1996). This would benefit dedicated investors, who would be attracted by a fairer market over those who as favoured investors normally have the privilege of selling for an immediate profit. Thus, a regionally based virtual stock market could very well be complementary to the established small-cap stock markets. An added advantage is that the system would provide an exit mechanism to founding investors so that these would not succumb so easily to acquisition offers from large firms. Besides, an efficient system might, eventually, be able to put so much pressure on the large banks that these would be forced to increase their productive efficiency and decrease their grip on the retail market.

## Conclusions

While traditional competition policies as well as academic work on the effects of mergers have typically addressed the allocative effects, this paper has stressed the effects of mergers and acquisitions on productive and dynamic efficiency. In principle, both types of effect can arise as a result of the existence or build-up of market power. That should make unproductive mergers a case for competition policies. Since the overwhelming evidence is that mergers are unproductive, competition policies should even be based on the presumption that (large) mergers and acquisitions create or enhance such market power. However, in order to prevent economically productive mergers being blocked as a result of this presumption, firms should be allowed to use an efficiency (and/or innovation) defence in antitrust investigations and proceedings.

Unfortunately, even recently introduced merger control regulations, such as the EU's Merger Regulation of 1989, have overlooked the connection between market power and the effects of mergers on productive and dynamic efficiency. The paper has suggested that this can be explained by the generally held beliefs in the virtues of large corporations, as evidenced by the merger predilections of past and current industrial policies. The introduction of a full efficiency test in competition policy will therefore very probably meet with substantial opposition from firms as well as authorities.

From a pragmatic point of view, it would therefore be advisable to try and compensate for the present half-heartedness of merger control by adapting current industrial policies to focus on the encouragement of those firms that can potentially challenge the merger-prone firms in the US and the EU. To this end, it has been suggested decentralising industrial policies to the regional or even local level and to adapt the micro-structure of financial markets to the needs of small and medium-sized firms. With respect to the latter, it has been suggested supporting the creation of a virtual internet-based stock market with regional entry counters for candidate firms.

## Notes

1 Mueller (1996) and Schenk (2000) provide extensive overviews of the literature. Most recently, Dickerson *et al.* (1997) found for a large panel of UK-quoted firms over the period 1948–77 that acquisitions have a systematic detrimental impact on company performance as measured by the rate of return on assets. Not only was the coefficient on acquisition growth much lower than that on internal growth, but there appeared to be an additional and permanent reduction in profitability following acquisition as well. More specifically, for the average company, the marginal impact of becoming an acquirer was to reduce the rate of return by 1.38 percentage points while the total reduction over time was 2.90 percentage points per annum. This translates into a shortfall in performance by acquiring firms of 17.7 per cent per annum. Decomposing growth into acquisition growth and internal growth showed that if a company were to double its rate of growth through growing internally, then its profitability would

rise by almost 6.9 per cent in the long run. If the same growth rate were to be realised by acquisition, then profitability would only rise by 0.2 per cent.

2 Bank loans equalled 90 per cent of nominal GNP at the end of September 1991 in Japan, compared to only 37 per cent in America; see Wood (1992).

3 Of course, firms can also be guarded against the market mechanism when government measures protect them against foreign competition. Similarly, government subsidies can provide shelter for suboptimal behaviour if they are not combined with strategic interventions.

4 For a somewhat different approach but a similar conclusion, see Kay (1993).

5 In this respect, also see Brenner (1990) who stresses the importance of a test for the effects of a merger on innovation performance.

6 Meanwhile notice that it has become less meaningful to distinguish horizontal from vertical and conglomerate mergers at all now that most large firms are vertically integrated conglomerates, thus making it possible for a single merger to be horizontal, vertical and conglomerate at the same time. See, for example, Karier (1993).

7 Ravenscraft and Scherer (1987: 227) have recommended that acquiring companies should file with the Securities and Exchange Commission (SEC) a report 'detailing all acquisitions made during the prior year, the consideration paid, the book value of the assets acquired, the method of accounting used, a description of each unit sold off during the year, and the loss or gain recorded in connection with each such divestiture'. They also recommend that certain acquisitions should be designated as distinct industry segments for which disaggregated sales, assets and operating income information would have to be disclosed in annual reports. These recommendations can only be supported, as owners of acquiring firms may be less willing to accept the managerial rationales that create merger waves if only they were better informed about what happens after a particular merger or acquisition has been realised (a particular firm's record in mergers and acquisitions remains obscure as all information on acquisitions normally vanishes into consolidated reports and forms). Yet, shareholders might easily get caught up in the same games as their agents are playing, especially when they represent large institutional holdings – which is increasingly the case. Therefore, one should not expect quick results from these recommendations.

8 Despite much lip service that is frequently being paid to small and medium-sized enterprises and several policy measures officially directed at this sector (such as tax facilities, loan guarantees, science parks, information diffusion offices, financial R&D support), the total of funds flowing to SMEs shrinks into insignificance when compared to the funds that flow towards large companies – at least when the experience of the 1980s is taken as evidence (see Schenk, 1993). For example, in the case of The Netherlands – applauded by the CEC (1989) for its extensive support of SMEs – it is remarkable that while many of these instruments were specifically developed for small and medium-sized firms, substantially more than 75 per cent of the funds committed went to companies with more than 500 employees during 1979–83, many of these firms moreover being just subsidiaries of large firms (Van Dijk and Kleinknecht, 1984). The Dutch situation does not seem to have been an anomaly either. For example, over £500 million of the £600 million allocated to the 1975-established and 1983-abolished UK National Enterprise Board – originally set up as a sponsor of innovation in the fields of advanced technology – was spent to rescue only a few large firms. On the level of Community-wide R&D subsidies, similar conclusions seem to hold (see Van Tulder, 1990).

9 According to *The Economist* of 25 January 1997, more than half of Europe's venture capital investment is used now to finance changes in firms' ownership

(especially by means of management buy-outs) and less than 6 per cent for starting up new firms.

10 Generally speaking, financial markets have an advantage over banks in the case of new technology-based firms (NTBFs) as making up an assessment of the potentialities of such firms is fraught with difficulties. By bringing together many analysts, investors and traders, financial markets are less dependent on individual judgements than banks (see, for example, Allen, 1993).

11 The lead in internet offerings was set by Spring Street Brewing, a New York beer maker, when it raised $1.6 million over the internet in February 1996, thus proving that even small offerings can succeed very well when they have access to the right type of market.

## References

Acs, Zoltan J. (1996) 'Small Firms and Economic Growth', in: Admiraal (ed). (1996): 1–62.

Adams, W. and J.W. Brock (1988) 'The Bigness Mystique and the Merger Policy Debate: an International Perspective', *Northwestern Journal of International Law and Business* 9 (1): 1–48.

Admiraal, Piet Hein (ed.) (1996) *Small Business in the Modern Economy*, Oxford: Blackwell.

Allen, F. (1993) 'Stock Markets and Resource Allocation', in: Mayer and Vives (eds) (1993): 81–116.

Brenner, Reuven (1990) 'Innovations and Anti-trust', in: Dankbaar, Groenewegen, and Schenk (eds.) 11(1990): 235–257.

Buigues, Pierre-André and Alexis P. Jacquemin (1996) 'Structural Interdependence Between the European Union and the United States: Technological Positions', Discussion Paper no. 9625, Louvain-la-Neuve: IRES, Université Catholique de Louvain.

Cecchini, P. *et al.* (1988) *The European Challenge*, Aldershot, Hants.: Gower.

Commission of the European Communities (1970) *Industrial Policy of the European Community* (Colonna Report), Brussels: CEC.

Commission of the European Communities (1989) *First Survey on State Aids in the European Community*, Brussels and Luxembourg: Commission of the European Communities.

Cowling, Keith, and Roger Sugden (eds) (1992) *Current Issues in Industrial Economic Strategy*, Manchester and New York: Manchester University Press.

Dankbaar, Ben, John Groenewegen and Hans Schenk (eds) (1990) *Perspectives in Industrial Organization*, Studies in Industrial Organization, vol. 13, Dordrecht, Boston and London: Kluwer Academic Publishers.

Dewey, D. (1996) 'Merger Policy Greatly Simplified: Building on Keyes', *Review of Industrial Organization* 11: 395–400.

Dickerson, A.P., H.D. Gibson and E. Tsakalotos (1997) 'The Impact of Acquisitions on Company Performance: Evidence from a Large Panel of UK Firms', *Oxford Economic Papers* 49: 344–361.

Dutch Ministry of Economic Affairs (DMEA) (1995) *Knowledge on the Move* [in Dutch], The Hague: Ministry of Economic Affairs.

Ergas, H. (1986) 'Does Technology Policy Matter?', Working Paper, Brussels: Centre for European Policy Studies.

Froot, K.A. (ed.) (1993) *Foreign Direct Investment*, Chicago and London: University of Chicago Press (for NBER).

Geroski, Paul A. (1989) 'European Industrial Policy and Industrial Policy in Europe', *Oxford Review of Economic Policy* 5 (2): 20–36

Hughes, Alan and D.J. Storey (eds) (1995) *Finance and the Small Firm*, London: Routledge.

Hughes, Kirsty S. (ed.) (1993) *European Competitiveness*, Cambridge: Cambridge University Press.

Ibbotson, R.G. and J.R. Ritter (1995) 'Initial Public Offerings', in: Jarrow, Maksimovic and Ziemba (eds) (1995): 993–1016.

Jarrow, R.A., V. Maksimovic and W.T. Ziemba (eds) (1995) *Handbooks in Operations Research and Management Science: Finance* (vol. 9), Amsterdam: North-Holland.

Karier, T. (1993) *Beyond Competition: The Economics of Mergers and Monopoly Power*, Armonk. NY: M.E. Sharpe.

Kay, N. (1993) 'Mergers, Acquisitions and the Completion of the Internal Market', in: Hughes (ed.) (1993): 161–180.

Kende, Michael (1996) 'Government Support of the European Information Technology Industry', paper presented to the CEPR/WZB Workshop 'Does Europe Have an Industrial Policy?', Berlin, 19–20 April.

Lawrence, R.Z. (1993) 'Japan's Low Levels of Inward Investment: the Role of Inhibitions on Acquisitions', in: Froot (ed.) (1993): 85–111.

Lichtenberg, Frank R. and D. Siegel (1990) 'The Effects of Leveraged Buyouts on Productivity and Related Aspects of Firm Behavior', *Journal of Financial Economics* 27: 165–194.

McVey, B. (1998) 'Finance and Entrepreneurship: the role of the new stock exchanges in local economic development', paper presented to the Third Biennial Conference of the Association of European Financial Centres, Manchester, 4–6 March.

Maddison, Angus (1987) 'Growth and Slowdown in Advanced Capitalist Economies: Techniques of Quantitative Assessment', *Journal of Economic Literature* 25 (June): 649–698.

March, J.G. (1978) 'Bounded Rationality, Ambiguity, and the Engineering of Choice', *Bell Journal of Economics* 9: 587–608.

Marchipont, J.-F. (1995) 'La stratégie industrielle de l'Union européenne: à la recherche d'un concept de politique de compétitivité globale', *Revue d'économie industrielle* 71 (1er trim.): 17–37.

Mayer, C. and X. Vives (eds) (1993) *Capital Markets and Financial Intermediation*, Cambridge: Cambridge University Press.

Mboweni, Tito (ed) (1993) *Antitrust, Monopolies, and Mergers*, Johannnesburg: UWC Press.

Mueller, Dennis C. (1986) *Profits in the Long Run*, Cambridge and New York: Cambridge University Press.

Mueller, Dennis C. (1996) 'Antimerger Policy in the United States: History and Lessons', *Empirica. Journal of Applied Economics and Economic Policy* 23 (3): 229–253.

Neven, Damien, R. Nuttall and Paul Seabright (1993) *Merger in Daylight: The Economics and Politics of European Merger Control*, London: Centre for Economic Policy Research.

Nooteboom, Bart (1994) 'Elements of Strategic Industrial Policy' [in Dutch], *Tijdschrift voor Politieke Ekonomie* 17 (3): 99–124.

Nooteboom, Bart and R.W. Vossen (1995) 'Firm Size and Efficiency in R&D Spending', in: Van Witteloostuijn (ed.) (1995): 69–86.

Odagiri, Hiroyuki (1992) *Growth through Competition, Competition through Growth: Strategic Management and the Economy in Japan*, Oxford: Clarendon Press.

OECD (1993) *National Systems for Financing Innovation* (restricted draft version), Paris: Organisation for Economic Co-operation and Development, Working Group on Innovation and Technology.

Porter, M.E. (1990) *The Competitive Advantage of Nations*, London: Macmillan.

Ravenscraft, D.J. and F. Michael Scherer (1987) *Mergers, Sell-offs, and Economic Efficiency*, Washington, DC: Brookings Institution.

Röell, A. (1996) 'The Decision to Go Public: an Overview', *European Economic Review* 40: 1071–1081.

Schenk, Hans (1992) 'Some Comments on the Competitive Strategy Aspects of Industrial Policy', in: Cowling and Sugden (eds) (1992): 33–53

Schenk, Hans (1993) 'West European Industrial and Competition Policies: Content and Assessment', in: Mboweni (ed.) (1993): 1–37.

Schenk, Hans (1995) *The Dutch Economy after the Turn of the Century. Pilot study: Financial Services and the Food Industry* [in Dutch], Rotterdam and The Hague: GRASP, Erasmus University Rotterdam/Dutch Ministry of Economic Affairs.

Schenk, Hans (1996) 'Bandwagon Mergers, International Competitiveness, and Government Policy', *Empirica. Journal of Applied Economics and Economic Policy* 23 (3): 255–278.

Schenk, Hans (2000) *Mergers, Efficient Choice and International Competitiveness*, Cheltenham: Edward Elgar (forthcoming)

Schenk, Hans, with Jean-Paul Warmenhoven, Marco Van Velzen and Cees Van Riel (1997) 'The Demise of the Conglomerate Firm' [in Dutch], *Economisch Statistische Berichten* 82 (4122): 736–740.

Servan-Schreiber, J.-J. (1967) *Le Défi Américain*, Paris: Denoël.

Sharp, Margaret (ed.) (1985a) *Europe and the New Technologies: Six Case Studies in Innovation and Adjustment*, London: Frances Pinter.

Sharp, Margaret (1985b) 'Technology Gap or Management Gap?', in: Sharp (ed.) (1985a): 263–297.

Thompson, S., Mike Wright and K. Robbie (1993) 'Buy-outs, Divestment, and Leverage: Restructuring Transactions and Corporate Governance', *Oxford Review of Economic Policy* 8 (3): 58–69.

Van Dijk, Asje and Alfred Kleinknecht (1984) 'The Position of Small and Medium Sized Enterprise in Dutch Innovation Policy' [in Dutch], *Economisch Statistische Berichten*, 26 September: 894–899.

Van Tulder, Rob (1990) 'Dutch Dilemmas: The Netherlands and European Technology Programmes', *Internationale Spectator* xliv (11): 671–678.

Van Witteloostuijn, Arjen (ed.) (1995) *Market Evolution: Competition and Cooperation*, Studies in Industrial Organization, vol. 20, Dordrecht, Boston and London: Kluwer Academic Publishers.

Vernon, R. (ed.) (1974) *Big Business and the State: Changing Relations in Western Europe*, Cambridge, MA: Harvard University Press.

Wassenberg, Arthur F.P. (1999) *Industrial Diplomacy*, Rotterdam: GRASP, Erasmus University Rotterdam (forthcoming).

Waverman, Leonard, William S. Comanor and A. Goto (eds) (1997) *Competition Policy in the Global Economy: Modalities for Cooperation*, London and New York: Routledge.

Williamson, O.E. (1968) 'Economies as an Antitrust Defense: the Welfare Tradeoffs', *American Economic Review* 58: 18–36.

Wood, C. (1992) *The Bubble Economy: The Japanese Economic Collapse*, London: Sidgwick & Jackson.

# Part IV
# Venture capital

# 12 Public policy and the development of the informal venture capital market

## UK experience and lessons for Europe

*Colin M. Mason and*
*Richard T. Harrison\**

## Introduction

The role of risk capital has recently emerged as a central issue in the debate on job creation and the reduction of unemployment in Europe. A paper from the European Commission in April 1998 entitled *Risk Capital: A Key to Job Creation in the European Union* (Commission, 1998) observed that there is an emerging consensus within the EU that the Union must become far more entrepreneurial if it is to create the jobs to reduce, sustainably and substantially, its unemployment levels. The report suggested that two conditions are required for this to happen. First, sources of risk capital have to be developed to ensure that appropriate financing instruments are available to European entrepreneurs, and second, risk capital investors need a stream of good investment opportunities as well as a fair reward for risk taking. Specifically, the report argued that:

> European entrepreneurs must be able to access the right financing, at the right price, at the right place and at the right time to develop their companies and their ideas. This means European entrepreneurs must be able to access start-up capital; intermediate and development capital as the company expands; and finally access institutional and private investors supported by a sizeable, liquid, secondary European stock market where their shares can be traded . . . In this field the European Union is weak on all fronts.
>
> (Commission, 1998: 2)

The availability of risk capital in Europe is much lower than in the USA across the entire financing spectrum. As the Commission's report noted, the

\* The research reported in this paper has been funded by the Department of Trade and Industry. We are grateful for their support. However, they are not responsible for the views expressed, which are solely those of the authors.

EU lacks a liquid stock market such as NASDAQ to attract growing entrepreneurial companies. There is also a lack of early-stage venture capital funds in the EU to invest in start-ups, especially in technology sectors. Although Europe has a sizeable venture capital industry, a disproportionate amount is invested in management buyouts (MBOs) and buyins (MBIs) (44.5 per cent in 1996) (EVCA, 1997). As a consequence, start-ups and growing businesses in Europe are over-dependent on bank loans and overdrafts (Aernoudt, 1999). Such finance is usually less flexible, more expensive and less secure than equity capital and is likely to be unobtainable by new and growing companies, particularly in technology sectors, on account of their negative cash-flow and lack of personal or business collateral (Commission, 1998).

Following the European Council meeting on Employment in Luxembourg in November 1997, the European Union has launched a risk capital initiative involving an investment of ECU160 million in venture capital funds specialising in early-stage technology investments. In addition, the Amsterdam summit extended the scope of the European Investment Bank to include the facility to invest in early-stage venture capital funds (the European Technology Facility). The European Investment Fund, whose role has been to provide long-term guarantees to banks and financial institutions funding investments in SMEs and Trans-European Networks, has since 1997 also provided finance to independent venture capital funds (Unwin, 1998; Aernoudt, 1999). New proposed regulations governing EU regional funds are also expected to give greater emphasis to venture capital (Aernoudt, 1999).

However, these developments have largely ignored the *informal* venture capital market. This market place is populated by high net worth, self-made individuals (referred to as *business angels*), most of whom have an entrepreneurial or business background, and who invest relatively small amounts of their own money, either individually or as part of an informal syndicate of friends and associates, in businesses in which they have no family connection (Wetzel, 1983; Gaston, 1989; Harrison and Mason, 1992; Mason and Harrison, 1994; Freear et al., 1995; Lumme et al., 1998). Business angels occupy a crucial part of the spectrum of sources of finance for business start-up and expansion by investing in the 'gap' below which it is uneconomic for venture capital funds to meet needs because of their cost base and the high transaction costs involved. Their investments are generally small (typically under ECU150,000) and they mainly invest in businesses at their start-up and early growth stages. Furthermore, most business angels are 'hands on' investors, using their business experience, skills and contacts to make valuable strategic, mentoring and supportive contributions to their investee businesses. Yet despite this evidence, measures to support informal venture capital in recent EU initiatives designed to increase the availability of venture capital are conspicuous by their absence, and it is mentioned just once in the Commission's Action Plan to improve conditions for the development of risk capital in the EU, where the proposal is simply 'to *review* measures to stimulate business angel networks' (Commission, 1998: 24, emphasis added).

The economic case for initiatives to increase the supply of informal venture capital is not simply because of the role played by business angels in the financing spectrum. Support is also justified because the effectiveness of initiatives to increase the number of venture capital funds specialising in early-stage investments requires an active informal venture capital market. Business angel investments are crucial in providing venture capital funds with a flow of pre-screened investment opportunities that have passed through the earliest, and most vulnerable, stages of business development. As Benjamin and Margulis (1996: 71) state:

> it boils down to this: angel investment runs the critical first leg of the relay race, passing the baton to venture capital only after a company has begun to find its stride. Venture capitalists focus . . . on expansion and later stages of development, when their contribution is most effective. In this way venture capital complements rather than conflicts with private investment.

In one US study it was noted that 35 per cent of firms that raised finance from venture capital firms had previously attracted finance from business angels[1] (Freear and Wetzel, 1989). By largely ignoring the informal venture capital market, current efforts to increase the supply of risk capital in Europe represent an incomplete response to the need to remove financial barriers to the start-up and growth of SMEs.

Business angels are involved in financing entrepreneurial businesses in the majority of EU countries, and in at least some of the countries where they appear to be absent this type of financing takes a different form and name (EBAN, 1998a). The informal venture capital market has been extensively researched in the UK (for example, Harrison and Mason, 1992; Mason and Harrison, 1994; Coveney and Moore, 1998; van Osnabrugge, 1998) and there have also been studies of business angel investment activity in Sweden (Landström, 1993; Landström and Oloffson, 1996), Finland (Lumme *et al.*, 1998) and The Netherlands (K+V organisatie adviesbureau bv/ Entrepreneurial Holding bv, 1996). These studies indicate that the informal venture capital market is a significant source of risk capital for businesses at their start-up and early growth stages when compared with other sources. In the UK (which probably has the most developed informal venture capital market in Europe) it has been estimated that there are approximately 18,000 active and potential business angels and that their current *annual* investment is in the order of £500 million in about 3,500 businesses. It is further estimated that business angels make ten times as many investments in early-stage ventures as the institutional venture capital industry and, on account of the smaller size of their investments, invest four times as much (Mason and Harrison, 1997a). In Finland there were estimated to be 1,500 business angels in 1994 who have invested a total of FIM850,000. This is equivalent to around 70 per cent of the capital managed by the Finnish venture capital industry at the time (of which only around two-thirds was in early stage investments) (Lumme *et al.*, 1998). In The Netherlands there are estimated to be at least 2,500 to 3,500 active business angels who have invested NLG3.5 billion in at least 2,500 businesses. In comparison, venture capital firms have invested in about 1,500 businesses (K+V organisatie adviesbureau bv/Entrepreneurial Holding bv, 1996).

Nevertheless, in comparison with the USA, the informal venture capital market in European countries is much smaller and SMEs in Europe are less likely to raise finance from business angels. Europe has significantly fewer angels per capita compared with the USA and on average they make smaller and less frequent investments. However, the UK, Finnish and Dutch studies all indicate that there is considerable potential to expand the supply of informal venture capital in Europe. First, a significant proportion of business angels report that they are unable to find sufficient investment opportunities. This reflects the inefficient nature of communication flows between investors and entrepreneurs seeking finance, allied to a desire amongst many business angels for anonymity, resulting in high search costs. Second, there is considerable scope for expanding the population of active business angels through measures which encourage and support individuals with the same self-made, high net worth characteristics as active investors but who have not entered this market.

This chapter develops this theme by considering how the European Union and Member States might best stimulate the informal venture capital market. It does this by drawing upon the experience of the UK, which has taken the lead in Europe in measures to encourage the supply of informal venture capital. There have been two strands of support during the 1990s (Harrison and Mason, 1996a). First, there are *tax incentives* for private individuals who invest in unquoted companies, which are intended to increase the supply of informal venture capital. Second, *business angel networks* (BANs) (sometimes termed business introduction services) have been created, in most cases with either direct or indirect government support, to overcome the inefficiencies in the informal venture capital market place which arise from the difficulties which business angels and entrepreneurs encounter in searching for one another. These types of initiatives are now being advocated, and in some cases implemented, in other EU countries (EBAN, 1998b). It is therefore an opportune moment to undertake a critical review of these initiatives. The UK's experience in promoting the informal venture capital market should provide useful lessons for policy development in the rest of Europe.

Against this background, this chapter therefore addresses three questions:

- Are these present initiatives to support the informal venture capital market in the UK effective?

- Are these initiatives still the most appropriate ways of supporting the informal venture capital market?
- If not, what directions should the support of the informal venture capital market take?

The evidence which this chapter draws upon to address these questions is a postal survey of business angels.[2] The managers of several business angel networks agreed to distribute questionnaires on our behalf to investors registered with their service.[3] Some other questionnaires were sent to investors who were identified through recommendations and informal contacts. It is based on 121 usable responses. In view of the way in which the survey was administered it is not surprising to note that 85 per cent of respondents are, or have been in the past, members of one or more BANs.

## Tax incentives: stimulating the supply side

Three measures were introduced in the 1994 Budget, replacing the largely discredited Business Expansion Scheme, to provide private individuals with tax incentives on qualifying investments in unquoted companies. The *Enterprise Initiative Scheme* (EIS) provided investors with up-front tax relief at 20 per cent on qualifying investments, capital gains are exempt from capital gains tax and losses from investments qualify for both income tax and capital gains tax (CGT) relief. *Capital Gains Tax Re-investment Relief* (RR) enabled investors to defer a CGT liability indefinitely, regardless of its source, by re-investing in unquoted companies. EIS investments also qualify for Re-investment Relief. *Venture Capital Trusts* (VCTs) are pooled investment vehicles which invest in unquoted companies (defined as including companies on the Alternative Investment Market, the London Stock Exchange's junior market) and in which the investor buys shares, in similar fashion to investment trusts. These measures were intended to encourage business angels to invest their money and expertise in small firms. The Chancellor, in his budget speech, stated that the three proposals 'could . . . generate substantial new investment in the unquoted company sector'.

The survey evidence indicates that 40 per cent of investors have used EIS to make a total of 85 investments, an average of 1.85 per investor who has used EIS. In aggregate, investments made using EIS accounted for 43 per cent of the investments made by all the business angels in the survey from the beginning of 1994. However, usage of the scheme has been limited by the rules concerning the types of investments and types of businesses which qualify. Nearly one-quarter of respondents reported that they had encountered specific investment situations in which the rules had prevented them from using EIS.[4] The main constraints were associated with the 30 per cent maximum shareholding rule, the 'not previously connected' rule, and restrictions (which were modified in the 1996 Budget) on companies with overseas subsidiaries and partly owned subsidiaries. The restriction on overseas subsidiaries was a particular issue for technology-based businesses, which often require to set up operations in the US at an early stage in their development. Problems can also arise if investee companies require follow-on finance: tax relief is lost if the 30 per cent shareholding is breached within the five-year qualifying period of the investment.

EIS has had a positive impact on investment activity in the informal venture capital market. Additionality would appear to be high: 77 per cent of the investors using EIS claimed that the scheme has encouraged them to make *more* investments than they would otherwise have done, and 56 per cent stated that the scheme has encouraged them to invest *larger* amounts per investment. However, the impact of EIS on the amounts invested is less significant. The extra amount that business angels identify that they have invested as a result of the EIS, in the form of more or larger investments, is about £1 million, equivalent to just 10 per cent of the total amount invested by the sample of business angels since the beginning of 1994. This limited impact on the amount invested is likely to be because the maximum size of shareholding allowed under the scheme is 30 per cent and only investments in ordinary shares qualify. Both restrictions are likely to discourage investors from using the scheme to make large investments as such investments typically involve an investor taking a larger shareholding and the share structure may require the use of more complex investment instruments (for example, preference-related share options) to ensure that the management is not required to give up a disproportionate amount of the equity (Mason and Harrison, 1996a). EIS has also had only a limited effect on altering investment preferences: despite the effect of the tax incentives on changing the risk–reward ratio, only 17 per cent stated that the scheme had encouraged them to make investments in businesses that they would not otherwise have considered.

Re-investment Relief[5] was used by just 22 per cent of business angels in the survey to make a total of 41 investments. However, because it is possible to combine RR with EIS there is an element of double-counting between the two schemes. On the face of it, EIS would appear to have had the greater impact, with almost twice as many investors using this scheme. However, it is unlikely that all the business angels in the survey would have had a capital gains liability; hence only a proportion would have been able to use RR. Thus, the proportion of *eligible* investors using RR will be significantly higher than one in four.

Nevertheless, given that fewer business angels used RR, it is not surprising that its impact on the overall level of informal investment activity is less than that of EIS. In aggregate, investments made using RR accounted for 23 per cent of the investments made by all the business angels in the survey from the beginning of 1994. However, the additional amount that business angels identify that they have invested as a result of RR, in the form of more or larger investments, is about £1.3 million, equivalent to 15 per cent of the total amount invested by the sample of business angels since the beginning of 1994. This is still a relatively small amount but is larger than the investment made under EIS, despite EIS being used by almost twice as many investors. Moreover, the additionality achieved by RR is extremely high: 88 per cent of those investors using RR stated that the tax incentive had encouraged them to make *more* investments and 56 per cent stated that it had encouraged them to make *larger* investments. This can be attributed to the rules concerning the types of investments which qualify for RR, which are less stringent than those for EIS. Indeed, only four investors (3.3 per cent) reported that the rules had prevented them from using RR to make investments. RR has also had more of an effect than EIS on changing investor preferences: 29 per cent of investors using RR stated that it had encouraged them to invest in businesses that they would not otherwise have considered. This is attributable, at least in part, to the time limit on re-investing their capital gains.

VCTs are managed on a discretionary basis: each trust's management makes the investment decisions and performs all of the due diligence and investment monitoring. As such, investing in VCTs is a passive form of investing, with no direct relationship between the angel and the trust's investee businesses. Consequently, it is not surprising to find that only 11 per cent of business angels in the survey had invested in VCTs, investing just over £500,000 in aggregate. Moreover, only a minority of this invest-ment displaced genuine business angel investment activity: 38 per cent of the investors investing in VCTs stated that this was an *alternative* to making direct investments in unquoted companies, with 62 per cent stating that their VCT investments were *additional* to their direct investments.

The tax reliefs currently available to UK business angels therefore do appear to have had a positive impact on informal venture capital invest-ment activity. There has been significant take-up of both the EIS and RR and additionality is high. However, the proportion of investments that can be attributed to the tax incentives is much greater than the proportion of funds invested, suggesting that the main impact of these measures, and of EIS in particular, has been at the margin, stimulating additional small invest-ments and encouraging some investors to make slightly larger investments than they would otherwise have done in the absence of the relief. VCTs, in contrast, have had much less of an effect in stimulating business angel investment activity. This is in line with expectations because this scheme does not allow investors to invest directly in companies and so there is no role for the investor to find and assess investment opportunities, make their own investment decision or contribute their skills and business know-how to the investee businesses. Indeed, one recent study found that only 14 per cent of business angels were passive investors (van Osnabrugge, 1998). However, this is not to deny that VCTs might be attractive to other types of investor, including those who do not have the requisite sources of information to enable them to identify their own investment opportuni-ties, as well as those who lack the necessary knowledge and confidence to undertake their own investment decisions and either do not have the skills and expertise to make useful hands-on contributions to investee companies, or do not wish to do so.[6]

The tax regime is undoubtedly a key influence on the flow of informal venture capital activity. Table 12.1 shows the responses of business angels to the effects of various macro-economic influences on their investment activity. The most significant influence is the capital gains tax regime. Around two-thirds of business angels indicated that the level of capital gains tax influences their informal investment activity, a much higher proportion than for any of the other potential influences listed.[7] Moreover, 30 per cent of business angels identify this as having a *major* impact on their willingness to make informal venture capital investments. This is two to three times higher than the proportion of investors who identify other factors as major influences which either encourage or discourage their willingness to invest. However, as previous studies have established that business angels invest primarily for capital gain (for example, Mason and Harrison, 1994), this should not be a particularly surprising finding.

Both EIS and VCTs do enable business angels to invest free from CGT; however, both schemes have significant limitations associated with the rules regarding qualifying investments, which has restricted their take-up. Business angels can defer existing CGT liabilities indefinitely by using RR, but by no means every business angel has a CGT liability. Moreover, investors will eventually be liable for CGT if their investment is successful. Thus, existing fiscal measures to stimulate the flow of informal venture capital are sub-optimal. First, the rules concerning qualifying investments are complex, and the effect is to create uncertainty amongst investors concerning whether particular investments will qualify for tax relief. To the extent that this uncertainty requires investors to take professional advice, this results in increased transaction costs. Second, at least some of the rules regarding qualifying investments appear to be unnecessarily restrictive, and have prevented some investors from using the schemes. Third, the schemes are unnecessarily expensive to the Treasury. Because of the various restrictions they are expensive to administer, and the emphasis which investors place on capital gains tax raises the question whether the front-end tax relief significantly adds to the attractiveness of EIS. Stimulating the supply of informal venture capital could be achieved more effectively simply by reducing, or even eliminating, CGT on all investments in unquoted companies: not only would this be expected to increase investment activity, increasing the tax take down the line as a result of increased economic activity, but would also save the cost of the front-end tax relief and much of the administrative cost involved with existing measures.

The March 1998 Budget is the first move in this direction: it proposes a tapering in the level of capital gains tax on assets held for long periods, falling from 40 per cent for short-term gains to 24 per cent after ten years for higher-rate tax payers. However, these new arrangements will replace

*Table 12.1* The influence of various economic conditions on the decision of business angels on how much of their investment portfolio to allocate to investments in unquoted companies

| | Discouraging investment | | No influence on investment | Encouraging investment | |
|---|---|---|---|---|---|
| | *(major)* | *(minor)* | *% of respondents* | *(minor)* | *(major)* |
| Rising interest rates | 6 | 40 | 52 | 2 | 0 |
| Falling interest rates | 0 | 1 | 55 | 38 | 5 |
| High real interest rates | 14 | 38 | 47 | 1 | 0 |
| Low real interest rates | 0 | 1 | 50 | 40 | 10 |
| Bull stock market | 0 | 18 | 62 | 19 | 1 |
| Bear stock market | 2 | 20 | 60 | 18 | 1 |
| High inflation | 11 | 23 | 47 | 16 | 3 |
| Low inflation | 3 | 8 | 55 | 27 | 6 |
| High rate of capital gains tax | 30 | 28 | 32 | 5 | 4 |
| Low rate of capital gains tax | 1 | 2 | 38 | 28 | 31 |
| Property prices rising above the rate of inflation | 6 | 20 | 57 | 14 | 3 |
| Static/falling property prices | 4 | 14 | 64 | 17 | 2 |

*Source*: Authors' survey.

*Note*: Based on between 110 and 114 responses: there were varying numbers of non-respondents in each row.

the indexation of capital gains. Most of the initial comment has been critical of the complexity of the new proposals. Moreover, the limited evidence available on exits by business angels suggests that angels exit from their successful investments in an average of five years (Lumme *et al.*, 1998), rendering these new proposals largely irrelevant to most angels.

## Overcoming information deficiencies: business angel networks

Stimulating the supply of informal venture capital through tax incentives is not a sufficient strategy for encouraging this market place. Various studies indicate that most business angels cannot find sufficient investment opportunities (Mason and Harrison, 1994a; Coveney and Moore, 1998; Lumme *et al.*, 1998). This situation is interpreted by most researchers as reflecting market inefficiencies (Wetzel, 1987; Mason and Harrison, 1994, 1995a). The invisibility of both business angels and entrepreneurs and the fragmented nature of the market place create high search costs both for business angels seeking investment opportunities and also for entrepreneurs seeking to locate business angels.

The other main strand of support for the informal venture capital market in the UK is therefore the establishment of business angel networks (BANs), or business introduction services. They provide a channel of communication between business angels seeking investment opportunities and entrepreneurs seeking to raise finance, thereby addressing the two main sources of inefficiency in the informal venture capital market, namely the invisibility of business angels and the high search costs of both business angels and entrepreneurs for one another. BANs use various methods, including personalised approaches, circulation of business plan summaries or investment opportunity publications, investment forums and fairs and computerised matching, to introduce entrepreneurs and business angels to one another (Mason and Harrison, 1996b). BANs normally charge registration fees to both entrepreneurs and investors, and some also take a 'success fee' which is calculated as a percentage of the amount that businesses raise from investors to whom they are introduced. However, all the experience to date indicates that it is not possible to operate BANs on a full cost-recovery basis (Mason and Harrison, 1996b). Thus, the establishment of BANs requires either government or corporate sponsors to contribute financially or in kind.

The Department of Trade and Industry has sought to encourage the establishment of this type of initiative, notably through its Informal Investment Demonstration Projects, launched in 1992, which provided pump-priming funding for a three-year period to enable five local Training and Enterprise Councils in England and Wales, selected on a competitive basis, to establish BANs. The objective was to encourage the establishment of such services throughout the country by demonstrating that BANs are a worthwhile way of enabling business angels to channel finance and their expertise to small firms. Linked to this initiative was the publication of a guide to the establishment of BANs (Mason and Harrison, 1993). Following a favourable assessment of these demonstration projects (Mason and Harrison, 1996c; Harrison and Mason, 1996b) the DTI has sought to encourage the establishment of BANs throughout the country. The second Competitiveness White Paper stated that: 'The DTI will work with the private sector, Business Links and TECs to ... develop national coverage of a local brokerage service throughout England' (HM Government, 1995: 105). This objective has largely been met: at the present time there are more than 40 BANs in the UK (BVCA, 1997a), more than half of which have been established by, or operate under contract to, Business Links. Most of the remainder have been established by private sector companies, generally as an adjunct to their mainstream corporate financial services activities. Indeed, the present concern is that the national provision of BANs is too fragmented.

Although the performance of individual BANs is variable, there is growing evidence to suggest that, when compared against appropriate benchmarks, their aggregate impact on informal venture capital activity is both positive and significant. Evaluation of the DTI's five demonstration projects reported significant impacts in terms of the mobilisation of a substantial pool of informal investment activity, stimulating demand for equity finance by SMEs that might otherwise have been latent, and facilitating a significant level of informal investment activity. In addition, there have been a range of indirect benefits, including advice and signposting to businesses that are inappropriate for the service, feedback from BAN staff and investors to whom the entrepreneur has been introduced, networking benefits (for example, resource acquisition) and the training of both entrepreneurs and business angels in equity investing (Mason and Harrison, 1996c; Harrison and Mason, 1996b). The BVCA's annual review of business angel investment activity confirms the large and growing volume of investments made through BANs (BVCA, 1997b). Moreover, public sector financial support for BANs is extremely cost-effective and compares favourably with other initiatives. LINC Scotland has calculated that the cost to the public purse per job created in businesses which have raised finance from business angels through its service as been £470 over two years; a similar calculation by the South West Investment Group was £700 over one year (IIVCRN, 1996). Moreover, the deadweight and displacement associated with businesses that have raised finance from investors that they have been introduced to through a BAN are likely to be low (Harrison and Mason, 1996b).

Furthermore, BANs that have been established by Business Links or by not-for-profit organisations are proving to be more effective than most commercially-focused BANs in helping to close the equity gap. The commercial orientation of private sector BANs requires them to be fee-driven. As a consequence, they are involved with larger investments, which are better able to support fees, and also with later stage deals (including MBOs/MBIs) and low-tech manufacturing (Mason and Harrison, 1997b). Thus, the involvement of the private sector in BANs has not eliminated the need for ongoing public sector involvement in the financing of BANs.

This favourable assessment of the impact of BANs in stimulating informal venture capital investment activity has to be qualified in two respects. First, most BANs are involved in relatively few deals. Second, investors registered with BANs make relatively few of their investments in opportunities that have been referred through BANs. It is therefore important to consider whether the effectiveness of BANs should be increased and, in turn, improve on the social and economic returns for the public funds invested in them. These issues are explored by means of responses from business angels to various statements in the questionnaire survey about their perception of the market place for informal venture capital investments. Five conclusions emerge.

First, the vast majority of business angels (79 per cent) agree that information availability on investment opportunities has increased. It seems plausible that this reflects the activities of BANs as most of the respondents are members of BANs. However, two-thirds of respondents who were not members of a BAN also agreed with the statement.

Second, nearly half of respondents (45 per cent) believe that competition for the best investment opportunities is increasing. This may reflect either an excess of (well-informed) business angels or a deficiency in the quality of small businesses seeking finance. A related finding is that one-third of investors had made offers of finance that were turned down by entrepreneurs, on an average of two occasions. In some cases the entrepreneur had considered that the terms and conditions of the investment were unacceptable (33 per cent). On other occasions the entrepreneur had obtained equity finance from an alternative source (29 per cent).

Third, there is a diversity of opinion amongst investors about the quality of investment opportunities. On the one hand, 37 per cent of business angels believe that the quality of investment opportunities that they are seeing is deteriorating. One possible interpretation is that the banks and other intermediaries may be encouraging inappropriate businesses to seek informal venture capital. However, 32 per cent of respondents agreed with the statement that the quality of investment opportunities is improving. One possible explanation for this diversity of opinion is that it reflects the geographical location of investors. The informal venture capital market is largely a local/regional market place, and different locations are likely to be characterised by different demand and supply conditions. It may also reflect the differing effectiveness of local BANs across the country. Alternatively, it might reflect investor differences, for example, in deal flow or in their investment criteria.

Fourth, two-thirds of business angels in the survey anticipate that they will encounter difficulties in finding sufficient investment opportunities that meet their investment criteria. There are three sets of reasons for this (Table 12.2). The first, and most significant, set of reasons are associated with opportunity quality and the match between investor preferences and opportunity characteristics. A second set of reasons are associated with the opportunity identification process. A significant minority of investors lack the time to search for and evaluate investment opportunities and lack reliable sources of information on investment opportunities. The third, and least significant, group of reasons are associated with putting the deal together, and arise from the lack of suitable co-investors and time constraints on evaluation and negotiating with the entrepreneur.

Fifth, for a significant minority of business angels membership of a BAN is not providing them with a superior quality of investment opportunities (Table 12.3). Whereas 55 per cent of investors considered that some or most of the opportunities that BANs provided were better than those that they saw from other referral sources, more than one-third believed that only a few were superior and almost one in ten investors considered that none of the opportunities that they received from BANs were better than those which they identified from other sources.

Reasons why membership of a BAN appears to have little or no impact on the ability of a significant proportion of business angels to make more

*Table 12.2* Reasons for anticipating difficulties in finding sufficient investment opportunities

| Reason | % of investors |
| --- | --- |
| Lack of match between my investment requirements and the investment proposals that I see | 78 |
| Low quality of investment proposals | 77 |
| Lack of time available to search for investment opportunities | 41 |
| Lack of reliable sources of information on investment opportunities | 40 |
| Lack of time available to evaluate investment opportunities | 27 |
| Lack of suitable co-investors | 18 |
| Lack of time available to negotiate deal structure | 13 |
| Other reasons | 10 |

*Source*: Authors' survey.

*Note*: Based on 78 respondents who anticipated difficulties in finding sufficient investment opportunities that met their investment criteria.

investments can be divided into two broad groups: investor characteristics and network characteristics. First, investor characteristics play a role. As noted earlier, some have very restrictive investment criteria. Others may have unrealistic expectations when assessing the 'quality' of opportunities. However, there was no evidence that those investors who reported that either few or none of the opportunities provided by BANs were better than those that they see from other sources shared any common characteristics or were distinctive in any way: neither were their stated investment preferences particularly restrictive. It should be recalled that angels were making a relative rather than an absolute judgement on the quality of opportunities that they received from BANs. Thus, an alternative explanation is that those angels who considered that most or all of the opportunities they received

*Table 12.3* The opinion of business angels about the quality of the opportunities they receive through BANs

| | % |
| --- | --- |
| *Most* of the opportunities are better than those that I see from other sources | 21 |
| *Some* of the opportunities are better than those that I see from other sources | 34 |
| Only *a few* of the opportunities are better than those that I see from other sources | 36 |
| *None* of the opportunities are better than those that I see from other sources | 9 |

*Source*: Authors' survey.

from BANs were poorer than those they saw from other sources possess a superior network of personal deal referral sources. This interpretation would seem to be strengthened by the fact that most are quite active investors, with a median of three informal venture capital investments.

Second, the evidence that membership of a BAN has little or no impact on the ability of a significant proportion of business angels to make investments may be linked to the characteristics of BANs themselves. It should be noted that individual BANs are not being singled out for criticism here. Indeed, those investors who considered that most or all of the opportunities they received from BANs were poorer than those they saw from other sources were members of a variety of different networks. The overriding problem is that the majority of BANs in the UK lack a critical mass of investment opportunities and investors: 62 per cent have 100 or fewer investors registered and 84 per cent have 100 or fewer investment opportunities available (BVCA, 1997a). This might reflect the limited marketing of the service, perhaps on account of a lack of resources. The lack of critical mass may also arise because some BANs are attempting to operate over too small a geographical territory. Whatever the reason, there will be a knock-on effect on the quality of the investment opportunities that they provide to their investors. BANs which have a limited flow of new investment opportunities are likely to have a lower acceptance threshold, accepting most businesses that wish to register with the network, in order to be able to provide their investors with a flow of new investment opportunities. Clearly, a BAN that does not provide investors with new opportunities is likely to be unable to retain them for long. The same pressure to provide investors with new opportunities on a regular basis also means that BANs which lack a critical mass are likely to show *all* opportunities to investors rather than only those which match investors' investment requirements. The latter approach might have the consequence that investors will receive information on opportunities on only a sporadic basis, reducing the probability that they will renew their membership.

The picture which emerges from these results is therefore one in which most business angels regard the overall quality of investment opportunities that they see as low and providing a poor 'fit' with their investment criteria, even though the volume of opportunities they receive may have increased, for example because of their membership of one or more BANs. In addition, business angels are encountering increased competition for the better-quality opportunities. Moreover, for a significant proportion of business angels, membership of one or more BANs has had little or no impact on increasing the volume of potential investment opportunities.

## Implications for policy and practice

Business angels are the main source of external risk capital for companies at their start-up and early growth stages. Moreover, through their hands-on involvement they also contribute valuable know-how, skills, contacts and support to the businesses in which they invest. However, this market is underdeveloped in Europe, with fewer investors per capita compared to the USA and a high proportion of investors reporting difficulties in finding investment opportunities. Promoting the informal venture capital market should therefore be a central feature of initiatives to increase the supply of venture capital at the earliest stage in the financing spectrum.

In this respect the UK leads the rest of Europe. However, encouraging the informal venture capital market is now on the policy agenda of several other European countries and there are signs that it is becoming recognised at the European level as having an important role to play in SME financing (Hemer, 1995; EBAN, 1998a, 1998b). UK policy has two strands: fiscal measures to increase the supply of informal venture capital and support for intermediary functions in the form of business angel networks to enhance information flows in what is an inefficient market place. This chapter has attempted to provide an assessment of the impact of such measures. The evidence that has been presented leads to the conclusion that both measures can be regarded as having had a positive but somewhat limited effect in stimulating the informal venture capital market in the UK. Fiscal measures to increase the supply of informal venture capital have had some impact, but this has been limited, at least in part, on account of the rules regarding qualifying investments. Some 200 investments a year have been made as a result of the introductions that BANs have facilitated between investors and entrepreneurs seeking finance (BVCA, 1997a), but a significant proportion of business angels are critical of the quality of investment opportunities that they receive from BANs.

Two conclusions can be drawn from the UK's experience of measures to stimulate informal investment activity which have relevance for the rest of Europe. First, the design, implementation and delivery of initiatives have been sub-optimal and this highlights the need for further experimentation and more effective diffusion of best practice. Second, existing measures are inadequate on their own and require to be complemented by other initiatives. This section suggests how the present measures to support informal venture capital in the UK should be built upon to achieve increased informal investment activity.

### Supply side

This chapter has confirmed the importance of the capital gains tax regime as the main influence on the supply of informal venture capital. By making the risk–reward ratio more favourable both EIS and RR have had a positive impact on informal venture capital investment activity, stimulating additional and larger investments. The time limit on re-investing the capital gain has also been useful in making investors look harder for investment opportunities and investing in situations that they would not normally consider. However, at the margin investing under time pressure may lead to sub-optimal decision-making which will reduce the overall impact of the scheme. The scope for RR is also limited because by definition it is restricted to business angels who have a capital gain liability. Beyond this, the potential impact of EIS has been limited by the rules regarding the types of investments and businesses that qualify under EIS, which has prevented investors from using the scheme to make larger investments. The consequence is that EIS has had only a marginal impact on the amounts invested by business angels. The rules have also discouraged investments in technology-based businesses. VCTs, in contrast, have had little impact on business angel investment activity. They have very limited attractiveness to business angels because they do not allow investors to participate in the investment decision or to become involved with the Trust's investee businesses, and are more likely to appeal to passive investors looking for a tax shelter. Moreover, VCTs are concentrating on larger investments in established businesses close to the maximum company size and funding limits because of the higher risk profile and the higher management costs associated with making smaller investments in early-stage businesses. There is also concern that promoters of VCTs are using loopholes and bending the rules in order to develop low-risk investment vehicles that are not within the spirit of the scheme (Guthrie, 1997) to invest in asset-backed businesses in exactly the same way as occurred with the BES.[8] Venture Capital Trusts therefore seems unlikely to have much effect on the supply of equity capital within the 'equity gap'.

These considerations raise the question whether such schemes are the most effective way in which to provide fiscal incentives to business angels. They are complex and costly to administer, restrictions often leave 'worthy' investments outside the scope of the scheme, and the financial services industry seeks to hi-jack such schemes through the creative use of loopholes and rule-bending to subvert them for low-risk investments. The attractiveness of the front-end tax breaks relative to the CGT relief is also uncertain. Moreover, because of the passive nature of managed investment funds, these will not attract genuine business angels. The most straightforward way in which to increase the supply of informal venture capital might therefore be to reduce, or eliminate, capital gains tax, which it has been argued is 'a tax that works directly against efforts to create an enterprise economy' (*Management Today*, 1997).

However, tax incentives for business angels need to be complemented by micro-level initiatives to assist those investors who view investing in unquoted companies as an attractive speculative investment but who, when it comes to the point, are reluctant to invest because they are not sure how to assess potential investments opportunities, undertake the due diligence or structure an investment. Some BANs are addressing these constraints by providing training events, such as 'investment master classes' led by experienced investors. A useful by-product of such events is that they may encourage investors to retain their membership of the BAN even if they are receiving few investment opportunities that meet their requirements. Inexperienced investors might also be encouraged to invest if they were able to join investor syndicates. Here again, some BANs are attempting to encourage the formation of investor syndicates by holding investor clubs. These additional services are valued by a significant minority of business angels, and are likely to have a positive effect on the level of investment activity, but clearly they hold less appeal for experienced investors (Table 12.4).

### Demand side

Policy, by and large, has not focused on measures designed explicitly to stimulate demand for informal venture capital, except as a by-product of improving the visibility of the supply. However, the survey findings clearly indicate that business angels are constrained by the lack of what they perceive to be good-quality investment opportunities. It is therefore essential that initiatives to stimulate informal venture capital activity are not restricted to supply-side measures but also include measures which address demand-side constraints.

There are two main explanations for demand-side constraints. First, very few growth SMEs are *investment ready*, by which it is meant that their 'owners are either not willing to, or do not know how to meet the requirements of external investors' (Marsden Jacob Associates, 1995: 19). Failure to be investment ready is primarily due to information deficiencies.

*Table 12.4* Forms of assistance that increase the ability of business angels to make more investments

|  | *No effect* | *Minor effect* | *Moderate effect* | *Strong effect* |
|---|---|---|---|---|
| Assistance in finding investment opportunities | 7 | 8 | 37 | 49 |
| Opportunities to co-invest with other business angels in a private investors' syndicate | 1 | 35 | 32 | 23 |
| Opportunities to co-invest with venture capital funds | 19 | 26 | 33 | 21 |
| Assistance with evaluating the merits and risks of investment opportunities | 18 | 24 | 35 | 18 |
| Assistance with the pricing and structuring of investments in unquoted companies | 19 | 21 | 41 | 18 |
| Assistance with monitoring the performance of your investments | 46 | 26 | 20 | 8 |

*Source*: Authors' survey.

Entrepreneurs need information on the advantages of attracting external equity capital and what it means to be investment ready, for example, in terms of governance arrangements, management skills and information availability, and how to become investment ready.

Increasing the proportion of growth SMEs that are investment ready is a major task and cannot be left to BANs to address on their own. Certainly, the better BANs in the UK do attempt to bring investment opportunities up to a 'good standard' through their one-to-one counselling sessions with entrepreneurs who contact the network and through the training courses that some BANs run for entrepreneurs. This should become a core activity for all BANs. However, all players in the small business support network, from central government down to Business Links and including banks, accountancy firms other private sector organisations, should be involved in educating entrepreneurs on the advantages of attracting external equity finance and on what is required to attract investors.

Second, there is a need to improve the quality of the SME stock. It is widely argued (for example, CBI, 1997) that there are insufficient incentives to encourage experienced managers in large firms – who have the skills and expertise to grow businesses that reach a significant size – to take the appreciable personal risks inherent in starting or joining a new business. They must weigh up the relative security of employment within a large organisation with its associated financial benefits against the risks of starting or working in a small business, which invariably involves accepting a lower initial salary and the loss of often considerable fringe benefits. Moreover, the entrepreneur is likely to be investing his or her long-term savings in the business and is likely to borrow money against the security of the family home. However, the rules regarding the granting of stock options, and the way in which they are taxed, may not be sufficient to attract experienced large-firm managers to start or join small entrepreneurial ventures (CBI, 1997). The present rate of CGT in the UK, at 40 per cent, is also claimed to be a deterrent to such entrepreneurial behaviour (BVCA, 1996; CBI, 1997). Capital gains tax on the gains made by entrepreneurs when they dispose of their business is a further constraint on the formation of new enterprises with growth potential. Because tax arises on the realisation of a gain there is a disincentive to realise the gain and reinvest the net amount. The effect of CGT liability is therefore to 'lock in' entrepreneurs who have the flair and talent for starting new growth businesses but may not have the necessary managerial skills to nurture successful growth by discouraging them from becoming serial entrepreneurs, forming new companies where they can repeat their success. This is not only a waste of their talents but is also detrimental to the company. The BVCA (1996) has proposed an 'entrepreneur's relief' which exempts entrepreneurs from CGT on the gains made on the disposal of their business.

Third, it is widely argued that there are insufficient incentives for entrepreneurs to seek equity capital to start and grow their businesses. The tax system should therefore avoid favouring debt finance over equity finance. Arguably, there is a need for incentives to encourage SMEs that would benefit from an injection of equity finance to seek out sources of supply. At present all the incentives to promote an equity culture are on the investor's side. One approach which should be explored is to introduce an 'equity allowance', equivalent to existing capital allowances, for unquoted companies that raise equity finance, which they could use to set against their tax liabilities (Mason and Harrison, 1995b). Both the BVCA (1996b) and CBI (1997) have proposed that unquoted companies should be able to deduct the costs of raising equity finance. However, this is more relevant in raising venture capital from institutional sources, where printing costs, travel expenses and professional fees are likely to be significant. The costs incurred by business angels and entrepreneurs in making an informal venture capital investment are much lower (Mason and Harrison, 1996a).

BANs must also become proactive in recruiting growth potential businesses seeking equity capital. They must develop strategies for identifying businesses that are likely to be attractive to investors on account of their growth potential and will benefit from the injection of business angel finance and expertise. Technology-based firms are one category of business which is likely to have a need for equity finance and also has the potential to generate significant returns to investors. BANs should therefore work closely with business incubators (Enterprise Panel, 1996) and technology commercialisation officers in universities. Some BANs have found that developing partnerships with the clearing banks has been a successful strategy.

Finally, closer co-operation between the informal and formal venture capital markets is required in view of the various complementarities that exist between business angels and venture capital funds. Many of the proposals received by venture capital funds are rejected not on quality grounds but because they do not pass their 'firm-specific' screening (Fried and Hisrich, 1994). For example, many proposals are rejected because the size of investment sought is too small and therefore uneconomic for the fund. However, business angels do not cost their time in the same way as an investment manager in a venture capital fund and so are able to consider opportunities that are too small to be of interest to a venture capital fund. Moreover, proposals which are explicitly rejected by venture capital fund managers may nevertheless be attractive to business angels. They may, for example, be prepared to invest in businesses where the prospective return is too low for a venture capital fund or where a gap in the expertise of the management team deters the venture capital fund from investing but the business angel is able to fill it. BANs should therefore establish close links with venture capital funds to develop mechanisms which enable proposals that are rejected by funds to be recycled for consideration by business angels.

## Intermediation

Successful stimulation of the supply of, and demand for, informal venture capital leaves the problem of bringing the two sides together, without which investments will not happen. The informal venture capital market is disorganised and fragmented, with high search costs for potential investors and entrepreneurs seeking finance. As Gaston (1989: 1) comments: 'the search for an angel can be an expensive, time-consuming, hit-or-miss affair . . . studded with pitfalls and dead ends that often result in failure and frustration.' This situation has a discouraging effect on both potential investors and would-be entrepreneurs, with society bearing the cost of these lost opportunities to establish new ventures or expand existing ones (Wetzel, 1986).

BANs are an attempt to overcome these difficulties and they have had some success in stimulating informal venture capital activity. Moreover, their cost-effectiveness in terms of the return to the tax payer has been impressive. BANs should be regarded as an essential element in the small business support infrastructure. However, they cannot be expected to recoup all of their costs through fees, even when success fees are levied.[9] But without a realistic level of public sector funding – which is extremely modest compared with other business support and more cost-effective and justifiable in terms of the social benefits of enabling small companies to raise risk capital – BANs will not be effective in stimulating the supply of and demand for informal venture capital and in providing introductions and facilitating investments. The need for BANs to become more proactive in marketing their service to businesses and to develop educational activities in order to increase their effectiveness in facilitating investments has been identified earlier as essential in raising their effectiveness. However, this adds to the costs of running a network. Governments must therefore accept the need to provide BANs with a realistic and ongoing level of funding in order for them to be effective in stimulating an increase in informal venture capital investment activity.

There are a number of factors that appear to be associated with successful BANs, some of which have been alluded to in this chapter. They include the level of resourcing, marketing and promotion of the service, involvement in the match-making process, type of host organisation, quality of staff and geographical location (Mason and Harrison 1995a, 1996b, 1996c; Brown and Stowe, 1996; Blatt and Riding, 1996; Wetzel and Freear, 1996). However, the single most important prerequisite for success is the development of a critical mass of investors and investment opportunities. It is likely that the dissatisfaction of many business angels with the investment opportunities provided by BANs and the limited number of investments of many BANs is to a large degree a function of the failure of most UK BANs to achieve critical mass. At least two implications follow. First, there is a need for BANs to devote considerable energy, creativity and resources to the ongoing marketing of the service to potential investors and entrepreneurs. Second, the geographical scale of operation is a key strategic decision for a BAN. There has been a long-standing debate in the UK concerning whether a single national service would be more effective than the present situation of various local/regional BANs co-existing alongside some national BANs. The predominantly local nature of the informal venture capital market, with most investors preferring to invest in businesses within about one to two hours driving time from their home, allied to the need for personalised approaches to marketing, would seem to favour either 'local' services, or else a national network with localised delivery. The operating territory of BANs must be sufficiently large to be able to attract a critical mass of investors and investment opportunities, but not too large, otherwise many investors will receive details of opportunities that they reject on distance grounds. Indeed, some of the longer-established Business Link BANs have recognised the need to operate on a 'regional' rather than a local basis and have therefore enlarged their operating area by collaborating with neighbouring Business Links (Mason and Harrison, 1995b). However, a significant minority of investors have no geographical limitations on their investment preferences (Coveney and Moore, 1998), and there are some types of businesses (for example, high-tech, those seeking larger amounts of finance) which have relatively fewer potential investors and so may require to undertake a more extensive spatial search for investors. Consequently, it is essential that local/regional BANs develop networking arrangements to enable the wider circulation of investment opportunities in appropriate circumstances.

## Conclusion

There is widespread consensus across Europe for the goal of creating a thriving SME sector. Within this broad objective there is a more specific goal, which again has a high degree of unanimity, to generate more growing businesses. This requires a range of complementary initiatives, of which the availability of venture capital, along with managerial ability, is key. This chapter has drawn attention to the important role of the informal venture capital market in the entrepreneurial process in providing both small amounts of risk capital for early-stage businesses and also management advice and know-how through the involvement of investors in the businesses in which they invest. However, in the current debate in Europe which links job creation with the availability of risk capital, the significance of the informal venture capital market is downplayed, and instead policy initiatives have concentrated on increasing the number of early-stage venture capital funds, despite the limitations of this approach (Mason and Harrison, 1995a; Murray, 1998; Murray and Marriot, 1998). The argument in this chapter is that initiatives to stimulate informal venture capital activity is an essential component in any strategy to increase the level of entrepreneurial activity in Europe.

This chapter has provided a critical review of the effectiveness of the fiscal and intermediation initiatives that have been introduced in the UK to stimulate informal venture capital activity with a view to highlighting what other European countries can learn when implementing their own initiatives. It has concluded that these initiatives have had positive, if somewhat modest, results. It has drawn attention to some of the shortcomings in design and implementation which can be linked to these sub-optimal outcomes and, in the final section, has proposed changes to existing UK initiatives and recommended a range of additional initiatives. There is a strong case for further initiatives to promote informal venture capital in the UK, and for replicating these and additional measures across the EU. Implementation of this policy agenda will result in a significant increase in informal venture capital activity over the medium-term and this, in turn, will generate substantial additional entrepreneurial activity.

## Notes

1   In a further 11 per cent of cases business angels and venture capital funds participated in the same round of financing.
2   Limitations on the length of this chapter prevent the survey findings from being reported in full: see Mason and Harrison (1997a) for a more detailed account.
3   In order to keep the names and addresses of their investors confidential, BANs were supplied with stamped envelopes containing the questionnaire, covering letter and FREEPOST reply envelope which they addressed and posted to their investors.
4   We do not have any information to indicate whether these investments went ahead without using EIS.
5   The March 1998 Budget has combined Re-investment Relief with EIS.
6   In the period August 1995 to September 1997 over £360 million was raised by 18 VCTs, of which £90.6 has been invested. However, only 16 per cent of the amount invested has been in early-stage businesses (Bank of England, 1997).
7   Those investors who gave the seemingly paradoxical response that a high rate of capital gains tax would *encourage* them to make investments explained that this is because they would be more inclined in such circumstances to use the various tax reliefs available.
8   The March 1998 Budget excluded the following types of property-backed investments from being eligible for investments by VCTs and through the EIS: nursing homes, hotels, forestry and farming, and property development.
9   Success fees add to the costs of running a BAN because of the need to monitor introductions over a period of time; any investments which result may not occur for several months. Some BANs have also reported they have sometimes been unsuccessful in extracting success fees from business clients.

## References

Aernoudt, R. (1999) 'European policy towards venture capital: myth or reality?', *Venture Capital: An International Journal of Entrepreneurial Finance*, 1, 47–57.
Bank of England (1997) *Quarterly Report on Small Business Statistics*, London: Industry Finance Division, Bank of England, December.
Benjamin, G.A. and Margulis, J. (1996) *Finding Your Wings: How to Locate Private Investors to Fund Your Business*, New York: John Wiley.
Blatt, R. and Riding, A. (1996) '" . . . Where angels fear to tread": some lessons

from the Canada Opportunities Investment Network experience', in R.T. Harrison and C.M. Mason (eds), *Informal Venture Capital: Evaluating the Impact of Business Introduction Services*, Hemel Hempstead: Woodhead-Faulkner/ Prentice-Hall, pp 75–88.

British Venture Capital Association (BVCA) (1996) *Taxation of Enterprise 1996/7*, London: British Venture Capital Association.

British Venture Capital Association (BVCA) (1997a) *Sources of Business Angel Capital 1997/98*, London: British Venture Capital Association.

British Venture Capital Association (BVCA) (1997b) *Report on Business Angel Investment Activity 1996/97*, London: British Venture Capital Association.

Brown, D.J. and Stowe, C.R.B. (1996) 'Private venture capital networks in the United States', in R.T. Harrison and C.M. Mason (eds), *Informal Venture Capital: Evaluating the Impact of Business Introduction Services*, Hemel Hempstead: Prentice-Hall, pp. 101–15.

Commission of the European Communities (1998) *Risk Capital: A Key to Job Creation in the European Union*, Luxembourg: Office for Official Publications of the European Communities.

Confederation of British Industry (CBI) (1997) *Tech Stars: Breaking the Growth Barriers for Technology-based SMEs*, London: Confederation of British Industry.

Coveney, P. and Moore, K. (1998) *Business Angels: Securing Start-up Finance*, Chichester: John Wiley.

EBAN (1998a) *Dissemination Report on the Potential for Business Angels Investment and Networks in Europe*, Truro, Cornwall: South West Investment Group.

EBAN (1998b) *Country Reports*, Truro, Cornwall: South West Investment Group.

Enterprise Panel (1996) *Growing Success: Helping Companies to Generate Wealth and Create Jobs Through Business Incubation*, London: Midland Bank.

European Venture Capital Association (EVCA) (1997) *Yearbook 1997*, Zaventem, Belgium: European Venture Capital Association.

Freear, J. and Wetzel, W.E. Jr (1989) 'Equity capital for investors', in R.H. Brockhaus Sr, N.C. Churchill, J.A. Katz, B.A. Kirchhoff, K.H. Vesper and W.E. Wetzel, Jr (eds), *Frontiers of Entrepreneurship Research*, Wellesley, MA: Babson College, pp. 230–44.

Freear, J., Sohl, J.E. and Wetzel, W.E. Jr (1995) 'Angels: personal investors in the venture capital market', *Entrepreneurship and Regional Development*, 7, 85–94.

Fried, V.H. and Hisrich, R.D. (1994) 'Toward a model of venture capital investment decision-making', *Financial Management*, 23 (3), 28–37.

Gaston, R.J. (1989) *Finding Private Venture Capital for Your Firm: A Complete Guide*, New York: John Wiley.

Guthrie, J. (1997) 'Venture capital trusts: too safe by far?', *Financial Times: Weekend Money*, 1–2 February, III.

Harrison, R.T. and Mason, C.M. (1992) 'International perspectives on the supply of informal venture capital', *Journal of Business Venturing*, 7, 459–75.

Harrison, R.T. and Mason, C.M. (1996a) 'Developments in the promotion of informal venture capital in the UK', in R. Cressy, B. Gandemo and C. Olofsson (eds), *Financing SMEs: A Comparative Perspective*, Stockholm: NUTEK, pp. 127–62.

Harrison, R.T. and Mason, C.M. (1996b) 'Developing the informal venture capital market: a review of the Department of Trade and Industry's Informal Investment Demonstration Projects', *Regional Studies*, 30, 765–72.

Hemer, J. (1995) 'Technology and market risks and their assessment', background paper to the EIMS Innovation Policy Workshop on Innovation Financing: Private Investors, Banks and Technology Appraisal, Luxembourg, 14–15 December.

HM Government (1995) *Competitiveness: Forging Ahead*, Cm 2867, London: HMSO.

International Informal Venture Capital Research Network (IIVCRN) (1996) *Newsletter*, 4, Southampton: Department of Geography, University of Southampton.

K+V organisatie adviesbureau bv/Entrepreneurial Holding bv (1996) *The Role of Informal Investors in the Dutch Venture Capital Market*, Arnhem: K+V organisatie adviesbureau bv.

Landström, H. (1993) 'Informal risk capital in Sweden and some international comparisons', *Journal of Business Venturing*, 8, 525–40.

Landström, H. and Olofsson, C. (1996) 'Informal venture capital in Sweden', in R.T. Harrison and C.M. Mason (eds), *Informal Venture Capital: Evaluating the Impact of Business Introduction Services*, Hemel Hempstead: Prentice-Hall/Woodhead Faulkner, pp. 273–85.

Lumme, A., Mason, C. and Suomi, M. (1998) *Informal Venture Capital: Investors, Investments and Policy Issues in Finland*, Dordrecht: Kluwer.

*Management Today* (1997) 'A chance for a canny chancellor', February, 3.

Marsden Jacob Associates (1995) *Financing Growth: Policy Options to Improve the Flow of Capital to Australia's Small and Medium-sized Enterprises*, Canberra: National Investment Council.

Mason, C.M. and Harrison, R.T. (1993) *Increasing the Supply of Informal Venture Capital: A Guide to Setting-up a Business Introduction Service*, Sheffield: Department of Trade and Industry, Small Firms Policy Branch.

Mason, C.M. and Harrison, R.T. (1994) 'The informal venture capital market in the UK', in A. Hughes and D.J. Storey (eds), *Financing Small Firms*, London: Routledge, pp. 64–111.

Mason, C.M. and Harrison, R.T. (1995a) 'Closing the regional equity gap: the role of informal venture capital', *Small Business Economics*, 7, 153–72.

Mason, C.M. and Harrison, R.T. (1995b) *Final Review and Evaluation of Five Informal Investment Demonstration Projects*, Sheffield: Small Firms Policy Branch, Department of Trade and Industry.

Mason, C.M. and Harrison, R.T. (1996a) 'Informal venture capital: a study of the investment process and post-investment experience', *Entrepreneurship and Regional Development*, 9, 105–26.

Mason, C.M. and Harrison, R.T. (1996b) 'Informal investment business introduction services: some operational considerations', in R.T. Harrison and C.M. Mason (eds), *Informal Venture Capital: Evaluating the Impact of Business Introduction Services*, Hemel Hempstead: Prentice-Hall, pp. 27–58.

Mason, C.M. and Harrison, R.T. (1996c) 'The Department of Trade and Industry's informal demonstration projects: an interim assessment', in R.T. Harrison and C.M. Mason (eds), *Informal Venture Capital: Evaluating the Impact of Business Introduction Services*, Hemel Hempstead: Woodhead-Faulkner/Prentice-Hall, pp. 248–72.

Mason, C.M. and Harrison, R.T. (1997a) *Supporting the Informal Venture Capital Market: What Still Needs to Be Done?*, Venture Finance Working Paper no. 15, Southampton: University of Southampton.

Mason, C.M. and Harrison, R.T. (1997b) 'Business angel networks and the development of the informal venture capital market in the UK: is there still a role for the public sector?', *Small Business Economics*, 9, 111–23.

Murray, G. (1998) 'A policy response to regional disparities in risk capital to new technology-based firms in the European Union: the European Seed Capital Fund Scheme', *Regional Studies*, 32, 405–19.

Murray, G. and Marriot, R. (1998) 'Modelling the economic viability of an early-stage, technology focused, venture capital fund', in R.Oakey and W. During (eds), *New Technology-based Firms in the 1990s*, vol. 5, London: Paul Chapman, pp. 97–121.

Unwin, Sir B. (1998) 'New policies on venture capital from the EIB/EIF', presentation to a UK Presidency of the European Union conference on 'Venture Capital, Growth and Employment in the European Union', 2 June, Guildhall, London.

van Osnabrugge, M. (1998) *Comparison of Business Angels and Venture Capitalists: Financiers of Entrepreneurial Firms*, Oxford: Venture Capital Report.

Wetzel, W.E. Jr (1983) 'Angels and informal risk capital', *Sloan Management Review*, 24, 23–34.

Wetzel, W.E. Jr (1986) 'Entrepreneurs, angels and economic renaissance', in R.D. Hisrich (ed.), *Entrepreneurship, Intrapreneurship and Venture Capital*, Lexington, MA: Lexington Books, pp. 119–39.

Wetzel, W.E. Jr (1987) 'The informal venture capital market: aspects of scale and market efficiency', *Journal of Business Venturing*, 2, 299–313.

Wetzel, W.E. Jr and Freear, J. (1996) 'Promoting informal venture capital in the United States: reflections on the history of the Venture Capital Network', in R.T. Harrison and C.M. Mason (eds), *Informal Venture Capital: Evaluating the Impact of Business Introduction Services*, Hemel Hempstead: Prentice-Hall, pp. 61–74.

# 13 The liability of small-scale investment

## A simulation model of the performance of an early-stage, technology-focused, venture capital fund

*Gordon Murray and Richard Marriott**

## Introduction

### Industry context and policy interests

Policy measures to improve the formation and growth rates of new technology-based firms (NTBFs) are increasingly popular in developed economies world wide. NTBFs have come to be recognised as a potentially important constituent of an innovative and advanced economy. However, growing government interest and intervention is also a recognition that technology-based businesses face particular difficulties. Provision of finance through established capital markets for these young enterprises, which by definition are highly speculative, frequently remains problematic. The traditional sources of finance for young firms at start-up, namely the entrepreneur (and his/her family and friends) usually followed by collateral-based bank debt, may be either insufficient or inappropriate to exploit fully the rapid growth potential of an attractive and novel technological product or service (Moore, 1993).

In these circumstances, the provision of risk capital by venture capital firms may be the most suitable form of external finance. However, outside the United States and a number of advanced Western economies, notably the United Kingdom, the venture capital industries of many countries remain immature and inexperienced. In addition, with the singular exception of the United States, the greater the experience of a venture capital sector, the more the tendency of the incumbent venture capital firms and their institutional

*    The authors would like to thank both the Department of Industry, Science and Technology and the Department of Workplace Relations and Small Business of the Federal Government of Australia for their sponsorship of this research. The collaboration of the Australian Technology Group and Nanyang Securities, Sydney, is also gratefully acknowledged. The views expressed remain solely those of the authors.

investors to move towards a preference for larger and less risky 'development capital'[1] deals. This has led to the situation where potentially attractive NTBFs have seen constraints placed on the availability of, particularly, longer-term risk capital. This capital scarcity has potentially serious, adverse consequences for the NTBFs' rate of growth. This phenomenon has been termed 'the equity gap'[2] (Macmillan, 1931).

A vigorous and growing community of NTBFs within an economy may produce significant 'externalities' of interest to government. This is in addition to any benefits reaped by the commercial investors in such firms. Accordingly, governments are frequently prepared to provide a range of incentives or subsidies to ensure that sufficient finance and support are made available to early-stage investments in technology-based, young firms. The alleviation or attenuation of market failure frequently becomes the economic rationale for such state interventions.

One major constraint to the supply of long-term or risk capital to NTBFs is the apparent inability of technology-focused, venture capital funds to provide attractive returns to their investors. Both the UK and European performance statistics indicate that early-stage investments have generated the lowest level of returns of any stage of venture capital finance. This raises the question as to whether *successful* investment in NTBFs is a peculiarly American[3] phenomenon. *In extremis*, is it solely a West or East Coast phenomenon? These are questions of profound importance regarding both industry and technology policy for many countries.

### A European Commission response

Small and medium enterprises (SMEs) have assumed a growing influence in the policy actions and instruments of the European Commission. This interest has come about through an increasing recognition of the major contribution of SMEs to total employment and to the net creation of new jobs (see Birch, 1979; Gallagher and Stewart, 1986; Storey *et al.*, 1989). SMEs are now firmly established as a major focus of the Commission's economic, technological and regional policies. This interest may also be superficially evidenced by the fact that there exists one Directorate General (DG XXIII[4]) with a specific remit to promote the interests of the 13 million SMEs in the Union. However, the actual or potential influence of SMEs impacts across a wide range of other DGs, notably DG XVI (Regional Policy) and DG XIII (Innovation).

The publication, *European Industrial Policy for the 1990s* (European Commission, 1991) notes the failure of European firms to bring high-technology, innovative products to the market as speedily as competitor nations (pp. 31 and 33). The document signals the shortage of small firms (that is, new technology-based firms) available to exploit and commercialise innovations in Europe. The problems of finance for these firms is also observed. However, no specific policy prescriptions relating to finance are tendered.

The subsequent White Paper *Growth and Employment: The Challenges and Ways Forward into the 21st Century* (European Commission, 1994) re-iterates both the need for more European NTBFs and policy makers' concerns that Europe does not convert sufficient of its science and technology base into commercially successful products and services. The validity of the American exemplar, particularly the positive impact of new (high-tech) firm formation on aggregate employment, is also again acknowledged. Specifically, the White Paper notes 'the lack of risk capital to help firms through the development phase and the reluctance of private-sector financiers to invest in activities if they consider the risks too great or the returns too uncertain' (p. 102).

It was left to the considerably more focused and bolder *Green Paper on Innovation* (European Commission, 1995) to articulate specific policies to address the perceived problem of Europe's weaker innovative infrastructure compared to the Japanese and, above all, the Americans. Acknowledging the importance of an appropriate financial environment, the Green Paper describes in detail a series of barriers to innovation in a section entitled: 'Problems with Financing: a) Financial Systems which Avoid Innovation' (p. 39). With rare candour the document observes 'that the European inno-vations system is full of holes'. Existing financial institutions, uncertainties and limits to public financing and an unfavourable European tax regime are seen to be the greatest financial barriers to innovation. Thirteen 'actions' are presented for discussion, with Action 6 proposing ten recommendations at national and/or Community level (pp. 52–3). Within the venture fund context of this paper, relevant Commission actions to promote the genesis and development of NTBFs included 'acquiring holdings in venture risk intermediaries' or 'the possible support of the creation of multi-national new seed capital funds'.

The *First Action Plan for Innovation in Europe* (European Commission, 1997) was the end result of the discussion process stemming from the Green Paper. Under the second of the three major foci of the First Action Plan, 'Establishing a Favourable Framework for Innovation', the Commission com-mitted itself to reinforcing European Investment Fund action in favour of inno-vation and co-operation between the European Investment Bank and the Structural Funds. The first tangible outcome of this statement was the launch in 1997 of the *Innovation and Technology Equity Capital* (I-TEC) scheme.

I-TEC explicitly recognises the additional costs in making early-stage venture capital investments in unproven NTBFs. Accordingly, a new or established venture capital fund which will contract to allocate at least 25 per cent of new capital raised to early-stage investments in a minimum of five technologically innovative SMEs can obtain up to a total of ECU500,000 in grant. This sum must be employed to defray the peculiar, additional costs to the investor of initial appraisal and 'hands-on' management of NTBF investee firms. I-TEC was announced in 1997. By the end of that year, nine venture capital funds had entered the Scheme, providing a potential extra source of risk capital of ECU186 million exclusively for early-stage, high-tech investments (*Innovation & Technology Transfer*, 1/98, p. 9).

It is interesting to note that, while the I-TEC scheme owes much to the political commitment engendered by Edith Cresson (the Commissioner responsible for DG XIII) via the vehicles of the Green Paper and Action Plan, the actual logic and operation of the new scheme was very heavily based on the experience the Commission gained from the European Seed Capital Fund Scheme (Murray, 1998). This 'pilot action' (1988–95) was sponsored by DG XXIII and DG XVI, and not by DG XIII. The ESCF scheme was the first European initiative to address the peculiar scale-related, cost problems of exceptional information search and investee governance which are experienced by early-stage technology venture funds. This issue is central to the present paper.

### Genesis and growth of the venture capital industry

The modern venture capital industry, starting from its post-war roots in East Coast America (Fenn *et al.*, 1995), has grown to become a significant element of the corporate financial services sector in virtually every major economy. The concept of speculative, but potentially well rewarded, equity investments (risk capital) in rapidly growing, unquoted companies has become increasingly popular with aggressively ambitious owner-managers and institutional investors alike. Venture capital firms have mushroomed not only in the traditional western economies of North America and Europe but also in the Pacific Rim and, latterly, the former Soviet-controlled states of central and eastern Europe.

While the USA continues to have the largest and longest-established venture capital industry, Europe, and particularly the United Kingdom, has similarly developed its own style of venture capital activity. European investment at nearly ECU7 billion in 1996 (EVCA, 1997) is now of a scale broadly equivalent in terms of the funds raised and invested each year to the United States. The growth that has characterised the US industry is also evident across the Atlantic (see Figure 13.1). Both regions have recently achieved record venture capital investment activity with the USA and the UK having invested $10.0 billion and £2.8 billion, respectively, in 1996.

### Demise of early-stage investment activity

As the European venture capital industries have grown in the scale and number of financing transactions, the nature of their investment activity has significantly changed. Over time, the 'venturing' aspect of this investment with its concentration on start-up and early-stage businesses has declined. Instead, this so-called 'classic venture capital' has given way to a predominant interest in later-stage or 'merchant capital' deals (Bygrave and Timmons, 1992). Classic venture capital focuses on very young enterprises

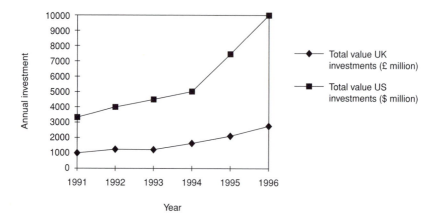

*Figure 13.1* The growth of UK and US venture capital investments, 1991–6
*Source*: BCVA and NVCA *Annual Statistics, 1977.*

with a high but risky potential for substantial sales and profit growth – what Storey *et al.* (1989) term 'fast trackers'. They will invariably represent a very small minority of all firm starts in an economy. In marked contrast, merchant capitalists concentrate on the considerably less risky refinancing of existing and established businesses. Financing management buy-outs and buy-ins (MBOs/MBIs) is the most popular and profitable activity within this latter category (see Table 13.1).

The magnitude of the trend away from start-up and early-stage investments has most clearly been seen in the dominant UK industry within Europe. However, with few exceptions (of which the United States is the most notable), this demise of early-stage investment can be viewed as the

*Table 13.1* Distribution of annual investments by 16 country members of the European venture capital industry, 1994–6

| Stages of venture capital investment | 1994 | | 1995 | | 1996 | |
|---|---|---|---|---|---|---|
| | *ECU million* | *% total* | *ECU million* | *% total* | *ECU million* | *% total* |
| Seed | 37.1 | 0.7 | 34.4 | 0.6 | 55.2 | 0.8 |
| Start-up | 273.3 | 5.0 | 286.5 | 5.2 | 385.8 | 5.7 |
| Expansion | 2,294.2 | 42.2 | 2,298.6 | 41.4 | 2,650.0 | 39.3 |
| Replacement | 434.1 | 8.0 | 354.5 | 6.4 | 653.3 | 9.7 |
| MBO/MBI | 2401.0 | 44.1 | 2,572.0 | 46.4 | 3,007.3 | 44.5 |
| Total investment | 5,440.0 | 100.0 | 5,546.0 | 100.0 | 6,751.6 | 100.0 |

Source: EVCA, 1996

prevalent mode of behaviour by venture capital sectors as they become established. Based on investment experience and a greater appreciation of the difficulties and costs of early-stage investment, maturing venture capital sectors appear to become more risk averse over time. This phenomenon embraces countries as far apart as Australia and Austria.

## Old and new worlds – old and new investments

It is the ability of the US venture capital industry to continue to invest predominantly in young, and as yet unestablished, technology-based enterprises which differentiates it so dramatically from its major European counterparts. This is in part a categorisation issue. The USA does not include refinancing and restructuring type acquisitions, commonly termed 'leveraged buy-outs', within the rubric of venture capital. However, this explanation is not sufficient. When these statistics are removed from country comparison, the US venture capital industry remains significantly more involved in technology-based investment activity than its European counterparts (see Figure 13.2).

The Bank of England in its 1996 report *The Financing of Technology Based Small Firms* specifically noted the very small proportion of monies that were allocated to seed and very early-stage, venture capital investments in the UK. The Bank also observed that this equity financing gap occurred at the most critical, early-growth stages for young entrepreneurial companies with potentially attractive technology ideas and future products/services but with insufficient track record or income with which to secure more traditional financial support such as bank debt.

## The value of new technology-based firms

For that minority of UK venture capital firms which are prepared to invest in start-up and early-stage ventures, very demanding investment 'hurdles' are imposed on those investee firms seeking their financial support. It is not uncommon for performance requirements to be of the order of 60 per cent per annum internal rates of return (Murray and Lott, 1995). Accordingly, in practice, the terms 'start-up' and 'early-stage' have largely come to mean investments in NTBFs by specialist venture capital firms. NTBFs may be defined by their high levels of investment in R&D as a percentage of sales and their predominance of 'knowledge workers' within the labour force (OECD, 1986; Butchart, 1987). Fontes and Coombs (1997) more generally define NTBFs as 'young independent firms involved in the development and/or diffusion of new technologies'. Despite the considerable risks and uncertainties of technology-based investments (see below), the 'upside' to the investors is the highly attractive prospect of investing in a firm with new and proprietary technology and which may come to command a dominant presence in large, profitable and rapidly growing international markets.

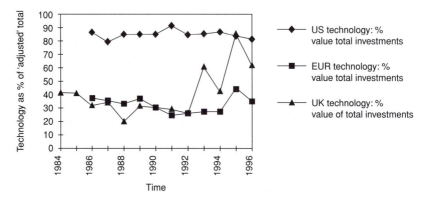

*Figure 13.2* Value of technology investments as a percentage of 'adjusted' total value (that is, excluding MBOs/MBIs in the UK and Europe and LBOs/acquisitions in the US) by venture capital industries, 1984–96

*Source*: BVCA, EVCA and NVCA *Yearbooks, 1977.*

*Note*: The marked increase in technology investments in the UK post-1992 is likely to be overstated, reflecting the difficulties of accurately classifying technology.

Further (but of no rational economic interest to professional, private sector investors), within the wider corpus of small and medium sized enterprises, NTBFs represent a peculiarly attractive focus for policy-makers. They are seen as offering significant potential benefits in four cardinal areas of governmental interest: employment creation, innovation, export sales growth and regional development (Rothwell and Zegveld, 1982; Freeman, 1983; OECD, 1986; Oakey *et al.*, 1988; Rothwell, 1989; Roberts, 1991; Coopers & Lybrand, 1996; Branscombe and Florida, 1997). This interest in NTBFs has in part stemmed from a widespread appreciation of their critical role from the early 1970s in the economic growth of regions of high-technology activity in the USA, particularly Silicon Valley, California, and Route 128 around Boston, Massachusetts (Oakey, 1984; Florida and Kenny, 1988; Roberts, 1991; Bygrave and Timmons, 1992; *The Economist* supplement on Silicon Valley, 29 March 1997), as well as their contribution to fast growth European regions (Meyer-Kramer, 1985; Keeble, 1989).

However, while successful NTBFs potentially offer material advantages to the host economy, their genesis and early years are potentially fraught with extremely high levels of uncertainty and risk in virtually all areas of activity including financing, technology and marketing (Huntsman and Hoban, 1980; Oakey, 1984; Sahlman, 1990; Roberts, 1991; Murray, 1995, 1998). For the individual NTBF, an exceptional technological offering is a necessary but not sufficient condition for economic success. Their entrepreneurial founders have also to manage organisational and product/market demands in both internal and external environments characterised by their complexity and rapid rates of change. Early-stage investment by venture capitalists is often termed 'capital and consulting'. Venture capitalists have come to appreciate both the uncertainties and very long odds of picking future technology winners. They have also had to accept the often very high level of governance-related costs of supporting young companies and their management teams through the early, and often difficult, stages of firm formation and growth.

### A renaissance for new technology-based firms?

As contemporary statistics for both UK and pan-European investments indicate, there have been some moves since 1993 towards a greater proportional involvement in early-stage and technology-based investments. In explaining this change, it is likely that both 'pull' and 'push' factors are at work. The very marked increase in the value of technology stocks on the dominant US 'small caps' market, NASDAQ, has underscored the attractions to investors of big technology 'hits' such as Netscape Communications Amazon.com and Yahoo! The opportunity to invest in the earliest years of what might be one of the dominant companies of the next millennium is a very attractive prospect despite the associated uncertainties.

Within the rapidly maturing European markets, lucrative MBO/MBI opportunities may no longer be available to other than a small number of entrenched and very large venture capital companies (Murray, 1995). The atomistic structure and information imperfections in the capital markets for start-up and young companies are such as to reduce the ability of a few providers of capital to dominate this market in a manner similar to that for MBOs/MBIs. In addition, Europe has seen a record growth in the value of new funds raised by venture capital firms. Since 1992, the level of funds raised by independent venture capital firms has increased by 52 per cent to a cumulative ECU58.6 billion in 1996 (EVCA, 1997). This creates considerable supply-side pressures on the recipient venture capital firms to invest finances on a regular base. This need may additionally have helped trigger a reappraisal of classic venture capital activity.

However, it would be unwise to infer from this partial evidence that a problem no longer exists for young companies seeking equity support. Particularly, the statistics available from the venture capital industries in Europe are highly variable in quality.[5] The increase seen in the number of technology investments in the UK is not mirrored in a commensurate increase in the proportionate value of financings at the earliest stages of investment categories. Early-stage financings have virtually remained constant at 5 per cent of total investment in the UK since 1993. The same is broadly true of continental Europe. This suggests that the broad definitions of technology investments used in the annual BVCA statistics are rather less related to novel, speculative technologies and new businesses than would at first be assumed.

# Factors in the demise of early-stage technology investments

### *Venture capital fund performance*

The comparative evaluation of the performance of venture capital firms as the agents managing term funds into which institutional investors have allocated finance is fraught with difficulties. Given the relative youth of the European industry, which did not reach a critical mass of investments until approximately the mid-1980s, the ability to evaluate the common form of ten-year closed funds has not been available until the last couple of years. Technical issues of interim capital gains, annual yields, provisions and write-offs and, particularly, tax treatments have made the constructing of an evaluation process both a theoretical and political minefield. However, the adoption by the BVCA and the EVCA of agreed industry valuation guidelines for unquoted portfolio companies has significantly assisted in the production of credible performance figures. It is likely that the rigour of these figures will increase over time (see Table 13.2).

What these fund performance figures have indicated unequivocally is that the historic returns to early-stage investments have been dramatically poorer than those allocated to later-stage, and less risky, alternatives – particularly MBO/MBI deals. Whatever the reason, the attraction of technology investments to US venture capitalists (record average returns to US venture capitalists of 41 per cent per annum were achieved in 1996, see *Red Herring*, December 1997, citing Venture Economics Inc.), their economically rational European equivalent has been correct to eschew such investments. And this is exactly how European venture capitalists have behaved until very recently.

### *The two tyrannies*

The challenge and difficulties of investing in NTBFs may be described with reference to 'two tyrannies': (i), project risk and, for the majority of small, specialist, early-stage technology, venture capital funds, (ii), the diseconomies of small size.

*Table 13.2* Mature European private equity funds pooled internal rates of return (IRR per cent) by stage of investment: cumulative net IRRs from inception to 31 December 1996

| Fund type | Sample size (no. of funds) | Pooled IRR(%) | Median IRR(%) |
|---|---|---|---|
| Early-stage | 27 | 25.7 | 4.5 |
| Development | 60 | 37.3 | 5.4 |
| MBOs/MBIs | 67 | 17.6 | 15.5 |
| Generalist | 48 | 19.4 | 1.3 |

Source: EVCA, 1997 (reporting a Venture Economics/Bannock Consulting study).

*Tyranny I: Project risk*

Professional investors are at their most vulnerable to 'adverse selection' problems at the earliest stage of investment in the life cycle of a new enterprise (Amit *et al.*, 1992). *In extremis*, an early-stage, technology investment will require the venture capitalist to come to a formal view on the economic attraction of:

a technology that has not been proven; which is to be incorporated into novel products and/or services which remain, as yet, solely in the mind of the entrepreneur; and will be eventually offered to markets and customers whose existence presently remains purely hypothetical. On top of these uncertainties, the new enterprise may not uncommonly be managed by a technological entrepreneur or a founding team whose experience of commercial practices and disciplines is negligible.

It is for these reasons that the venture capitalist has little choice other than to be highly 'hands on' or interventionist in his/her relationship with the management of the investee firm. Payments to the new venture will commonly be staged and will each be conditional on meeting mutually agreed performance and/or development deadlines. The initial and subsequent rounds of investment may be seen as the venture capitalist taking out and exercising a number of 'real options' to invest in the new business

---

**The first tyranny: project risk**

- Exceptional technical entrepreneurs are rarely competent business persons – they're frequently commercially naïve boffins.
- Project assessment and due diligence is highly problematic in areas concerning 'leading edge' technologies.
- Uncertainty is compounded by the need to analyse both technological feasibility and the existence of a sufficiently large and attractive market (often for a product which does not yet exist).
- The speed of the 'technology trajectory' often requires an extremely rapid rate of commercial exploitation before the advent of competitor products and/or technological redundancy.
- Successful NTBFs need to grow, internationalise and develop second-generation products in a very short time horizon. This places exceptional managerial, financial and technical demands on a new business.
- The limited availability of appropriate capital markets increases the uncertainty of the future financing of the investee and the profitable 'exit' of the venture capital firm.

(Bergemann and Hege, 1997). As the emergent technology metamorphoses into potentially attractive new products and services, the venture capitalist will commonly attempt to build a functionally balanced team of experienced, professional managers to augment (or if necessary replace) the creativity and innovation of the founder team.

### *Tyranny II: Scale-related costs of the venture capital fund*

It is for the reasons described above that the management of an early-stage venture capital fund is involved in a range of highly time-consuming activities in order to manage the considerable levels of project uncertainty and risk. Given the complexities of the technologies, it is critical that the professional investor is highly informed on both technical and economically related issues. Thus, a number of venture capitalists manage risk by technology specialisation rather than by diversification. The information and networking advantages of specialisation are generally seen to be greater than the forgone benefits of diversification. (For example, there are several 'life sciences only' funds in existence and a growing number of exclusively internet-related, venture funds.)

Governance costs in relation to enterprise revenues are extremely high at the early stages of an NTBF's genesis and growth, and there is little opportunity for the investor to commit large sums in the investee companies. Yet, an annualised internal rate of return (IRR) to the project of over 50 per cent is only satisfactory if commensurately large sums of money can be invested. If this high IRR figure is achieved only on a few tens of thousands of pounds or dollars, the potential rewards will never match the greater certainty of the high project costs which will be incurred. Potentially attractive returns are only likely to be possible after product/service prototypes have been proven and a major marketing and sales drive launched. This is likely to be several years after initial R&D activity. Given the time cost of money, extended research and development cycles demand a commensurately high project return. (Short-termist investors are likely to have very little interest in early-stage technologies.) These first marketing exercises may well be international in scope (Oviatt and McDougall, 1994) thereby adding a further source of uncertainty.

### *NTBFs as a 'special case'*

While it has taken some time for the technical argument that market imperfections in the allocation of capital to NTBFs do exist and are material (particularly information asymmetries and existence of socially valuable externalities), there appears now to be a more widespread and sympathetic acceptance of this position. This is not to argue that a firm, merely because it may be categorised as being an NTBF, should automatically be financed. Venture capital firms are uniform in their assertion that the majority of

> ## The second tyranny: diseconomies of small fund size
>
> * The high costs of information in complex and imperfect markets;
> * the high levels of management support and guidance required by early-stage investees;
> * the limited ability to attenuate project risks by diversifying the fund;
> * the limited ability to invest large sums early in the life cycle of the investee firm;
> * the skewed risk/return profile resulting in the need for a big success by the VC;
> * the long NTBF cycle and its implications on fund structure/ behaviour;
> * the demand for 'quantum leaps' in follow-on financing and the consequent danger of excessive dilution of ownership for the financially constrained original investors (and the entrepreneur);
> * the wholesale unattractiveness to institutional investors of early-stage, technology specialist, venture capital funds – other than in the USA.

businesses they see are not viable investment opportunities given the exceptional *fund* returns demanded by their institutional investors. But these high returns are a consequence of the risks and uncertainties incurred by the venture capital firm, which will expect to see the majority of its portfolio underperform against the original performance targets sold to the institutional investors in its fund. Therefore, individual firm applicants for venture capital finance incur a pricing penalty for reasons intrinsic to this investment activity and outside their individual control. In short, market inefficiencies (for example, imperfect and asymmetric information) and the consequent additional governance costs imposed on the venture capital firms oblige them to demand a price for their capital that excludes all but a handful of investee firms. It is not improbable that venture capital firms reject as many, if not more, potentially good firms as they accept.

As noted, the Bank of England has recently (November 1996) prepared a report on the financial needs of NTBFs. A paper entitled *Government Programmes for Venture Capital,* which looks at the financing needs of NTBFs and the role of venture capital, has also been produced by the Working Group on Innovation and Technology Policy of the OECD in December 1996. The European Commission, in its 1995 Green Paper on Innovation (and the follow-on operational document *The First Action Plan for Innovation in Europe* published in 1997) cited the limited provision of finance as a major potential impediment to the adequate supply of NTBFs within the European Union. In this regard and from the perspective of the

NTBFs, the substance does not yet appear to reflect fully the apparently increased level of contemporary government interest and concern. While the majority of European Union member states have a range of financial instruments to support small and medium sized enterprises, Storey and Tether (1996) found only eight countries with direct financing support schemes which included NTBFs. This number of countries dropped to four (Germany, The Netherlands, Sweden and the UK) if only explicit and exclusively focused NTBF schemes were considered.

Implicit in Storey and Tether's observations is the fact that fast-growth NTBFs are different from other types of SME. Effective policy instruments need to reflect and address the peculiar strengths and, particularly, the weaknesses of NTBFs in Europe. This present paper will only allude to indirect support instruments given their relevance to venture capital fund performance.

## Policies to alleviate economic constraints: three generic (indirect) instruments

Policies to incentivise the supply of venture capital from established capital markets (primarily via institutional investors), and which specifically focus on the venture capital firm, commonly rely on three generic instruments (see Figure 13.3).

### *Down-side protection*[6]

Early-stage investments in NTBFs carry a range of firm- and industry-specific risks. Thus, it is not uncommon for a very significant proportion of the investee firms in a portfolio to result in full or partial loss of the venture capitalist's investment (Sahlman, 1990). This malign outcome skews the risk/reward distribution strongly towards poor fund returns in both theory and practice. Recognising this peculiar reality, a number of governments have either instituted publicly supported insurance schemes (SOFARIS in France) or measures for the state to share in the cost of investment and, thus, of potential failure (the terminated PPM scheme in The Netherlands and the current BTU scheme in Germany).

Down-side protection is extremely important for smaller funds in particular. Because they are already constrained by limited finances, the write-off of a significant number of investments can reduce the level of residual operating funds available for investment to below a viable limit. Also, the very nature of early-stage investment requires that significant risks are taken and a high level of uncertainty is accepted. A fund that is not losing a proportion of investments is probably acting in too conservative a manner in emerging technology markets.

It is common for these schemes to assume a substantial proportion of the costs of project failure. SOFARIS provides a 50 per cent cover as did

---

Policies tend to be concentrated in five areas of resolution, relating to:

- financial constrains;
- management weaknesses;
- market imperfections;
- access to technology;
- access to information.

In addition, policies may be classified by their target group into:

- *direct* policy instruments;
- *indirect* policy instruments.

The vast majority of schemes to support NTBFs are direct, that is, they involve some type of assistance to the entrepreneur/business. Indirect policies are more commmonly aimed at infrastructure improvements.

---

*Figure 13.3* Typology of government support measures for new technology based firms

the PPM scheme (which ended in 1995). The BTU scheme assumes a maximum cover of 75 per cent of total project investment cost (although calculated in different ways for the two variants of the scheme). Both the BTU and the PPM schemes extended this guarantee for five years from the time of the first venture capital investment in a portfolio company. After five years, cover under the PPM scheme declined by 10 per cent a year to disappear at year 10. The critically vulnerable first year of the investment was also removed from the cover in the post 1988 variant of the Dutch scheme. All schemes instituted a ceiling level of cover per portfolio firm.

### Upside leverage

Underwriting project losses puts a floor or safety net under the fund. However, this measure can produce the unfortunate consequence of reducing the venture capitalists' incentive to ensure that they make good investments because 'adverse selection' mistakes become significantly less costly. Upside leverage instruments, conversely, do not protect the venture capital firm against the costs of project failure but multiply the financial benefits of success to the disproportionate advantage of the venture capital firms and their private equity investors. Given that a relatively small number of invest-ments will typically provide the majority of capital gain for the fund, this leverage again can be critically important for the smaller fund.

Leverage schemes usually allow each dollar of a venture capitalist's fund to be matched with one or more dollars of the government's money. The BTU scheme (co-financing variant) will match the venture capitalist *in each investment* on a parity, that is, 1:1, ratio to a ceiling of DM3 million federal investment. In the SBIC Scheme, the leverage is 2:1 for most licensed US venture capitalists outside special development areas, up to a ceiling of a state contribution of US$90 million *per fund*. Thus, a US$45 million fund of private investors can attract the maximum leverage of US$90 million publicly guaranteed monies to become a $135 million US fund. In 1997, the Australian government formally adopted a local equivalent of the revised SBIC Scheme by creating the Industrial Investment Fund with A$130 million available for leveraged investment on a 2:1 state:private ratio.

In addition, these schemes materially assist the fund in being able to provide portfolio companies with successive rounds of finance. This dearth of follow-on finance is a major problem for a small venture fund supporting an exciting, and invariably cash demanding, investee company (Murray, 1994). Given that the government finances are in effect loans, the venture capitalists pay an annual interest charge. However, this source of capital is less costly than that provided by private equity co-investors in the event that the fund is profitable.[7] The state may insist on a share of the capital gain of the fund. While increasing the cost of the state's participation, the benefits of leverage outweigh the incremental costs – provided that attractive investments are made and realised by the fund. Thus, the loan allows the fund to 'gear up or leverage' the returns from the investment to the benefit of the private equity investors. Zero Stage Capital, a Boston based, early-stage venture capital firm, and one of the first managing partners to be awarded a license under the new leverage scheme, has estimated that the benefit of this instrument can translate into a one-third improvement on the terminal IRR of an average performing fund.[8]

In the latter two generic schemes, the state leverage may be either directed at the fund itself or at a specific portfolio company. Underwriting schemes are commonly authorised on a specific deal by deal basis. Thus, each portfolio company has individually to be accepted into the scheme by the underwriter. In the case of the upside leverage, this is addressed at the level of the fund in the case of the SBIC scheme and one of the variants (KfW 'refinancing') of the BTU Scheme. The other BTU scheme ('co-investment') participates directly in the portfolio company in parallel with the venture capitalist.

### Support for the fund's operating costs

Specialist early-stage technology funds are commonly characterised by their small size. The great majority of seed capital funds in Europe have been capitalised at under ECU20 million. Some funds in Europe have as little as ECU2 million under management (Murray, 1998). As such, they are able to exploit few of the scale and scope economies available to larger development capital funds of $200 million upwards. However, industry norms for the level of fee income available to the managing partners (that is, the venture capital firm) are based on the precedents set by these larger and more influential funds. In addition, in most venture capital communities, the managing partners have seen significant downwards pressure on the percentage of fee incomes negotiable and an increase in the stringency of the conditions under which these fees are provided. These pressures are in no small part a consequence of early abuses of inexperienced institutional investors by aggressive venture capital firms.[9] The bargaining power of the institutional investors is either applied directly (in the case of larger investors) and/or via the agency of a 'gatekeeper': a specialist private equity consultant advising several institutions on an optimal asset allocation programme.

The 'going rate' management fee for development or merchant capital funds is around 2 to 2½ per cent of the total value of the funds raised. Several institutions have negotiated 'tapering' fee incomes over the life of the fund. (The model described also employs a taper from the sixth year.) The appropriate figure for specialist, early-stage technology funds in order to cover the operating costs of the venture capital management activity is probably about 4 to 5 per cent of finance raised (Hook, 1992) depending on the scale of the funds managed (see below). This latter figure has appeared totally unacceptable to the vast majority of institutional investors or their advisers.

The European Seed Capital Fund pilot programme of the European Union (1988–95) was a pan-European attempt to address this issue of the relatively (high) cost of managerial governance in small funds. Half of the eligible operating costs of the 23 early-stage funds in the programme were paid for by the European Commission through the provision of a non-interest-bearing term loan to the fund. This subsidy on operating costs was paid for start-up costs and the first five years' running costs of the fund. The loan to cover a part of the costs was only repayable if the fund subsequently made a profit on its investments over the ten years of the fund's life. The focus of this scheme proved very popular, and was appreciated by early-stage fund managers and private investors alike. They argued that the *imprimatur* of the EU allowed them to increase substantially the level of private finance raised (Murray, 1998).

The initial review of the European Seed Capital Fund Scheme carried out by the author in 1991 for the European Commission placed considerable emphasis on the economic vulnerability of small, grant-dependent funds (ibid.). The observation was made that both regional and commercial funds would run out of finances within their ten-year horizons *even without making any investment in portfolio companies*. Essentially, the administrative cost of the funds was strongly out of kilter with the level of finances available. The average size of the 21 funds surveyed was ECU1.7 million (range ECU0.5–7 million).

A further study by the author of technology specialist start-up and early-stage venture capital funds in the UK in 1992 (that is, funds which did not undertake MBO/MBI, replacement equity or rescue finance) indicated that the UK population of independent management companies controlling closed end funds was only nine businesses.[10] If the four largest funds which ranged from £5 to 21 million were removed, the average size of the five remaining funds is £1.41 million (range £0.5–1.6 million). A review of the *BVCA Directory 1996/7* some four years later again identified only nine specialist early-stage funds. Removing one very large international fund of £285 million, gave eight funds with an average size of £8.2 million (range £1–19 million). While the average size of these technology specialist funds has grown nearly sixfold in four years, there remains a continuing question of fund viability, given the absolute small size of these funds.

## The model

### Research objectives and organisation

In order to explore in more detail the determinants which influence the scale and viability of an early-stage specialist technology fund, it was decided to construct a spreadsheet model in Microsoft Excel which could closely mirror the financial characteristics of a 'typical fund' and the likely range of economic outcomes of the investment activity. The model's architecture was designed to allow both practitioners and other academics to augment or customise the data to their own needs.

Additionally, it was planned to use the model to explore the impact of the two major types of state support for early-stage funds, that is, guarantee and leverage assistance on a 'typical' fund. Accordingly, two state-supported variants of the model have also been produced.

### Sources of fund information

The original determination of the cost and revenue items was modelled on the experience of the Australian Technology Group. This specialist venture capital fund was set up with £15 million (A$30 million) of Australian federal government support in 1995. Despite government financial involvement as the sole investor, ATG was conceived as, and was expected to develop into, a fully commercial investment activity. The authors were given full access to fund costs and portfolio firm investment details to assist in defining the original model. However, characteristics of the fund which were peculiar and exclusive to ATG or to the Australian environment were excluded in order to retain the generic character of the model. Cost structures were subsequently referenced to a second independent, fixed term, early-stage Australian fund which was set up in 1996 without state support and operated with a more parsimonious cost structure.

Both of the Australian funds were too early in their investment and real-isation cycles to provide useful statistics on portfolio firms' successes and failures. In consequence, a senior investment executive from each of four established (that is, more than one investment/realisation cycle concluded) UK specialist early-stage technology funds was contacted. They were asked for their views as to the distribution of investment outcomes which could typically be expected from early-stage technology deals. They were also invited to agree with or make amendments to a table of probabilities of capital gains/losses over three rounds of finance (see Table 13.3). The purpose of this request was not to get an exact match with the respondents' funds and information of this detail was not requested. Rather, the views of these correspondents on the credibility of such early-stage portfolio outcomes and probabilities was sought. Overall, there was surprisingly strong agreement as to the reasonableness of the assumptions in Table 13.3. Observations were restricted to minor variations in estimates of probabili-ties or capital multiples. All respondents confirmed the plausibility of the three-stage, six-year project investment cycle for a ten-year closed fund (see below).

The four respondent funds were also asked to confirm the credibility of four structural characteristics of a 'typical' early-stage fund (see Table 13.4).

Of the four questions, strong agreement was again provided on the assump-tions made, with one exception. It was decided to increase to 10 per cent the maximum percentage of the fund allocated to any one investment in the model.

## *Structure of the model*

### *The model's specification and assumptions*

Based on an examination of the academic and practitioner literature of venture capital and subsequent investigation of the actual operation of several specialist, fixed-term, independent[11] funds, a generic model specification was derived.

*Table 13.3* 'Suggested' distribution of investment outcomes by stage of investment

| Alternative outcomes | Stage 1 (First round/year 0) | | Stage 2 (after 2 years) | | Stage 3 (after 4 years) | |
|---|---|---|---|---|---|---|
| | Capital multiple | Probability % | Capital multiple | Probability % | Capital multiple | Probability % |
| Very poor | 0.2 | 10 | 0.2 | 10 | 0.5 | 10 |
| Poor | 0.5 | 40 | 0.75 | 40 | 1.5 | 40 |
| Good | 1.5 | 40 | 2.0 | 40 | 3.0 | 40 |
| Excellent | 2.5 | 10 | 3.0 | 10 | 4.0 | 10 |

*Table 13.4* Confirmation of the structural characteristics of a typical early-stage fund

| Assumption | Murray estimate | Credible? (Y or N) | Respondents' estimate of typical tech. early-stage fund? |
|---|---|---|---|
| Number of ongoing investments per VC executive | 5 | Y | n.a. |
| Maximum % of fund into one investment | 5% | N | 10% |
| Maximum investment per investee company over three stages | £2m | Y | n.a. |
| Typical % allocation of three staged payments per investee firm | 20/40/40 | Y | n.a. |

FUND STRUCTURE

The fund is structured as a ten-year, fixed life fund with the investment capital contributed progressively over the first eight years.

Capital from poor investments (defined as a zero or negative net present value when the two-year investment outcome is discounted back to year zero using a nominal cost of capital and employing the appropriate beta rating) is 'returned' as the investments are liquidated.[12] The capital still invested at the end of the ten-year horizon is returned at that date by the sale/flotation of the remaining investments. Thus, it is assumed that all investments are liquidated by the end of the ten-year period. In practice, this is a rather strong assumption and fund managers usually negotiate a period of discretion in fully liquidating the fund.

INVESTMENT AND EXIT TIMING

In order to model the sequential investment behaviour of the fund, the total capital is divided into five 'mini-funds', each running for six years and sequentially offset by one year. Accordingly, the first mini-fund runs from year 0 to year 6, the second from year 1 to year 7, and so on. The fifth and final mini-fund runs from year 5 to 10 inclusive. This timing reflects the staged investment activity of a typical fund including the time constraints on investment executives in assessing and effecting new investments in the earlier stages of a fund. As a fund comes towards its concluding years, the activities of the investment executives are increasingly directed to ensuring that portfolio companies successfully exit the fund.

Each mini-fund consists of three investment rounds, spaced at two-yearly intervals. The first round takes place in the start or zero year for the mini-fund, the second round occurs at the end of the second year of the mini-fund, and the third round occurs at the end of the fourth year of the mini-fund. The amounts drawn down in each round (tranche proportion) is user-defined in the model. This investment arrangement allows for a total of 15 (3 rounds of finance × 5 mini-funds) capital draw downs during the life of the fund, the timings of which are assumed to be known at the outset but could be varied by the model user.

INVESTMENT OUTCOMES AND PROBABILITIES

The mini-fund is taken to be the unit of investment activity, and the combination of all five 'mini-funds' constitutes a portfolio of investments (that is, the total fund). To model the probabilities and capital gain outcomes relating to successful and unsuccessful investments, a table of 'probability versus capital multiple' was established for each round within a mini-fund. Thus, three separate tables each corresponding to successive investment rounds within the mini-fund were created.

For each table there are four possible outcomes, or states, over the two-year period immediately following the draw-down of the round of finance. Each outcome has an associated probability of occurrence (the total of which is 1.0), and a 'capital multiplier' which was defined as being equal to:

$$\frac{(\text{Value of investment at } t + 2 \text{ years}) - (\text{Value of investment at } t + 0 \text{ years})}{(\text{Value of investment at } t + 0 \text{ years})}$$

Those occasions where the principal sum or less is returned from the discounted investment cashflows are designated as 'failures'. Any residual capital left after the expiry of the two-year investment period is returned to the limited partners with interest at the end of the ten-year period. These residual sums are not available for further investment and are subtracted from the total funds available. In the case of the 50 per cent and the 100 per cent guarantee variants of the model, a part or the whole of the losses incurred in failed investments are returned to the limited partners, with interest, at the end of the ten-year period.

The alternative outcomes where the discounted investment returns exceed the original capital are designated as 'successes'. The total capital generated or 'pay out' (principal + gain) is then applied to the next round of investment activity. This process is repeated until the three rounds of finance for each mini-fund are concluded over the six-year investment period. For example, if £1 million is invested in an investment round, and the appropriate table is as below, then the four payoffs will be:

| | |
|---|---|
| £0 | with 40 per cent probability |
| £1 million | with 30 per cent probability |
| £2 million | with 20 per cent probability |
| £4 million | with 10 per cent probability |

The probability of 'failure' is 70 per cent (40 per cent + 30 per cent) and will result in an expected return of capital to investors of £300,000 (£0 × 0.4 + £1 million × 0.3). The probability of 'success' is 30 per cent (20 per cent + 10 per cent) which will place an expected value on the investment of £800,000 (£2 million × 0.2 + £4 million × 0.1). The expected outcome is discounted (including the beta value) back to the time of the investment in order to produce a net present value (NPV). Only aggregated outcomes with a positive NPV continue to the next decision point up until the third and final round of finance. The model conducts an analysis on the basis of the 'expected' outcome. This is the average of the 64 possible outcomes with the weighting applied to each outcome being the probability of this outcome occurring (Figure 13.4).

The probability/pay out table for each round of finance is allowed to be different. It is assumed that, as the investors become increasingly familiar with the prospects of their portfolio companies, the risk of investment failure decreases progressively in Rounds 2 and 3 (Table 13.5). This is also reflected in the deployment of declining investment betas for each successive round (that is, 2.0, 1.6 and 1.4) when calculating the cost of capital to the investors.

MANAGEMENT FEES LEVIED ON THE FUND

The fee structure consists of two parts. For the first five years of the fund, the fee is a fixed annual percentage of the total capital committed to the fund. The management fee charges are incurred by the fund irrespective of whether or not finance is actually drawn down from the fund and invested in portfolio companies. For the remaining life of the fund from year 6, the management fee levied is a 'fixed annual percentage of the total capital

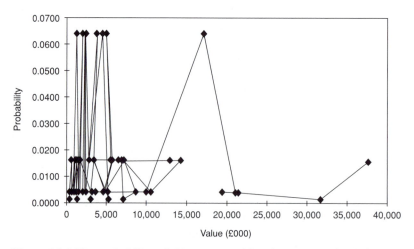

*Figure 13.4* The probability of 64 outcomes of an investment simulation for a fund of £20 million

*Table 13.5* 'Agreed' distribution of investment outcomes by stage of investment

| Alternative outcomes | Stage 1 (First round/year 0) | | Stage 2 (after 2 years) | | Stage 3 (after 4 years) | |
|---|---|---|---|---|---|---|
| | Capital multiple | Probability % | Capital multiple | Probability % | Capital multiple | Probability % |
| Very poor | 0.0 | 10 | 0.2 | 10 | 0.5 | 10 |
| Poor | 0.5 | 40 | 0.75 | 40 | 1.0 | 40 |
| Good | 2.0 | 40 | 2.0 | 40 | 2.0 | 40 |
| Excellent | 4.0 | 10 | 3.0 | 10 | 3.0 | 10 |

committed less any capital nominated for return from the fund to the investors'. Thus, the managers receive a tapering fee income from year 6 as the fund becomes fully invested and investee companies increasingly exit from the portfolio.

The fees for the whole investment period must be paid from the initial capital raised by the fund. Therefore, the actual or net amount of capital available for investment is reduced by the cumulative fee costs.

'CARRIED INTEREST' RECEIVED BY THE MANAGING PARTNERS

In common with normal operating practice in independent funds, the managing partners are acting as agents on behalf of the limited partners (institutional investors). Management is incentivised to perform in a manner consistent with the interests of the fund's investors. Accordingly, the management fee is designed to cover the legitimate operating costs of the management team but not to reward them for making investments *per se*. It is the incentive structure which is designed to reward management for making *good* investments. Thus, managers are allowed to retain 20 per cent of the capital gain of the total fund after the limited partners' fee levies have been repaid and the performance of the fund has exceeded a 'hurdle' of the cost of capital to the fund. This hurdle represents the 'opportunity cost' of access to their capital forgone by the investors or a time value of their money invested.

FUND PERFORMANCE CRITERIA: INTERNAL RATE OF RETURN AND NET PRESENT VALUE

The model computes an annualised internal rate of return (IRR per cent) for the mini-funds and the total fund based on capital invested and returned net of fees. However, internal rates of return can be misleading. Particularly in circumstances where both negative and positive cashflows are recorded over successive periods, multiple IRRs can be generated. Therefore, the model also computes the net present value (NPV) for each of the mini-funds and for the combined portfolio. NPV represents the additional wealth created for the investors, over the life of the fund, in present value terms.

In addition to computing the private partners' IRR and NPV for the mini-funds and then the aggregated fund, the model also recognises the disparate financial interests of the venture capitalist managing partner and the institutional investors or limited partners. Thus the managers' IRR is also calculated. These returns are based on the net fee income generated and the managers' opportunity for a minority participation in the 'carried interest' or net capital gain of the fund.

Irrespective of the merits of NPV calculations, the venture capital industry almost exclusively measures fund performance in terms of net IRRs, that is, total cash invested and total cash received after all costs. Accordingly, both measurements are employed in presenting the results of the model (see pp. 250–9).

The section on investment, outlined above, provides the basis for estimating the cashflows expected from the 'mini-funds' and total fund. The determination of an appropriate discount rate is accomplished with reference to the weighted average cost of capital (WACC) and the capital asset pricing model (CAPM).

The CAPM is commonly used to estimate a cost of equity from the following formula:

$$r_e = r_f + (r_m - r_f) \times \beta$$

where:
$r_e$ = cost of equity
$r_m$ = rate of return on the market portfolio
$r_f$ = risk-free interest rate
$\beta$ = a measure of relative risk.

The model allows the input of these variables in order to compute the cost of equity. Given the cost of debt, and the ratio of debt to equity in the funding of the capital for the total fund, the weighted average cost of capital can be computed and applied to the expected cashflows. Only a pre-tax analysis is included in the model. Similarly, it is assumed for the purposes of the present model that the funds invested are exclusively via equity instruments. Thus, gearing applied by either the venture capitalist or the portfolio companies is not included in the model. This is considered a valid simplification. The use of debt for gearing purposes is likely to be highly inappropriate in young and research-intensive enterprises which commonly experience extended periods when the cashflows are exclusively negative.

## The 'base case' model: structure of the excel spreadsheet

The model is organised in the spreadsheet around eight linked worksheets:

1 *General worksheet*
   Allows the setting of general inputs to the model and presents key outcomes of IRR and NPV values for the mini-funds and overall portfolio.
2 *Probability worksheet*
   Allows key inputs in terms of probabilities and capital multiples for each of the three potential stages of financing.
3 *Decision tree worksheet*
   Calculates the 'expected value' of the mini-funds and the decision as to whether to continue or terminate the mini-fund.
4 *Graph worksheet*
   Presents a graphic representation of the distribution of the 64 possible outcomes to the model and their probability of occurrence.
5 *Deal worksheet*
   Shows the expected value of a deal. The net cashflow to investors is also computed.
6 *Mini-fund worksheet*
   Takes the Deal worksheet and multiplies the results by the number of individual deals in a mini-fund. The number of deals per mini-fund is set by the user in the General worksheet.
7 *Portfolio worksheet*
   Accumulates the mini-fund worksheet and lags each mini-fund by one year. The fees payable to the management are calculated in this worksheet.
8 *Manager worksheet*
   Determines the costs of the management function and their dependency to the fund, the number of deals and the number of investment executives. Data in this worksheet allow the managers' IRR to be computed.

Tables 13.6 and 13.7 illustrate the inputs to the base-case model including both capital and cost structures. Table 13.8 illustrates the output from the model expressed in portfolio NPVs and IRRs.

## Variants on the base case model: impact of state support schemes

In order to look at the implications of state support for early-stage funds, the following two variants of the models were created:

1 Generic support scheme 1: a guarantee and underwriting of individual project failure:

   • The venture capital firm receives in part or full (50 per cent or 100 per cent is specified in the model) the original equity participation

*Table 13.6* Base case model input (*ex* worksheet 1)

| | |
|---|---:|
| Base fees (% fund) | 2.5 |
| Capital hurdle rate (% p.a.) | 15.00 |
| Capital return rate (% p.a.) | 10.00 |
| Management share of capital gain (%) | 20.00 |
| Debt rate (% p.a.) | 10.00 |
| Risk-free rate (% p.a.) | 8.00 |
| Market premium (% p.a.) | 7.00 |
| Portfolio capital size (£000s) | 20,000 |
| Average deal size (% capital) | 10.00 |

*Table 13.7* Management fund costs (*ex* worksheet 8)

| | |
|---|---:|
| Establishment costs | |
| Start-up (£000s) | 75 |
| Capital raising costs (% of fund) | 2.00 |
| Overhead costs | |
| Minimum staff | 2 |
| Minimum salary bill (£000s) | 115 |
| Minimum rent and utilities (£000s) | 25 |
| Information/research (£000s) | 25 |
| Computer system (£000s) | 5 |
| PR (£000s) | 12.5 |
| Per deal costs | |
| Staff per deal | 0.25 |
| Salary per extra staff (£000s) | 60 |
| Pre investment costs (£000s) | 10 |
| Per person costs | |
| Travel (£000s) | 2.5 |
| Rent, furniture and utilities (£000s) | 15 |

on termination of an unsuccessful project within the five mini-funds. The guarantee is eventually returned to the limited partners and is not reinvested by the fund managers;

- the venture capital firm pays an up-front charge for the guarantee which is calculated as a percentage of the total finance raised by the fund. (This percentage is modelled as a variable. The guarantee cost is taken off the total sum available for investment);
- On realisation of successful portfolio investments, the guarantor receives a proportion of the value-added generated. Unlike the contribution of 'carried interest' going to the managers, the value-added in which the guarantor participates contains no 'hurdle' prior to distribution. This share of capital gain is no longer available to the investors. (The proportion is modelled as a variable and can be set at zero per cent.)

*Table 13.8* Model outcomes (*ex* worksheet 1)

| | |
|---|---|
| Number of mini-funds | 5 |
| Deals per mini-fund | 2 |
| Total number of deals | 10 |
| Gross deal size (£000s) | 2,000 |
| Management fees per deal (£000s) | 300 |
| Net deal size (£000s) | 1,700 |
| Deal IRR (% p.a.) | 21.32 |
| Deal NPV (£000s) | 163 |
| Gross mini-fund size (£000s) | 4,000 |
| Management fees per mini-fund (£000s) | 600 |
| Net mini-fund size (£000s) | 3,400 |
| Mini-fund IRR (% p.a.) | 21.32 |
| Mini-fund NPV (£000s) | 326 |
| Gross portfolio size (£000s) | 20,000 |
| Management fees for portfolio (£000s) | 3,000 |
| Net portfolio size (£000s) | 17,000 |
| Portfolio IRR (% p.a.) | 21.32 |
| Portfolio NPV (£000s) | 1,406 |
| Managers' IRR (% p.a.) | 29.38 |

2   Generic support scheme 2: state 'leverage' of the private equity of the fund:
   - Matching equity is provided by the state and is drawn down at the time of an investment;
   - the ratio of state to private equity is a variable. A ratio of 2:1 is used in the results discussed in the next subsection;
   - state equity receives a preferred, annual coupon approximating to the ten-year bank rate – say 8.00 per cent. This annual charge is paid by the fund. The model allows this annual charge to be set as a variable percentage including a value of zero;
   - the venture capital firm can charge an annual management fee on the state's equity at the time of drawdown. This is set as a variable with the normal venture capital firm's management fee as the default but with the option to have a zero management fee levied on state finance;
   - the state participates in any value-added as a percentage of total capital gain to the fund. This is set as a variable with default at 20 per cent but with the option for a zero allocation;
   - in the event of project failure, all investors share pro rata, based on their contribution of total equity, in the net loss.

## *Interrogation of the model(s)*

The objective in constructing the model was to seek to understand, on the cost and investment return assumptions stated, a number of the key dynamics of early-stage venture capital funds. Of particular interest were the following relationships:

1   total fund size to investment returns/performance;
2   key cost and investment drivers on investment returns/performance;
3   impact of support schemes on investment returns/performance.

The investment performance must necessarily be seen from two perspectives, that is, the investment returns reaped by the institutional investors (limited partners in the fund) or the venture capital firm (managing partners to the fund). The terms limited partners' IRR and managers' IRR are used to differentiate these two performance metrics. It should be noted that the burden of scale diseconomies most directly fall on the management agents in that they cannot levy additional charges on their institutional investors to meet a cost over-run. However, in practice, a very poor return to the managers is likely to impact directly on the institutional investors. Managers would seek to reduce and claw back some of the losses incurred and/or reduce their commitment to the fund investors and portfolio companies under management. *A desirable investment performance for an early stage technology fund is pragmatically rather than theoretically set at an IRR of 25 per cent.*

It was hoped to use any enhanced understanding of this particularly challenging stage of investment activity to inform the activities of both industry practitioners and state collaborators. The specific and additional needs of these two interest groups can be built into further refinements of the model.

In the data that follow, the base case figures are applied to a fund of £20 million and with a management fee of 2.5 per cent unless either of these two variables is the subject of the simulation. See Table 13.6 for a full specification of the base case.)

## *The effect of fund size*

The management's IRRs only start to become positive at a fund size of just under £10 million, and the rate of growth of the management's IRR starts to decline rapidly beyond £20 million. The scale effect on management's IRR is 0.36 per cent per million of additional funding. The base case suggests that a fund is not likely to be economically attractive to either institutional investors (limited partners) or the managing partners (venture capital firm) on probable cost and revenue assumptions below a scale of £15 million. In practice, for the managing partner to receive an IRR of 30 per cent, requires a minimum fund size of £20 million (see Figure 13.5).

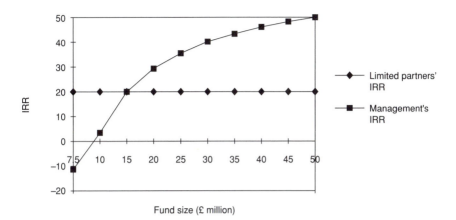

*Figure 13.5* Effect of fund size on management's and limited partners' returns on 'base case' model

The IRR return to the limited partners is insensitive to an increase in the size of the fund. Scale effects are not captured in IRR calculations if no other variables are changed. However, if the return to the limited partners is measured by net present value (NPV), the scale effects are immediately evident. The NPV increases in direct proportion to the increase in size of the fund. For example, in the base case model, the NPV to a £10 million fund is computed as £1.4 million. Doubling the fund size to £20 million results in a doubling of the NPV to £2.8 million. There is a straight-line relationship between fund size and the limited partners' NPV.

### The effect of management fee income

This effect can also be illustrated when the management fee rate is changed. An increase of management fee of 0.5 per cent serves to reduce the NPV of the limited partners by £200,000 This can be expressed as a reduction in the limited partners' NPV of 6.6 per cent per 1 per cent fee increase to the managing partner. Again, the IRR calculation does not pick up this effect on the limited partners' returns.

The benefit of this transfer of resources to the management partner via an increase in fee income is captured both in a near doubling of its IRR between 2.5 per cent and 5 per cent and an increase in the NPV. A 1 per cent increase in the management's fee results in an incremental gain of £945,000 to the management. Management, in NPV terms, is nearly five times more sensitive to a fee rate change than the limited partners (Figure 13.6).

This would suggest that limited partners have some discretion regarding the appropriate level of management's fee income on early-stage funds

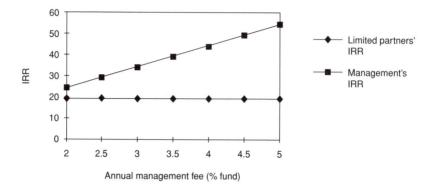

*Figure 13.6* Effect of fee income on fund performance

when a documented case is presented regarding the additional costs incurred. In purely nominal terms, the gain to management significantly outweighs the consequent loss to the limited investors of such a change. However, the venture capital agent's fees are levied to cover the costs of managing the fund on behalf of the institutional investors. These fees are not paid to provide a source of additional profit after operational costs are fully met.

### Effect of increasing fund costs

The raising of the total fund operating costs clearly impacts significantly on the returns to the management (Figure 13.7). Management alone bear the adverse outcomes of any cost over-runs as the responsibility of limited

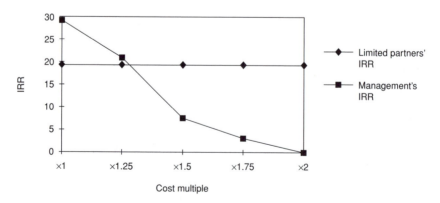

*Figure 13.7* Effect of increasing fund costs on performance

partners is limited to the cost of the management fee incurred. The limited partners' IRR and NPV is insensitive to an increase in costs for which management are alone responsible. On the existing cost and income structures, the raising of total costs by 50 per cent rapidly destroys the economics of a £20 million fund to the venture capital agent. In the event of the fund's total costs doubling, the management's IRR is reduced from a satisfactory 29 per cent to a catastrophic 0.28 per cent. The model again corroborates the critical need of early-stage funds to ensure that costs are balanced against revenues and positive cashflow.

### Effect of management's carried interest

Again, the negative impact of an increase in the amount of carried interest paid as a performance incentive on the returns of limited partners is much less than the consequent gain to the management (Figure 13.8). When measured by IRR, the difference is fourteenfold with IRR increases to the limited partners and the management of –0.34 per cent and +3.4 per cent, respectively, per percentage change in the carried interest. In NPV terms, every 1 per cent increase in the carried interest negotiated by management costs the limited partners a reduction in NPV of £54,000.

This suggests that, if the fund's performance is measured in terms of IRRs, 'the carry' is a highly cost effective means of incentivising the management to undertaken profitable investments within the fund, as measured by the incremental benefits gained and forgone to the two parties. Given that each percentage increase in the carried interest from the industry standard of 20 per cent reduces the limited partners, NPV by approximately 2 per cent, such a change may be less attractive.

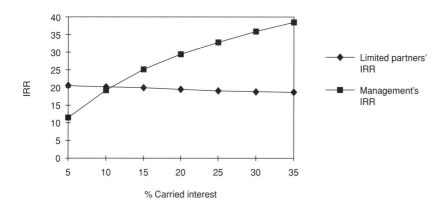

*Figure 13.8* Effect of management's 'carried interest' on fund performance

*Effect of a 'star' investment on fund performance*

In this simulation the investment outcomes were altered to produce a more binary outcome of success or failure.

Capital multiple returns by investment stage were either zero or negative on 50 per cent of occasions. Conversely, there was a one in a thousand chance of a 100 times capital gain over three rounds of finance:

| Probability | Capital multiples by stage of finance | | |
|---|---|---|---|
| | *Round 1* | *Round 2* | *Round 3* |
| 0.1 | 0 | 0 | 0 |
| 0.4 | 0.5× | 0.5× | 0.5× |
| 0.4 | 1× | 1.5× | 1.5× |
| 0.1 | 1× | 10× | 10× |

While a one hundred times capital gain appears attractive, the probability ascribed of a thousand to one chance of achievement reduces the impact of such an occurrence. However, there still remains a positive impact despite the long odds. At a fund size of £20 million, the management gains approximately 14 percentage points with the IRR increasing to 43.6 per cent. The increase in returns to the limited partners is a more modest 5.7 per cent to produce a revised IRR of 25.26 per cent (Figure 13.9).

However, if the limited partners' returns are assessed in terms of NPV, the star investment produces material benefits. The limited partners' NPV on a £20 million fund increases from £2.8 million to £8.5 million. A £10 million increase in fund size results in a marginal improvement of NPV in the star investment of £4.2 million. This gain is threefold larger than when compared to the marginal improvement of £1.4 million in the base case investment.

While a 100 × capital gain is improbable, it can occur. This extreme outcome is in addition to the two additional opportunities to achieve a 10 × capital gain at the end of rounds 2 and 3. It would appear that the benefits of a 'star' investments are material to limited partners and managers alike. Such a desired outcome should remain a sensible goal of the investment managers but in reality is largely outside their control.

*Effect of providing a guarantee to the fund*

Unlike the base case model, the guarantee scheme requires that the fund pays both a fee for the provision of the guarantee and gives a share of any ensuing capital gain to the guarantor. Thus, the guarantor participates in the success of the fund in part recompense for the inevitable losses of the fund and the subsequent underwriting costs incurred by the guarantor.

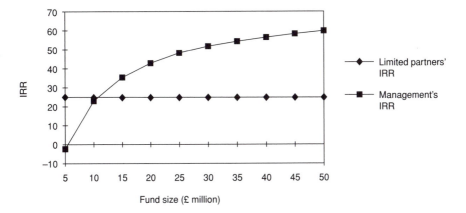

*Figure 13.9* Effect of impact of a 'star' investment

*Table 13.9* Model inputs (*ex* worksheet 1: guarantee option)

| | |
|---|---|
| Basic fees (% capital) | 2.50 |
| Capital hurdle rate (% p.a.) | 15.00 |
| Capital return rate (% p.a.) | 10.00 |
| Management's share of capital gain (%) | 20.00 |
| Fee for capital guarantee (% capital) | 2.00 |
| Guarantor share of capital gain (%) | 20.00 |
| Debt rate (% p.a.) | 10.00 |
| Risk free rate (% p.a.) | 8.00 |
| Market premuim (% p.a.) | 7.00 |
| Portfolio capital size (£000s) | 20,000 |
| Average deal size (% capital) | 10.00 |

### Effect of fund size on a guaranteed fund

The effect of the 100 per cent guarantee is to increase significantly the impact of the fund size on the returns to management. This is to be expected as a full 100 per cent guarantee on speculative investments essentially means that these risky decisions are costless. While the IRR to the limited partners is little changed at 20.7 per cent from the base case of 19.5 per cent, the NPV of the portfolio increases by 31 per cent at each level of fund size compared to the base case (Figure 13.10).

However, when a 50 per cent guarantee scheme is put in place, the results are more ambivalent. At a fund size of £20 million, the IRR to the limited partners increases marginally from 19.52 per cent to 20.65 per cent but the resultant NPV is only 70 per cent of that achieved by the base case. The NPV of the base case is £2.82 million and the 50 per cent guarantee scheme is £1.96 million. This is likely to be due to the consequent charges incurred from the guarantor both in the percentage fee levied and the guarantor's share of the eventual capital gain (if any) of the fund. At a full underwriting of failed investments, these charges remain acceptable. At a 50 per cent guarantee, investors would be materially better off (in NPV terms) if the guarantee was forgone.

EFFECT OF 2:1 LEVERAGE ON FUND PERFORMANCE

The model was adapted to reflect the key elements of the revised Small Business Investment Company (SBIC) scheme, post-1992, whereby US federal government funds are used to leverage the 'upside' returns of the management and limited institutional investors. The model allows a range of government contributions to total equity to be computed (Table 13.10).

The following charts are based on a 2:1 government:private investment ratio. Government funds are charged at a long-term bond rate of 7 per cent although this variable can be changed in the model. As with the guarantee option, the state is paid an interest coupon on the leveraged funds provided. The state contributor participates in any capital gain of the fund. However, the state in turn pays the prevailing fee to the managing partner for the management of the state's contribution to the whole fund. The model is based on a £20 million fund size. All other parameters, such as the 20 per cent management carry, remain unchanged as in earlier model specifications.

While the size of fund needed for a positive management's IRR is slightly higher than for the base case, the major effect of leverage is in the marked

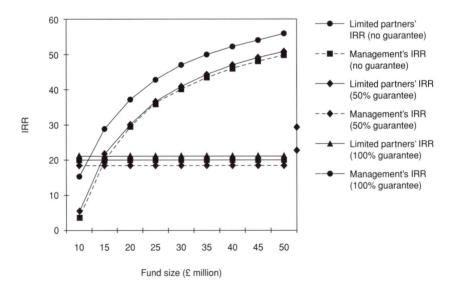

*Figure 13.10* Effect of 100 per cent and 50 per cent guarantee on fund performance

*Table 13.10* Base case model input (*ex* worksheet 1: 2:1 leverage option)

| | |
|---|---:|
| Basic fees (% fund) | 2.50 |
| Capital hurdle rate (% p.a.) | 15.00 |
| Capital return rate (% p.a.) | 10.00 |
| Management's share of capital gain (%) | 20.00 |
| Proportion of capital from state (%) | 67.00 |
| Annual return on state capital (% p.a.) | 5.00 |
| Management fee on state capital (% capital) | 2.50 |
| State share of capital gain (%) | 20.00 |
| Debt rate (% p.a.) | 10.00 |
| Risk free rate (% p.a.) | 8.00 |
| Market premuim (% p.a.) | 7.00 |
| Portfolio capital size (£000s) | 20,000 |
| Average deal size (% capital) | 10.00 |

increase in IRR returns to the private investors (Figure 13.11). Their annualised returns increases from 18 per cent to 28 per cent at each level of
fund size – a material increase of 55 per cent. The effect on management's
IRR to fund size is 1.3 per cent per £1 million increase. However, if the
leverage effect is measured in NPV terms, the effect of the 2:1 leverage
is to increase the NPV to the limited partners by a rather more modest
6.9 per cent, or £0.2 million, across the range of fund sizes.

Increasing the leverage of the fund raises the IRR to the limited partners
but slightly decreases the management's IRR (Figure 13.12). The IRR
changes per percentage increase in state leverage are 0.26 per cent to the limited partners and –0.063 per cent to the management. If appraised in NPV
terms, the move from a zero contribution of funds from the state to a 90 per
cent contribution changes the limited partners' NPV from £1.75 million to

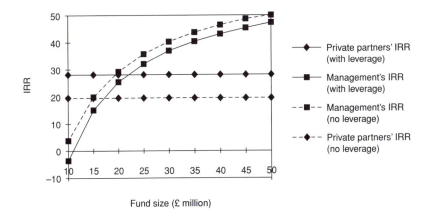

*Figure 13.11* Effect of 2:1 state:private leverage on fund performance

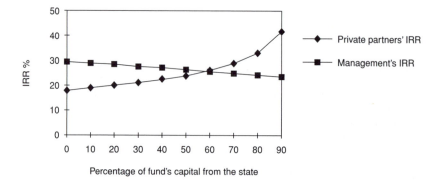

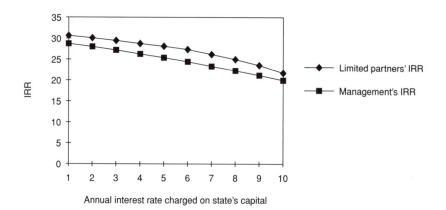

*Figure 13.12* Effect of scale of government leverage on the performance of a £20 million fund

£1.32 million. This is a 52 per cent change or £10,000 per percentage increase of state leverage.

The effect of increasing the payment to the state via the annual interest charge on the leveraging fund supplied is to lower the IRRs to both public and private investors (Figure 13.13). The effects of a 1 per cent increase in the cost of state capital is –0.84 per cent and –1.32 per cent for the management's and the limited partners' IRRs, respectively. None the less, the IRR returns to both parties still remain attractive. However, assessing performance in IRR terms disguises the NPV impact of increasing interest charges levied by the state. If the state interest rate is changed from 1 per cent to 10 per cent, there is a 82.5 per cent reduction in the value of the

*Figure 13.13* Effect of interest cost of state's leveraged funds on the performance of a £20 million fund

limited partner's NPV which decreases from £4.77 to £0.84 million. The positive leverage effects of the state's contribution is larger than the negative effect (on investors' returns) of increasing the cost of state capital. Thus, the state may charge a commercial (that is, risk adjusted) or at least bond rate level of interest payment without prejudicing the commercial returns of the private investors or their venture capital agents.

## Concluding observations

The nature of the above simulations are such that categorical conclusions are dangerous without clearly specifying all the model parameters of importance. In addition, a level of prudence is necessary, given that financial models invariably remain a crude analogue of reality. The model should not be used in a primarily prescriptive fashion. Rather, its value is as one means of systematically exploring the relationships between costs and revenues for an early-stage fund under various operating assumptions and policy alternatives.

However, making the strong assumption that a flow of attractive investments is available to the fund managers, the most important findings from a policy focus concern the *importance of fund size* on the returns to the venture capital management company (the managing partner). It is stressed that the return goals of *both* limited and managing partners have to be met to ensure long-term viability of such fixed-term fund-based technology investments. Management cannot be expected to bear an unreasonable burden of risk from the fixed and variable costs incurred without adequate recompense.

On the cost and performance data supplied, it is suggested that the desired minimum size of a specialist, technology focused, early-stage venture capital fund should be approximately £20 million (equivalent to US$33 million or ECU28 million). A fund with under £15 million (US$25 million or ECU21 million) under management is of increasing vulnerability regarding its ability to return investment rewards commensurate with the levels of risk and illiquidity incurred. Meeting commercial returns remains difficult for funds of this small size, even with the imposition of 2:1 leveraged government funding.

The level of annual fee income which the managing agent is paid also remains of considerable importance. For every 1 per cent increase in management fee, the IRR of the venture capitalist managing the fund increases by 3.74 per cent from 17 per cent (at a 1 per cent fee) to 33 per cent (at a 5 per cent fee) without changing any other parameters. In this context, a fee income for the managing agents in a small, technology specialist, early-stage fund above the development capital funds' standard of 2–2½ per cent appears equitable to both management and investors.

The simulations suggest that state assistance via the use of a leverage mechanism is preferable for a number of reasons: 2:1 leverage has a more direct impact on the IRR returns of the limited partners than a guarantee scheme; importantly, leverage exclusively rewards successful investment activity and incentivises both the limited and managing partners. Further, in contrast to guarantee schemes, management is not insulated from the negative outcomes of poor decision-making.

It is important to note that this study has only dealt with commercial funds, that is, those funds which seek to attract investors in international capital markets. On a number of occasions (see Murray, 1998), local and national governments will further impose parochial development remits on venture capital organisations in which they are commonly the sole or largest institutional investor. Given that these organisations may well be obliged by their investors to pursue goals which are in conflict with commercially optimal behaviour, this research can make no substantive comment on the structural requirements of such funds.

The model is flexible to a wide range of interrogations. Both input (cost) and output (returns) variables can be changed by the user to reflect the peculiarity of individual fund circumstances. Future refinements could seek to use options theory rather than decision tree analysis to explore dynamic outcomes of an investment process. Further work could also be done on empirically validating the beta values used in the model at each stage of investment. However, these interesting elaborations remain outside the initial model specification.

## Model software

The authors are prepared to share their Excel spreadsheet model with academic colleagues and other interested parties in the hope that it may be refined and improved by co-operative action. Requests for the model from commercial users will be met on the condition that a contribution is made to Amnesty International. Enquiries should be directed to Dr Gordon Murray (e-mail: gordon.murray@warwick.ac.uk).

## Notes

1 Development capital investments are generally described as those transactions involving established companies but not start-up or early-stage enterprises.
2 It should be noted that several academics harbour significant reservations regarding the existence and the degree of an equity gap for small firms (see, for example, Aston Business School, 1991).
3 The importance of recent Israeli activity must be recognised, including the very strong links with American commerce and academe.
4 DG XXIII also has a remit for the promotion of tourism.
5 The USA is also not above criticism. Investment activity figures for comparable years, 1991–5, compiled by Venture Economics and Venture One and made available by the National Venture Capital Association show major inconsistencies.
6 In addition to the described schemes, there is also a 50 per cent guarantee scheme, the *Udviklingsselskaber*, in Denmark.
7 In practice, the number of sources of equity co-investment available at the early stages of investment can be severely constrained.

8  Correspondence with Paul Kelley, President of Zero Stage Capital, Cambridge, MA.

9  These circumstances led one industry commentator to observe memorably that the UK venture capital industry had 'mugged' the institutional investors (Initiative Europe, 1994).

10  These figures only related to specialist, early-stage venture capital firms registered as full members of the BVCA. In reality, there exist a number of other such firms which are not members of the BVCA. However, these firms which are often publicly supported initiatives are likely to be significantly smaller, in terms of funds under management, than full BVCA members.

11  The term 'independent' is used to denote a fund structure whereby professional managers, acting as agents, seek the commitment of institutional investors as limited partners in a fund. The subscribed fund operates for a fixed period, normally ten years, over which time investments are made and then realised. The limited partners are returned any capital gains net of the costs of the fund managers and less any distribution of capital gain awarded to the manager (the 'carried interest').

12  In practice, the model did not return any residual from 'failed' investments until the end of the ten-year fund period. However, residual monies so held were not available for further investment and earned a market cost of capital, that is, the opportunity cost to the investors, while still held in the fund.

# References

Amit, R., Glosten, L. and Muller, E. (1990) Does Venture Capital Foster the Most Promising Entrepreneurial Firms?, *Californian Management Review*, Spring, 102–11.

Aston Business School (1991) *Constraints on the Growth of Small Firms*, London: HMSO.

Bank of England (1996) *The Financing of Technology Based Small Firms*, London: Bank of England.

Bergemann, R. and Hege, U. (1997) Venture Capital Financing, Moral Hazard and Learning, Discussion Paper no. 1738, Centre for Economic Policy Research, London: CEPR.

Birch, D. (1979) The Job Creation Process, in *MIT Program on Neighbourhood and Regional Change*, Cambridge, MA: MIT Press.

Branscombe, L.M. and Florida, R. (1997) Challenges to technology policy in a changing world economy, in L.M. Branscombe and J.H. Keller (eds), *Investing in Innovation: Creating a Research and Innovation Policy that Works*, Cambridge, MA: MIT Press, pp. 1–18.

British Venture Capital Association (1996) *BVCA Directory 1996/7*, London: BVCA.

British Venture Capital Association (1997) *Report on Investment Activity 1996*, London: BVCA.

Burns, P. and Dewhurst, J. (1993) *Financial Characteristics of Small Companies in Britain*. 3i plc/ Cranfield School of Management, England.

Butchart, R.L. (1987) A New Definition of the High Technology Industries, *Economic Trends* 400, February, 82–8.

Bygrave, W.D. and Timmons, J.A. (1992) *Venture Capital at the Crossroads*. Boston, MA: Harvard Business School Press.

Coopers & Lybrand (1996) *Sixth Annual Economic Impact of Venture Capital Study*, Boston, MA: Coopers & Lybrand.

European Commission (1994) *Growth and Employment: The Challenges and Ways Forward into the 21st Century*, White Paper, Brussels: European Commission.

European Commission (1995) *Green Paper on Innovation*, Brussels: EC.

European Commission (1997) *First Action Plan for Innovation in Europe*, Brussels: EC.

European Commission (1998) High-tech Investment Capacity Boosted, *Innovation & Technology Transfer*, 1/98, p. 9, Luxembourg: EC.

European Venture Capital Association (1996) *Performance Measurement Survey*, Zaventem: EVCA.

European Venture Capital Association (1997) *Venture Capital in Europe: 1996 EVCA Handbook*, London: KPMG.

Fenn, G., Liang, N. and Prowse, S. (1995) *The Economics of the Private Equity Market*, Washington, DC: Board of Governors of the Federal Reserve System.

Florida, R. and Kenney, M. (1988) Venture Capital, High Technology and Regional Development, *Regional Studies,* 22, 33–48.

Fontes, M. and Coombs, R. (1997) The Coincidence of Technology and Market Objectives in the Internationalisation of New Technology-based Firms, *International Small Business Journal*, 15, 4, 14–35.

Freeman, C. (1983) *The Economics of Industrial Innovation*, Cambridge, MA: MIT Press.

Gallagher, C. and Stewart, H. (1986) Jobs and the Business Life Cycle in the UK, *Applied Economics*, 18, 875–900.

Hook, R. (1992) Management Costs of Early Stage Funds, paper presented at the Sixth Seminar of the European Seed Capital Fund Network, Liege, December.

Huntsman, B. and Hoban, J.P. (1980) Investment in New Enterprises: Some Empirical Observations on Risk, Return and Market Structure, *Financial Management*, Summer, 44–51.

Initiative Europe (1994) *UK Venture Industry Review,* February, London: Initiative Europe.

Keeble, D.E. (1989) High-technology Industry and Regional Development in Britain: the Case of the Cambridge Phenomenon, *Environment and Planning*, 7, 153–172.

Macmillan, H. (1931) *Report of the Committee on Finance and Industry*, Cmnd 3897, London: HMSO.

Meyer-Kramer, F. (1985) Innovation Behaviour and Regional Indigenous Potential, *Regional Studies* 19, 523–34.

Moore, B. (1993) *Financial Constraints to the Growth and Development of Small, High-technology Firms*, Small Business Research Centre, Cambridge University, England.

Murray, G.C. (1994) The Second 'Equity Gap': Exit Problems for Seed and Early-stage Venture Capitalists and their Investee Companies, *International Small Business Journal,* 12, 4, 59–76.

Murray, G.C. (1995) Evolution and Change: an Analysis of the First Decade of the UK Venture Capital Industry, *Journal of Business Finance and Accounting*, 22, 8, 1077–1107.

Murray, G.C. (1998) A Policy Response to Regional Disparities in the Supply of Risk Capital to New Technology-based Firms in the European Union: the European Seed Capital Fund Scheme, *Regional Studies*, 32, 5, 405–19.

Murray, G.C. and Lott, J. (1995) Have UK Venture Capital Firms a Bias Against Investment in New Technology Based Firms?, *Research Policy*, 24, 283–99.

National Venture Capital Association (1997) *Annual Report 1996*, San Francisco, CA: Venture One.

Oakey, R.O. (1984) *High Technology Small Firms*, London: Francis Pinter.

Oakey, R.O., Rothwell, R. and Cooper, S. (1988) *Management of Innovation in Small Firms*, London: Francis Pinter.

Organisation for Economic Co-operation and Development (OECD) (1986) R&D,

Innovation and Competitiveness, in *Science and Technology Indicators*, 2, Paris: OECD.

Organisation for Economic Co-operation and Development (OECD) (1996) *Government Programmes for Venture Capital*, Working Group on Innovation and Technology Policy. Paris: OECD.

Oviatt, B.M. and McDougall, P. (1994) Towards a Theory of International New Ventures, *Journal of International Business Studies*, 25, 1, 45–64.

Roberts, E.B. (1991) *Entrepreneurs in High Technology*, New York: Oxford University Press.

Rothwell, R. (1989) Small Firms, Innovation and Industrial Change, *Small Business Economics* 1, 51–64.

Rothwell R. and Zegveld, W. (1982) *Industrial Innovation and Small and Medium Sized Firms*, London: Francis Pinter.

Sahlman, W.A. (1990) The Structure and Governance of Venture Capital Organisations, *Journal of Financial Economics*, 27, 473–521.

Storey, D., Watson, R. and Wynarczyk, P. (1989) *Fast Growth Businesses: Case Studies of 40 Small Firms in the North East of England*. Paper no. 67, Dept of Employment, London.

Storey, D.J. and Tether, B. (1996) *New Technology Based Firms (NTBFs) in Europe*, EIMS, Brussels: European Commission (DG XIII).

**Part V**

# Creating the infrastructure and economic environment for a dynamic, diffuse economy

# 14 Universal service, universal access and the Internet

*Jonathan Cave*

## Introduction

The perennial topic of universal access or universal service (UA/S) policy has received renewed attention as a result of the growth of the electronic highway, here referred to by the slightly-inaccurate term 'Internet'. This attention stems in part from the fact that services available over the Internet are seen by some as valuable candidates for universal provision, or at least for targeted subsidies to certain groups. Another factor is that increasing competition is progressively undercutting the provider subsidies that have been the traditional means of paying for UA/S: conventional providers of telecommunications services face eroding profit margins, while their UA/S provision or payment obligations provide a regulatory cost advantage to 'unconventional' providers. This bypass effect is strengthened by the current non-economic pricing of Internet access and usage, leading some to suggest that Internet service providers (ISPs) should be subjected to the same obligations to contribute to UA/S funds as other providers of telephony services. Others commentators, viewing the same developments, have concluded that the innate efficiency of these alternative providers and the nearly complete solution of the access part of the UA/S problem signal the end for UA/S policies, or at least suggest that ISPs should be considered as alternative UA/S providers.

This paper develops some of the resulting policy issues. Throughout, it concentrates on two of the emerging technological possibilities: Internet Voice Telephony (IVT) and electronic mail (E-mail). The first section discusses arguments for universality and the implications of new developments. These implications are used in a second section to describe elements of UA/S policy most likely to be affected: the service bundle; eligible group(s); provider(s); and the payment mechanism(s). The third section gives a brief summary of the current state of play in terms of the economics of messaging and recent policy initiatives in the EU, three member states and the United States. The paper concludes with a discussion of policy considerations in general and with specific regard to network standards, interconnection, portability, and marginal customers.

Overall, it is our belief that these new developments pose unavoidable challenges to policy: current UA/S philosophies have outgrown their technical basis, and there are some reasons to believe that neither continuation of existing policies nor full *laissez-faire* will meet the challenge.

The literature in this field is vast, and this paper owes a significant debt to many articles. Since the object is to give an overview focused on practical policy questions rather than a survey, we have not provided extensive citations. However, there are a few specific sources that strongly influenced the point of view adopted here, particularly the analyses of the 1996 Telecommunications Act cited in the references section, the OFTEL/Analysys report on Universal Service, and Anderson, *et al.* (1995).

## The policy basis for universal access or service

### Background

The concept of UA/S as a public good and the particular shape of policy reflects the historic distinction between *telecommunication* in the sense of one-to-one or peer-to-peer two-way communication and *broadcasting* in the sense of one-to-many, one-way transmission of information, usually initiated by the sender.

Telecommunications policy was historically based on a natural monopoly model involving large economies of scale and inescapable 'bottlenecks' allowing network operators the power to exercise vertical foreclosure. Under those circumstances, even the entry of new technologies is distorted: if used to provide new services over the existing network the incentives to invest will be too low (dynamic inefficiency), while technologies used to provide an alternative may be subject to productive or allocative inefficiency in the short run. The original policy problem was insufficient access resulting from this monopoly power; over time, the issue of affordability assumed more prominence, particularly with regard to special groups of 'marginal consumers'. By and large, subsidies were paid by a combination of direct government funding and payment obligations imposed on a single 'provider of last resort', often the incumbent monopolist.

Broadcasting was traditionally viewed as a merit good, where the social problem was to ensure free or affordable access to pluralistic, unbiased information supporting social and/or cultural goals. Over the course of time, this was amplified to include a natural monopoly argument based on spectrum scarcity. The natural emphasis on content and usage as opposed to access was manifested in various standards as to acceptable content. Interestingly, the public broadcast obligation was not always concentrated on a single firm, but was transferred in exchange for regulatory relief. It is unusual for the costs of universal broadcast access to be visited on providers of alternative broadcast content, which may be provided by public broadcasters funded by a mix of general tax revenues and subscriber contributions, or by commercial broadcasters as a condition of licence (that is, in exchange for access to the airwaves).

In both cases, doubts about the feasibility and desirability of *competition* outlived their technical basis as penetration of the wireline network became virtually complete, alternative information outlets and commercial pressures undermined the merit good argument and new technologies effectively eliminated spectrum scarcity (except as a rationing device). The result was a series of regulations that increasingly lacked technical neutrality, favouring specific technologies for specific functions and altering the path of integration or convergence and, in some cases, even the emergence of new technologies or services.

Another interesting feature is the tendency for the policy debate to centre on *facilities* while market developments emphasise *services*. Despite this, liberalisation starts with services, leaving facility competition restrained. In the emerging liberalised environment, market power is more likely to reflect integrated horizontal dominance as opposed to inescapable bottlenecks through which all services must flow. This trend is particularly marked as the functions of telecommunications and broadcasting *converge* – a term used to indicate that they share each others' characteristics and offer overlapping, complementary or substitute services. This convergence has produced changes in the pre-existing separate regulatory structures covering telecommunications and broadcasting. It remains an open question whether convergence favours unified or symmetric regulation and, conversely, what impact regulatory changes will have on the speed and nature of convergence. In addition, regulation is increasingly affected by legal and economic issues of privacy, security, IPR, content, contract and similar concerns that are not discussed here.

### Benefits of universality

Universal Access or Service policies typically take the form of regulatory relief, outright subsidy or legal barriers to competition designed to ensure that 'uneconomic' customers receive a particular bundle of services. In practice, access is often conflated with either service or usage; arguments for the merits of access are used to justify provision or subsidy of specific services and the benefits of access are often computed on the basis of notional levels of usage. In this section, we review some of the principal economic and social justifications for universality, distinguishing as far as possible among access, service and usage.

### Economic

The principal economic rationale for universality is that connection offers externalities. The most obvious of these is the positive network externality of *interconnection*: each user who connects to a network derives the benefit of being able to contact all other users; but the additional benefits current users derive from being able to contact the newcomer are not represented in his or her willingness to pay for connection. Together with the belief that calling patterns expand and evolve as networks grow, this provides a rationale for passing some of the costs of network expansion on to existing users, and for continuing the process until maximum penetration is achieved. This argument is normally phrased in terms of access. A related benefit is the so-called call externality: the excess of the mutual benefit of a call over the benefits accruing to the initiator of the call. This provides an argument for usage subsidies, particularly for low-income consumers.

These externalities are relatively insensitive to the technology used to provide communications services, though they are quite responsive to changes in the bundle of services delivered over the network. Another set of arguments based on economies of scale and scope are much more sensitive to technology and other cost factors. Scale economies, typically ascribed to the large fixed costs of network infrastructure, lead to the allocative inefficiency associated with classic natural monopolies. The implications for universality are twofold. In the first place, the larger volumes associated with wider penetration should drive down average costs. Second, the larger consumer base may provide greater scope for effective competition, particularly when a vertically integrated incumbent's cost advantage is compensated by a UA/S obligation. Scope economies stem in part from the ability of networks to be used for a wide variety of services that may be complementary from the consumers' point of view or synergistic in their use of network capacity,[1] and provide an impetus for broadening the bundle qualifying for universal provision and the range of organisations involved in the provision and funding of UA/S.

In addition to these relatively static and inward-looking considerations, there are arguments for universality based on dynamic and/or general economic grounds. One is that demand for and supply of electronically provided goods and services evolve together. This suggests that subsidies aimed at building new demand can induce further growth and development of the 'value-added' sector. More generally, the success of electronic commerce depends on effective functioning of the communications network. The UA/S argument is that the 'reach' of electronic commerce should be as broad as possible, embracing individuals who are not currently economic to serve, but who may become profitable as their use of electronic commerce expands. By the same token, it is often argued that including a broader range of consumers and inducing firms to exploit opportunities for electronic marketing on a broad front will lead to more effective and more equitable competition.

*Social*

Social arguments for UA/S include the need to increase contact with people in remote regions and thus to encourage their social as well as economic development. By the same token, familiarity with modern communications systems will help to prepare the next generation for new technologies. At a more direct level, electronic communications systems are increasingly used for delivery of local public goods such as medicine, education and access to government services (including emergency services), to head off the widening gap between the wired and the unwired, and to promote visions of electronic democracy. Other general social goals include reducing the isolation of people with limited opportunities for 'face-to-face' social access.

*The concept of universal access*

EVOLUTION

In the early days[2] of electronic communications, there were many alternative providers and the major concerns were the extent of *coverage* (a result of the failure of local monopolists to internalise network externalities), especially the need to promote *interconnection* of different systems. This is consistent with a policy goal of universal access. After interconnection proceeded to monopoly, this emphasis was superseded by something closer to the current idea of *affordable* access by almost everyone to a specific set of services, which seems more naturally connected to universal *service*. In the US, this was realised by a combination of universal service obligations and a price structure regulated to provide the necessary subsidies. The balance between access and usage charges and the structure of the latter was skewed by the influence of local interests on the public utility commissions, resulting in very low charges (often no charge) for local calls, which led to the concept of an *access deficit* requiring subsidy. The potential loss of these subsidies formed part of the argument against the introduction of competition. After the vertical break-up of the incumbent monopolist, these subsidies were protected by entry restrictions and regulated access charges to ensure that the local exchange monopolist could discharge its duties as the 'carrier of last resort'. While the evolution of liberalised telecommunications took a different course in Europe, the same evolution from the need to promote penetration (access) to a desire for greater affordability (service) has taken place. Ultimately, this evolution found expression in a variety of formal universal service obligations and funding mechanisms. It is important to note that the current form and reform of UA/S policy often appeals to policy goals appropriate to a much earlier phase in the industry's life cycle. This is reflected in general design features such as:

- *universal service obligations* – for example, conditions under which low-income and/or rural subscribers must be served, public (pay) telephone provisions, 'lifeline' service/billing requirements, disconnection restrictions, and so on;

- *funding structure* – particularly the extent to which subsidies are provided by different classes of users, other service providers or general tax revenues; and
- *payment structure* – especially whether subsidies are paid to providers or subscribers and whether they are directed at access or usage.

FOCUS

Current UA/S policies concentrate on payments to single carriers of last resort for access provided via (analogue) wireline connections to homes. The underlying view of UA/S delivery assumes the presence of a single, dominant, vertically integrated firm. This firm usually offers a menu of two-part tariffs that separate access from usage. This distinction has several practical implications. First, it has clear connections with the distinction between universal access and universal service: the latter requires usage surcharges, whereas the former merely involves allowing providers to recover (relatively) fixed access deficits. Moreover, usage charges are imposed on callers while access charges also affect those who wish to receive calls. Finally, different classes of usage are distinguished (especially in the US) in ways that reflect local politics – typically, long-distance charges subsidised local calls, which were (until the rebalancing that followed local loop competition) heavily subsidised. Of course, most types of classic universal access/service arguments are implicitly aimed at promoting local communication.

### *Recent developments*

Recent developments hold the potential to upset the assumptions underlying current UA/S policies. The following are important market developments.

- *Shared access* by many users – studies of telephone use in developing countries indicate that call volumes per telephone roughly decline with income (at low income levels), indicating that telephones are shared, and that universal access need not involve a telephone in every house, with consequent capital savings.
- *Number and service portability* – offering the possibility of card-based access for marginal consumers, possibly in combination with card-based access to other public and commercial services.
- *Value-added usage services* – increasing the service quality and bandwidth needed for universal access.
- *Alternative means of access* – including public access ports in libraries, government offices, and so on.
- *Infrastructure growth* that virtually solves the access problem in most areas, supports effective competition in service provision, rolls back the threshold of uneconomic customers and provides alternatives to wireline access that offer superior cost characteristics for remote customers.

- *Withering of dominance* – the large single incumbents who formed the natural focus of UA/S policy face increasing competition. As a result, they may no longer be able to pay for UA/S from, for example, profits on long-distance or international calls. By the same token, the identity of the 'carrier of last resort' is no longer obvious – indeed, it has been suggested that incumbents using new technologies may be able to serve 'uneconomic customers' profitably if their entry is facilitated.
- *International consortia* – increasingly, major players in national telecommunications markets are multinational in character. The ability to effectively subject them to provision or contribution requirements may be limited, and they may enjoy unfair cost advantages as a result of the UA/S burdens on domestic players that threaten both effective competition and the financial soundness of the UA/S system.
- *Alternative payment schemes* – as the ability to collect money from low-income customers (for example, by advance payments) and technologies for earmarking benefits payments to specific expenditure categories (for example, to calls, to local calls or to incoming and/or emergency calls only) increase, the risk faced by UA/S providers can be reduced.

On balance, access is currently satisfactory in most developed countries but use and, for some, affordability are not. Attention is thus shifting to such questions as the extent to which call charges should be equalised across geographical areas, and the pursuit of new public interests associated with new services. In addition, non-economic regulation with an overtly technological or social flavour is increasingly important. On the economic side, new relationships between suppliers and users are evolving, including: different mixes of credit and debit payment; enhanced approvals and reallocation of customer classes; alternatives to disconnection; and alternative liability rules for risks associated with UA/S provision. Finally, new pricing structures are emerging that involve access–usage and local–distance rebalancing for telephony and usage – and/or content-based pricing for value-added services. These developments can provide a clearer view of the costs and benefits of alternative arrangements.

With regard to access, most residences continue to use analogue wireline connections that naturally limit the feasible services and the congestion and other external costs of their delivery. Despite this, there are many near-term alternatives such as ISDN, xDSL, cable, wireless, xMDS, DirectPC and so on. ISDN, for example, uses existing wires but promises end-to-end digital connections at modest cost. Its small penetration to date is probably due to a combination of low standards, installation problems, prices well above costs[3] and a charge structure with a very high usage component that prevents realisation of network externalities. In other words, there is a chicken-and-egg problem, with demand and supply sides waiting on each other before endorsing any particular alternative. This lag is no doubt enhanced by regulatory uncertainty, but the history of UA/S policy to date illustrates the dangers of regulatory endorsement of specific technologies.

## Policy elements

In general terms, a UA/S policy contains several distinct elements:

- *recipients* – service bundles and groups eligible for UA/S support;
- *providers* – who provides UA/S, how they are selected, what requirements they are subject to, what relief they receive, and so on;
- *costs and benefits* relevant to determination of charges, payments, and so on;
- *payments out* – who receives them and on what basis;
- *payments in* – who pays for UA/S and on what basis, other aspects of the funding mechanism; and
- *policy tools*.

### Service bundle

The service bundle includes the level of services available to specified eligible groups. Most current UA/S policies are limited to analogue voice-quality telephone service delivered by wire and capable of supporting fax/modem traffic at 9600 baud. Here, we consider two possible extensions of the service bundle: Internet voice telephony (IVT) and universal electronic mail (UEM).

#### Internet voice telephony

This refers to the use of the Internet to deliver voice (and sometimes video) messages. This niche market came into being as a result of technological advances permitting near-synchronous transmission of voice messages over packet-switched circuits combined with the current flat-rate pricing that makes IVT calls virtually free. Market penetration is proceeding at a fair pace, especially among 'closed' networks (for example, small groups of firms) for whom the main network externalities have already been internalised. Broader development will depend on the resolution of legal and economic uncertainties. These include:

- the relation of IVT charges to regulated voice telephony tariff structures;
- whether ISPs offering IVT most contribute to universal service funds;
- whether IVT providers should be liable for the same access charges as other telecommunications service providers;
- whether IVT providers are eligible to participate in 'pay or play' arrangements for universal service provision;

- whether the analogy between IVT providers and other switchless resellers of telecommunications services will hold up; and
- whether the quality, reach[4] and ease-of-use associated with IVT will reach the level of conventional voice telephony.[5]

From the economic point of view, IVT is not free, just inefficiently priced. Indeed, there is something quite perverse about a system that uses circuit-switched connections for data (fax/modem) transmissions and packet-switched Internet connections for (IVT) voice.

There have been many reports of IVT and similar high-bandwidth Internet uses leading to local loop congestion, particularly as a result of the greater mean duration of Internet calls. This congestion is not simply a matter of low prices, since the common US pattern of free local calls did not produce congestion. It also reflects a mismatch among switching protocols, network architectures and call distributions that is at least partially technological in origin. As to whether IVT represents a more efficient use of available capacity, a standard voice telephony connection occupies a 56 KBPS channel while an IVT connection runs at 4 KBPS without taking the 'interleaving' possible as a result of packet-switching into account, so IVT would seem to dominate in the local loop. However, current long-distance circuits may actually outperform IVT compression.

Finally, any legal or regulatory separation that attempts to distinguish between voice and data transmission will be very hard to enforce.

From the UA/S point of view, IVT plays two roles: as a potential means of delivering voice telephony services forming part of the current service bundle; and as a sector that may either contribute to or undercut UA/S funds.

*Universal E-mail*

This has recently been advocated as an addition to the universal services bundle. It does not necessarily require any extension of existing communications networks, and may complement or substitute for such existing means of communication as voice telephony, mail and facsimile. The implications are spelled out at length in Anderson *et al.* (1995).

### *Eligible groups (poor, remote, public access)*

Universal service policies typically contain, in addition to a bundle of services to which all people should have access, specific groups who should receive a possibly expanded bundle of services on particularly favourable terms. The distinction depends in part on whether UA/S policy is viewed primarily as a means by which everyone may gain an entitlement to some services or by which some may gain access to all communications services. This depends in turn on perceived problems of free-riding (like the current Internet-spawned local loop congestion), adverse selection (for example, when high-valuation customers 'opt-out' of those portions of the telecommunications system that support UA/S) and moral hazard (for example, when 'lifeline' phone or 'public service' Internet services are used for 'frivolous' or even criminal purposes).

These perceptions also affect the structure of subsidies and the balance between access and usage charges. In particular, use subsidies have been characterised as particularly vulnerable to moral hazard problems, but provide the only practicable and equitable means of dealing with the common problems associated with capacity saturation.

Once it is decided to provide differential treatment, it is necessary to establish the basis for this distinction. There are examples of policies that discriminate on the basis of income, location and profession. There are also policies that avoid subsidies to specific users by providing public access points. In the future, there seems no clear reason why determination, provision, monitoring and enforcement of personal or household eligibility for UA/S support should not be bundled with eligibility for other forms of social support. This may become particularly true as new forms of payment[6] make payments to users rather than providers easier to implement. However, problems remain in estimating need, allocating payments and limiting use to 'approved' communications. These problems are both practical and theoretical in nature – in particular, the classic distortions associated with in-kind transfers can be expected to recur if communications subsidies are targeted at specific uses.

### *Providers*

As liberalisation of the telecommunications market proceeds, UA/S provision by a single dominant firm is increasingly untenable. It is not even obvious that local monopoly is efficient, provided the reliability of the network is maintained. For instance, it certainly seems reasonable that wireless operators would have a significant advantage in providing UA/S in rural areas, while local network providers in urban areas could be expected to provide access (if not usage) at very low marginal cost. Indeed, as the service bundle expands one might expect different services to be provided by different firms using the same physical network or collection of networks.

At one level, this means that it may no longer be possible to implement subsidies within a given firm without unacceptable costs to competition. In addition, it seems that competition for specific aspects of the UA/S market could be implemented by, for instance, an auction mechanism. If this were coupled with multiple-source provision, benchmarking during the life of the contract and renewal options, it should be possible to preserve incentives to invest in new plant and equipment and to develop service bundles specifically aimed at making UA/S customers profitable in their own right; for example, by allowing advertising or direct marketing over UA/S lines or for subscribers choosing 'lifeline' packages.

### Payments out

One critical aspect of UA/S policy that receives increasing attention is whether payments should be made to customers or to providers. Briefly, providers are deemed to know how much UA/S provision costs, while customers know their own demand and can benefit from the flexibility provided by user subsidies. There are long-term consequences as well, because provider subsidies create incentives to isolate and maintain the UA/S market as a separate part of total telecommunications demand. On the other hand, the uncertainty connected with user subsidies may deter providers from fixed capital investment, particularly when the UA/S right or obligation may be reassigned within the lifetime of those assets.

### Payments in

The central issue relating to the Internet is whether ISPs are liable to pay for UA/S funds and on what basis they should be charged. Such payments could either be direct contributions or as surcharges to access or usage fees paid to the UA/S provider.

### Range of policy tools

Among the most interesting suggestions for adapting UA/S policies to the Internet age are modifications of pay-or-play rules allowing a wide range of UA/S activities (for example, wiring up schools, libraries, and so on) to be credited against the firms' UA/S fund payment obligations, and the specific direction in the 1996 US Telecommunications Act to use regulatory relief to compensate regulated UA/S providers.

## Current state of play

### Economics of messaging

In this section, we mention some of the salient aspects of messaging for the main technologies.

### Telephony

Voice telephony costs tend to be concentrated in network provision (cables, switches). The large fixed costs are common to business and home uses, and support a natural monopoly model, though emerging new technologies such as cable and wireless[7] telephony may change this picture. Cable offers very high bandwidth and is already nearly universal in some areas. Wireless telephony, while it has some fixed costs associated with switching and gateways to the wired network, does not involve large-scale investments in wires and cables. On the demand side, voice telephony is characterised by a wide range of willingness-to-pay. The resulting price discrimination favours homes and local calls at the expense of businesses and long-distance calls. This provides an additional cost advantage for Internet communications that has created a network structure with a few large players, each of whom has many local points of presence.

### Facsimile

Facsimile (fax) transmission was developed 33 years before voice telephony. However, the supply was well in advance of the demand and today it can best be characterised as a value-added overlay to existing infrastructure. Network externalities required development of standards – for the most part, these are self-regulated. The role of fax transmission continues to evolve, with emergent mailbox and broadcast services and convergence with other PC-based messaging technologies.

### E-mail

Electronic mail is also delivered as a value-added overlay using circuit-switched local and packet-switched (PS) leased-line LD transport, cellular, GSM, cable and even satellite telephony. The inherently digital nature of electronic mail allows it to make use of PS to attain cheap, efficient, asynchronous transmission, leading to much better capacity utilisation, especially during peak-load times. The asynchronous nature of the communication can also reduce total traffic, though the ability to attach and freely deliver highly formatted text and multimedia documents is beginning to undercut this.

Network externalities realised via growth of non-regional user groups are boosting interconnection and enforcing the use of common transmission and addressing protocols. At the local loop level, inappropriate use of CS circuits, and shifts in call duration distributions are currently causing congestion, delay, churn[8] and poor sorting. In the near future, the use of electronic mail will expand to embrace user–agent data searches, mailing lists, 'broadcast-like' one-to-many distributions of material valued more by recipients than senders and MIME and other high-bandwidth types of messaging.

### Technology

At the technological level, the scale and right-of-way economies that supported existing policies are beginning to wane due to shared facilities, microwave transmission, fibre/digital switching and the ability of wireless and/or cable telephony providers to enter local markets while bypassing the local fixed network.

*Policy*

In broad policy terms, the concept of universality is shifting away from access and coverage towards equity, affordability and expanded service bundles. At the same time, telecommunications policy in general is increasingly reliant on market forces or market-like mechanisms. Finally, the structure of the regulated telecommunications industry is changing rapidly: international consortia weaken the power of national regulators; industrial concentration continues to increase on a global scale; and political pressures for harmonisation of regulation are increasing.

*Structure*

The ownership structure is evolving too, from publicly owned and operated providers to local monopolies and thence to competing private firms. In some cases, multiple networks compete at the local level, while in other situations local monopoly networks compete for business between their subscribers using the interconnection provisions of emerging open network policies. The implications of these developments for the desirability and feasibility of UA/S have yet to be spelled out. In addition, the industry is being integrated along four dimensions: layer (service, switching, transport); distance; geography; and bundling of non-substitute services for consumers.

*Interconnection*

One particular focus of new policies that echoes the earliest concerns behind UA/S policy is interconnection. An interconnecting new entrant offering similar services to the incumbent will share its reach and tend to compete on the basis of price and quality, subject to the incumbent's attempts to foreclose entry or expropriate rents via access prices. By contrast, an unconnected entrant must differentiate its products so that customers will buy them *as well as* the incumbent's.

In the case of IVT, interconnection to the ordinary voice telephony system remains limited, and the necessary product differentiation is achieved via bundling with other Internet services. The general network externalities of the Internet will probably produce substantial interconnection in time, particularly as different types of messaging converge, but at the moment IVT is confined to a narrow group of individuals.

Judging by the current state of E-mail, it is quite possible to have market equilibria without fully connected networks. There are strong motivations for businesses to attempt to restrict free-riding, so that universal penetration could be achieved without fully realising the benefits of ubiquity.

For both services, increases in interconnection could reduce the internal subsidies on which universal service provision to marginal customers currently rests. This will be offset to some extent by overall rate reductions that reduce the number of such individuals and expand the range of affordable services, but the spillover effects of increased concentration will lead to patchy growth of universal service funds as an alternative funding mechanism for the remaining individuals and services.

On the demand side, the existence of network and call externalities imply that in general networks will be too small. In addition, the original users of telecommunications services (including IVT and E-mail) didn't value ubiquity. On the other hand, increasing integration due to liberalisation (and also in part to the Internet), limited possibilities for capture and user demand for ubiquity mean that the market has (almost) solved the maximum reach problem. Whether this proceeds to, for example, complete E-mail coverage depends on the limiting influence of: terminal equipment costs; content, privacy, security, intellectual property right and contract concerns; recurrence of old externalities; congestion; and on future developments among substitute complementary and messaging services and equipment. The identity of substitute services shifts with the uses of E-mail. In 1986, Huber found the following origins of E-mail: telephone 55 per cent; telex 10 per cent; mail, courier and other electronic services 5 per cent. Recent developments such as voicemail increase substitution by making voice telephony more asynchronous. Important complements that will increase the utility of E-mail include: gateways linking E-mail with regular mail and telephone networks; unified messaging systems; and new standards that increase the ranges of interactions[9] and content (for example, multimedia) that can be exchanged via E-mail.

On the supply side, costs differ across the various layers required for the new services, which are subject to differing types and degrees of regulation. The *computer infrastructure* is characterised by relatively large fixed costs to users but small incremental cost per application. In other words, purchase of the necessary computer and communications equipment may not be justifiable for IVT or E-mail on their own. Without pricing schemes to spread the joint costs, development depends on the introduction and widespread use of so-called 'killer applications' whose benefits are sufficient to induce large-scale investments on which other services can free-ride. The *communications infrastructure* also has large fixed costs incident on providers, but these are shared with other, widely used services. The *service infrastructure* adds fixed costs of routing, storage and addressing – here, too, incremental costs are very low. In the future, the costs associated with services such as IVT and E-mail will be affected by the type of supplier. Traditional suppliers of communications services offer scope economies (shared hardware, networks and marketing), and thus tend to provide these services in highly integrated form. Network owners, 'value-added network service providers' and firms who buy signal transport from network owners provide a second type of supplier, typically facing higher marginal but lower fixed costs. Finally, Internet service providers (ISPs) have sprung up, with various target markets, degrees of coverage and organisational structure;

they buy communications services and simply provide the overlay necessary to use the Internet. Their fixed costs are the lowest, and so is their ability to control service quality. This accounts in part for the high degree of 'churn' among their clientele and provides a quality-based alternative to the price- and quantity-based regulatory models currently in use. For ISPs, the most successful structures combine localisation (to save on link costs) with meta-networks (to save on support cost); 25–40 per cent of their costs go for transport, and all are shared among the applications/services the ISP provides. The emerging size distribution is bimodal, with both large and small ISPs coexisting.

To the extent that an equilibrium pattern can be detected, it seems likely to involve a few vertically integrated firms with a fringe of smaller, less-integrated ones. Scope economies will lead to bundling, making revenues insensitive to changes or differences in demand mix. This trend towards bundling is reinforced by sunk costs, excess capacity and oligopolistic co-ordination. In terms of network utilisation, these factors and the current inappropriate pricing schemes are producing increasing congestion. In the medium term this will produce pressures for extra capacity, real-time pricing, multiple service 'qualities', peak-load pricing and similar innovations. In terms of pricing, the current structure involves 'hidden discounts' for value-added network service providers meeting term and volume conditions. These discounts share risks and reduce churn (AT&T estimates 20–50 per cent per year). Such discounts are spreading to ISPs. In addition, there is widespread secrecy of prices, and substantially higher prices for 'marginal' customers.

## Recent developments in selected European and US settings

### Europe

EU policy provides a 'common denominator' for the member states. The service bundle includes ordinary voice telephony and lines capable of supporting modest fax/modem services. This bundle serves two functions: a *minimum* service level to be provided throughout the Union and a *maximum* basis for computing transfers between market parties. The definition of eligibility is mainly geographical and income-based, and affordability is left to local determination. Costing is based on the specified service bundle and harmonised according to the rules in the Voice Telephony Directive. The object of harmonisation is to prevent uneven development following liberalisation. The rules implicitly assume payments to incumbent providers (rather than new entrants or customers). Payments for universal services may be required of organisations providing public telecommunications networks and/or voice telephony – they are distinguished from interconnect charges. Access deficit charges are only allowed where national regulatory authorities have constrained retail tariffs to smooth rate rebalancing. Foreign operators that 'merely interconnect' are exempt, and charges should not reflect traffic from other member states. The choice of funding mechanism (surcharge, formal UA/S fund, and so on) is left to individual states. The policy recognises the possible need to adjust interconnect, access and settlement fees. EU policy does not address new services, save for a determination that IVT does not qualify as voice telephony for the purposes of satisfying UA/S requirements. By the same token IVT providers are specifically exempt from universal service contribution requirements. This position may change as interconnection between IVT and conventional telephone networks expands and as the quality of IVT improves – indeed, these gaps may narrow more rapidly due to the cost advantage this policy creates for IVT providers.

French UA/S policy in the context of the Internet is discussed in the Théry (1994) report, which foresees full deployment of the electronic super-highway by 2015 with equality of access across income, location and profession. However, the report envisages no concrete steps towards this goal. The 1996 Telecommunications Act uses the EU definition, extended to include leased lines, ISDN, PS and telex. Universal service surcharge rates must be approved by two government entities. Services provision by the dominant incumbent, France Télécom, is mandated by law. There is no universal service fund.

German UA/S policy has recently been codified in two laws. The *Telekommunikationsgesetz* governs the transition to competition, while the *Informations- und Kommunikationsgesetz* (especially the *Teledienstegesetz*) governs new services. These laws paper over the issue of convergence, especially since telecommunications are regulated at the federal level, while broadcasting is left to the Länder. The *Telekommunikationsgesetz* contains the first formal statement of universal service policy; it is almost identical to the EU position. Germany pays for universal services using a formal fund.

In the United Kingdom, UA/S policy stipulates the EU standard bundle, with additional 'Information Society Initiatives' for public access to advanced services. The UK has no universal service fund. Even if such a fund were to be established, ISPs would be exempt. Recently, the telecommunications regulator reviewed universal service scope, costing, provider selection and funding. The review did not call for any major extension or revision, and found no basis for universal service funds or any other form of external subsidy to the dominant incumbent (BT, except in Hull). For the future, the emphasis seems to be on prior market endorsement of new services – thus, UA/S policy should follow rather than lead the market.

## United States

The first formal endorsement of UA/S in US law can be found in the 1934 Telecommunications Act, which distinguished telecommunications from broadcasting along the lines indicated in Table 14.1.

*Table 14.1* Distinctions between telecommunications and broadcasting

|  | *Telecommunication* | *Broadcast* |
|---|---|---|
| Medium | Wires | Wireless |
| Basis for regulation | Natural monopoly | Scarce public good (spectrum) |
| Regulatory structure | Common carrier | Competition |
| Nature of communication | Private | Open |
| Content control | None | FCC control |

The principle perceived economic conduct threats to UA/S in the following years were predation and cream-skimming, and policy responded by erecting entry and diversification barriers. Later years saw increasing emphasis on market forces and major technological shifts that largely reversed the columns of Table 14.1. By 1996, a broad consensus had emerged along the following lines:

- some telecommunications services have social benefits that exceed their cost, which in turn exceeds their market value – these may require some form of subsidy, protection or favourable treatment;
- market forces are the best tool for dealing with problems of market convergence and/or splitting; and
- regulation is still needed to control anticompetitive behaviour.

The 1996 Telecommunications Act embodied this consensus, giving the first formal definition of UA/S.

- Everyone should have access to high-quality services at just, affordable rates.
- Access to advanced telecommunications and Internet services should be provided in all geographic areas and at specific public access points.
- Rates should be comparable across geographic areas (especially for services provided to the health care sector).
- Rates for services provided to the education sector should be discounted.
- Necessary subsidies should be provided by equitable, non-discriminatory contributions to predictable support mechanisms.

The Act also provides for periodic redefinition of the service bundle and partial 'pay or play' provisions that provide incentives for more efficient providers to supplant incumbents. Of particular interest is sec. 254, which calls for revenue-based *contributions* from all telecommunications carriers, including wireless carriers and possibly others in future. The same section offers *support* to any common carrier providing universal services and to non-telecommunications carriers providing, for example, Internet services to schools. In addition to this direct financial support to and from market players, sec. 706 directs the Federal Communications Commission and the states to support UA/S using:

- price cap regulation;
- regulatory forbearance;
- pro-competitive measures; and
- removal of barriers to infrastructure investment.

These provisions lay the foundation for a bold expansion of the UA/S provision and even, in principle, for a solution to the UA/S problem through reallocation of the costs and claims to benefits for Pareto-improving services. Nonetheless, there remain certain causes for caution or concern. First, the funding provisions of the Act may bias consumer choices away from contributing providers; their cost disadvantage could even promote inefficient bypass. The wording of the Act mentions 'equitable and non-discriminatory' taxes; this may be construed as a recognition of this problem but evaluation of such taxes is at best a very complex matter, particularly when it involves identifying superior technologies or the case for adding new services or recipients.

Even in strictly economic terms, it will be difficult to maintain (or establish) competitive equity between telecommunications operators and ISPs, or between content and conduit service. The Act attempts to relax legal barriers to allow market forces to operate, but appears to do so in a discriminatory fashion. For local loop competition, local exchange carriers are required to offer non-discriminatory interconnection, *but not to wireless operators*. Diversification constraints on RBOCs (regional Bell operating companies, or 'Baby Bells') have been relaxed, but they remain subject to heavy regulatory burdens. These continuing burdens on wireless operators and RBOCs will affect their roles in providing and paying for UA/S. The Act ostensibly tries to use market forces to direct technology while preserving UA/S, but does so in a way that may undercut natural experiments while removing local flexibility. Finally, the application of existing antitrust law (market definition, interpretation of structural and conduct restrictions, application of performance-based indicators of anticompetitive conduct) may be hard or inappropriate under the circumstances, since in the context of UA/S there is no natural presumption that competition is either efficient or feasible.

## Policy issues

These considerations lead to the identification of a number of practical policy issues. It seems evident that the necessary communication infrastructure is already in place in most western countries. However, the structure of telecoms prices is skewed by a regulatory heritage that no longer fits the market, a combination of poor incentives and regulatory capture and the persistence of extraneous political agendas. The service gap between IVT and ordinary voice telephony is narrowing rapidly, spurred on by differential treatment. Connectivity and interoperability remain problematic, and this can lead to equilibria in which large segments of traffic 'opt out' of those portions of the network where they may be required to contribute to UA/S. As far as E-mail is concerned, connectivity is rising (if not complete), but subscription and use remain problematic (in extent and focus). There has been only modest penetration of terminal equipment for both services; while there are many PC owners, the bulk of them are not signed up to receive Internet services. Those who are comprise a selected population made up, on one side, of those with well-defined needs sufficient to differentiate them from UA/S recipients and, on the other, of those whose use of Internet services is as yet unstable and casual. Neither group offers a clear indication of the future role of Internet-based UA/S.

In economic terms, those who (currently) have good substitutes display very elastic demand, which inhibits profitability and service development; those using Internet services in more essential ways may do so largely because they face artificially low prices. Further demand infrastructure development seems to wait upon cuts in set-up and recurrent costs, as with the cellular market. Currently, IVT and E-mail require some form of set-top, PC, fax or other terminal. There may be arguments for subsidising the acquisition and support of this equipment, particularly as the rapid pace of technology produces large amounts of surplus equipment that is perfectly adequate to provide these services.

In the development of network standards, there seems to be a clear choice between oligopolistic and government inefficiency. Unfettered competition may lead to excessive differentiation and loss of connectivity. Vertical integration and service bundling may raise switching costs and reduce innovation incentives. Long-run policy options include promulgation and enforcement of *minimum* standards, strategic use of government procurement (especially with multiple suppliers and auction-like contract allocation and renegotiation mechanisms) and activities designed to foster co-operative standards. However, in terms of the latter, the dismal record of high-definition television (HDTV) standardisation should be borne in mind; national competition for standard-setting virtually halted the development of this technology for many years.

As far as interconnection is concerned, policy development must recognise the tension between the social advantages of a fully-connected network and the likely effects of rent-seeking and regulations focused solely on interconnection. For example, long-distance voicemail costs include access charges, while E-mail is much cheaper – this cost advantage is based on a regulatory distinction between interexchange carriers and extended service providers rather than differences in the resource costs of service provision. Another example is provided by EU rulings exempting IVT providers from universal service fund payments, combined with the perceived necessity of avoiding international subsidies in an environment involving strategic multinational alliances. This tension may produce biased regulation, inappropriate prices and higher net costs. On one side, the resulting cost asymmetries do promote extended service provider use and the development of this sector of the market, but the same factors may weaken universal service funds and thus the very network facilities used by extended service providers.

Another policy issue is portability. Ostensibly, *telephone number portability* cuts consumer search and switching costs, reduces entry barriers and stabilises ubiquity (at the cost of some churn). In combination with card-based access, it can also promote universal service goals in areas where terminal equipment costs are high relative to individual subscriber incomes, providing a boost to shared-telephone equipment programmes in less-developed areas. These advantages have led to rapid progress, in the form of new regulatory rules,[10] experiments and interim measures. By contrast, there appears to be nothing comparable for *E-mail address portability*; addresses are assigned by providers and the consequences are magnified by service bundling.[11] Furthermore, provisions for E-mail forwarding are far more primitive than those for either voice telephony or regular mail. Some have suggested a future government policy providing all citizens with unique addresses, but this is a long way off at present. An alternative model can be found in Internet domain name assignment, which is handled by self-regulation, but the sheer size of the task when extended to universal services makes this an unlikely future.

A final set of policy issues concern so-called marginal customers. In the first place, new technologies, services and regulations call for updating current definitions of 'uneconomic' customers, areas and services. Ideally, UA/S policy could be aimed at promoting a future in which the goal of universality can be achieved without any subsidies or protection from competition. In terms of *geographically marginal customers*, one area for affirmative policy is regulation of maximum toll charges for remote customers to reach Internet service providers. This form of price cap regulation can offer incentives for development of new technologies. Another set of policies gaining acceptance obligate service providers to offer below-cost rates to certain groups. There are several outstanding questions.

- Which costs should rates take into account, and how are they assessed?
- How are these rates provided to consumers – geographical, income-based or other discounts?
- How should access deficits be made up – fees from competitors and/or other beneficiaries,[12] subsidies paid from general revenues, rebalancing of access and use fees, and so on?
- How should equality, transparency, credible and accurate monitoring and effective entry regulation be maintained?

As mentioned earlier, new technologies and the possibility of viable competition[13] suggest that subsidies may be better directed to users than to providers. Such subsidies may involve vouchers, resale of used equipment and other indirect mechanisms. The costs of such schemes may be met through specific taxes, surcharges, general tax revenues or allowing advertising access. Determination of subscriber eligibility and provision of earmarked subsidies may be bundled with social support assessment for certain classes of individuals (for example, the poor), while subsidies for others (for example, those living in remote areas) may be provided more indirectly to make efficient use of existing social support overhead structures.

Finally, the extended concept of universal services may facilitate the delivery of a wide range of government services. It is even possible that the savings available in this way may make the entire enterprise self-funding, providing issues of security, identity verification, fraud prevention and competitive fairness can be resolved.

## Notes

1 For example, circuit-switched voice calls are notoriously wasteful of circuit capacity; their efficient management depends on being able to induce a sorting by duration and willingness-to-pay through, for example, time-of-day pricing. Internet calls are typically of long duration, but are very 'patchy' and thus can be transmitted by breaking messages into small packets; these can be interspersed in ways that dramatically increase capacity utilisation. This shift can be sustained by a breadth of services sufficient to sustain the needed traffic volume.
2 This refers to the US context.
3 Probably due to self-fulfilling beliefs that existing demand is relatively inelastic and future demand is uncertain.
4 At the moment, IVT users can only connect to other IVT users, but plans are under development to create 'gateways' connecting IVT callers with the general voice telephony network. These gateways are not free, however, and will pass their hardware and access charges along to consumers in some manner.
5 This argument forms the basis for most current exemptions of IVT from UA/S obligations and applies equally to cable telephony.
6 For example, credit, debit, prepaid, and other card-based access provisions.
7 As used here, the term refers to cellular and 'PCS' telephony and to tight-beam radio.
8 This is particularly evident in the market for ISPs, who compete in part on response time and modem pool capacity. Because sign-up conditions are attractive and contractual constraints weak, market shares are very unstable: subscribers sign up for a new provider, whose service deteriorates due to congestion, whereupon the subscriber base evaporates. Under these conditions, incentives to invest in adequate capacity are weakened.
9 Virtual real-time exchanges, multiple-user conferencing via E-mail, and so on.
10 For example, 'equal access rules' (1+ dialling) for chosen long-distance carriers.
11 For example, telecommunications and Internet service providers often include 'E-mailboxes' with addresses including the providers' name.
12 For example, service providers whose markets expand through subsidised access to new customers.
13 Competition to become the designated 'provider of last resort', competition among alternative providers of 'universal' services and/or competition between more or less vertically integrated providers of basic and enhanced services.

# References

Alliance for Public Technology (1996) 'Connecting each to all: principles to implement the goal of advanced universal service' Washington, DC: APT, and http://www.apt.org/publica/each2all.html

Analysys (1995) 'The costs, benefits and funding of universal service in the UK', report to OFTEL, London: OFTEL.

Anderson, R.H., Bikson, T.K., Law, S.A. and Mitchell, B.M. (1995) *Universal Access to E-Mail: Feasibility and Societal Implications*, Report MR-650-MF, Santa Monica, CA: RAND.

Borrows, J., Bernt, P. and Lawton, R. (1994) 'Universal service in the United States: dimensions of the debate', working paper 124, Bad Honnef, Germany: Wissenschafliches Institut für Kommunicationsdienste.

British Telecom (1997) 'Internet voice telephony: comments on Draft Notice 97/V 140/06', London: BT.

Catinat, M. (1997) 'The reform of the telecommunications regulatory frameworks: the American and European approaches', presentation to Harvard Information Infrastructure Project conference on 'The Impact of the Internet on Communications Policy', Cambridge, MA, December.

Council of the European Union (1994) *Council Resolution on Universal Service Principles in the Telecommunications Sector*, Brussels, CEC.

Cruikshank, D. (1997), Remarks to FT World Telecommunications Conference, London, December.

Ducey, R. (1997) 'Internet broadcasting', presentation to Harvard Information Infrastructure Project conference on 'The Impact of the Internet on Communications Policy', Cambridge, MA, December.

European Commission DG XIII (1994) *Commission Statement Concerning Council Resolution (1) on Universal Service Principles in the Telecommunications Sector*, Brussels: CEC.

——— (1995) *Theme Paper on Universal Service Issues*, Brussels: CEC.

——— (1997a) *Status Report on European Union Telecommunications Policy*, Brussels: CEC.

——— (1997b) *The Future of Universal Service in Telecommunications in Europe*, Brussels: CEC.

Federal Communications Commission (1997) *Commission Implements Telecom Act's Universal Service Provisions, Adopts Plan to Ensure Access to Affordable Telecommunications Service for All Americans* Report no. CC 97–24 Common Carrier Action, 7 May, Washington, DC: FCC (CC docket no. 96-45).

Golden, R. (1996) 'Telecommunications Act of 1996 and the Internet', Palo Alto, CA: Fenwick & West LLP, http://www.fenwick.com/pub/april.html.

Greenstein, S. (1997) 'Universal service', presentation to Harvard Information Infrastructure Project conference on 'The Impact of the Internet on Communications Policy', Cambridge, MA, December.

Greguras, F. (1997) 'An introduction to hot issues in electronic commerce', presentation to Computer Law Association's CyberCopia conference, San Francisco, CA, 23–24 October.

Hammond IV, A. (1995–6) 'Universal access to infrastructure and information', part I *DePaul Law Review*, 45: 923.

——— (1996) 'Universal access to infrastructure and information', part II, *DePaul Law Review*, 45: 1067.

HM Government (1997), *The Telecommunications (Open Network Provision and Leased Lines) Regulations 1997*, SI 1997: 2932, London: Stationery Office.

Horrigan, J. and Rhodes, L. (1995) 'The evolution of universal service in Texas', unpublished working paper, Lyndon B. Johnson School of Public Affairs.

Hundt, R. (1997) 'The Internet: from here to ubiquity', presentation to the Institute of Electrical and Electronic Engineers Symposium on Hot Chips, Palo Alto, CA, August.

Krattenmaker, T. (1994) *Telecommunications Law and Policy*, Durham, NC: Carolina Academic Press.

—— (1996) 'The telecommunications act of 1996', *Federal Communications Law Journal* 1, November.

McIntyre, B. (1996) 'Utilities unleashed: the answer to customers' Internet and broadband services needs?', paper presented to 'The Last 100 Feet' conference, organised by the Harvard Information Infrastructure Project, Arlington, VA, 29–30 October; to be published in D. Hurley and J.H. Keller (eds), *The First 100 Feet: Options for Internet and Broadband Access*, Cambridge, MA: MIT Press, forthcoming.

McKnight, L. (1997) 'Internet telephony', presentation to Harvard Information Infrastructure Project conference on 'The Impact of the Internet on Communications Policy', Cambridge, MA, December.

May, A. (1997) 'Comment on Notice 97/V 140/06: Voice on the Internet', Washington, DC: Federal Communications Commission, mimeo.

Mitchell, B. and Vogelsang, I. (1991) *Telecommunications Regulation: Theory and Practice*, Cambridge and New York: Cambridge University Press.

Mueller, M. (1993) 'Universal service in telephone history', *Telecommunications Policy*, July.

Nogueira, J. and Calvalcanti, J. (1997) 'The safety net approach to Internet pricing', mimeo, Universidade Federal de Pernambuco.

OECD (1996) *Local Telecommunications Competition: Developments and Policy Issues*, OCDE/GD(96)179, Paris: OECD.

OFTEL (1997a) *Promoting competition in services over telecommunications networks*, London: OFTEL.

—— (1997b) *BT Internet Services Investigation: Statement Following Investigation into the Pricing of BTNet, BT Internet's Plan 180 and Campus World*, London: OFTEL.

—— (1997c) *Report of the Work of OFTEL's Consumer Panel on Retail Price Controls and Universal Service, 1995–1997*, London: OFTEL.

—— (1997d) *Universal Telecommunications Services: Proposed Arrangements for Universal Service in the UK from 1997*, consultative document, London: OFTEL.

Théry, G. (1994) *Les Autoroutes de l'information*, Report to the Prime Minister, Paris: Documentation française.

Werbach, K. (1997) *Digital Tornado: The Internet and Telecommunications Policy*, Office of Plans and Policy Working Paper 29, Washington, DC: Federal Communications Commission.

Williams, H. (1997) 'USO in a competitive environment', *World Communications*.

# 15 Market structure, corporate objectives and cost efficiency*

*Johan Willner*

## Introduction

This contribution focuses on the basic assumption that lies behind the present dominant tendency to privatise and deregulate, namely the belief that public ownership leads to inefficiency, in particular if there is a monopoly. While there are strong incentives to cut costs in a firm which is managed by its owner and exposed to competition, the notion of private sector cost efficiency does not stand up to critical examination under other and more realistic conditions. For example, large companies or organisations in both private and public ownership are in general led by a manager whose efforts may or may not conform to the targets set by the owners. The way in which this delegation problem is affected by privatisation and deregulation has not always been understood properly.

Some authors, such as Frey (1997), have recently emphasised that many organisations actually rely on so called *intrinsic work motivation* rather than on external intervention in the form of rewards and punishments (*extrinsic work motivation*). To use sticks and carrots can even be counter-productive, because they may crowd out the intrinsic motivation, thus making an assumption of opportunism self-fulfilling. Consequently, it seems that performance-related pay is actually less wide-spread in the business world than is usually believed (Jensen and Murphy, 1990). However, the traditional approach to analyse agency problems is based on the assumption that all individuals are greedy and lazy. It is obvious that this rules out the possibility that any organisation based on, for example, a public service commitment could perform well. An unbiased analysis should therefore be extended beyond the traditional framework, but few contributions have done this.

On the other hand, the standard approach still deserves attention as an important special case with implications that have not yet been fully understood. Some theoretical research has already shown that private ownership

* The first draft of this paper was presented at the conference 'Practical Proposals for Industrial Policy in Europe', University of Warwick, 11–15 December 1997, arranged by EUNIP. I am grateful for constructive comments by the participants.

and/or competition will not always make a company more efficient. For example, Ellen Pint (1991) suggests that a public monopoly would outperform a (regulated) private monopolist if the weights in the objective function were appropriate. While public ownership might lead to excessive labour intensity, there would be an opposite bias after privatisation.[1] Giovanni De Fraja (1993) has shown that wider objectives than profit maximisation can actually make a firm more efficient, at least in a good state of nature. It is sometimes believed that competition might have a greater impact on performance than ownership, but Stephen Martin (1993) has shown that an increase in the number of firms in an oligopoly will actually increase managerial slack if demand is linear.

The present contribution focuses on the combined effects of ownership and competition on cost efficiency, if welfare is included in the objective function at least to some extent under public ownership. The company or companies are assumed to be managerial; the manager (the agent) may or may not have intrinsic work motivation. The only relevant source of cost differences is assumed to be managerial slack (X-inefficiency).[2] The analysis is inspired by the contributions by Frey (1997), De Fraja (1993) and Martin (1993) that were referred to above; these ideas are combined and developed to a model for analysing privatisation and deregulation under different kinds of motivation.

Unlike De Fraja's analysis, we deal explicitly with the market in which the company operates and formulate the objective function using inverse demand schedules. Demand is assumed to be linear, but a generalisation is provided elsewhere (Willner, 1998b). Moreover, we analyse maximising with and without break-even constraints, including the case where public ownership means free provision and a fixed budget. It turns out that public ownership would actually reduce managerial slack and possibly unit costs if there is any effect at all.[3] The exception is the case where the output is provided free of charge with too small a budget. It also follows that an increase in the number of oligopolistic (and managerial) firms will reduce efficiency. Of course, private companies are often more efficient than what follows from a proper understanding of how managerial firms with opportunistic managers work, but managers may in practice, like other types of agents, be genuinely interested in good performance and not only in money and leisure.

The nature of the agents' motivation may sometimes have a greater impact on efficiency than the ownership and objectives of an organisation. It is not necessarily the case that only public organisations rely on intrinsic motivation and private firms on rewards and punishments or vice versa. The opportunistic motives of the agent in a conventional model are not necessarily seen as examples of simplistic modelling only. Alternatively, they can be seen as representing cases where the intrinsic work motivation has been crowded out through monitoring, rewards and punishments. Differences in efficiency between public and private sector organisations may therefore go both ways.

## The basic model: intrinsic and extrinsic work motivation

Most of the earlier literature adopts the conventional approach in which the manager is assumed to be motivated only by rewards and punishments. If there is asymmetric information on the true state of nature, the manager can reduce his or her efforts and pretend that high costs are actually explained by unfavourable conditions. The employer must therefore adhere to an incentive compatibility constraint which ensures truthful revelation. In general, this implies performance-related pay, which causes the manager to bear some of the risk.

However, it is well known that individuals may work for other reasons than to gain rewards and avoid punishments. Artists, scientists, managers and many other professionals are not necessarily motivated by pecuniary rewards. Thus, while traditional models associate high performance with costs for the individual, there may be benefits as well, as in a model described by Bruno S. Frey (1997).[4] To introduce extrinsic motivation may under such circumstances reduce or crowd out the intrinsic motivation.

Our analysis applies a simplified model that is inspired by De Fraja (1993) and further elaborated in a number of ways, including allowing for intrinsic motivation. We shall ask how changes in ownership and market structure affect cost efficiency in a managerial company with asymmetric information about costs. The company operates in a monopoly or in an oligopoly with a demand function which is known both by the owner and the manager. For illustrative purposes, we shall adopt the version $p = a - x$, where $p$ is price, $x$ is output and $a$ a positive parameter. A more general version is provided elsewhere (Willner, 1998b).

Marginal costs consist of two parts. One part is dependent on the state of nature, which will be indexed by $L$ ('low-cost') and $H$ ('high-cost') respectively, and not affected by the manager's efforts. These non-avoidable marginal costs are either $c_L$ or $c_H$, with the probabilities $q$ and $1 - q$. The owner knows $c_L$, $c_H$, $q$ and $1 - q$ but the state of nature is known only by the manager. The second part depends on the manager's efforts to increase efficiency, or reduce managerial slack $s$. We shall assume that production is feasible in both states of nature.

The manager's utility function is usually quasi-linear and additive separable in this type of model. It can then be written as the sum of the salary, which is either $y_L$ or $y_H$, and a function which is related to effort or slack. In a conventional model, the manager's utility would be decreasing in effort or increasing in slack. However, if there is intrinsic work motivation, good performance causes both costs and benefits. This part of the utility 'function is therefore assumed to be first increasing and then decreasing. Reformulated in terms of managerial slack, this means that the manager's utility can be expressed in terms of a function which is maximised for some value $\bar{s}$. Thus, if the manager is allowed to choose the effort level without intervention, marginal costs will be $c_L + \bar{s}$ or $c_H + \bar{s}$.

It is reasonable to assume that the extent to which the manager is in control affects utility. To be controlled and manipulated causes disutility. This notion could be expressed in terms of some variable that stands for the degree of independence. However, following Frey (1997) we introduce a shift parameter $E$ which expresses the degree of control, or in his terminology, external intervention. This parameter will be omitted when it is kept constant, but the full version of the utility function is:

$$u = y + v(s, E). \tag{15.1}$$

An increase in the extent to which the agent is controlled may be associated with a cost for the company even if there is no intrinsic motivation or any monitoring costs. Suppose that there is a binding participation constraint requiring that utility is at least $\bar{u}$. Less independence then means that the agent must be compensated either by a higher salary or by more managerial slack, in which case marginal costs are higher.

Suppose that the degree of control associated with sticks and carrots is $E_1$ and the level associated with intrinsic motivation only $E_2$. Depending on the sign of $\partial^2 v / \partial s \partial E$, $v'(s, E_1)$ may be either below or above $v'(s, E_2)$. It seems plausible to assume that an increase of control causes the marginal utility of managerial slack to increase in most situations. Independence and slack are then *substitutes* in the sense that a reduction of either of them requires compensation in terms of the other. This means that $\partial^2 v / \partial s \partial E$, is positive, in which case $v'(E_1)$ lies above $v'(E_2)$. In other words, an increase in the level of control crowds out intrinsic motivation to some extent.

It is also possible that $\partial^2 v / \partial s \partial E$, is of the opposite sign, in which case the increased amount of control (lost independence) actually increases the motivation by allowing for more efforts to reduce slack for a given level of utility. This can be described as a *crowding-in* effect. However, it seems reasonable to accept Frey's conjecture that this situation is less likely (Frey, 1997).[5]

Assumptions 1(a) and 1(b) below summarise this discussion, while (c) and (d) are fairly innocuous simplifications.

**Assumption 1(a)** There exists an $\bar{s}$ such that $v'(\bar{s}) = 0$; **(b)** $\partial^2 v / \partial s \partial E > 0$; **(c)** $v'(0)$ is finite; **(d)** $v(0) = 0$.

## A simple principal–agent model: the case of monopoly

In this and the following two sections we focus on the case where the employer relies on extrinsic motivation only. The level of control is then kept constant at $E_1$ and will consequently be omitted from the utility function. Consider – to begin with – a monopoly which can be either in private or public ownership. In the latter case, the company is at least to some extent concerned with welfare (the total surplus).

Instead of comparing welfare and profit maximisation, we assume that the company's objective function is a weighted sum. Pure welfare or profit maximisation are then special cases. The manager's utility is seen as part of the total surplus. This means that $y_k$ cancels out, because salaries appear with the same weight as a cost and benefit. Thus, the total surplus $T_k$ in a given state of nature $k$ can be written as follows:

$$T_k = \int_0^{x_k} a - x\,dx - (c_k + s_k)x_k + v(s_k).$$  (15.2)

The manager's utility must be sufficiently high to prevent him or her leaving the firm (the *participation constraint*). The manager must also have an incentive to reveal truthfully that the (non-avoidable) marginal costs are $c_L$ instead of reporting that they are $c_H$ (the *incentive compatibility constraint*). In other words, truthful revelation of low costs must be more rewarding than cheating by pretending that circumstances have been unfortunate, which would make additional slack of the size $c_H - c_L$ possible. This can be achieved by paying a sufficiently high salary, but it may actually turn out to be cheaper to satisfy these restrictions by allowing for some slack. Therefore, the optimal contract will maximise the objective function with respect to the permitted slack levels $s_L$ and $s_H$ as well.

Profits in a given state of nature are denoted $\pi_k$. Further, let the weight associated with the total surplus and the profits be denoted by $\rho$ and $(1 - \rho)$ respectively. We can then analyse small increases in $\rho$ without break-even constraints, because the company is assumed to be profitable in a neighbourhood of $\rho = 0$. However, higher values of $\rho$ will also be dealt with, with and without break-even constraints.

Total marginal costs will be $c_L + s_L$ or $c_H + s_H$. There are no other fixed costs than $y_L$ or $y_H$. Let $\bar{u}$ be the utility level that can be reached in some alternative employment. The participation constraints are then $u(y_L, s_L) \geq \bar{u}$ and $u(y_H, s_H) \geq \bar{u}$. The incentive compatibility constraint requires $u(y_L, s_L) \geq u(y_H, s_H + c_H - c_L)$ to hold true. It is obvious that $u(y_H, s_H + c_H - c_L) > u(y_H, s_H)$, which means that the participation constraint will automatically be satisfied in the good state of nature.

In this version of the model we assume that the constraints are binding and substitute the solutions for $y_L$, and $y_H$ into the objective function. We focus on a small increase in $\rho$ for a company that is able to make profits; inequality constraints and break-even constraints are dealt with in Willner (1998b).

We introduce the abbreviations $a_L = a - c_L$, $a_H = a - c_H$ and $\Delta c = c_H - c_L$. The objective function is then:

$$W = q\left\{ a_L x_L - \frac{2-\rho}{2} x_L^2 - s_L x_L - (1-\rho)\left[\bar{u} - v(s_L) + v(s_H + \Delta c) - v(s_H)\right] + \rho v(s_L)\right\}$$

$$+ (1-q)\left\{ a_H x_H - \frac{2-\rho}{2} x_H^2 - s_H x_H - (1-\rho)[\bar{u} - v(s_H)] + \rho v(s_H)\right\}.$$  (15.3)

The first-order conditions with respect to $x_L$, $x_H$, $s_L$ and $s_H$ are, after some minor rearrangements:

$$q[a_L - (2 - p)x_L - s_L] = 0. \tag{15.4}$$

$$(1 - q)[a_H - (2 - p)x_H - s_H] = 0. \tag{15.5}$$

$$-qx_L + qv'(s_L) = 0. \tag{15.6}$$

$$-(1 - q)x_H + (1 - pq)v'(s_H) - q(1 - p)v'(s_H + c_H - c_L) = 0. \tag{15.7}$$

We can now solve for output in both states of nature as functions of the level of managerial slack:

$$x_L^*(s_L) = (a_L - s_L) / (2 - p). \tag{15.8}$$

$$x_H^*(s_H) = (a_H - s_H) / (2 - p). \tag{15.9}$$

It is obvious that both expressions are decreasing in managerial slack. It is useful to observe that the derivatives with respect to $s_L$ and $s_H$ are $-1/(2 - p)$.

Next, consider the levels of managerial slack. It is straightforward to solve for $s_L$ from (15.6), but deriving $s_H$ might need some elaboration. It will be convenient to approximate $v'(s_H + \Delta c)$ as $v'(s_H) + v''(s_H)\Delta c$. Combining with (15.8) and (15.9) and introducing an abbreviation then yields:

$$x_L^*(s_L) = v'(s_L). \tag{15.10}$$

$$x_H^*(s_H) = v'(s_H) - [(q(1 - p)v''(s_H)\Delta c)] / [(1 - q) = f'(s_H, p)]. \tag{15.11}$$

Note that concavity requires $f''(s_H, p)$ to be negative. Differentiating and rearranging yields:

$$(ds_L)/(dp) = [(a_L - s_L)/(2 - p)^2] / [v''(s_L) + 1/(2 - p)]. \tag{15.12}$$

$$(ds_H)/(dp) = [[(a_H - s_H)/(2 - p)^2] - \partial f'/\partial p)] / [f''(s_H) + 1/(2 - p)]. \tag{15.13}$$

It is obvious that the numerator of both derivatives is positive. The signs of the denominators are negative if the functions $v'(s_L)$ and $f'(s_L, p)$ are steeper than $x^*(s_L, p)$ and $x^*(s_H, p)$. At first sight it seems as if the effect of ownership depends on whether the manager's marginal utility with respect to slack is a steep or a flat function.

However, checking the second-order conditions shows that one of the cases can be excluded. The Hessian determinant is:

$$|H| = \begin{vmatrix} -q(2 - p) & 0 & -q & 0 \\ 0 & -(1 - q)(2 - p) & 0 & -(1 - q) \\ -q & 0 & qv''(s_L) & 0 \\ 0 & -(1 - q) & 0 & (1 - q)f''(s_H, p) \end{vmatrix}. \tag{15.14}$$

Let the principal minors be denoted by $|H_1|$, $|H_2|$, $|H_3|$ and $|H_4|$. It is obvious that $|H_1|$ is negative and $|H_2|$ positive, as should be the case. However, rearranging the conditions for $|H_3|$ to be negative and $|H_4|$ to be positive yields:

$$v''(s_L) < -1 / (2 - \rho). \tag{15.15}$$

$$f''(s_L, \rho) < -1 / (2 - \rho). \tag{15.16}$$

Thus, the second-order conditions are not satisfied unless $v'(s_L)$ and $f'(s_L, \rho))$ are steeper than $x^*(s_L, \rho)$ and $x^*(s_H, \rho)$. This means that the nationalised company is actually more cost efficient. This also applies to the case when the company sets $\rho = 1$.[6]

This means either that cost efficiency may be a non-issue or that wider objectives than profit maximisation are actually beneficial from the standpoint of cost efficiency as well. It might also be surprising that there is no trade-off between underprovision and excessive costs in a monopoly. This holds true because the monopolist would not be able to restrict output without increasing managerial slack as well.

As is elaborated elsewhere (Willner, 1998b), similar results hold true if break-even constraints are imposed, at least in the low-cost case.[7] To ensure that an intersection means a global maximum in such a case, we have to guarantee the concavity of the objective function and the constraints. If the objective function is non-concave, it follows that slack is zero, so that ownership does not matter. Otherwise, a company with constrained welfare maximisation ($\rho = 1$) will be more efficient than a private monopoly, but less efficient than if the constraint is removed.

It is often argued that public enterprises should not be allowed to make losses, because these would have to be financed by distortionary taxation. However, the break-even constraint may produce more slack and a further reduction of output in addition to the reduction because of prices being higher than marginal costs. It is not self-evident that these costs are overshadowed by the costs related to taxation.

To understand the intuition, note that the role of asymmetric information is to create an opportunity to cheat and thus make the implementation problem non-trivial. This increases the salary in the good state of nature. However, the basic result about the potentially beneficial effects of wider objectives is not driven by uncertainty and asymmetric information. Without uncertainty, the first-order conditions are simply $a - (2 - \rho)x - c - s = 0$ and $x(s) = v'(s)$; the objective function is concave if and only if $v'(s)$ is steeper than $x(s)$. The welfare maximising firm would then choose to pay more in salary in order to reduce the amount of slack.

Intuition might suggest that unit costs could become higher if slack is lower, because of what it costs to induce the manager to cut slack. However, this is not the case, at least if there is full-information. To see that costs $C = c + s + y/x$ are actually decreasing in $\rho$, note that the result is obvious if $s = 0$ because $x$ is then larger. To see that the same is true when $s > 0$, differentiate with respect to $\rho$:

$$dC/d\rho = (ds)/(d\rho) - [v'ds/d\rho x - [(\partial x/\partial s)(ds/d\rho) + (\partial x/\partial \rho)]y]/(x^2). \tag{15.17}$$

Rearrange and note that $v'(s^*)x^* = x^{*2}$. We get:

$$dC/d\rho = [(\partial x/(\partial s)(ds/d\rho) + (\partial x/\partial \rho)]y / x^2. \tag{15.18}$$

This expression is negative. Thus, unit costs are decreasing in $\rho$. The result can be generalised to the case of asymmetric information, provided that $v''(s_H)\Delta c$ is small in comparison with $y_L/x$.

## The case of free provision

Public utilities are sometimes provided free of charge and financed by the taxpayers. This may or may not be a good policy, but what matters for the present analysis is whether it would inevitably mean low cost efficiency as compared to private sector standards. Thus, suppose that there is a given and fixed budget which will cover variable costs, including managerial slack, and salaries. The fixed budget is denoted by $B_L$ and $B_H$ respectively; $B_L$ and $B_H$ may but need not be equal. This case is more complicated, because $s_H$ will depend on $B_L$. Therefore, we focus on the good state only.

Suppose that the objective is to maximise welfare in terms of the area under the demand schedule minus costs. The Lagrange-function is then:

$$L = q\left[a_L x_L - \tfrac{1}{2}x_L^2 - s_L x_L + v(s_L)\right] + (1 - q)\left[a_H x_H - \tfrac{1}{2}x_H^2 - s_H x_H + v(s_H)\right]$$
$$+\lambda_1[B_L - (c_L + s_L)x_L - \bar{u} + v(s_L) - v(s_H + \Delta c) + v(s_H)]$$
$$- \lambda_2[B_H - (c_H + s_H)x_H - \bar{u} + v(s_H)] \tag{15.19}$$

The first-order conditions with respect to $x_L$, $x_H$, $s_L$ and $s_H$ are, after some rearrangements:

$$q(a_L - x_L - s_L) - \lambda_1 (c_L + s_L) = 0. \tag{15.20}$$

$$(1 - q)(a_H - x_H - s) - \lambda_2 (c_H + s_H) = 0. \tag{15.21}$$

$$(q + \lambda_1)[- x_L + v'(s_L)] = 0. \tag{15.22}$$

$$(1 - q + \lambda_2)[-x_H + v'(s_H)] - \lambda_1 v''(s_H)\Delta c = 0. \tag{15.23}$$

The budget may be generous enough to make the constraints non-binding. The result is then the same as in the previous section if $\rho$ is set equal to one. The only difference is that the company's revenues are not covered by the customers but by the taxpayers. In the opposite case, the Lagrange multipliers are non-zero. Note that any solution in which the willingness to pay $(a - x_L)$ is positive means rationing.

We either get $\lambda_1 = -q$, which is possible only if the budget allows for $x_L$ to equal $a$, or we get $x_L = v'(s_L)$, as in the previous section. The latter case means that output also is maximised given the budget. This can be understood by solving for $x_L$ from the constraint, differentiating with respect to $s_L$ and using the condition $x_L = v'(s_L)$. The derivative is then zero. Let us introduce the abbreviation $\bar{u}_L = \bar{u} + v''(s_H)\Delta c$. Checking the second derivative shows that $x_L(s_L)$ is concave in $s_L$ in the point $x_L = v'(s_L)$ if $B_L < \bar{u}_L$, which means that $x_L(s_L)$ intersects $v'(s_L)$ at its maximum point.

The results from the previous section may now hold, but the outcome depends on the size of the budget. Thus, it is now possible to get solutions with more slack and less output than in a private monopoly without violating the second-order conditions. The reason is obvious: the organisation can then neither afford a high output nor a great amount of slack-reducing activity with such a low budget. This situation is represented by point A in Figure 15.1.

The effect of adjusting the budget is not completely straightforward, because the terms relating to the bad state of nature in $y_L$ may depend on $x_L$, $s_L$ and $B_L$ via the Lagrange multiplier $\lambda_2$. However, if the approximation of $\bar{u}_L$ is appropriate, it will not be greatly affected by an increase in the budget. Thus, $\partial x_L^* / \partial B_L$ is positive. This means that an increase in $B_L$ will increase output for a given level of slack, and cause the equilibrium to be shifted from point A to point B in the figure. Conversely, a budget cut would then not only reduce output but increase the amount of slack as well.

If $v'(s_L)$ is flat, $v(0)$ is relatively small. Thus, a large enough $B_L$ means that there will be no intersection between $x^*(s_K, B_L)$ and $v'(s_L)$. Both a welfare maximising organisation and a private monopolist would then choose $s_L = 0$. On the other hand, if $v'(s_L)$ is steep, a sufficiently large $B_L$ ensures that we get a higher output and lower slack than in a private monopoly.

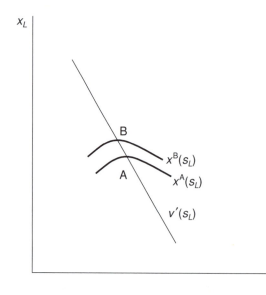

*Figure 15.1* Free provision with a restricted budget

This suggests that the present tendency to cut budgets in order to make the non-commercial public sector more efficient may be counter-productive in the sense that this may increase managerial slack.

## Competition

Competition and public ownership are often seen as alternative approaches to reduce the welfare costs of imperfect competition. However, competition is often seen as a way to reduce managerial slack as well. In this section we shall reformulate the principal–agent model in terms of an *n*-firm oligopoly so as to examine a deregulation that aims at creating more competition. This version shows that earlier results can easily be included so as to enable us to study the joint impact of privatisation and deregulation, but a generalisation of Martin's (1993) results about competition is provided elsewhere (Willner, 1998b).

Consider a market with *n* profit-maximising and managerial firms. They are identical in the sense that the non-avoidable marginal costs are the same everywhere, as are the managers' utility functions and outside options and the probabilities for each outcome. All companies have Cournot conjectures. Assuming that it is possible to break even, the Lagrange function for a firm *i*, $i = 1, 2, \ldots n$ is:

$$\pi_i = q[(a_L - x_L - s_{Li})x_{Li} - \bar{u} + v(s_{Li}) + v(s_{Hi}) - v(s_{Hi} + \Delta c)]$$
$$+ (1 - q)[(a_H - x_H - s_{Hi})x_{Hi} - \bar{u} + v(s_{Hi})]. \qquad (15.24)$$

The first-order conditions with respect to $x_{Li}$, $x_{Hi}$, $s_{Li}$ and $s_{Hi}$ are, after some rearrangement:

$$q(a_L - x_L - x_{Li} - s_{Li}) = 0. \qquad (15.25)$$

$$(1 - q)(a_H - x_H - x_{Hi} - s_{Li}) = 0. \qquad (15.26)$$

$$q[-x_{Li} + v'(s_{Li})] = 0. \qquad (15.27)$$

$$(1 - q)[-x_{Hi} + v'(s_{Hi})] - qv''(s_{Hi})\Delta c = 0. \qquad (15.28)$$

The *n* equations represented by (15.25) now yield the oligopolistic output $x_{Hi}^c$ $(s_{L1}, s_{L2}, \ldots s_{Ln}, n)$ as functions of the level of managerial slack in each firm and the number of firms. Combining with (15.27) yields the following condition:

$$x_{Li}^c (s_{L1}, s_{L2}, \ldots s_{Ln}, n) = v'(s_{Li}). \qquad (15.29)$$

$$x_{Hi}^c (s_{H1}, s_{H2}, \ldots s_{Hi}, n) = v'(s_{Hi}) - [q(1 - \rho)v''(s_{Hi})\Delta c]/(1 - q)$$
$$= f'(s_{Hi}, \rho). \qquad (15.30)$$

There are *n* such pairs of equations, which can be used to determine the level of slack in each firm. However, as the equilibrium is symmetric, we can add the conditions and divide by $n$ to get the following condition for the general level of slack:

$$(a_L - s_L) / (n + 1) = v'(s_L^c). \tag{15.31}$$

$$(a_H - s_H) / (n + 1) = f'(s_H^c). \tag{15.32}$$

Differentiating yields:[8]

$$ds_L^c / dn = - (a_L - s_L)/(n + 1)^2 / n[v'' + 1/(n + 1)]. \tag{15.33}$$

$$ds_H^c / dn = - (a_H - s_H)/(n + 1)^2 / n[f'' + 1/(n + 1)]. \tag{15.34}$$

It is a simple exercise to show that concavity requires $|v''(s_L)| > 1/2$ and $|f''(s_H)| > 1/2$. As $1/(n + 1) \leq 1/2$, the denominators of (15.33) and (15.34) must then be negative. This implies that an increase in the number of firms will increase the amount of managerial slack.[9] If there are no solutions to (15.29) and (15.30) while production is still feasible, or if the second-order conditions are not satisfied, slack is zero. The number of firms does not then affect the solution.

Note that a private monopoly will be less cost efficient than a welfare-maximising firm if the second-order conditions are satisfied. Thus, to privatise a public monopoly reduces cost efficiency, but to split it so that we get oligopolistic competition then makes matters worse. This result runs contrary to the popular fashion to privatise and deregulate. Note, however, that it does not mean that competition is inefficient if it is possible to get a large number of entrepreneurial rather than managerial firms to run an activity. Moreover, industrial output may both increase and decrease after an increase in the number of managerial firms in an oligopoly.

## Intrinsic work motivation

So far, the analysis has yielded a number of fairly strong conclusions which can be generalised beyond linear demand. If managers are opportunistic as in pp. 293–300, good management becomes a commodity that is bought and sold on the market. It is then no surprise that a monopolist can afford to pay more than an oligopolist for cost-reducing activities. Profit maximisation limits the willingness to pay for lower costs, because only part of the slack-reducing activity benefits the owner. On the other hand, if a company has wider objectives, as made possible under public ownership or in the voluntary sector, the benefits of lower costs to the rest of society strengthen the incentives to reduce slack.

As shown in the next section, there exists a number of empirical studies suggesting that this analysis is actually not too far from the truth. Nevertheless, the model may do some injustice to decision-makers both in the public and the private sector. For example, why are some oligopolistic companies highly efficient? Why can some public sector organisations perform well without paying fat-cat salaries?

In this section we shall focus on the possibility that managers are driven by other forces than salaries and slack. If the agent is sufficiently motivated, no incentive compatibility constraint is needed. This is associated with the low control level $E_2$ (see pp. 291–3). On the other hand, managers might quit if they get other more attractive offers, so there still has to be participation constraints for both states of nature. Thus, the agent will choose $\tilde{s}$, which means that the salary is determined from the participation constraints. We get the following solution for both states of nature:

$$y = \bar{y} = \bar{u} - v(E_2, \tilde{s}).$$

(15.35)

If there is no break-even constraint, we can replace $y_L$ and $y_H$ by (15.35) in the objective function above (pp. 293–7). The first-order conditions imply:

$$x_L^*(\tilde{s}) = (a_L - \tilde{s}) / (2 - \rho).$$

(15.36)

$$x_H^*(\tilde{s}) = (a_H - \tilde{s}) / (2 - \rho).$$

(15.37)

On the other hand, if the principal tries to manipulate the agent, the degree of independence is $E_1$. The analysis is then the same as on pp. 293–7, with the exception that the utility of slack should now be explicitly written as $v(E_1, s)$. Assumption 1(b) implies that $v'(E_1)$ lies above $v'(E_2)$.

Crowding out can cause $\tilde{s}$ to lie to the left of the intersection between $v'(E_1)$. and $x_L(s)$, as illustrated by Figure 15.2, where $x_L^M(s_L)$ and $x_L^*(s_L)$ represent profit and welfare maximisation respectively.[10]

For example, if privatisation means that the organisation introduces extrinsic motivation, slack increases from $\tilde{s}$ to $s_L^M$. To introduce extrinsic

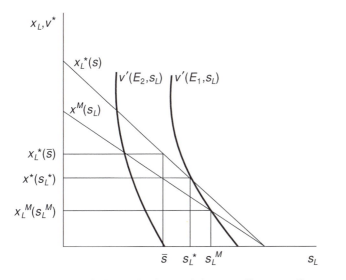

*Figure 15.2* Intrinsic motivation and the crowding-out effect

motivation without privatisation means a change from $\bar{s}$ to $s_L^*$. On the other hand, if sticks and carrots are used only under public ownership, privatisation would reduce slack from $s_L^*$ to $\bar{s}$.

If the principal relies on intrinsic work motivation, the model predicts that a change of objectives would not affect cost efficiency. However, a strong crowding-out effect, as in the figure, means that privatisation matters if $E$ also changes. In some cases, public ownership is associated with intrinsic work motivation, as often happens in universities and in some service production. However, there is not necessarily any simple relationship between ownership and type of motivation. While some public sector organisations rely on intrinsic motivation, others may be more bureaucratic and focused on reward and punishment than some private firms or voluntary organisations. The notion of public sector inefficiency may even work as a self-fulfilling prophecy, if the authorities respond by introducing rewards and punishments with a strong crowding-out effect.

Thus, both forms of ownership may be associated with either intrinsic or extrinsic work motivation. The outcome then depends on the size of the crowding-out effect and the slopes of $v'(E_1, s)$ and $x_L^M(s)$. If the crowding-out effect is weak, $\bar{s}$ lies to the right of both intersections with $v'(E_1, s)$. The principal would then not rely on intrinsic motivation. A strong effect means that $\bar{s}$ lies to the left of both intersections, while a moderately strong effect means that it lies between them.

Demand shifts and changes in the number of firms leave $\bar{s}$ unaffected if there is intrinsic work motivation. However, this does not necessarily mean that the actual level of managerial slack is unaffected. The reason is that a change in the position of the relationship between output and slack might reverse the ranking between $\bar{s}$ and the intersection point with $v'(E_1, s_L)$. Thus, a company which relies on intrinsic motivation might have an incentive to adopt sticks and carrots after a change in demand or market structure and vice versa, and this may change the level of slack.

## A discussion of empirical results

There exists a body of empirical research on comparative cost efficiency, which has gained surprisingly little attention given its policy relevance. We would expect strong and unanimous support among investigations from different institutional settings for the superiority of private ownership if this were an economic law. However, the empirical research in the area has been surveyed a number of times, and the verdict seems to be that there is no simple relationship between cost efficiency and ownership (Millward, 1982; Boyd, 1986; Yarrow, 1986; Vickers and Yarrow, 1988; and Willner, 1996).[11]

Most surveys of the existing literature consider both services and industrial production, and differences between public and private ownership then tend to go both ways. For example, refuse collection is often more cost efficient under private ownership, but insurances are not. However, the nature of industries such as urban transport, health care and insurances might be changed to such an extent by privatisation or nationalisation that we are no longer comparing the costs for producing the same service.[12]

Table 15.1 is based on Willner (1996), but it now includes only industrial production of homogeneous goods whose nature is not dependent on ownership. Moreover, a public service commitment (some weight attached to welfare) might be more likely in utilities such as water and electricity than in other state-owned companies. As the table shows, with such a focus, the empirical findings tend to yield similar conclusions to the theoretical analysis.

It might be too early to evaluate the effects of privatisation in countries other than Britain, where its history is sufficiently long. If privatisation improves efficiency to such an extent that it overshadows any benefits of public ownership, we would expect strong and unanimous support from the studies that have been made. However, their results are far from conclusive. For example, some evidence suggest that total labour productivity may have increased, as a result of stronger incentives to shed labour (Parker and Martin, 1996). However, analysing total factor productivity rather than just labour productivity suggests that privatisation does not make the overall use of inputs more efficient (Parker, 1995). A data envelopment analysis suggests that some companies may have become more efficient, while others have even deteriorated (Parker *et al.*, 1997). Martin and Parker's (1995) analysis of performance throughout the business cycle yields similar results. In many cases, the improvements actually took place before privatisation. Some cost-cutting might have taken place without privatisation, or has taken place in firms without any history of public ownership.

There are fewer empirical studies which evaluate the impact of competition on cost efficiency in oligopolies, but some results suggest that it is not self-evident that an increase in the number of firms is beneficial. Some evidence from Switzerland and Germany suggest that the administrative costs of running insurance services might actually have become higher after deregulation (Epple and Schäfer, 1996; Felder, 1996; and von Ungern-Sternberg, 1996). Moreover, some monopolies like British Telecom improved their performance after privatisation in Britain, while a number of companies which were exposed to competition did not, contrary to what Vickers and Yarrow (1988) expected in their early analysis of privatisation in Britain.[13]

## Concluding remarks and practical suggestions

The virtues that are usually associated with private ownership relate to the ability of a market to generate decentralised decision-making and an allocation which reflects the preferences in society. However, these advantages might best be reached under public ownership when the market mechanism is too far away from this ideal, as in a natural monopoly or in markets which become increasingly concentrated because of mergers and acquisitions.

*Table 15.1* Cost efficiency in industrial production

| Author(s) | Country | G | ND | P |
|---|---|---|---|---|
| Cement | | | | |
| Çakmak and Zaim, 1992 | Turkey | | x | |
| Electric utilities | | | | |
| Atkinson and Halvorsen, 1986 | US | | x | |
| Färe *et al.*, 1985 | US | x | | |
| Foreman-Peck and Waterson, 1985 | UK | | x | |
| Hausman and Neufield, 1991 | US | x | | |
| Meyer, 1975 | US | x | | |
| Moore, 1970[a] | US | | x | |
| Neuberg, 1977 | US | x | | |
| Pescatrice and Trapani, 1980 | US | x | | |
| Peters, 1993[b] | US | x | | |
| Spann, 1977 | US | | x | |
| Yunker, 1975 | US | | x | |
| Gas | | | | |
| Millward and Ward, 1987 | UK | | x | |
| Plastics | | | | |
| Tyler, 1979 | Brazil | | x | |
| Steel | | | | |
| Rowley and Yarrow, 1981[c] | UK | | x | |
| Tyler, 1979 | Brazil | | x | |
| Water utilities | | | | |
| Bruggink, 1982 | US | x | | |
| Byrnes *et al.*, 1976 | US | | x | |
| Crain and Zardkoohi, 1978 | US | | | x |
| Feigenbaum and Teeples, 1983 | US | | x | |
| Lynk, 1993 | UK | x | | |
| Mann and Mikesell, 1976[d] | US | x | | |
| Teeples and Glyer, 1987 | US | | x | |

*Notes*:
[a] Borcherding *et al.* (1982) interpret this source as less favourable for public production.
[b] Strictly speaking, the original source is an unpublished report which is cited by its author in Peters (1993).
[c] This source can also be interpreted as suggesting that private ownership might be more efficient, but we follow Aylen (1994) in emphasising the ambiguity of the result.
[d] Borcherding *et al.* (1982) give the opposite interpretation, but we follow Crain and Zardkoohi (1978), Boyd (1986), Yarrow (1986) and Boardman and Vining (1989). The original source is P.C. Mann and J.L. Mikesell, 'Ownership and Water Systems Operation', *Water Resources Bulletin*, vol. 12, 1976, pp. 995–1004.
*Explanation of symbols*: G = public production superior; ND = no difference or ambiguous results; P = private production superior.

Important strategic decisions are then made by unelected managers who may control companies with a turnover that exceeds the GDP of a medium-sized European country. The presence of a non-profit-maximising company might then enforce discipline within the industry, as suggested for example by Cremér *et al.* (1989), De Fraja and Delbono (1989) and Willner (1992, 1994).

However, motives other than microeconomic market failures may in practice have been even more important for understanding why there has been public ownership in some industries. For example, many state-owned companies in Finland and Sweden have been part of a development strategy. They were established because of a lack of private venture capital, but their behaviour has been largely commercial. Efficiency has not been an issue and plays no major role as an argument for privatisation in these countries (Willner, 1998a).

In recent years there has been a tendency to dismiss market failures and other arguments for public ownership because of perceived cost inefficiency. Nevertheless, as the present analysis and most empirical studies of cost efficiency in industrial production suggest, public ownership is not inherently inferior.[14] The dominant view seems to be formed not by empirical evidence but by the general performance of the centrally planned economies, which is not necessarily relevant for mixed economies. The fact that dictatorship, rigid central planning, an over-sized defence sector, an emphasis on industrial conglomerates and macroeconomic mismanagement (and an excessive reliance on rewards and punishment) led to bad performance does not imply that state-owned companies and public utilities in the west should be privatised.

Public ownership in Britain is often seen described as less successful than in, for instance, Scandinavia. As in the centrally planned economies, nationalisation in Britain was, however, to some extent motivated by misguided attempts to create large conglomerates. Unlike in Scandinavia, state-owned companies were also constrained to being financed mainly through the state budget. Moreover, they were often given objectives that interfered with cost minimisation. This is not always a bad policy, but the companies became targets for criticism once cost efficiency was given higher priority than other political objectives.

Selfish behaviour has often been interpreted as implying that economic activity should in general be commercial. Our analysis suggests that the converse is true: the market mechanism would more often perform well without opportunism, which requires managers to be bribed in order to induce efforts. If pay has to be performance-related, productive efficiency becomes analogous to environmental protection. A profit maximiser is not then interested in paying enough for benefits – in this case cost-reducing activity – that spill over to other agents. The optimal amount cannot therefore be achieved unless other stakeholders than the owner have a say.

The present obsession with cost efficiency in activities which remain in the public sector might be counterproductive. Such a development can mean lower budgets, which can yield more managerial slack, and a strong emphasis on rewards and punishments. The latter can in fact provide good examples of how intrinsic motivation is crowded out by external intervention. The traditional principal–agent model can even be seen as describing cases where this has happened: the agent's own motivation has been burned out and replaced by an ambition to earn rewards and avoid punishments.

Competition is usually seen as the best remedy for failures created by profit maximisation, but this may be wishful thinking in industries characterised by mergers and acquisitions. Moreover, it is not self-evident that competition is always beneficial, even if a market is not a natural monopoly in any strict sense. For example, free entry might lead to cream skimming since no company can afford the less-profitable activities. The quality of services like public transport may in addition be reduced because of coordination problems. Finland is often mentioned as a front-runner in deregulating telecommunications, but the process has also led to questionable changes such as incompatible telephone cards and a need to use complicated codes.

Needless to say, the fact that popular views about public sector inefficiency are prejudiced should not be used as a motive for a new orthodoxy which is a complete reversal of the present trends. Cost efficiency is a bad motive for privatisation but also for nationalisation.[15] Thus, there are no good ideological shortcuts to excuse ignorance about how specific industries work.

## Notes

1 She suggests that the trend to privatise is explained by attempts to get electoral benefits and to restrict the scope for future governments.

2 While the most popular arguments for private ownership are based on the management's incentives to cut costs if there is a profit motive, there are some other explanations as well. These include diffuse ownership, vague objectives and the lack of bankruptcy and takeover threats, but it is not self-evident that these factors make private ownership more efficient (see, for example, De Fraja, 1993, and Vickers and Yarrow, 1988).

3 If managerial slack can be lowered only by paying high salaries, intuition might suggest that unit costs can be higher under public ownership and lower under competition, but this intuition is false.

4 More precisely, benefits $B$ and costs $C$ are then described as functions of work performance $P$ and external interventions $E$. The agent then maximises $B - C$, which means that $B_p = C_p$.

5 Frey's analysis is formulated in terms of performance rather than slack. Suppose that slack is a function $g(P)$ of performance as defined in Frey's model (Frey, 1997); $g_p < 0$. Performance can then be written as $g^{-1}(s)$ or $f(s)$. Utility is maximised if $B_p - C_p = 0$; the corresponding derivative in our model is $v' = (B_p - C_p)f_s$. The benefits of a higher performance are then seen as costs of increased slack, which are absent if there is no intrinsic work motivation. Simplifying by setting $C_E = 0$, there is a crowding out effect if $\partial^2/\partial s \partial E = B_{PE}f_s > 0$, which means that $B_{PE} < 0$ as in Frey's model.

6 As shown elsewhere (Willner, 1998b), the analysis can be extended to cases where $v'$ is flat. It then follows that the best solution is to set managerial slack equal to zero.

7 This case is very close to De Fraja's analysis (De Fraja, 1993), but the proof is much simpler, without essential loss of generality.

8 The number of firms can of course take only integer values, but we can treat (15.31) as including a variable $n$ which can take any value. The sign of the derivative would than tell whether managerial slack would increase or decrease as $n$ changes from, say, $n_0$ to $n_0 + 1$.

9 This result is to some extent dependent on linearity because an increase in the number of firms then always reduces the output of each firm. As shown elsewhere (Willner, 1998b), the entry of a second firm in a monopoly can under certain conditions more than double output, in which case slack would be reduced.

10 In the case of free provision would get $x_L = [B_L - \bar{u} + v(\bar{s})]/(c_L + s_L)$; the expression is similar for the high-cost case. Managerial slack may be lower or higher than under profit maximisation. Slack can no longer be affected by the size of the budget, but output is linear in $B_L$.

11 Many authors' beliefs about relative cost efficiency are based on an early survey by Borcherding et al. (1982), which cites a large number of non-academic reports as well. These tended to favour private ownership. However, like other authors, Borcherding et al. warn against simplistic interpretations and suggest that competition might be more important than ownership.

12 The postal services in Finland could be a case in point. They are not yet privatised, but are organised on a commercial basis. This has meant large reductions in the number of service points, which shifts the transport costs to the customers.

13 Amersham, British Aerospace, Cable and Wireless, Enterprise Oil and Jaguar were among the firms in Britain that were expected to improve their performance. Actually, British Aerospace improved its performance, but it is doubtful whether the same can be said of Jaguar. Rolls Royce experienced a relative decline in productivity growth as compared to the rest of the economy, and the experiences of the other companies on the list were mixed while some monopolies improved their performance (Parker and Martin, 1995; and Martin and Parker, 1995).

14 The focus on industrial production rather than services also explains why this analysis has ignored factors such as differences in service quality, wage bargaining or other cases where cost-cutting cannot be an end in itself. These have been dealt with elsewhere (Willner, 1998a and 1999).

15 For example, the catering organisation within the army in Finland is cost efficient, but most customers would not see this as an ideal of how restaurant services should be organised.

# References

Atkinson, S. and R. Halvorsen (1986), 'The Relative Efficiency of Public and Private Firms in a Regulated Environment: the Case of US Electric Utilities', *Journal of Public Economics*, vol. 29, pp. 281–294.

Aylen, Jonathan (1994), 'Privatization of British Steel', in Matthew Bishop, John Kay and Colin Meyer (eds), *Privatization and Economic Performance*, Oxford: Oxford University Press, pp. 162–187.

Boardman, Anthony and Aidan Vining (1989), 'Ownership and Performance in Competitive Environments: a Comparison of the Performance of Private, Mixed and Share-owned Enterprises', *Journal of Law and Economics*, vol. 32, pp. 1–33.

Borcherding, Thomas E., Werner W. Pommerehne and Friedrich Schneider (1982), 'Comparing the Efficiency of Private and Public Production: the Evidence from Five Countries', *Zeitschrift für Nationalökonomie*, Suppl. 2, 127–156.

Boyd, Colin W. (1986), 'The Comparative Efficiency of State Owned Enterprises', in Anant R. Negandhi (ed.), *Multinational Corporations and State-owned Enterprises: A New Challenge in International Business*, Greenwich, CT and London: Research in International Business and International Relations, JAI Press.

Bruggink, Thomas M. (1982), 'Public versus Regulated Private Enterprise in the Municipal Water Industry: A Comparison of Water Costs', *Quarterly Review of Economics and Business*, vol. 22, no. 1, pp. 111–125.

Byrnes, Patricia, Shawna Grosskopf and Kathy Hayes (1976), 'Efficiency and Ownership: Further Evidence', *Review of Economics and Statistics*, vol. 68, no. 2, pp. 337–341.

Çakmak, Erol H. and Osman Zaim (1992), 'Privatization and Comparative Efficiency of Public and Private Enterprise in Turkey: The Cement Industry', *Annals of Public and Cooperative Economy*, vol. 63, no. 2, pp. 271–284.

Crain, W. Mark and Asgkhar Zardkoohi (1978), 'A Test of the Property Rights Theory of the Firm: Water Utilities in the United States', *Journal of Law and Economics*, vol. 21, no. 2, pp. 395–408.

Cremér, H.M., M. Marchand and J.F. Thisse (1989), 'The Public Firm as an Instrument for Regulating an Oligopolistic Market', *Oxford Economic Papers*, vol. 42, April, pp. 283–301.

De Fraja, Giovanni (1993), 'Productive Efficiency in Public and Private Firms', *Journal of Public Economics*, vol. 50, no. 1, pp. 15–30.

De Fraja, Giovanni and Flavio Delbono (1989), 'Alternative Strategies of a Public Enterprise in Oligopoly', *Oxford Economic Papers*, vol. 41, April, pp. 302–311.

Epple, Karl and Reinhard Schäfer (1996), 'The Transition from Monopoly to Competition: the Case of Housing Insurance in Baden-Württemberg', *European Economic Review*, vol. 40, nos 3–5, pp. 1123–1131.

Färe, R., S. Grosskopf and J. Logan (1985), 'The Relative Performance of Publicly Owned and Privately Owned Electric Utilities', *Journal of Public Economics*, vol. 26, no. 1, pp. 89–106.

Feigenbaum, Susan and Ronald Teeples (1983), 'Public versus Private Water Delivery: a Hedonic Cost Approach', *Review of Economics and Statistics*, vol. 65, no. 4, pp. 672–678.

Felder, Stefan (1996), 'Fire Insurance in Germany: a Comparison of Price-performance between State Monopolies and Competitive Regions', *European Economic Review*, vol. 40, nos. 3–5, pp. 1133–1141.

Finsinger, Jörg (1984), 'The Performance of Public Enterprises in Insurance Markets', in Maurice Marchand, Pierre Pestieau and Henry Tulkens (eds), *The Performance of Public Enterprises: Concepts and Measurement*, Amsterdam: North-Holland.

Foreman-Peck, J.O. and Michael Waterson (1985), 'The Comparative Efficiency of Public and Private Enterprise in Britain: Electricity Generation Between the World Wars', *Economic Journal*, vol. 95, Supplement, pp. 83–95.

Frey, Bruno S. (1997), 'On the Relationship Between Intrinsic and Extrinsic Work Motivation', *International Journal of Industrial Organization*, vol. 15, no. 4, pp. 427–440.

Hausman, William J. and John L. Neufeld (1991), 'Property Rights versus Public Spirit: Ownership and Efficiency of US Electric Utilities Prior to Rate or Return Regulation', *Review of Economics and Statistics*, vol. 73, no. 3, pp. 414–423.

Jensen, M.C. and K.J. Murphy (1990), 'Performance Pay and Top-management Incentives, *Journal of Political Economy*, vol. 98, pp. 225–264.

Lynk, E.L. (1993), 'Privatisation, Joint Production and the Comparative Efficiencies of Private and Public Ownership: the UK Water Industry Case', *Fiscal Studies*, vol. 14, no. 2, pp. 98–116.

Mann, P.C. and J.L. Mikesell (1976), 'Ownership and Water Systems Operation', *Water Resources Bulletin*, vol. 12, no. 5, pp. 995–1004.

Martin, Stephen (1993), 'Endogeneous Firm Efficiency in a Cournot Principal–Agent Model', *Journal of Economic Theory*, vol. 59, no. 2, pp. 445–450.

Martin, Stephen and David Parker (1995), 'Privatisation and Economic Performance Throughout the UK Business Cycle', *Managerial and Decision Economics*, vol. 16, pp. 225–237.

Meyer, Robert A. (1975), 'Publicly Owned versus Privately Owned Utilities: a Policy Choice', *Review of Economics and Statistics*, vol. 57, no. 4, pp. 391–399.

Millward, R. (1982), 'The Comparative Performance of Public and Private Ownership', in Lord E. Roll (ed.), *The Mixed Economy*, London: Macmillan.

Millward, R. and R. Ward (1987), 'The Costs of Public and Private Gas Enterprises in Late 19th-century Britain', *Oxford Economic Papers*, vol. 39, no. 4, pp. 719–737.

Moore, Thomas G. (1970), 'The Effectiveness of Regulation of Electric Utility Prices', *Southern Economic Journal*, vol. 37, April, pp. 365–375.

Neuberg, Leland Gerson (1977), 'Two Issues in the Municipal Ownership of Electric Power Distribution Systems', *Bell Journal of Economics*, vol. 8, Spring, pp. 303–323.

Parker, David (1995), *Measuring Efficiency Gains from Privatization*, Research Centre for Industrial Strategy, Occasional Papers in Industrial Strategy, no. 36, University of Birmingham.

Parker, David and Stephen Martin (1995), 'The Impact of UK Privatisation on Labour and Total Factor Productivity', *Scottish Journal of Political Economy*, vol. 42, no. 2, pp. 201–220.

Parker, David and Stephen Martin (1996), 'The Impact of UK Privatization on Employment, Profits and the Distribution of Business Income', *Public Money and Management*, January–March, pp. 31–37.

Parker, David, Aziz Boussofiane and Stephen Martin (1997), 'The Impact on Technical Efficiency of the UK Privatization Programme', *Applied Economics* (forthcoming).

Pescatrice, Donn R. and John M. Trapani (1980), 'The Performance of Public and Private Utilities Operating in the United States', *Journal of Public Economics*, vol. 13, no. 3, pp. 259–276.

Peters, Lon L. (1993), 'For-profit and Non-profit Firms: Limits of the Simple Theory of Attenuated Property Rights', *Review of Industrial Organization*, vol. 8, no. 5, pp. 623–634.

Pint, Ellen M. (1991), 'Nationalization vs. Regulation of Monopolies: the Effects of Ownership on Efficiency', *Journal of Public Economics*, vol. 44, no. 2, pp. 131–164.

Rowley, C.K. and Yarrow, G.K. (1981), 'Property Rights, Regulation and Public Enterprise: the Case of the British Steel Industry 1957–1975', *International Review of Law and Economics*, vol. 1, no. 1, pp. 63–96.

Spann, Robert M. (1977), 'Public versus Private Provision of Public Services', in Thomas E. Borcherding (ed.), Budgets and Bureaucrats, Durham, NC: Duke University Press, pp. 71–89.

Teeples, R. and D. Glyer (1987), 'Cost of Water Delivery Systems: Specification and Ownership Effects', *Review of Economics and Statistics*, vol. 69, pp. 399–408.

Tyler, W.G. (1979), 'Technical Efficiency in Production in a Developing Country: an Empirical Examination of the Brazilian Plastics and Steel Industries', *Oxford Economic Papers*, vol. 31, no. 3, pp. 477–495.

Vickers, John and George Yarrow (1988), *Privatization: An Economic Analysis*, Cambridge, MA: MIT Press.

von Ungern-Sternberg, Thomas (1996), 'The Limits of Competition: Housing Insurance in Switzerland', *European Economic Review*, vol. 40, nos 3–5, pp. 1111–1121.

Willner, Johan (1992), 'To Create Competition Without Regulation: a Mixed Oligopoly with Endogenous Cost Differences', in Keith Cowling and Roger Sugden (eds), *Current Issues in Industrial Economic Strategy*, Manchester and New York: Manchester University Press, pp. 54–69.

—— (1994), 'Welfare Maximisation with Endogenous Average Costs', *International Journal of Industrial Organization*, vol. 12, no. 3, pp. 373–386.

—— (1996), 'Social Objectives, Market Rule and Public Policy: the Case of Ownership', in Pat Devine, Yannis Katsoulacos and Roger Sugden (eds), *Competitiveness, Subsidiarity and Objectives: Issues for European Industrial Strategy*, London and New York: Routledge, pp. 12–41.

—— (1998a). 'Privatisation in the Nordic EU-countries: Fashion or Necessity?, in David Parker (ed.), *Privatisation in the European Union: An Industrial Policy Perspective*, London and New York: Routledge, pp. 172–190.

—— (1998b), 'Privatisation, Deregulation and Cost Efficiency', Turku: Åbo Akademi University, mimeo.

—— (1999), 'Policy Objectives and Performance in a Mixed Market with Bargaining', *International Journal of Industrial Organization*, vol. 17, no. 1, pp. 137–145.

Yarrow, George (1986), 'Privatization in Theory and Practice', *Economic Policy*, no. 2, pp. 324–364.

Yunker, J.A. (1975), 'Economic Performance of Public and Private Enterprise', *Journal of Economics and Business*, vol. 28, pp. 60–75.

# 16 Regulating transnationals

## Free markets and monitoring in Europe[1]

*David Bailey, George Harte and
Roger Sugden*

## Introduction

A central objective of recent industrial polices across Europe (at regional, national and European levels) has arguably been the promotion of the activities of both 'domestic' and 'foreign' based transnational firms. This has come via two routes: first, the dash to attract inward investment from the rest of the world, to bring foreign transnationals into the EU; and second the desire to build so-called 'Euro-champions' through the 1992 Single Market Programme, with these Euro-firms supposedly then capable of competing with US and Japanese firms (Ramsay, 1992). Indeed, it can be argued that the aim of completing the Single Market has come in response to vigorous lobbying from the leaders of European-based transnationals such as Volvo and Phillips who have been eager to exploit the added flexibility it will bring them (see Bellak, 1997), suggesting that the European agenda of integrating markets has actually been the agenda of the élites controlling decision-making within transnationals. This faith in Euro-champions – and the decisions of élites within them – has rested on a mistaken distinction between 'European' and 'non-European' transnationals (Ramsay, 1992). Furthermore, the push to attract inward investment has gained momentum with governments and regions scrambling to attract jobs as unemployment rates across Europe have soared, most recently because EU governments have imposed severe monetary and fiscal policies in an attempt to meet the Maastricht criteria for membership of the imminent European Monetary Union (EMU).

It is not the aim of this chapter to analyse in depth the consequences arising from such a heavy emphasis on promoting transnationals in an increasingly 'free' European economic environment. Rather, the aims are: (a) to show that certain key issues arise which necessitate a policy response from different tiers of government across Europe; (b) to show that an appropriate first step in devising such policy responses might be the creation of monitoring bodies at the national and European levels to understand more fully the forces being unleashed and to inform and catalyse policy debate; and (c) in doing so to outline what functions a monitoring unit might usefully perform and what implications for industrial policy might arise from its activities. Our view is that, while information may not mean power, without the right kind of information governments and communities cannot hope to develop appropriate policies and attitudes towards transnationals.

## Transnationals and industrial development: some key issues facing the EU

The Single Market, to which the finishing touches are still being added, creates increasing freedom from intervention by government, workers and others – that is, greater 'negative' freedom[2] – for strategic decision-makers in transnational firms over investment, output, employment and so on. As control over such decisions becomes more firmly enshrined in the hands of a few élite decision-makers within these increasingly dominant and mobile firms, the risks of 'strategic failure' become more likely, with the objectives of the élites who make those strategic decisions conflicting with the wider interests in society (Cowling and Sugden, 1994). The end result is social inefficiency, with the economic system yielding inappropriate outcomes for the society (or societies) served by that economy. At the heart of this is the 'industrial' versus 'corporate' strategy issue. 'Corporate' strategies are seen here as strategies for industrial development conceived by and in the interests of strategic decision-makers within large transnational corporations, whereas 'industrial' strategies are those devised by and in the interests of a wider set of actors in the community. If strategic decision-making is the preserve of only a few, there arises the potential for 'strategic failure', where the objectives of the élite making strategic decisions conflict with the wider interests in society, with the result that the economic system fails both to consider the range of possibilities available and to deliver the most appropriate outcomes for the community.

At the European level, such strategic failure is being manifested in (at least) two key forms. First, there is 'divide and rule' of workers and regions as well as governments by transnationals. Second, there is the reinforcing of centripetal tendencies through the centralisation of strategic decision-making. The first issue, divide and rule, is evident in a number of ways; workers and regions are being played off against each other by firms eager to reduce costs. One prominent example was Ford's actions in relocating production of different models around its European plants; this can be interpreted as significant in bringing to bear an implicit 'threat effect' on workers in British factories to catch up with productivity levels elsewhere; similarly with BMW and Rover, where the parent firm threatened to produce the new Mini model elsewhere if new work patterns and payments were not accepted by Longbridge workers. In another recent case, Hoover shifted production from France to Scotland to exploit lower wage and social security costs. As Bellak (1997) notes, the Hoover case was particularly interesting for the sophistication of the tactics used: Hoover announced in advance the closure of one of its three plants without specifying which one, trying 'to black-mail the workers by creating a situation where each plant (and region) had to bid down costs (and social protection) against the others', a sort of transnational-controlled Dutch-auction.

National and regional governments are also being played off against each other, via a race to attract new inward investment as well as trying to hang on to existing transnationals' activities. Fiscal policies are increasingly being designed specifically to serve transnationals' interests, through both subsidy packages[3] and downward pressure on corporation and income taxes across Europe.[4] With an evaporating tax base, a consequence of divide and rule is that the scope for redistributive and social expenditure by governments is also drying up, and it is possible to observe the emergence of both social dumping and tax competition (Willner, 1994). Of course, this is not solely inspired by transnational firms, but they are an important factor contributing to the intensification of such tendencies as well as to the move towards further deregulation.

In this regard, transnationals are homing in on their ultimate objective; the Multilateral Agreement on Investment (MAI), currently under discussion at the OECD, would give transnationals complete freedom (again 'negative' freedom, or freedom from control) over investment decisions, with governments given no power to challenge them. The 'free' market being constructed is negatively free for élite decision-makers in transnationals. The real danger is that this over-emphasis on negative freedom for the few ignores and indeed restricts positive freedom for the many; that is, the freedom for communities to make strategic decisions. The increasing emphasis on only one type of freedom for just a few intensifies the risks of strategic failure in the system as a whole (see Bailey, 1998).

A second dimension of strategic failure comes through the concentration of strategic decision-making in key locations in Europe by transnationals, which may serve to reinforce centripetal tendencies: with production located so as to serve the objectives of strategic decision-makers, different sorts of activities are located in different locations, leading to a Hymerian distribution of activity (Hymer, 1975). This latter process is suggested by recent trends across Europe. As Young and Hood (1993) note, location consultants advising transnational firms produce separate listings of sites across Europe for different activities. Regarding R&D activity, German and French locations score highly; for regional headquarters, locations close to main commercial centres are attractive; for greenfield assembly operations, the peripheral areas of northern Britain, Ireland, Spain, Portugal and Greece are most attractive; and so on. If transnationals have followed such advice, it would imply that higher value-added and decision-making activities have located closer to the central core of Europe.

There is some limited evidence to favour such a hypothesis. For example, the peripheral regions of the EU have attracted mainly low-order assembly operations, with strategic decisions made elsewhere. In the British case, Barrell and Pain (1997) found that Britain has been successful in attracting labour-intensive investment but has fared poorly in attracting capital-intensive activity, and has been unattractive in sectors where R&D has been more significant. Another finding (ibid.) is that Britain has done well in attracting investment in the non-manufacturing sector, yet this is the very sector 'where the evidence for the existence of beneficial supply-side effects from foreign investment is weakest'. It seems somewhat perverse that the only justification for subsidising inward investment by transnationals is the positive spillover effects of their activities, but that the type of inward investment attracted by Britain has few such spillovers. Other evidence is available in Young and Hood (1993), who summarise the effects of inward investment in Britain, pointing to some significant static gains (such as jobs and exports) but few dynamic benefits and little in the way of spin-off and demonstration effects. They conclude that transnational investment has not enabled the mature industrial regions of Britain to break free from their peripherality.

It could be argued that through strategic decision-making power being held in the key sites where transnationals locate European headquarters (or their home bases outside Europe), that very peripherality is being reinforced by transnationals' activities, with strategic decision-making, R&D and assembly operations taking place in different locations, and with that spatial pattern of development being in the interests of transnational firms. This Hymerian pattern of different activities need not correspond to wider community wishes nor with the goals of EU regional policy. Simply 'privatising' the industrial development process by handing over decision-making to transnationals (Cowling and Sugden, 1993), as is now happening, will not reverse the process of centripetalism, but is more likely to intensify it. If widening regional disparities and the concentration of decision-making in key sites is of concern – as we would suggest it is in terms of economic democracy, freedom and competitiveness – then it suggests that other industrial policies will be needed to deconstruct a transnationals-controlled pattern of development and to rebuild one in the interests of, and controlled by, regions and communities.

These are only two facets of the strategic failure problem; also of concern are monopolisation of markets and control over trade and technology.[5] Such effects are likely to intensify with developments currently taking place. In particular, the new division of labour unfolding across Europe as central and east European countries join the free trade area and integrate with the west gives strategic decision-makers in transnational firms added flexibility, with further opportunities to engage in divide and rule and other activities. Transnational investment in transition countries may bring new jobs but it also brings a raft of dangers in terms of monopolisation, outdated technological development and the capture of trade and other policies (see Bailey *et al.*, 1998). It also raises some fundamental policy issues for western countries; for example, if Britain has been 'successful' in selling itself to mobile transnationals at the lower end of the division of labour through low wages and social conditions combined with subsidies, it will find it increasingly difficult and expensive to continue as new competitor nations emerge to undercut it. What this also suggests is that it will be the transnationals themselves that will benefit from such trends, and not taxpayers or workers.

Another development, which will intensify the problems of strategic failure discussed above, is the proposed MAI, which is likely to be signed by OECD members in some form in 1999. The agreement is intended to remove all national controls on foreign investors and is seen by its advocates as an important step in the development of the global economy.[6] Its central theme is the 'protection of investment, investment liberalisation and dispute settlement' (Shelton, 1997), and is based around three principles: nondiscrimination; no entry restrictions; and an absence of special conditions. An aim is to seek to ensure a 'uniform, stable and predictable environment in which (transnational) enterprises can conduct their activities' (Kang, 1997).

In this way, the MAI extends trade liberalisation measures such as GATT and NAFTA into investment liberalisation. As Bleifuss (1998) notes, the MAI 'subordinates the rights of elected governments to set national economic policy to the right of transnational corporations and investors to conduct business'. The fear is that regions and nations will be forced to bid down social conditions even further in order to attract investment, but will be unable to impose sanctions on firms which behave undesirably in economic, social or environmental terms. Experience with both the GATT and NAFTA has not been encouraging in this respect. The GATT removed non-tariff trade barriers so as to maximise world trade, and in doing so threatened social and environmental legislation, while NAFTA has seen Canadian and Mexican governments sued by transnationals over their environmental protection measures.[7] Yet no restrictions on subsidies are included in the MAI, and as a result a one-sided market is being created, with transnationals gaining greater rights (more negative freedom) without accepting any further responsibilities. Governments are bound to resort to greater use of subsidies and grants so as to attract transnationals, as these would be the only instruments left available to them. This suggests that, following the MAI, governments will have a greater incentive to monitor the impact of subsidy-giving in order to assess their effectiveness and to inform policy-making in the limited area where policies could still be made.

## Facilitating appropriate policy responses: a European monitoring unit

In the short term, addressing the causes of strategic failures necessitates governments[8] negotiating with élites of strategic decision-makers in these firms so as to obtain as much benefit as possible for society from their presence, using existing points of contact with such firms. In the longer term, strategies need to encourage bottom-up approaches, broadening participation in strategic decision-making. They also need to encourage alternative forms of internationalisation, such as multinational webs, particular types of production networks envisaged by Sugden (1997) as a potential alternative to the internationalism of transnationals (see also Cowling and Sugden, 1998); a multinational web would be a large-scale production process comprising a myriad of smaller firms in a nexus of criss-crossing relationships which span international borders, a multinational (rather than a transnationals-controlled) production process. A significant first step in developing such policies towards transnationals would be the creation of transnational monitoring units at regional, national and European levels. These units would be designed to collect information on transnationals' performance and impact, to prepare accounts, and to use these to influence economic policy and attitudes of and towards transnationals.

Such a move could bring with it significant benefits as there remains – despite the increased imbalance of power between transnationals and governments in recent years – both a valid role for governments and *some* scope for them to try to obtain their objectives. As Ietto-Gilles (1997) notes, transnationals do require certain support services from governments, for example to reduce national and international uncertainty; to protect their foreign interests; to ensure a stable low-risk macro-environment; and to provide a necessary infrastructure for their operations. Similarly, Hirst and Thompson (1996) note that the bulk of transnationals' activities remain specific to the country of origin (although we would argue that the potential to relocate is important in heightening such firms' power), and that to see transnationals as beyond the control of governments is excessively pessimistic. Governments should realise this does give them a degree of leeway, both directly and indirectly (for example, in helping to build 'countervailing power' for other actors, that is, enabling other groups to have an input into strategic decision-making).

If anything, however, governments appear to be moving in the opposite direction. Historically, in Britain it would seem that successive Labour governments of the 1960s and 1970s were paralysed by the fear of being perceived as hostile (and subsequently deterring investment) if they were to adopt a more proactive bargaining position. The view that transnationals had to be accepted 'warts and all' was hence a dominant idea amongst policy-makers keen to attract inward investment for its perceived employment benefits. However, during the 1980s and 1990s under Conservative governments and now under 'New Labour', there appears to have been a different ideology; the government is not afraid to act, as it sees no reason to act in the first place. The Thatcherite agenda of minimal government intervention and an arguably blind belief in so-called free markets is now firmly entrenched in Britain and other countries.[9]

Even if earlier British governments had wanted to act so as to address some of the deficiencies arising from the presence of transnationals, nothing was done to make this possible. In particular, the lack of monitoring of such firms meant that governments were unable to create bargaining power. This is not something which is given for governments and other actors, but rather is endogenous; governments can manipulate their environments to maximise such bargaining power. A key aspect of this is monitoring so as to have the necessary information needed to understand and anticipate transnationals' activities, to be prepared for negotiations, and if need be to devise policies to affect the public's opinion of transnationals, and therefore demand for their products and hence the strategies of firms themselves. Governments, workers, consumers and others would then be better informed and prepared and thus more able to negotiate with, and put pressure on, transnationals. Bargaining strength could thus be built up over time, moving governments in particular away from positions of ignorance, which have characterised both their previous inactivity and their blundering interventions, such as the fiasco in British policy over Chrysler in the 1970s (see Hodges, 1974).

One approach might be for governments themselves to use the information collected by a monitoring unit to publicise the activities of transnationals and thus to influence public perception of such firms, an approach which would learn from successful firms in oligopolistic markets. The strategies of transnational corporations themselves might then be altered, by dispelling ignorance and possibly affecting the firm's markets. The effects of such tactics have been illustrated recently by way consumer groups and charities publicising the use by sportsware manufacturers such as Nike of low-wage and child labour in the Far East in manufacturing goods, action which apparently forced such firms to alter their strategies because of fears of a consumer boycott.[10] Image may be the Achilles' heel for such oligopolistic firms, as they are predominantly engaged in non-price competition, being highly dependent on marketing and advertising to enable premium prices to be charged so as to earn higher profits. Such isolated incidents are being formalised in a number of ways. Most recently Amnesty International has developed human rights principles for companies (Amnesty International, 1998) and the Council on Economic Priorities has developed a wide ranging standard (SA 8000) on social accountability (CEPAA, 1997).

However, governments which use information in this way would potentially raise a number of problems. Suggesting such a proactive role for the monitoring unit may well illegitimise the very idea of creating a unit in the minds of those who might otherwise see the unit as relatively harmless. Many would be sceptical of whether governments should be engaged in such activities. For such activity to be successful, it would require detailed government involvement in marketing and advertising issues, with the dangers seen in top-down propaganda dissemination in authoritarian countries.[11] It might seem heavy-handed and in some way to threaten free speech. An alternative approach, potentially avoiding these dangers, would be for monitoring units (established as public agencies but separated from government itself) to act as 'clearing houses', disseminating information for other actors (workers, consumers, pressure groups such as environmental activists, even the legislature such as through parliamentary select committees) to use to affect transnationals' image. In that sense a monitoring unit would simply be an extended form of the Registrar of Companies.

This would be a step towards redressing the imbalance between such firms and other actors in terms of how these firms portray themselves. However, potential users of information on transnationals' activities (such as on wages, conditions of work, environmental impact, links with political parties and so on) face a hostile legal environment. Recent events in Britain, such as the Maxwell pensions scandal, 'McLibel', and the Marks & Spencer versus *World in Action* case,[12] illustrate how powerful transnationals can be in quashing criticism of their activities. A range of measures are required to enable actors to hold transnationals to account, for example in rewriting the contract between society and such firms; the privilege of incorporated limited liability status might be offered in return for giving up the protection of libel law. The control of the media, both TV and newspapers, by transnationals through the increasing concentration of power in communications would also need to be tackled (see Cowling, 1985). Therefore, a monitoring unit could only be effective in enabling other actors if wider and deep-rooted legal and democratic imbalances between transnationals and communities were also addressed.

Such considerations illustrate a rationale for creating monitoring bodies, in order to provide governments and other actors in the community with information concerning transnationals' activities, so that they can make rational decisions or negotiate with or pressure transnationals, if need be, to change corporate strategies so as to reflect wider community interests. Furthermore, if multinational webs or other processes are to be encouraged as alternatives to transnationals as forms of internationalism, then transnationals are likely to resist such developments, because they threaten their markets and profitability. Production units in alternative forms of internationalism would need advice and assistance on market research and planning, legal and cultural factors, understanding of transnationals' pricing strategies and so on. Monitoring bodies, networked with community players, could be well placed to provide some of these services relating to transnationals' activities. This would also avoid the government–firm dichotomy and help fuse actors in new forms of industrial development.

A specific possibility is that multinational webs might be developed as networks which cross national boundaries but which in other respects have similarities to the industrial districts of the Third Italy, in terms of the diffusion of strategic decision-making, and a fusion of the social and economic into one integrated process growing from the histories, traditions and cultures of the localities making up a web (see Sugden, 1997; Cowling and Sugden, 1998). Lessons could also be learned from how districts have evolved; for example, how they have succeeded in international markets without the economies of scale which benefit transnationals. To do this, firms in certain districts have co-operated in providing marketing and other support services. Webs might have similar needs at a multinational level, and monitoring bodies might be in a position to meet such needs through the provision of information on markets dominated by transnational firms, such as on the activities of such firms and market opportunities.

We might also envisage monitoring bodies catalysing wider community groups, such as consumers and workers. Some action in monitoring transnationals has already been started in Europe by consumers' and workers' organisations and ethical consumption/investment advisers such as EIRIS and PIRC, New Consumer and Ethical Consumer, as well as SOMO, an information exchange on transnationals which is based in The Netherlands. Complementing this, there has also been a resurgence of interest in social accounting, prompted by organisations such as the New Economics Foundation and Accountability. This activity could be further encouraged through creating monitoring bodies across Europe that could network with such community groups. If an important goal is to foster multinational webs as alternatives to transnational-controlled internationalism, we need to think beyond just corporate webs, and to think also about webs involving various actors in communities. This could help to build the 'countervailing' power which such players need, and taking it further, to begin to build coalitions between such players. For example the environmental pressure group, Greenpeace, built a coalition involving itself, consumers and some European governments to oppose Shell dumping the Brent Spar oilrig at sea. We can envisage the fostering of multinational, multi-actor webs as a form of countervailing power.

Another possible advantage arising from the evolution of monitoring bodies is in catalysing policy debate. Issues of concern could be identified and policy options explored. Dynamism might then be created, with this quite simple policy initiative leading to more detailed and coherent future strategies, going beyond merely collating and discussing information. Issues to explore could include the impact of transnationals on pre-existing regional networks of small firms, which might lead into a discussion of what – if any – are appropriate policy responses. Linking back to the encouragement of multinational webs, another issue could concern how transnational-controlled hierarchical networks (which are usually international in nature) might be transformed into more democratic multinational webs.

Our suggestions can be seen as steps towards a free economy. If strategic failure arises because élites of strategic decision-makers in transnationals are 'negatively' free (that is, free from control), then an appropriate strategic response is to re-emphasise the 'positive' freedom (the right) of communities (workers, consumers, suppliers and so on) to participate in strategic planning. To obtain positive freedom for these different groups would mean both restoring a balance at the macro-level in what is meant by economic freedom, and also encouraging diversity at the micro-level in both who enjoys freedoms and how such freedoms are realised (see Bailey, 1998, for an exploration of the relationship between freedom, markets and industrial policy). It might be seen as involving both a top-down approach in curtailing the negative freedom of élites in transnationals, and a bottom-up approach in facilitating community groups' participation.

To ensure the positive freedom of groups currently excluded from strategic decision-making would imply a radical restructuring of what is meant by the 'free' market and is clearly well beyond any current ideas or proposals for policy towards transnationals. However, in pursuing policies today which may lead to the attainment of longer-term strategies in the future, then it is crucial to bear in mind those longer-term objectives, even if in the short run they are infeasible. In this sense, time inconsistency in industrial policy design could be avoided or, more accurately, time consistency could be *created*. For this reason we would consider monitoring bodies desirable.

If a free economy has negative and positive dimensions, economic freedom requires monitoring because it is an aspect of positive freedom in the context of an economy where transnational corporations are central actors. For different community actors to be free to participate in strategic decision-making, they need first to be informed and to understand the range of options available – a basis from which they can then develop their own strategies. Monitoring is needed to provide that basis. Thus developing a monitoring approach in the short run might lead to a dynamic process that later promotes positive freedom for community actors. Accountability and its links with freedom can in this way be seen as a two-stage process, with 'freedom of information' provision in the short term leading on to the ability for communities to act on that information (that is, positive freedom) in the longer term. Monitoring is therefore a necessary but not sufficient requirement for positive freedom for communities.

In this context, it has to be remembered that in fact markets are not ends in themselves, but rather means to ends. In the scramble to the market now under way throughout the world economy via the processes of privatisation, liberalisation, deregulation and globalisation, those ends seem to have been somewhat forgotten. 'Competitiveness' is usually referred to as the goal, but we would suggest that this depends as much on positive freedom (freedom to legal protection, health, education, and participation in the economy) for the many as it does on negative freedom for the few. Current debate not only confuses means and ends, but also obscures the nature of markets being created. A common argument is that negatively free markets for élite decision-makers deliver efficiency and competitiveness. We would counter that, even if it were accepted that competitiveness requires free markets, free markets have different dimensions, both negative and positive. The latter depends on health, education and training, legal and corporate governance systems, many of which involve us with the activities of transnational corporations. Monitoring the performance of transnationals on such issues would therefore be important in assessing whether an economy is competitive; it would be important to know how well the economy is delivering in terms of a range of factors which determine positive freedom.[13]

## The form of monitoring in a European context

Following from our recognition of the different interests of transnationals and communities, we would argue that the interests of community actors are not served simply by taking publicly available information that is primarily reported for the benefit of capital markets. Indeed, post-modern society is much less satisfied with profit as an appropriate indicator of economic performance even for the owners of capital, let alone as being an unsatisfactory indicator of overall corporate performance. In effect we know very little about transnationals, other than what might be useful for investment or lending purposes. Despite much recent publicity and advocacy, particularly with regard to the environment, there is little evidence of widespread, comprehensive, systematic and reliable reporting on the wider economic, social and environmental impact and performance of firms. What limited reporting does occur is substantially voluntary and so depends for its existence, let alone its nature and form, on managerial discretion. Such discretion is influenced in the main by narrow, financial incentives. The problem is that in a society characterised by unequal distributions of freedom, power and influence and by conflicts of interest, voluntary disclosure is likely to reflect the values of dominant groups, and so be used to 'mislead, mystify and legitimate' certain interests and actions (Cooper, 1984). Control over information is used to protect the negative freedom of élite strategic decision-makers. It is therefore critical not just to rely on the limited amount and range of information which transnationals voluntarily report. Indeed, as Deborah Leipziger of the Council of Economic Priorities notes in relation to transnational firms' own codes of conduct: 'Monitoring is the key thing. Even the best codes are worthless if there is nothing to back them up.'[14]

Just as equity analysts monitor the performance of firms in which investments are made, so too governments and other actors might monitor the performance of transnational firms. This is a useful parallel because equity analysts and institutional investors take the corporate report prepared by management together with a variety of other quantitative and qualitative information, and construct their own account of the performance of firms. They are actively encouraged to do so by the principal regulators of financial reporting practice, the Accounting Standards Board. The monitoring bodies might thus prepare 'economic and social accounts' of transnational firms' activities, drawing on approaches in the social auditing literature to investigate the wider economic and social impact of firms. The exact format of such accounts should be decided by monitoring bodies in conjunction with community players, and could cover issues such as: ownership and control; competition; research and development; employment and industrial relations; and the balance of payments (all of these have been consistent concerns for governments in a number of countries, see Bailey *et al.*, 1994a), as well as other issues such as environmental impact, contribution to regional development, impact on small firm webs or networks, and so on.

Much could be learnt from pursuing such an approach at the national level and – where political realities allow – at regional levels,[15] but added benefits would arise in the European context, for example, through a co-operative approach between European nations, coordinated by a European-level monitoring unit. The first benefit of such an approach is that the cost of gathering information is likely to be reduced for cooperating countries; by bringing different dimensions to the exercise, information may be unearthed more speedily and with less trouble. Second, the content of any monitoring is likely to be of a better quality and quantity. Third, the potential for policy development in the longer term has an international dimension, whether in countering divide and rule, building coalitions of countervailing power, or fostering multinational webs; a European monitoring body could begin to nurture this international co-operation.

A final advantage is that policy flexibility would be preserved through a co-operative monitoring approach. For example, as the strategy is flexible, it could accommodate different countries' attitudes, leaving all future options open and positively facilitating their consideration. This is important, as EU countries' attitudes have varied considerably, such as when Britain blocked the Vredeling proposals. In addition, the prisoners' dilemma of countries fearing to act on an individual basis might be overcome through an EU-wide monitoring approach; firms would then have no incentive to switch production to another EU country. Whilst transnational firms might have an incentive to switch production outside the EU, it could be argued that the sheer size of the EU market would provide a major incentive to keeping production within the Union. Moreover, if large-scale disinvestment were to begin to take place, threatening employment and welfare, the units could be quickly disestablished, with little sunk cost. Either way, there is flexibility, both in a positive sense in promoting a dynamism in policy design, or conversely, in a negative sense, in allowing a rapid exit if governments become too concerned over any negative impact.

## Conclusions

The promotion of transnationals across Europe in recent years brings with it increased risks of strategic failure as élites of decision-makers are (negatively) free from control. Such strategic failure in the EU context is evident particularly in terms of corporations' divide and rule strategies and an intensification of centripetal tendencies. Governments therefore have an important role – and responsibility – in negotiating with transnationals to secure wider benefits for communities in the short run, and in democratising decision-making and encouraging alternative forms of internationalisation in the longer run. To fulfil such a role, a useful first step would be the creation of monitoring units across Europe at different tiers of government, regional, national and European.[16] These units would investigate the impact of transnationals on economies, and in doing so could network with other community monitoring bodies. The longer-run objectives of building countervailing power for communities and catalysing policy debate and initiatives may then become possible. Such an approach would thus retain flexibility in providing a platform for future action in moving towards a truly free market, free in both a negative and positive sense. Above all, the proposal seeks to provide an openness and accountability that will facilitate a dialogue and debate, ensuring that markets will be more likely to operate in an open and equitable manner and for a wider variety of interest groups.

## Notes

1  This updates and develops further the ideas contained in Bailey *et al.* (1994a). We would like to thank Christine Oughton and Lisa De Propris for useful comments and suggestions.
2  Following Berlin's (1969) distinction between negative and positive freedom. The former concerns freedom of choice, or freedom *from* constraint by others, whereas the latter concerns the right *to* do something, to make plans and to realise them.
3  A recent case was the 'bidding war' which erupted in 1997 between two British regions, Wales and the North-East, to win a plant of the Taiwanese-based computer firm Acer (*Guardian*, 8 November 1997). The intense regional competition over subsidies offered prompted the Department of Trade and Industry to try to take control of subsidies given to incoming transnationals, but it eventually backed down in the face of opposition from the Welsh, Scottish and Northern Ireland Offices (ibid., 18 November 1997).
4  As well as other policies, such as training packages specifically tailored to meet the needs of transnational firms. For example, a key role for the forthcoming Regional Development Agencies in Britain will be to design training packages to suit foreign investors (DETR, 1997).
5  At a more general level we see policy debate being conducted in terms of what is best for transnational firms, and not what is best for communities, workers and so on. For example, the recent impasse at the Kyoto global climate talks has been attributed in part to the lobbying of the US by car, oil and energy transnationals keen to avoid stringent new emissions-reduction requirements (*Guardian*, 29 November 1997 and 5 December 1997).
6  For example, the Director-General of the WTO, Renato Ruggerio, claimed: 'we are writing the constitution of a single global economy' (*Guardian*, 13 February 1998).
7  *Guardian*, 13 February 1998.
8  Assuming there is no agency problem between governments and the communities they are supposed to represent.
9  In contrast, evidence on the historical development of policies in Japan and France suggests that underlying concerns in those countries over the impact of transnationals may not have changed much, even though policies have (see Bailey *et al.,* 1994b).
10  See *International Herald Tribune*, 15 May 1998.
11  Actually, governments are already heavily involved in advertising, for example health education authorities can be seen to be acting in a manner which is against the interests of tobacco and alcohol companies.

12 Robert Maxwell deployed legal tactics which suppressed details of how employees' pension funds were raided until after his death (see *Guardian*, 17 December 1997). On 'McLibel', see Vidal (1997) which questions the use by transnationals of libel writs as a form of censorship. More recently, Granada Television was successfully sued by Marks & Spencer after its investigative programme *World in Action* revealed that the retailer was selling clothes made outside the UK with 'Made in the UK' labels, and that child labour was being used by a supplier in Morocco. The programme makers claimed that they did not intend to suggest that the firm was aware that this was happening, but was denied the chance to present a defence case as a libel 'short-cut' was taken in court (see *Guardian*, 4 March 1998).

13 See also Nexus Theme Group on Britain in the World (1997) which called on the incoming Labour government in Britain to undertake a 'social audit' of foreign direct investment to inform debate about British competitiveness and industrial policy. In a similar vein, Marquand (1998) argues that public policy should aim to maximise well-being, not GDP per head, and calls for 'a mechanism for social audit, from which appropriate indicators of well-being should be derived'. In turn, policy should then be evaluated on the basis of measurable improvements in such indicators of well-being.

14 *Guardian*, 13 June 1998.

15 For example, devolution of economic power to Scotland might facilitate a monitoring strategy at a regional level, again involving co-operation with other European monitoring units. This was explicitly suggested by the Standing Commission on the Scottish Economy in its 1989 Final Report. It suggested the creation of a Scottish monitoring unit to provide detailed knowledge on a wide variety of issues and to stimulate discussion on the role, effects and policy implications of transnationals' activities for the Scottish economy.

16 This would accord with the view of Hirst and Thompson (1996) that governance is possible at different levels, from the international economy down to the industrial district.

# References

Amnesty International. 1998. *Human Rights Principles for Companies*. London: Amnesty International.

Bailey, David. 1998. *Freedom, Markets and Industrial Policy*, Industrial Development Policy Discussion Paper no. 4. Universities of Birmingham and Ferrara: Institute for Industrial Development Policy.

Bailey, David, George Harte and Roger Sugden. 1994a. *Making Transnationals Accountable*. London: Routledge.

——, —— and —— 1994b. *Transnationals and Governments*. London: Routledge.

Bailey, David, Roger Sugden and Rachel Thomas. 1998. Inward Investment in Central and Eastern Europe: the Compatibility of Objectives and the Need for an Industrial Strategy. In Michael Storper, B. Stavros, Thomadakis and Lena, Tsipouri eds, *Latecomers in the Global Economy*. London: Routledge.

Barrell, Ray and Nigel Pain. 1997. Foreign Direct Investment, Technological Change, and Economic Growth within Europe. *Economic Journal*, vol. 107, no. 445, pp. 1770–1786.

Bellak, Christian. 1997. Reeling in the Transnationals. *New Economy*, vol. 4, no. 1, pp. 17–21.

Berlin, Isaiah. 1969. *Four Essays on Liberty*. Oxford: Oxford University Press.

Bleifuss, J. 1998. Building the Global Economy. *In These Times*, 11 Jan. pp. 13–15.

Cooper, D. 1984. Information for Labour. In B.V. Carlsberg and T. Hope, eds, *Current Issues in Accounting*, 2nd edn. Deddington: Philip Allan.

Council on Economic Priorities Accreditation Agency. 1997. *Social Accountability 8000*. London: CEPAA.

Cowling, Keith. 1985. Economic Obstacles to Democracy. In R.C.O. Matthews, ed., *Economy and Democracy*. Basingstoke: Macmillan.

Cowling, Keith and Sugden, Roger. 1993. Industrial Strategy: a Missing Link in British Economic Policy, *Oxford Review of Economic Policy*, vol. 9, pp. 83–100.

—— and ——. 1994. *Beyond Capitalism*. London: Pinter.

—— and ——. 1998. The Wealth of Localities, Regions and Nations: Developing Multinational Economies. In Jacques De Bandt, Christine Oughton and Marco Di Tommaso, eds, *Bottom-up versus Top-down Approaches to Industrial Strategy*, London: Routledge (forthcoming).

Department of the Environment, Transport and the Regions (DETR). 1997. *Building Partnerships for Prosperity: Sustainable Growth, Competitiveness and Employment in the English Regions*. London: Stationery Office.

*Guardian*. 1997a. Ministers Raging Turf War. 8 November, p. 26.

—— 1997b. DTI Surrenders in Turf War. 18 November, p. 20.

—— 1997c. US Threatens to Scupper Climate Talks. 29 November, p. 14.

—— 1997d. Temperature Rises at Global Warming Talks. 5 December, p. 17.

—— 1997e. The Dogs of Libel. 17 December, p. 17.

—— 1998a. Meet the New World Government. 13 February, p. 15.

—— 1998b. Buried by Libel. 4 March, p. 16.

—— 1998c. Code Breaks the Ethics Ploys. 13 June, p. 30.

Hirst, Paul and Grahame Thompson. 1996. *Globalization in Question: The International Economy and the Possibilities of Governance*. Cambridge: Polity Press.

Hodges, Michael. 1974. *Multinational Corporations and National Government*. Farnborough: Saxon House.

Hymer, Stephen. 1975. The Multinational Corporation and the Law of Uneven Development. In Hugo Radice, ed., *International Firms and Modern Imperialism*. Handsworth: Penguin.

Ietto-Gilles, Grazia. 1997. Working with the Big Guys. *New Economy*, vol. 4, no. 1, pp. 12–16.

*International Herald Tribune*. 1998. Swoosh! Public Shaming Nets Results. 15 May, p. 11.

Kang, K.S. 1997. Opening Address. In OECD, *Multilateral Agreement on Investment: State of Play, April 1997*. Paris: OECD.

Marquand, David. 1998. Some Concluding Thoughts, *Nexus Third Way Debate*. http://www.netnexus.org/

Nexus Theme Group on Britain in the World. 1997. The Politics of Globalisation. *Renewal*, vol. 5, no. 2, pp. 71–77.

Ramsay, Harvey. 1992. A Critical Assessment of the 1992 Project Agenda for Industry Policy. In Keith Cowling and Roger Sugden, eds, *Current Issues in Industrial Strategy*. Manchester: Manchester University Press.

Shelton, J.R. 1997. Opening Address. In OECD, *Multilateral Agreement on Investment: State of Play, February 1997*. Paris: OECD.

Standing Commission on the Scottish Economy. 1989. *Final Report*. Glasgow: Standing Commission on the Scottish Economy.

Sugden, Roger. 1997. Economias Multinacionales y la Ley del Dessarrollo sin Equidad, *FACES (Revista de la Facultad de Ciencias Económicas y Sociales, Universidad Nacional de Mar del Plata)*, vol. 3, no. 4, pp. 87–116.

Vidal, John. 1997. *McLibel: Culture on Trial*. Basingstoke: Macmillan.

Willner, Johan. 1994. Does a Reduced Public Sector Increase Welfare in an Open Economy? In Patrizio Bianchi, Keith Cowling and Roger Sugden, eds, *Europe's Economic Challenge*. London: Routledge.

Young, Stephen and Neil Hood. 1993. Inward Investment Policy in the European Community in the 1990s. *Transnational Corporations*, vol. 2. no. 2, pp. 35–62.

# 17 Industrial strategy in the era of transnationals

## Analysis and policy issues

*Grazia Ietto-Gillies*

## Introduction

An industrial strategy for the twenty-first century must begin by taking stock of the major changes in the industrial and macro environment that have occurred in the last two decades in order to achieve consistency between the modern business/economic structure and the development of such a strategy.

The changes that we have witnessed are many and they relate to both the political and economic spheres. The major ones include the new political and economic order following events in central and eastern Europe; the growing relevance of China as an economic power; the establishment and strengthening of economic integration within regional blocs, particularly the European Union; the increasing relevance of information and communication technologies (ICTs) in all aspects of production, consumption and business activities in general; the decreasing share of manufacturing in the level of output and employment.

There is one other development that is of great relevance for most aspects of business life and which, moreover, impacts on all the changes just mentioned. This is the role of transnational companies (TNCs) in economic activity.

This chapter deals with the increased participation of TNCs in world production and integration and how this may affect the development of a strategy on industrial policy. The chapter starts with an analysis of key elements in TNCs' activities and their role in production and integration. The section below (pp. 332–4) discusses advantages of multinationality for companies. Implications for analysis and for industrial policy are considered subsequently, and conclusions follow the final section.

## The increasing role of TNCs in the economy: some key elements and issues

The impact of TNCs in world economic activities relates to employment, production, research and development, and technology spread as well as most aspects of international integration.

World-wide the transnational companies are responsible for well over 70 million employees. The total number of employees has been increasing steadily in the last few decades with the affiliates taking an increasing share compared to employment in the parent companies. Though the share of employment in affiliates of TNCs is larger in developed than developing countries, the latter have seen their share of affiliates' employment increasing faster than in the developed countries (UNCTAD-DTCI, 1994, table IV.3, p. 175).

Table 17.1 gives values of various indicators of activities by TNCs in relation to world economic activity. All indicators show increasing trends, whether the comparison is with world output or with world gross domestic capital formation or with exports. The growth in foreign direct investment (FDI) has tended to outstrip the growth in many other significant indicators of world economic activity. In particular, world sales of foreign affiliates have overtaken exports (see last row in Table 17.1). Moreover, the growth of FDI flows is proceeding at a faster pace than the growth of trade world-wide (second last row in the table) though trade is still a much larger component of international transactions than FDI (OECD, 1994: 19).

The growing shares of TNCs' involvement in world employment, output and international flows is an indication of their increased role in key aspects of economic life. There are many issues attached to this role and some will be considered here.

## TNCs and international integration

There appears to be a new pattern of international integration in which the mechanisms and flows of business integration are evolving from the traditional

*Table 17.1* International production and world economic activity, selected indicators, 1960–95

| Indicator | 1960 | 1975 | 1980 | 1985 | 1990 | 1991 | 1993 | 1994 | 1995 |
|---|---|---|---|---|---|---|---|---|---|
| World FDI inward stock as % of output | 4.4 | 4.5 | 4.6 | 6.3 | 8.3 | 8.5 | 9.2 | 9.4 | 10.1 |
| World FDI inflows as % of output | 0.3 | 0.3 | 0.5 | 0.5 | n.a. | 0.7 | 0.9 | 0.9 | 1.1 |
| World FDI inflows as % of gross fixed capital formation | 1.1 | 1.4 | 2.0 | 1.8 | 4.0 | 3.1 | 4.4 | 4.5 | 5.2 |
| World FDI outflows as % of exports | n.a. | 2.7 | 2.2 | 3.2 | 7.1 | 6.1 | 6.1 | 5.5 | 5.8 |
| World sales of foreign affiliates as % of exports | 84 | 97 | 99 | 99 | 129 | 122 | 128 | 121 | n.a. |

*Sources*: GATT/WTO, various issues; UNCTAD-DTCI, 1992–7.

exports and imports towards FDI and collaborative agreements. The OECD report (1992) sees the internationalisation of industry proceeding in 'three broad stages with profound effects on the nature of global competition' (p. 11). The three stages are identified as trade, foreign direct investment and industrial linkages. The first stage extends up to the late 1960s, the second up to the early 1980s and the third stage since the 1980s.

This 'stages' analysis reinforces the tendency to see the three aspects of international integration as substitutes for each other: as an either or situation. In particular some authors (Mundell, 1957; Hirst and Thompson, 1996) appear to see a dichotomy between trade and FDI.

Are trade and FDI substitutes or complements? The answer depends partly on the level of analysis we are interested in (at the company or macro level) and partly on the categories of production or products used. Cantwell (1994) bases his analysis and conclusions on the classification of international production[1] into (a) resource-based production; (b) market-orientated production; and (c) rationalised or integrated international production. The analysis in UNCTAD (1996) is based on the distinction between manufacturing versus services products. In general, the following considerations and conclusions apply.

At the company level, direct production can take over from exports for market sourcing purposes, and thus substitute for it. However, there are plenty of opportunities for trade and FDI to move alongside each other and reinforce each other for various reasons, including the following. Direct production may encourage exports/imports of components or capital goods. Moreover, a production foot in one country may increase the TNCs' ability to trade with third countries; for example, Japanese and US FDI in the UK increased in the run up to the single market in order to give the investing companies the opportunity to export from the UK to the rest of the EC/EU (Thomsen and Woolcock, 1993). In addition, vertically integrated international production strategies by companies lead to exports and imports of components thus increasing world-wide trade. Some low-wage countries develop export-orientated inward FDI strategies in order to enhance growth. This results in increase in trade and in changes in the structure of trade (Barry and Bradley, 1997). There may, in fact, be effects on the geographical pattern of trade as well as on the share of intra-firm and intra-industry trade as the components traded belong to the same industrial category and are often exchanged across countries on an intra-company basis.

Where does the balance between complementarity and substitution lie? World-wide the TNCs are responsible not only for all the FDI but also for most trade (UNCTAD, 1992 and 1995) and indeed a large share of world trade – at least 30 per cent – takes place on an intra-firm base (UNCTAD-DTCI, 1996). Whatever the underlying company strategies, it appears that, at the industry and macro levels, trade and FDI have moved alongside each other in a complementary rather than a substitution pattern (Graham, 1997; Petri, 1994; Thomsen and Woolcock, 1993). Molle and Morsink (1991) find a non-linear relationship of complementarity in which FDI takes over once trade has reached a minimum level.

However, the main changes in this new pattern of integration are not so much because the old pattern was trade-based and the more recent one is FDI-based or linkages-based, because the new one is indeed both trade- and FDI-based as well as based on new forms of interaction and collaboration. Thus if we want to analyse integration by stages, what happens is that at each historical stage new forms and mechanisms of integration are being added to old ones.

The main distinguishing feature is now to be sought in the fact that both trade and FDI and indeed international linkages originate with TNCs. In the past, trade originated mainly with uninational companies (UNCs). Now trade, as well as other components of cross-country flows, originates mainly with TNCs. So the real dichotomy is between integration based on the activities of UNCs and integration based on the activities of TNCs. Thus the different stages ought to be identified by the involvement and role of TNCs in the various mechanisms of integration. Such a role has been increasing in various respects: (a) because the TNCs are responsible for wider mechanisms and components of integration (such as FDI and collaborative agreements in addition to trade); (b) because their involvement in traditional mechanisms such as world trade is also increasing; (c) because a considerable amount of activity across borders now takes place on an intra-company basis; (d) because large TNCs are increasing the geographical scope of their operations by investing in a larger number of countries (Ietto-Gillies, 1996).

If we want to capture key differences between different stages of internationalisation and integration, we must look at the attributes and power of the TNCs as the agents most responsible for the new integration. Moreover, we must consider how this wide role of TNCs affects the qualitative nature of integration, the geographical distribution of economic activity, the competitive environment and the position of other players in the economic system. These are all issues relevant to a strategic industrial policy.

### The impact of profits from foreign investment

The increased role of foreign investment – particularly FDI – in internationalisation has automatically brought about increased flows of earnings[2] from those investments. The growth in international investment, whether direct or portfolio, has led to a cumulative growth in the flow of earnings from those investments. None the less, investment earnings tends to be a rather forgotten element in the assessment of the effects of FDI and in international integration. Yet, it is a very large component. The OECD (1994, p. 19) provides comparisons between two decades which show that the average value of investment earnings in both decades 1970–9 and 1980–9 is higher than the world average flows of the total portfolio and direct investment.

The relevance of profits from foreign investment lies not only in the size of the transfers but also in the fact that this is a component of international integration that shows strong *cumulative and intertemporal patterns* in which history plays a very relevant role. Countries with a long history of FDI will have large amounts of profits on the cumulative stock of FDI, whether on the inward or outward sides: the profits continue throughout the life of the investment. At the macro level for some countries – such as the UK – the profits on cumulated outward FDI are large enough to support all or most of the new outflows of FDI: thus new foreign assets are acquired without any further deployment of resources (Ietto-Gillies, 1999). This outcome is considered in the Reddaway Reports (1967 and 1968) as one of the reasons for encouraging outward FDI.

The assessment of the effects of investment on the balance of payments are far from straightforward. They involve considering both direct and indirect effects such as those on trade level and patterns. The outcome is also likely to depend on the implicit or explicit hypotheses made on counterfactual, alternative scenarios[3] as in Hufbauer and Adler (1968). In any case, the effects must be looked at in terms of their cumulative and intertemporal pattern. Moreover, the balance of payments effects are mirrored by strong effects on the real sector of the economy and possibly on its industrial structure. Rowthorn and Wells (1987) point out some negative effects on the UK of being caught in a 'wealth trap' and becoming a 'rentier nation' through large inflows of net earnings linked to cumulative outward FDI going back for decades. In the absence of an active industrial policy the impact of such earnings on the balance of payments may contribute to squeeze out the manufacturing balance with de-industrialising effects on the real economy.

The effects of earnings from foreign investment must, however, take account of both inward and outward flows. Both the Reddaway reports (1967, 1968) and Rowthorn and Wells (1987) tackle this issue by concentrating on the effects on the UK of profits from outward FDI. However, given the recent large and increasing flows of inward FDI, any positive or negative effects on the balance of payments and/or the real sector ought to be taken into consideration.

For a good number of developed countries – and particularly for the UK – FDI is, in fact, a two-way process with growing involvement at both the outward and inward sides. Table 17.2 shows that the developed countries' ratio of outward to inward stock of FDI is decreasing, with corresponding opposite patterns for the developing countries. Within the major developed countries, the UK and the US stand out as the two countries in which the ratio is decreasing faster; Germany and France show opposite patterns. Japan exhibits the well-known pattern of outward FDI far greater than inward ones.

A more detailed study (Ietto-Gillies, 1999) looks at the distribution pattern of earnings between different countries and finds that the position of EU

*Table 17.2* Ratio of outward to inward FDI stock, major regions and selected countries, 1980–96

| Region/country | 1980 | 1985 | 1990 | 1996 |
|---|---|---|---|---|
| Developed countries | 1.36 | 1.23 | 1.18 | 1.28 |
| EU | 1.15 | 1.26 | 1.09 | 1.15 |
| UK | 1.28 | 1.57 | 1.06 | 1.03 |
| Germany | 1.18 | 1.62 | 1.36 | 1.69 |
| France | 1.04 | 1.11 | 1.27 | 1.23 |
| US | 2.65 | 1.36 | 1.10 | 1.23 |
| Japan | 5.76 | 9.35 | 20.78 | 18.32 |
| Developing countries | 0.07 | 0.11 | 0.20 | 0.31 |

*Source*: UNCTAD-DTCI (1997).

*Table 17.3* Outward and inward FDI and earnings from outward and inward FDI; ratios, total EU and member countries, 1988–96; averages

| Country | Earnings on outward FDI/ earnings on inward FDI | |
|---|---|---|
| | 1988–92 | 1993–6 |
| Austria | 0.27 | 0.34 |
| Belgium-Luxembourg | n.a. | 0.60[a] |
| Denmark | n.a. | n.a. |
| Finland | −0.88 | 0.45 |
| France | 1.23 | 1.55 |
| Germany | 0.76 | 1.67 |
| Greece | 0.15 | 0.29 |
| Ireland | 0.07[b] | 0.08 |
| Italy | 0.34 | 1.62 |
| The Netherlands | 1.16 | 1.71 |
| Portugal | 0.01 | 0.26 |
| Spain | 0.16 | 0.23 |
| Sweden | 5.39 | 1.66 |
| United Kingdom | 2.09 | 1.90 |
| Total EU countries[c] | | |
| ratios | 1.29 | |
| values | 83,462/ 64,719 | |

*Source*: IMF, *Balance of Payments Statistics*, selected issues.

*Notes*:
n.a. = not available.
[a]   Average 1995–6 only.
[b]   1990–2 only.
[c]   EU total is average of 1995 and 1996 figures; it excludes Denmark and Greece.

countries as regards net earnings from FDI differs considerably (Table 17.3). Some countries are net receivers of earnings from FDI (ratios greater than one for France, The Netherlands, Sweden and UK) and some are net payers (Austria, Finland, Ireland, Greece, Portugal and Spain). For some countries the pattern seems to change considerably through time (for example, Sweden and Germany). The study finds that the UK is a net receiver of earnings from the world as a whole, from the EU and indeed from each EU country.

In summary, the position of different countries as net receivers or payers of direct investment earnings vary according to their history of FDI (length of time and values of investment), and the pattern regarding inward and outward involvement. The effects of earnings should be considered alongside those on FDI; they both impact on the balance of payments and on the real economy including its industrial structure.

### TNCs and competition

Many aspects of TNCs' activities and their characteristics – such as size, variety of modes of entry and their role in world trade – raise issues of competition for the industries in which they operate (Cowling and Sugden, 1987; Graham, 1978; Knickerbocker, 1973). Here I would just like to empha-sise two other issues relevant to competition. The first one relates to inter-company collaborative agreements, which are on the increase, partic-ularly the technology-based ones (Hagedoorn, 1996; UNCTAD-DTCI, 1994 and 1995). This new pattern of organisation of activities at the firm and industry levels raises a variety of issues including those related to the effects on the competitive environment and on the power of TNCs *vis-à-vis* other players in the economic system, on which more in the next section.

Effects on the competitive environment can come about also via the form taken by FDI. The FDI statistics include data on both greenfield invest-ments and mergers and acquisitions; this means that, conceptually, FDI is rather different from domestic capital formation. It is, in fact, capital forma-tion for the company whose capacity increases whether the FDI takes the form of acquisitions or of greenfields. However, only the greenfield type of FDI will result in capital formation at the macro level, for the host economy and the world as a whole. Essentially, the statistics on FDI take a micro rather than macro stance on the link between investment and capital forma-tion. This issue is not a minor one when we consider that mergers and acquisitions across borders contributed approximately 65 per cent to the total FDI flows in the period 1988–96 (UNCTAD, 1997). Foreign invest-ment via mergers and acquisitions has a direct impact on competition.

## Advantages of multinationality

Most analyses of TNCs and their location strategies are based on the under-lying assumption that producing in foreign countries has costs and disadvantages attached to it and that we must look for counterbalancing elements to see why they invest abroad. This assumption goes back to Hymer (1960) and is more implicit in the works of Dunning (1977 and 1980). The counterbalancing elements are seen in specific locational advantages and/or in advantages linked to the ability of the company to exploit its ownership advantages in foreign locations.

To what extent is it still realistic to assume that operating abroad involves extra costs and risks? And if it does not, are there consequences for the way we analyse the TNCs and their effects? In the 1960s, at the time of the pioneer analysis by Hymer, it was very reasonable to emphasise the costs, risks and disadvantages of foreign direct production; but is it now? International production has been increasing at a very fast pace; it is involving a growing number of companies from a larger number of countries. The number of countries in which each large TNC operates is growing, thus the geographical spread of their operation is increasing. As internationalisation becomes more significant and easier, it permeates down the scale of companies: an increasing number of smaller and medium-size companies are investing in foreign countries. Moreover, international involvement also spreads across a variety of mechanisms ranging from trade to FDI to portfolio investment to inter-firm collaborative agreements.

This growing push towards internationalisation in all directions means that companies have learned more about the international environment. Their experience as foreign direct investors can be used for future foreign activities in the same and/or new countries. Vernon (1979) looks at large TNCs as 'global scanners' capable of scanning the world for investment opportunities; Cowling and Sugden (1987) emphasise TNCs' 'detection power', that is the power to obtain, process and use information to their own advantage particularly *vis-à-vis* rivals. Thus, TNCs learn to become more involved in international production partly through their own experience: because they have been investing abroad, they are at an advantage in further investment. Moreover, there are also spill-over effects and external economies in two respects. First, in the sense that market penetration through one mode – for example exports – eases the way to (and cuts the transaction costs of) other modes of market penetration (direct production or licensing). Second, because internationalisation by big companies may help to pave the way for smaller ones to branch abroad.

Large TNCs gain advantages from two different sources of diversification. The first one relates to the different mechanisms and modes of market penetration. History and accumulated knowledge through one mechanism helps to diversify into another. The second one refers to the diversification by country of operation. The advantages gained give the large TNCs extra power *vis-à-vis* rivals, uninational companies (UNCs), governments, consumers, and labour.

The advantages towards rivals derive from the actual and potential penetration of new markets, from their knowledge and lower marginal costs of extra foreign investment or of other modes as well as from the spreading of risks in many locations or throughout different modes. Moreover, any advantage towards other players such as governments or labour put a company in a stronger position towards rivals.

The advantages towards governments derive again from their knowledge of different countries and their ability to play one government against the other, in the search for grants and favourable conditions.

Their power towards labour derives from the fact that labour is fragmented in dealing with the TNCs. There are two sources of fragmentation: geographical by nation-states and structural/organisational. Transnational companies operate across different nation-states and thus across different regulatory regimes: the regulatory framework refers to labour (and the bargaining boundaries of its trade unions), to taxation and to currencies.[4] The knowledge of conditions in nation-states and the ability to operate across them is likely to give TNCs advantages compared to players who cannot operate internationally, or not to the same extent. In particular, the different regulatory regimes as regards labour are likely to give considerable advantages because a truly transnational organisation faces a labour force which is fragmented by its inability to organise across borders.

The structural/organisational fragmentation of labour is connected with inter-company agreements, particularly with sub-contracting or licensing which can take place within the national boundaries or across nations. These contractual arrangements – whether national or international – weaken labour compared to a situation in which all the production is internalised and labour is employed by one large company within which labour organisation becomes easier (Ietto-Gillies, 1992, ch. 14; Cowling and Sugden, 1987).

The combination of these two diversification mechanisms puts labour in a weaker position because it faces a double fragmentation: fragmentation by regulatory regimes (nation-states) and fragmentation by contractual arrangements linked to the organisation of production.

In summary, the activities of transnational companies have created a situation in which some players are able to plan, organise and control activities across national boundaries while others are less able to do so due to a variety of reasons. Multinationality gives advantages which the companies can then use to their benefit in dealing with other players such as UNCs, labour, consumers, governments and rivals.

## Implications for analysis

The points made in the previous sections have various implications for economic analysis, in particular with regard to the following issues: the modelling of location strategies by multinational companies in the context of the new trade and location theories; assessment of the degree of multinationality; the effects of profits from foreign investment and their impact on the real economy and its industrial structure. These issues and their implications for analysis and policy will be touched on here, though considerably more research is needed on them.

Location and trade theory have received a great boost in the last decade or so (Krugman, 1985, 1991; Helpman and Krugman, 1985). The new trade theories with their emphasis on external and internal economies have changed the way we look at location and agglomeration and the way we analyse international trade. Transnationals must figure prominently in any theory of location and trade for two reasons. First, because they are responsible for location decisions of a large and growing share of world activity. Second, because a very large share of world trade originates with them whether on an intra- or inter-firm basis. There are, in fact, various attempts to incorporate TNCs into the new location/trade theories (Krugman, 1985; Helpman and Krugman, 1985; Markusen, 1995).

The models designed to explain multinational activities are usually based on a multi-plant framework deriving from assumptions on spatial transaction costs (including transportation costs) and size of markets; there is also a specific, key assumption that companies have joint inputs and thus fixed costs at the level of the firm. In these models it appears that the same type of assumptions are made – and thus the same conclusions reached – as regards multi-plant production whether the locational framework refers to different regions of the same nation-state or to different nation-states. This is fine if the location strategies of TNCs are not affected by the possible advantages of operating *across* different regulatory regimes; if, in other words, the only specific issue in multinationals' location is an issue of spatial transaction costs which may apply to different degrees to the inter-national and the inter-regional economy.

However, if TNCs pursue strategies of location across different regulatory regimes – different nation states – because this gives them advantages *vis-à-vis* other players and in particular labour, then inter-national location must be analysed differently from inter-regional (within the same nation-state) location. The issue of advantages of operations across nation-states may have to come at the forefront of explanations of TNCs' location strategies. If we want to understand such strategies and their impact on patterns of location and agglomeration of activity, we cannot confine ourselves to locational comparative advantages whether of a static or dynamic type. We must add to them elements related to advantages and disadvantages of operating across nation-states. These are not a prerogative of localities, geographical space or nations, but a prerogative of operating *across* nations; for example, if labour fragmentation is part of an overall strategy, then the advantages of such a strategy are not connected with spatial transaction costs or with barriers to entry into a market, but with the spreading of activities across different regulatory regimes. In this perspective, the degree of multinationality of a firm becomes relevant.

How do we assess the degree of transnationality? Many authors have tried to develop synthetic indices designed to assess and compare the degree to which companies and/or industries and/or countries are internationalised (Sullivan, 1994; Dunning and Pearce, 1981; UNCTAD, 1995). All these indices have in common the fact that they are built as a ratio of foreign to home activities (whatever the nature of the activity chosen by a specific index and whatever the complexity of the index). Therefore they consider internationalisation as a dichotomy between home and direct foreign production/activities. Though the share of foreign to home activities is important in a variety of contexts, any measure of transnationalisation relevant to the understanding of strategic behaviour should also capture a different dimension, the degree to which companies' activities are spread throughout the world (Ietto-Gillies, 1998).

The effects of FDI should be considered in conjunction with the full impact of profits from FDI. The effects of profits are usually analysed in relation to their contribution to the balance of payments (Reddaway, 1967, 1968). However, there are also considerable effects on the real economy and on the cross-country distribution of resources. Much noise is made about the distribution of resources across the EU, yet this is a considerable source of re-distribution which is hardly emphasised in the literature. Net profits from foreign investment affect the level of consumption, and their contribution to the balance of payments affects the long-term structure of the economy (Rowthorn and Wells, 1987).

## Implications for policy

There is now a good deal of literature on the need for an industrial strategy (Cowling, 1987; Cowling and Sugden, 1992) and indeed on the theoretical underpinning of different approaches to industrial policy and strategy (Sawyer, 1992; Dietrich, 1992). One general point made (Cowling, 1990) is that the need for a strategic stance on the part of governments derives partly from the fact that TNCs themselves act strategically; this means that unless governments develop a strategic type of industrial policy, the TNCs' strategies might become the nations' strategies by default. Of course, the fact that each TNC has its own strategy does not mean that the combined result at the industry and macro level is a coherent industrial strategy. On the contrary, the inconsistency between different uncoordinated strategies will generate problems for other players (including governments) as well as for the TNCs themselves.

There are several dimensions to TNCs' activities which are relevant to their strategic behaviour and for the government response to it. In the previous pages I have concentrated on a specific one: the advantages and power that derive from strategies of diversification, particularly across different regulatory regimes. Such strategies affect the location and agglomeration of activity as well as the degree of embeddedness into the local economy. Moreover, it greatly affects the distribution of power between different players.

Some problems derive from the fact that powerful TNCs confront less-powerful players such as labour, UNCs, consumers and governments themselves. I see as an important part of any strategic industrial policy that the government should enable other players in the economic system (UNCs, labour, consumers) to develop countervailing power in the international arena. A first step in this direction is to put them in a position of having access to full information and being able to process it and use it; such access implies transparency and accountability on the part of TNCs, which, inevitably, involves some monitoring of their activities (Bailey *et al.*, 1994). It also implies that UNCs, consumers and labour should be encouraged and helped to develop intra- and inter-company networks across national and international boundaries. Access to the information and communications infrastructure and the development of the relevant skills for its use, become essential to this aim.

If TNCs' location strategies are influenced by issues of power, then the location of activity world-wide and the resultant uneven development cannot automatically be assumed to respond to efficiency criteria. Moreover, companies that have a high degree of transnationality (spread of activities) are less likely to be embedded in the local/national economy, particularly when this spread is combined with an international, vertically integrated organisation of production.

The degree of embeddedness may also be related to the entry mode into a market. For example, Yamawaki (1997) finds that the probability of exit is influenced by the entry mode; specifically, it finds a high probability of exit for those subsidiaries of Japanese TNCs in the US and EU established through diversifying acquisitions.

The TNCs' choice of entry mode may become a constraint for regions, countries and governments. The different modes have profound effects on the distribution of activity and employment across regions and countries. Both their short-run level of activity and their long-term development are at stake.

Enabling other players to develop countervailing power is not just a distributional issue *per se*. A more balanced distribution of power will inject transparency into locational decisions. The scope for highlighting and debating possible inefficiencies in location strategies and possible long-term negative effects of such strategies on agglomeration patterns and/or on the degree of embeddedness of TNCs in local economies will be enhanced.

The 1960s and 1970s analyses of the effects of TNCs' activities saw a considerable concentration on the issue of nationality of ownership. Given the fact that many developed countries are now both home and host to TNCs and their activities and that most large TNCs are increasing the geographical spread of their operations, the issue of ownership seems less relevant than the issue of degree of multinationality considered above. The degree to which TNCs are embedded in a location (Phelps, 1997) or are footloose, their relationship with the local and national economies, with their governments, with labour, with the UNCs may, to an extent, depend on the degree to which they have opportunities for (and are committed to) activities in other countries. In this perspective the nationality of the TNC may matter less than the degree to which activities are spread across different nation-states: the latter gives more of an indication of potential locational mobility and possible footlooseness than the nationality of the company.

Is a strategic industrial policy possible in a world dominated by TNCs? My answer is positive. First, because, though the number of TNCs is growing, the very large players are relatively few. It is possible to monitor their activities and strategies, to engage in dialogue with them and involve them in a medium-term to long-term industrial strategy. Second, governments can begin to bargain by offering a stable macroenvironment and a congenial physical, research and human infrastructure instead of grants and subsidies; indeed, more collaboration between government and TNC can be achieved by stressing that the elimination of inefficient locational strategies and the active promotion of industrial development can favour private business (Sawyer, 1992) as well as local and national economies. Moreover, governments can use levers connected to access to the markets which companies need (Cowling, 1990).

A strategy of attracting foreign investment through grants is a negative-sum game for the governments and taxpayers of the world. It leads to distribution from the public to the private sphere and is unlikely to affect the total sum of world investment or of world foreign direct investment. There are also doubts as to the extent to which it affects the geographical distribution of FDI across the world.

Guisinger (1986) finds that incentives have little effect on the location decisions of companies. Marginson, *et al.* (1995) in a survey of large UK companies, find that the majority of companies cite labour skills as the most common factor for the location of investment or the closure of plants. The more widespread the practice of grants is among governments, the less likely it is to be effective in the geographical allocation of FDI. A policy of grants and sweeteners always reminds me of Francis Bacon (1561–1626), the English philosopher, 'who was prosecuted for accepting bribes from litigants' in his role as Lord Chancellor. 'He admitted the truth of the accusation, pleading only that presents never influenced his decisions' (Russell, [1946] 1984, p. 526).

Co-operation between governments and international agencies in dealing with transnational issues is necessary whether it relates to the reduction of competition between government through grants or to the empowerment of other players, particularly in relation to networking across nations. However, the modern TNC-based configuration of integration can be used to generate a co-operative stance between governments. This is particularly the case between countries linked by two-way FDI as each side is home to companies with assets at stake in the other.

# Conclusions

The paper starts by looking at some elements of the new environment which are considered relevant in shaping the strategic framework for industrial policy. It deals with issues related to the complementarity between different entry modes and in particular between trade and FDI. It develops the thesis that the major changes must be looked at not so much in terms of the mode of penetration and operation but in terms of its TNC-based rather than its UNC-based configuration. The paper also considers the impact of profits from foreign investment and touches on the issue of competitiveness.

A section emphasises the need to shift the focus of analysis from the costs to the advantages of operating multinationally. Advantages derive to companies from diversification across many nations (regulatory regimes) and across different modes of market penetration (trade, FDI, inter-company linkages).

A further section is devoted to considering some implications for analysis; the need for further research is highlighted. The following issues of analysis are discussed: the role of advantages of operating across nation-states in the new theories of trade and location which incorporate transnational companies; the impact of profits from foreign investment on the real economy and its industrial structure as well as on the distribution of resources across the world and the EU; emphasis on the spread of activities in the assessment of the degree of multinationality of companies. Issues of competitiveness are briefly touched on.

The implications for policy concentrate on issues of the distribution of power between different players in the economic system; the embeddedness of TNCs and their activities in certain regions/countries; and the relevance of the nationality of ownership of the TNCs. A strategy of countervailing power for other players in the economic system (UNCs, consumers, labour) is advocated. The aims of such a strategy are partly to achieve some redistribution of power, partly to achieve a more efficient distribution and agglomeration of economic activity, and partly to increase the level of embeddedness of TNCs in the local and national economies.

# Notes

1  Cantwell (1994) correctly points out that international production cannot be entirely measured by FDI because production can take place without FDI flows.
2  Earnings from FDI include profits on FDI as well as interest on loans between parent and affiliates. The interest component is usually relatively small.
3  For a clear survey on this point see Dunning (1993, ch. 14).
4  Aliber (1970) develops a theory of FDI based on customs and currency regimes.

# References

Aliber, R.Z., 1970, A theory of direct foreign investment. In C.P. Kindleberger (ed.), *The International Corporation*. Cambridge, MA: MIT Press, 17–34.

Bailey, D., Harte, G. and Sugden, R., 1994, *Making Transnationals Accountable: A Significant Step for Britain.* London: Routledge.

Barry, F. and Bradley, J., 1997, FDI and trade: the Irish Host-country experience, *Economic Journal,* 107, 445: 1798–1811.

Cantwell, J., 1994, The relationship between international trade and international production. In D. Greenaway and L.A. Winters (eds), *Surveys in International Trade.* Oxford: Blackwell.

Central Statistical Office/Office for National Statistics, various issues, *Business Monitor, MA4: Overseas Direct Investment.* London: HMSO.

Cowling, K., 1987, An industrial strategy for Britain, *International Review of Applied Economics,* 1.

Cowling, K., 1990, The strategic approach to economic and industrial policy. In K. Cowling and R. Sugden (eds), *A New Economic Policy for Britain: Essays on the Development of Industry.* Manchester: Manchester University Press.

Cowling, K. and Sugden, R., 1987, *Transnational Monopoly Capitalism.* Brighton: Wheatsheaf.

Cowling, K. and Sugden, R. (eds), 1992, *Current Issues in Industrial Economic Strategy,* Manchester: Manchester University Press.

Dietrich, M., 1992, The foundations of industrial policy. In K. Cowling and R. Sugden (eds), *Current Issues in Industrial Economic Strategy,* Manchester: Manchester University Press, 16–32.

Dunning, J.H., 1977, Trade, location of economic activity and the MNE: a search for an eclectic approach. In B. Ohlin, P.O. Hesselborn and P.M. Wijkman (eds), *The International Allocation of Economic Activity.* London: Macmillan, 395–431.

Dunning, J.H., 1980, Explaining changing patterns of international production: in defence of the eclectic theory. *Oxford Bulletin of Economics and Statistics,* 41 (4), 269–95.

Dunning, J.H., 1993, *Multinational Enterprises and the Global Economy.* Wokingham: Addison-Wesley.

Dunning, J.H. and Pearce, R.D., 1981, *The World's Largest Industrial Enterprises,* Farnborough: Gower.

GATT/WTO, various issues, *International Trade.* Geneva: United Nations.

Graham, E.M., 1978, Transatlantic investment by multinational firms: a rivalristic phenomenon?, *Journal of Post-Keynesian Economics,* 1, 1.

Graham, E.M., 1997, US direct investment abroad and US exports in the manufacturing sector: some empirical results based on cross-sectional analysis. In P.J. Buckley and J.-L. Mucchielli (eds), *Multinational Firms and International Relocation.* Cheltenham: Edward Elgar, 90–102.

Guisinger, S., 1986, 'Host-country policies to attract and control foreign investment'. In T.H. Moran (ed.), *Investing in Development: New Roles for Private Capital.* New Brunswick: Transaction Books, 157–72.

Hagedoorn, J. 1996, Trends and patterns in strategic technology partnering since the early seventies. *Review of Industrial Organization,* 11: 601–16.

Helpman, E. and Krugman, P.R., 1985, *Market Structure and Foreign Trade. Increasing Returns, Imperfect Competition and the International Economy.* Cambridge, MA: MIT Press.

Hirst, P. and Thompson, G., 1996, *Globalization in Question.* Cambridge: Polity Press.

Hufbauer, G.C. and Adler, M., 1968, *Overseas Manufacturing Investment and the Balance of Payments.* Washington, D.C.: US Treasury Department.

Hymer, S.H., 1960, *The International Operations of National Firms: A Study of Direct Foreign Investment.* Cambridge, MA: MIT Press (published 1976).

Ietto-Gillies, G., 1992, *International Production. Trends, Theories, Effects.* Cambridge: Polity Press.

Ietto-Gillies, G., 1996, Widening geographical trends in UK international production: theoretical analysis and empirical evidence, *International Review of Applied Economics*, 10, 2: 195–208.

Ietto-Gillies, G. 1998, Different conceptual frameworks in the assessment of the degree of internationalization: empirical analysis of various indices for the top 100 TNCs. *Transnational Corporations*, 7, 3: 17–39.

Ietto-Gillies, G., 1999, Earnings from foreign direct investment: patterns in EU countries and their implications. In F. Chesnais, G. Ietto-Gillies and R. Simonetti (eds), *European Integration and Global Corporate Strategies*. London: Routledge.

International Monetary Fund (IMF), various issues, *Balance of Payments Statistics Yearbook*. Washington, DC: IMF.

Knickerbocker, F.T., 1973, *Oligopolistic Reaction and Multinational Enterprise*, Boston: Harvard University Press.

Krugman, P., 1985, Increasing returns and the theory of international trade. *NBER Working Papers*, no. 1752, November.

Krugman, P., 1991, *Geography and Trade*. Cambridge, MA: MIT Press.

Marginson, P., Armstrong, P., Edwards, P. and Purcell, J., 1995, Facing the multinational challenge. In P. Leisink, J. van Leemput and J. Vilrokx (eds), *Innovation or Adaptation? Trade Unions and Industrial Relations in a Changing Europe*. Aldershot: Edward Elgar, ch. 11.

Markusen, J.R., 1995, The boundaries of multinational enterprises and the theory of international trade, *Journal of Economic Perspectives*, 9, 2: 169–89.

Molle, W. and Morsink, R., 1991, Intra-European direct investment. In B. Burgenmeier and J.L. Mucchielli (eds), *Multinationals and Europe 1992*. London: Routledge.

Mundell, R.A., 1957, International trade and factor mobility. *American Economic Review*, 47, June: 321–35.

Organization for Economic Co-operation and Development (OECD), 1992, *Globalization of Industrial Activities: Four Case Studies: Auto Parts, Chemicals, Construction and Semiconductors*. Paris: OECD.

Organization for Economic Co-operation and Development (OECD), 1994, *The Performance of Foreign Affiliates in OECD Countries*. Paris: OECD.

Petri, P.A., 1994, The regional clustering of foreign direct investment and trade, *Transnational Corporations*, 3, 3: 1–24.

Phelps, N.A., 1997, *Multinationals and European Integration: Trade, Investment and Regional Development*, London: Jessica Kingsley and Regional Studies Association.

Reddaway, W.B., 1967, *Effects of UK Direct Investment Overseas: An Interim Report*. University of Cambridge, Department of Applied Economics, Occasional Paper no. 12. Cambridge: Cambridge University Press.

Reddaway, W.B., 1968, *Effects of UK Direct Investment Overseas: Final Report*. University of Cambridge, Department of Applied Economics, Occasional Paper no. 15. Cambridge: Cambridge University Press.

Rowthorn, R.E. and Wells, J.R., 1987, *De-industrialization and Foreign Trade*. Cambridge: Cambridge University Press.

Russell, B., [1946] 1984, *A History of Western Philosophy*. London: Counterpoint, Unwin Paperbacks.

Sawyer, M., 1992, On the theory of industrial policy. In K. Cowling and R. Sugden (eds), *Current Issues in Industrial Economic Strategy*. Manchester: Manchester University Press.

Sullivan, D., 1994, Measuring the degree of internationalisation of a firm, *Journal of International Business Studies*, 25, 2: 325–42.

Thomsen, S. and Woolcock, S., 1993, *Direct Investment and European Integration: Competition among Firms and Governments*. London: Royal Institute of International Affairs and Pinter Publishers.

UNCTAD-DTCI, *World Investment Report, 1992, 1994, 1995, 1996 and 1997*. Geneva: United Nations.

Vernon, R., 1979, The product cycle hypothesis in a new international environment. *Oxford Bulletin of Economics and Statistics*, 41: 255–67.

Yamawaki, H., 1997, Exit of Japanese multinationals in US and European manufacturing industries. In P.J. Buckley and J.-L. Mucchielli (eds), *Multinational Firms and International Relocation*. Cheltenham: Edward Elgar, 220–37.

# 18 Multinational enterprise investment and industrial policy

*Cormac K. Hollingsworth**

## Introduction

In the last decade there has been a surge in foreign direct investments throughout the world economy. In the late 1980s, the flows were concentrated in the developed countries (Graham and Krugman, 1993). Since then developing countries have increased their share of inward investment flows from 17.5 per cent of world FDI in 1988 to 37.4 per cent of world FDI in 1994 (*The Economist*, 16 December 1995). These large investment flows have drawn attention to the importance of multinational enterprises (MNEs) in the world economy and to the opportunities available for individual countries if they can attract those investment flows.

At the macroeconomic level, MNEs have progressively centralised production and investment decisions in manufacturing. In the early 1960s, US firms began to increase their investment overseas; this was followed in the 1970s by European firms, and then in the 1980s by Japanese firms. The integration of the world economy by MNEs has been accompanied by a liberalisation of trading arrangements. The change in the structure of production coupled with trade liberalisation has had real effects on the level of investment and wages in individual economies (Hollingsworth, 1997).

At the microeconomic level, regional development agencies often encourage MNEs to invest in depressed regions. An MNE's investment is seen as part of an economic strategy to re-invigorate the region. Substantial subsidies are offered to MNEs for an investment in a depressed region. The subsidies are justified by referring to the benefits for the regional economy created by the MNEs presence: positive externalities such as a pool of skilled labour; new technology and so on.

Despite these developments there has been little comment on how government policy should react to the interaction between MNEs and regional development agencies, and between MNEs and the local communities in the regions

* The views expressed in this chapter are those of the author alone. The author is grateful to Keith Cowling, Roger Sugden, David Bailey and conference participants for their comments.

in which each MNE invests. In this chapter we discuss both issues. We begin with a discussion of the level of subsidies given to MNEs by regional development agencies. We describe a number of cases of subsidies given to MNEs to invest in certain regions. In particular we describe the case of Ford's 1997 negotiations with the UK government on a subsidy for Ford's Halewood plant. We suggest that there may be a problem of a 'winner's curse' for regional development agencies whose subsidy bid wins an MNE's investment. We extend our analysis of MNE investments to discuss how an MNE can become engaged in a bargain with the local community. The case of the Ford Halewood negotiations highlights this problem. Ford's investment in Halewood was brought to Liverpool by subsidies in the early 1970s in the hope of encouraging economic development in the region. However, the region remained relatively dependent on the plant for employment (*Financial Times*, 3 April 1997), and there was little development during the next two decades. To explain this we consider the bargain between an MNE and the local community in which one of its plants is situated. We show that it is quite likely that the bargain results in the welfare of the local community becoming a cost that the MNE tries to minimise. We also suggest that local welfare may be reduced *ceteris paribus* because of the MNE's multi-plant structure.

We conclude the chapter with a discussion of how industrial policy should take account of the effects of MNEs. In general, industrial policy should be concerned with creating dynamic regional economies. MNEs can aid policy-makers to achieve this goal, by providing employment in the short run and aiding the creation of a regional pool of knowledge. However, in this chapter we highlight how MNEs may hinder the long-term policy of creating dynamic regional economies. The problems of a winner's curse in an auction for an MNE's investment and the lack of regional development independent of an MNE's investment have implications for industrial policy towards MNEs. That MNEs have a role to play in creating dynamic economies, by reducing learning externalities for a region, means that subsidies should allow them to share in the economic benefit of reducing those learning externalities. However, this implies that the level of subsidies should be calculated according to the benefits to the region concerned. Furthermore, the continued effect of an MNE on a region's development should be monitored. We suggest that the proposal of Bailey *et al.* (1994) to create an MNE monitoring unit would allow governments to estimate the economic effect on a region of an MNE's investments. The success of the MNE's investment should be continuously audited, and the monitoring unit's main role should be to perform these audits (ibid.).

## Multinational bargaining with governments: investment subsidies

The level of subsidies provided to MNEs is becoming a serious issue. A high level of subsidy is provided to many MNE investors in the UK. For example, the investment by Lucky Goldstar in Wales in 1996 received over £200 million (*Financial Times*, 10 June 1996); Mercedes was paid $250 million for an investment in Alabama; BMW was paid $130 million for an investment in North Carolina; and Ford was paid £80 million ($130 million) to attract the production of a new Jaguar model to Birmingham.

Regional development agencies usually compete in an auction for an MNE's investment. The Welsh Development Agency faced intense competition from the Scottish Development Office for Lucky Goldstar's investment (*Financial Times*, 22 May 1996). Indeed, *The Economist* has pointed out that plans to create Regional Development Groupings within England could increase competition for investment, and is quite likely to raise subsidies even further (*The Economist*, 7 June 1997).

Each agency's bid is based on an estimate of the value to their region of the employment the MNE promises to provide. If we assume that this is a common value auction then the winner is likely to suffer the 'winner's curse'. The winner of the auction will be the regional development authority that has the largest positive error in the estimate of the value of the investment, and so will have over-bid *ex post*. *The Economist* refers to this problem: 'if governments end up in an auction for a foreigner's favour, the "winner" may pay more than the value of any spillovers [in new technology or in new skills brought by the MNE]' (*The Economist*, 16 December 1995). In the case of Ford's investment in a new Jaguar model in Birmingham, the £80 million subsidy paid to attract the production represented a substantial portion of Ford's £500 million investment.

Governments and MNEs can also be involved in a bargain over the level of subsidies. This framework is implied by the work of Ruigrok and Tulder (1995), Stopford and Strange (1991) and Porter (1990). For example, Ford has developed a strategy of bargaining for new subsidies from governments for improvements to actual plants (and GM has followed Ford's strategy to receive additional subsidies: *Financial Times*, 14 March 1997).

Ford announced on 8 January 1997 that its Halewood plant would be closed, because production of the new Escort would take place in Germany and Spain (*Financial Times*, 8 and 17 January 1997). On 20 January Ford announced that it would seek subsidies for the plant from the UK government. Ford's UK manager of corporate affairs was reported as saying: 'the availability of aid is one of the factors which will decide which route we take' (*Financial Times*, 20 January 1997). The *Financial Times* (8 February 1997) suggested that any deal with Ford over a new subsidy 'is likely to increase competition for subsidies as carmakers lobby governments for aid for factories in sensitive areas'. As it pointed out (22 January 1997): 'It all begins to fit together: Ford does not want a strike. The government does not want bad publicity ahead of the election. And Ford, of course, needs the [subsidy].' Ford was offered £15 million from the government on 28 March, but it announced that the money was not enough (*Financial Times*, 29 March 1997).

The common-value auction for an MNE's investment can result in a region overpaying for the benefits of the MNE's investment. Also an MNE may use its bargaining position to increase the subsidy further. This is likely to result in large subsidies going to large firms, overpaying for the short-term benefits, and perhaps preventing longer-term development.

## MNEs and local development

The case of Ford's Halewood investment is an interesting one. Ford was provided with subsidies in the early 1970s to invest in Halewood, and the investment was expected to help regenerate the region; however twenty years on, the region 'relies heavily' on the Halewood plant and would suffer greatly if the plant closed (*Financial Times*, 3 April 1997). This suggests that we should analyse an MNE's interaction with the local community.

A community that is employed by an MNE may have lower welfare than a community employed by locally based firms. The reasons for this are both related to the difference in structure between a locally based firm and an MNE. First, the senior managers of the MNE usually are not members of the local community. Second, the multi-plant structure of the MNE confers bargaining advantages which lowers local welfare.

The distance of the managers from the local community means that the utility of an MNE's management (the MNE's strategic decision-maker: Cowling and Sugden, 1994) is not usually coincident with that of the local community welfare. Therefore, beyond any efficiency effects of unobserved effort, the local community's welfare becomes a cost that the MNE will seek to minimise. We can model this interaction between the MNE and the local community as a bargain. This allows us to consider how the MNE's structure will reduce a community's welfare.

The MNE has a multi-plant structure with plants in many different countries. This increases the MNE's outside option above that of a locally based firm in a bargain with any local community. We shall illustrate this by considering the bargain between the local community at plant $i$, with welfare $U_i$ and outside welfare $\bar{U}_i$, and an MNE which gains a profit $\pi_j$ from each plant $j$, which gives it total profits, $\Pi = \Sigma \pi_j$. The Nash bargain over total profits and the wage and employment at plant $i$ can be described in terms of a Nash product, $\Omega_i$:

$$\Omega_i = [U_i - \bar{U}_i]^\beta \left( \Pi - \tilde{\Pi}_i \right) \tag{18.1}$$

where $\beta$ is the relative bargaining strength of each community, and $\tilde{\Pi}_i$ is the MNE's inside option for the bargain at plant $i$. If the MNE has a horizontal structure, then its multi-plant structure means that its inside option may be written as follows:

$$\tilde{\Pi}_i = \sum_{j,j \neq i} \pi_j . \tag{18.2}$$

Of course, if vertical links exist between the different plants, then the MNE's inside option will be smaller.[1] However, if there are no vertical links, then the bargain in equation (18.1) may be simplified by using (18.2) to the following:

$$\Omega_i = \left[U_i - \bar{U}_i\right]^{\beta} \pi_i . \tag{18.3}$$

This is just the bargain in a locally based firm. The level of local welfare bargained at plant $i$ depends only on the conditions at plant $i$, and it appears that whether there is a local firm or an MNE is of no consequence to the level of local welfare.

However, the case depicted in equations (18.1)–(18.3), where the MNE's inside option is the continued profits at each plant, is the outcome of an efficient bargain between each local community and the MNE (McDonald and Solow, 1981). The efficient bargain assumes that the MNE cannot change the level of employment at any plant once each bargain has been completed. The MNE is committed to the level of employment at every plant, so it cannot change the level of employment to compensate for a strike at a plant where a disagreement with the local community has resulted in that strike.

However, if the MNE has the 'right-to-manage' (Nickell and Andrews, 1983), the MNE can set the level of employment and output at each plant independently of the bargain over the welfare of the local community. This means that, in the event of a disagreement at one of its plants, the MNE can expand employment and output at all its other plants to compensate for the lost profit at the striking plant. Provided that the local community does not involve itself in the production decisions of the MNE, then the 'right-to-manage' assumption is valid. In that case, the MNE's inside option is very different from that in equation (18.3):

$$\tilde{\Pi}_i > \sum_{j, j \neq i} \pi_j . \tag{18.4}$$

The form of the bargain (equation (18.1)) in the 'right-to-manage' welfare bargain has consequences for the level of the local welfare. The bargain now no longer simplifies to equation (18.3). Comparing (18.2) and (18.4), it is clear that the level of bargained local welfare for the community at plant $i$ must be lower with inside option (18.4) rather than (18.2). The MNE organisational form lowers the level of local welfare.

There is some evidence of the bargaining advantages that the multi-plant structure of MNEs confer. The ILO (1992) suggests that 'even when it means forgoing some economies of scale, the advantage for the [MNE will be] that a strike or other form of work stoppage can be met by redirecting production' (see also Scherer *et al.*, 1975). The opportunities for improving the bargaining position of the firm may be a strategic reason for becoming an MNE. It is tempting to suggest that the motivation behind FDI is to acquire these bargaining advantages. However, most initial FDI by a MNE is used to gain access to markets (see, for example, the Bureau of Economic Affairs' latest survey of MNEs; BEA, 1996, Healy and Palepu, 1993, and Pain, 1993, for empirical evidence. For evidence of this bargaining advantage motivating FDI, see Estrin *et al.*, 1997).

We can conclude that the development of local firms is preferable to MNE investment for two reasons. First, the management of the local firms and the interests of the local community are more closely aligned. Second, in a bargain between the local community and its firms, the welfare of the local community will, *ceteris paribus*, be lower if the firms are MNE rather than local single-plant firms.

## Policy: a MNE monitoring unit

Industrial policy should have as its aim the maximisation of the welfare of local communities. We have concluded that MNEs are not necessarily consistent with this policy goal. An MNE's structure may result in welfare for a local community being lower if it depends on MNEs for employment than if it has an independent dynamic economy. The encouragement of MNE investment in a region should only be the initial action in a long-term plan to develop the productive potential of each region. MNEs have a role to play in the creation of dynamic economies. First, MNEs can quickly provide employment to depressed economic regions. Second, the MNE can bring with it knowledge that would otherwise have taken a community a long time to acquire. A region can be developed in partnership with any MNEs, but the policy goal should remain the creation of an independent dynamic community.

We have shown how the actions of MNEs can lead to a loss of welfare. So, although MNEs may be involved in the economic development of a region, policy-makers should take steps to prevent MNEs hindering its continued development. To prevent MNEs exploiting their bargaining advantages when dealing with individual governments the provision of subsidies should be co-ordinated at a European level. A subsidy that is provided should reflect the future effect that the MNE will have on the local economy. The purpose of the subsidy is to share with the MNE some of the benefits from any positive externalities that result from the investment.

In addition, individual investments by MNEs should be monitored to audit the effects on the development of the local community. The MNE monitoring unit suggested by Harte and Sugden (1990) and Bailey *et al.* (1994) should be the model for this. Both the financial success of the MNE's subsidiary and its effects on the local community should be monitored. Research by Bailey *et al.* (1994) has shown that the audits are of equal use to both managements of individual MNEs and to policy-makers. In particular, those MNEs that are receiving subsidies should be monitored to ensure that the continued public support for the MNE investment is justified. The monitoring unit could also undertake the role of advising on how the level of each subsidy should be calculated.

A European monitoring unit would also be very useful in examining some of the current trends in investment and the links within the world economy.

It would be a mistake for the MNE monitoring unit to examine only investments by non-European MNEs within the EU. Since investments by MNEs around the world affect the bargains of EU governments and unions with the MNEs, all investments should be monitored and audited.

## Conclusions

The goal of industrial policy is to create dynamic regional economies. Encouraging MNE investment with subsidies should only be a short-term measure, bringing much-needed employment and knowledge to a region. However, the economic inefficiencies of providing MNEs with large subsidies to fulfil a role of 'employers of last resort' are contrary to the long-term policy goal. Long-term policy should be seeking to encourage each region to develop an independent dynamic economy, in partnership with MNEs.

We have documented in this chapter that individual countries are making offers of subsidies in a repeated bidding contest for foreign direct investment. It is quite likely that the 'winner's curse' is striking often, with many countries that gain an MNE's investment providing much larger subsidies than the social value of the investment to the region concerned. Also, although MNEs may provide employment to a depressed region, the presence of the MNE may not be enough to increase the welfare of the local community and independent local development should be encouraged alongside the MNE's investments.

We suggested two policy approaches. The first was a co-ordination of subsidies at a European level to prevent the 'winner's curse' striking too often. The second was the creation of Bailey *et al.*'s (1994) MNE monitoring unit. The MNE monitoring unit would monitor investments by both EU and foreign MNEs. The monitoring serves two purposes: first, it allows a regular assessment of the effect of the MNE's efforts to reinvigorate local economies, efforts for which some MNEs are receiving a substantial subsidy; second, it allows a general assessment of the relative bargaining strength of each MNE, and to make sure that those powers are not abused.

On a theoretical level it seems likely that structures may be designed where the auction for an MNE's investment is not subject to the winner's curse and also encourages the development of the local regional economy. It is likely that some form of monitoring agency would be part of the design to achieve a better outcome to the auction and to the long-term development of a region.

Looking to the future, access to the large EU market will continue to attract foreign investment. The size of the market means that attempts to audit the activities of MNEs at an EU level will be accepted by the MNEs as part of operating in Europe. Also the evidence shows that MNEs will find useful the information collected. An approaching problem for the EU is that central and eastern Europe and east and south-east Asia will attract more foreign investment in the future. Some of these markets are growing fast and so they will attract investment to supply their markets directly; cost advantages, such as lower wages, over the rest of Europe will persist 'for years to come' (*Financial Times*, 6 March 1997). These investments are likely to change the bargaining power of unions and governments within western Europe.

## Note

1   As GM found to its cost at a strike at the plant that was its only supplier of brake pads in Dayton, Ohio. GM's US production ground to a halt. The strike was about GM's plans to source some of the production at another plant (*International Herald Tribune*, 8 July 1996, p.15: 'GM facing tough contract sessions').

## References

Bailey, David, George Harte and Roger Sugden (1994) *Making Transnationals Accountable: A Significant Step for Britain*, London: Routledge.

Bendiner, Burton (1988) *International Labour Affairs, The World Trade Unions and the Multinational Companies*, Oxford: Clarendon Press.

Bureau of Economic Affairs (BEA) (1996) 'Operations of US Multinational Companies: 1994 Benchmark Survey, Preliminary Results', *Survey of Current Business*, vol. 76, no. 12.

Cowling, K. and R. Sugden (1994) *Beyond Capitalism Towards a New World Economic Order*, London: Pinter.

Estrin, Saul, Kirsty Hughes and Sarah Todd (1997) *Foreign Direct Investment in Central and Eastern Europe: Multinationals in Transition*, London: Royal Institue of International Affairs and Pinter Publishers.

*Financial Times* (22 May 1996) 'Korean Group Plans', p. 1.

*Financial Times* (10 June 1996) 'Welsh Fear Move to Poach Korean Plant', p. 9.

*Financial Times* (8 January 1997) 'Ford Warns of Action to Cut Capacity', p. 17.

*Financial Times* (17 January 1997) Shorts: 'Escort to Go from UK', p. 1.

*Financial Times* (20 January 1997) Shorts: 'Ford Seek State Aid for Halewood', p. 1.

*Financial Times* (22 January 1997) Leader: 'Affording Ford', p. 21.

*Financial Times* (8 February 1997) 'Ford and Unions Agree Halewood Deal', p. 4.

*Financial Times* (6 March 1997) Leader: 'Renault's Row', p. 27.

*Financial Times* (14 March 1997) Observer: 'Hush Money', p. 21.

*Financial Times* (29 March 1997) 'Ford to Review Vehicle Plans for Halewood', p. 4.

*Financial Times* (3 April 1997) Survey – Merseyside: Knowsley: 'Jobs Blackspot Relies Heavily on Ford'.

Froot, Kenneth A. ed. (1993) *Foreign Direct Investment*, New York: NBER and Chicago University Press.

Graham, Edward M. and Paul R. Krugman (1993) 'The Surge in Foreign Direct Investment in the 1980s' in Froot (1993) pp. 13–37.

Harte, George and Roger Sugden (1990) 'A Proposal for Monitoring Transnational Corporations', in Keith Cowling and Roger Sugden, eds, *A New Economic Policy for Britain: Essays on the Development of Industry*, Manchester: Manchester University Press.

Healy, Paul M. and Krishna G. Palepu (1993) 'International Corporate Equity Associations: Why, Where, and How?', in Froot (1993).

Hollingsworth, Cormac K. (1997) 'The Effects of Multinational Enterprises in the

Industrialised World: Theory and Empirics', unpublished PhD thesis, University of Warwick.

International Labour Office (ILO) (1992) *Industry on the Move*, Geneva: ILO.

Kassalow, Everett M. (1978) 'Aspects of Labour Relations in Multinational Companies: an Overview of Three Asian Countries', *International Labour Review*, vol. 117, no. 3, pp. 273–287.

Lawrence, Robert Z. (1993) 'Japan's Low Levels of Inward Investment: the Role of Inhibitions on Acquisitions' in Froot (1993)

McDonald, I.M. and R.M. Solow (1981) 'Wage Bargaining and Employment', *American Economic Review*, vol. 100, no. 4, pp. 1115–1141.

Nickell, S.J. and M. Andrews (1983) 'Trade Unions, Real Wages and Employment in Britain 1951–1979', *Oxford Economic Papers*, November (supplement), pp. 183–206.

OECD (1996) *Indicators of Tariff and Non-tariff Trade Barriers*, Paris: OECD.

Pain, Nigel (1993) 'Econometric Analysis of Foreign Direct Investment in the UK', *Scottish Journal of Political Economy*, 40, 1–24.

Pankert, Alfred (1977) 'Some Legal Problems of Workers' International Solidarity', *International Labour Review*, vol. 116, no. 1, 67–74.

Porter, Michael E. (1990) *The Competitive Advantage of Nations*, London: Macmillan.

Ruigrok, Winfried and Rob van Tulder (1995) *The Logic of International Restructuring*, London: Routledge.

Scherer, Frederic M., Alan Beckstein, Erich Kaufer and R.D. Murphy (1975) *The Economics of Multi-plant Operation*, Cambridge, MA: Harvard University Press.

Stevens, Guy V.G. and Robert E. Lipsey (1992) 'Interactions Between Domestic and Foreign Investment', *Journal of International Money and Finance*, vol. 11, pp. 40–62.

Stopford, John and Susan Strange (1991) *Rival States, Rival Firms: Competition for World Market Shares*, Cambridge Studies in International Relations, 18, Cambridge: Cambridge University Press.

*The Economist* (16 December 1995) 'Helping Handouts'.

*The Economist* (7 June 1997) 'English Devolution', p. 36.

UNCTAD (1993) World Investment Directory, vol. III: Developed Countries, New York: UNCTAD.

# 19 The macroeconomics of industrial strategy

*Philip Arestis and Malcolm Sawyer**

## Introduction

The purpose of this chapter is to explore the macroeconomics of industrial strategy. In particular, it is argued that an industrial strategy can potentially ease the constraints of capacity which lie behind inflationary pressures and the foreign trade position on the achievement of full employment. An implicit assumption behind our approach is that high levels of demand can help to underpin an industrial strategy and its promotion of investment and economic change.

There has been a general separation between macroeconomic analysis and industrial economics. At the academic level, with a few exceptions, macroeconomic analysis has proceeded with little regard to the industrial economics literature. This is not another way of saying that macroeconomics did not have microeconomic foundations. It is rather that the foundations which have been most often used have been those of atomistic competition, though there has been considerable use recently of models of imperfect competition (cf. Dixon and Rankin, 1994). It is also the case that there has been a general focus on the operation of labour markets rather than of product markets. For its part, the study of industrial economics has generally ignored macroeconomic considerations.

This separation is also apparent at the level of policy discussion and policy implementation. Macroeconomic policy is a matter for the treasury and the central bank, industrial policy for the industry department. The discussion of macroeconomic policy has rarely given thought to the effects of that policy on industrial policy or strategy even though the macroeconomic stance provides the backcloth against which industrial policy must necessarily be conducted. In a similar vein, the implications of industrial policy for macroeconomic policy are rarely evaluated. An outstanding example of this separation is the granting of operational independence to

*   The contribution of Malcolm Sawyer to this paper draws heavily on work which he undertook whilst Research Fellow at the Jerome Levy Economics Institute, USA, and he is grateful for the research environment which the Institute provided.

the Bank of England and the prescribed policy objective of the Bank to meet the government's inflation target. The policy instrument to be employed is the rate of interest, which is set with little, if any, regard to the effects on production and investment. But, also, no consideration is given to the effects which supply-enhancing policies could have on the achievement of the inflation target.

We do not offer any precise definitions of industry policy or strategy or of macroeconomic policy, nor do we seek to define industrial economics and macroeconomics. However, industrial policy would be viewed in an encompassing fashion to potentially include all those microeconomic policies which impact on industrial performance. The term industrial strategy is used to signify a more strategic approach to industrial policy, where the government sets out the broad parameters of industrial development and where, in effect, a wide range of policies (including, for example, education and training, interest rate policy) are designed to underpin the achievement of the overall strategy. Macroeconomic analysis is defined here as what macroeconomists do, even though much of what is now described as macroeconomics is little more than simplified microeconomics (for example, new classical macroeconomics, new Keynesian concerns with efficiency wages). In this chapter, we focus on two aspects of macroeconomic analysis: the idea of an inflation barrier to high levels of employment and the role of the trade sector in the determination of the rate of growth.

Three broad approaches to macroeconomics can be readily identified: first, the new classical macroeconomics (including monetarism) which views markets as being perfectly competitive and clearing rapidly at full employment in the labour market; second, the new Keynesian approach with a focus on wage determination through efficiency wages, insider–outsider models and the like and notions that wages and prices do not adjust rapidly (if at all) to the level of demand. These two approaches share two features which are particularly relevant for this chapter. First, any occurrence of unemployment is ascribed to features of the determination of wages. In the new classical macroeconomics case, this would be problems of misperceptions, trade unions and other market 'imperfections', unemployment benefits and the like. In the new Keynesian approach, unemployment arises from a range of labour market 'imperfections' (in the sense of features which would not be present under perfect competition) but many of which are almost inevitable features of an industrialised economy. The link between wages and productivity postulated in the efficiency wage literature is not a feature of the real world which can be 'wished away'. Hence many of the so-called imperfections which are identified are intrinsic ones which cannot be removed by appropriate public policies. Second, the supply-side of the economy dominates in the determination of the level of economic activity (at least in equilibrium) and the level of aggregate demand plays, at most, a passive role in adjusting to the available supply. A related aspect of this is the general view that the level of savings sets the constraint for the level of investment, and hence any attempts to raise capital accumulation and growth require some prior increase in savings.

The third approach, which we label as post-Keynesian, adopts a rather different general perspective and in particular a different approach to the relationship between microeconomics and macroeconomics. Whilst the two approaches just referred to begin with atomistic micro units and through aggregation arrive at macro relationships, the post-Keynesian approach does not draw a distinction between the two. The level of economic activity is heavily influenced by the level of effective demand, and the market economy is subject to cycles in economic activity. In the sphere of production, pricing is linked to investment: for a given level of unit costs, the higher the level of investment, the higher the price level desired by firms. Investment is related to distribution, growth and the cyclical behaviour of the economy. An economy with ambitious investment programmes will have a high growth rate, and there will be stronger upward pressure on prices than in an economy which is growing more slowly or is stagnating. The growth process brings inflationary pressures, even if the economy is operating at less than full capacity levels. In a capitalist system investment is essentially determined by expected profit rates and uncertainty. Both imply instabilities, and government involvement and other institutions are thought desirable to ameliorate the degree of instability. There is an absence of self-righting mechanisms to bring the economy to full employment, and there are a range of constraints which can operate to prevent the achievement of full employment, including lack of productive capacity, and inability of the economy to balance its trade at full employment income. Disparities between regions and areas also means that even if full employment is secured in some more prosperous regions, unemployment would remain in the less prosperous. Another set of institutions are the trade unions and the monetary sector. Trade unions are important in wage determination; monetary institutions in creating money through bank credit, where the underlying mechanism is via the demand for bank credit to finance working capital requirements. Thus, there is an intimate link between the real sector and the monetary sector.

Our general approach is a post-Keynesian one, which has two particular implications in the context of this chapter. First, the level of aggregate demand is viewed as relevant for the level of economic activity and also for the rate of investment, which in turn determines the future productive capacity of the economy. Second, the labour market is given little role in the determination of the level of employment (and indeed we would cast doubt on the usefulness of the notion of a labour market).

## On the operation of market economies

The view of the operation of market economies which underpins the approach adopted here has three strands. First, competition within a market economy is a process of rivalry, with winners and with losers. There are significant

economic, social and political forces which generate and reinforce disparities and inequalities, whether between individuals, regions, sectors or
countries. This is an application of the notion that success breeds success
and the corollary that failure breeds failure. In the economic sphere, the
operation of market forces generates processes of cumulative causation
(Myrdal, 1957) and centrapetalism (Cowling, 1987, 1990). An economically
successful region generates profits which stimulate further investment; it
can attract mobile, often highly skilled, workers from other regions and it
can benefit from static and dynamic economics of scale (Kaldor, 1972).
Unemployment and low wages are both characteristics of relatively less
prosperous regions. In the more specific areas of industrial economics, there
is a variety of routes through which 'first mover advantage' spills over into
cumulative causation. Frank and Cook (1995) argued for the widespread
effects of the 'winner-takes-all' situation, and they particular apply their
ideas to explain the widening disparities of individual incomes. When the
winner takes all, there are no prizes for being second. In so far as the
process of competition has some 'winner-takes-all' features, then it will
generate disparities but with the added ingredient that the winner can reinvest the winnings to secure future advantages.

The dynamic interplay between investment and productivity growth reinforces inequalities which are thus explained by endogenous factors in the
process of historical development rather than by the exogenous 'resource
endowment' (Kaldor, 1970: 343). Economies which are already developed
enjoy competitive advantages so that the growth that takes place generates
'dynamic increasing returns' to scale (Kaldor, 1972). These induce higher
productivity and rate of profit in the faster-growing countries, making it
progressively harder for the slower countries to compete. An inflow of
capital and skilled labour ensues which allows still further expansion
of production and the reaping of further economies of scale, higher productivity and rate of profit. These effects, labelled as 'backwash', are
thought to be contained by certain advantages accruing to the slower countries. These are the 'spread' effects, which can accrue, for example, from
expanded markets, the transfer of new technology from the advanced regions,
and so on. The 'spread' effects are not thought to be strong enough
to outweigh the negative effects emanating from 'cumulative causation'.
Even if by chance the 'spread' and 'backwash' effects are in balance, this
would not be a stable equilibrium, for any change in the balance of the two
forces would be followed by cumulative movements. 'Cumulative causation' thus creates a situation whereby the equilibrating forces of the market
no longer perform the role attached to them, so that a core–periphery relationship emerges. The dependence of the periphery on the core reduces the
ability of the periphery to pursue independent development policies and
'cumulative causation' generates the need for redistributive policies.
Consequently, the market mechanism reinforces regional disparities and
imbalances rather than eliminating them and the continuing North–South

divide is understandable in these terms. Further 'cumulative causation' in economic terms generates inequalities in non-economic terms, such as political power, cultural domination and so on (Cowling, 1985). It is thus expected that those economies which are relatively rich dominate, not just in the economic power sense, but also in terms of their ability to exert political superiority. In this way they are in a position to impose their policies and culture over the less-powerful countries.

The operation of the forces of cumulative causation indicates that there will be disparities of employment and capacity across regions and so on, and that the achievement of full employment requires policies which ensure the reduction of those disparities.

Second, many of the factors which would be labelled as 'imperfections' based on the benchmark of perfect competition (in the sense that they would be absent from perfect competition) often have a positive role to play in the operation of a market economy. A particular example would be the use of long-term contracts in the labour market, which would be absent from a so-called flexible labour market that mimics the spot market of perfect competition. Long-term contracts can help to promote training, the involvement of workers in the functioning and decision-making within the enterprise and the reduction of an adversarial relationship between employees and employers, all of which could reasonably be expected to have a positive impact on productivity. Similar arguments can be applied to trade unions, minimum wages and so on. One of the 'imperfections' of particular relevance to industrial policy clearly refers to the relationship between firms. Whereas agreements between firms are often dismissed as collusion designed to raise prices (which they may well be), there may be a more positive aspect of such agreements in the promotion of, for example, common standards, over the provision of specialised training and so on.

Each of these considerations raises severe problems for competition and monopoly policy. Since competition itself generates winners and losers, and thereby a process of concentration and centralisation, an initial position of atomistic competition is generally unstable. The policy dilemma emerges as to how to deal with the market power which the successful in the competitive struggle possess. As Marris (1972) argued, monopoly policy appears to involve the notion that, whilst success should be rewarded, excessive success should be punished. Relationships between firms may be mutually fruitful as well as collusive, and there is no clear way of distinguishing between them. But a further policy implication is a warning across attempts to create an economy which resembles perfect competition, destroying the supposed 'imperfections'.

Third, the perspective adopted here is that there are no automatic forces which ensure that there will be adequate aggregate demand to underpin the full utilisation of labour and of capital equipment. Unlike the first two approaches to macroeconomics identified above, we do not assume that Say's Law will operate and that aggregate demand will adjust to the supply-side determined equilibrium. But neither do we assume that a high level of aggregate demand is sufficient for full employment of labour, which we would see as also requiring supply-enhancing measures to ensure adequate capacity (see Arestis and Sawyer, 1997, 1998).

## Linking macroeconomic policy and industrial strategy

There are numerous possible links and interdependencies between macroeconomic policy and industrial strategy; in this chapter we are selective and focus on two of these. Our general perspective is that there are supply-side constraints on the achievement of full employment which can be alleviated through supply-enhancing measures, many of which would be associated with an industrial strategy. There are also demand constraints which need to be addressed but fall outside the scope of this chapter, but which we would view as crucial for the achievement of full employment (see Arestis and Sawyer, 1997, 1998).

In the next section, we discuss the non-accelerating inflation rate of unemployment (NAIRU), and argue that it can be viewed as a capacity constraint which is reflected in inflationary pressures. Industrial strategy is then seen as a mechanism by which the capacity constraint can be lifted with consequent beneficial effects on the inflationary picture. In the subsequent section, we briefly review the constraints on economic activity arising from balance of trade considerations.

## The NAIRU and capacity constraints

One of the major constraints on the achievement of full employment is often seen as the non-accelerating inflation rate of unemployment (NAIRU). In some respects, it may not be so much whether the NAIRU does exist (whatever that might mean), but rather that policy-makers and others respond as though it did.[1] In this section, we develop an analysis which suggests that this form of inflation barrier should be viewed as arising from a lack of capacity rather than as a labour market phenomenon. The argument advanced here is that productive capacity has a significant effect on the inflation barrier.[2] The policy implications of such analysis are clear: means have to be found to raise the level of capacity in the economy, even though the effect of a lack of capacity is expressed as an inflation problem rather than a capacity problem.

The key features of the usual formulations of the NAIRU are that it is a supply-side equilibrium position with an emphasis on the operations of the labour market. The usual suggestion is that either the NAIRU has to be accepted as a 'fact of life' or, in so far as it can be changed, that it requires some policy responses directed towards the labour market (such as reducing unemployment benefits or improved training). We would wish to view the NAIRU as a theoretical representation of the idea that there may be an inflation barrier to the achievement of full employment. Where the economy operates relative to any calculated NAIRU would depend on, *inter alia*, the level of effective demand, and we would not have any presumption that the NAIRU is a 'strong attractor' for the actual rate of unemployment.

The focus of the analysis here is on the role of capacity, and as such we pay most attention to the production side and to price formation, and little to wage determination. For our purposes here, it will suffice to postulate that wage determination considerations give rise to a positive relationship between the real product wage and employment. The equilibrium wage relationship can be viewed in one of two ways, but in both cases the level of unemployment restrains wages relative to some reference level. The first alternative is an equilibrium relationship between real wages relative to some target or reference level and the level of unemployment,[3] and this can be expressed as $w - p - T = g(U)$ where $w$ is log of money wage, $p$ is log of the relevant price level, $T$ the log of the target real wage and $U$ is the rate of unemployment. The second alternative is an equilibrium relationship which starts from the enterprise level where money wages are treated as a mark-up over alternative income $a$. This alternative income is a weighted average of alternative wages if employment can be found and of unemployment benefits $b$ if employment cannot be found, where the weights depend on the level of unemployment.[4] In equilibrium it is usually assumed that all enterprises offer the same wage, which enables a relationship to be derived which of the general form $w - b = h(U)$. When the level of unemployment benefits in real terms is set by the government, the relationship can be re-written as $(w - p) - (b - p) = h(U)$, which has the same basic form as the target real wage equation above. When the ratio of benefits to wages is fixed by the government, then the equation $w - b = h(U)$ immediately yields the level of unemployment. In each case there are a range of other variables which enter these relationships but are not of particular relevance to the discussion here. For each of the relationships specified above, the expected sign of the relationship between real wage and unemployment is a negative one, and thereby a positive one between the real wage and employment. These relationships can be summarised as $(w - p) - T = G(L)$ and $(w - p) - (b - p) = H(L)$, respectively with $G'$ and $H'$ positive. In Figures 19.3 and 19.4, the curve labelled RWE (real wage employment) is a representation of either of these relationships.

In the modelling of enterprise behaviour with regard to price, real wage, employment and output determination (which are, of course, interdependent) we wish to allow for varying returns to scale (and the related possibility that the productivity of labour may vary either positively or negatively with the volume of employment). At the level of the enterprise we make explicit allowance for the capital stock, and at the aggregate level for changes in the number of enterprises. In effect, this distinction corresponds to capacity-replacing (though productivity-enhancing) investment and capacity-enhancing investment. The general environment within which the enterprise is assumed to operate is that of imperfect competition: the position of the demand schedule facing the individual enterprise is assumed to depend on the decisions of other enterprises and on the level of aggregate demand.

The short-run profit-maximising decision facing the enterprise is modelled as involving the maximisation of $\Pi = p(q,Z).q - w.l$ where $q = f(l^\alpha k^{1-\alpha})$; $Z$ is a vector of variables influencing the demand facing an enterprise including the level of aggregate demand, lower-case letters refer to the enterprise level. We do not include material inputs since their inclusion would complicate the analysis without being of importance to the points which we wish to explore here. Using the level of employment as the key decision variable, with the capital stock and $Z$ held constant, the first order condition for profit maximisation yields:

$$\frac{(e-1)}{e} \alpha l^{\alpha-1} k^{1-\alpha} f'(l^\alpha k^{1-\alpha}) = \frac{w}{p(q,Z)} . \tag{19.1}$$

This first-order condition looks rather like a demand for labour schedule but should not be so regarded since the enterprise does not face parametric output prices, though it is assumed to face a given nominal wage (and hence sets the real product wage through its actions over its price). Further, this equation provides a 'point' outcome: it is an equation in $l$($k$ being exogenous as this point, $p,q$ being functions of $l$) which can be solved to give the level of employment, from which the level of output, real product wage and price can be derived.

One way to map out a relationship between the real product wage and the level of employment is to vary the $Z$ variable. In particular, movements in the level of aggregate demand would generate movements in employment, real product wage and so on. Making such variations in $Z$ would lead to a relationship, labelled the p-curve, as sketched in Figure 19.1, where it is assumed that the function $f$ is such that it initially displays increasing returns to labour and then diminishing ones. If there is a constant elasticity of demand then the relationship in Figure 19.1 is merely the inverted U-shaped short-run cost curve. The significance of the role of aggregate demand here is that it provide the mechanism for the generation of a curve such as the one in Figure 19.1: without that (or analogous) mechanism, the decisions of the enterprise would merely yield a point outcome (in terms of real product wage and employment). Further, any point on the p-curve has to be supported by a particular level of aggregate demand.

It is readily apparent from equation (19.1) that an increase in the capital stock would lead to an upward shift in the real product wage–employment relationship (and in the case of a Cobb–Douglas production function with $f' = 1$, a 1 per cent rise in $k$ would lead to a 1 per cent rise in $l$ for a given real product wage). However, for a given level of $Z$, an increase in $k$ would lead to a combination of higher real product wage (induced by the lower price required to sell the increased output) and of employment.

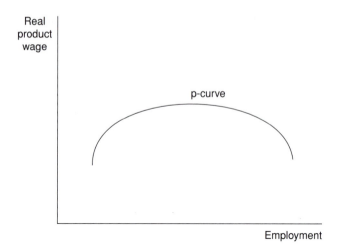

*Figure 19.1* Real product wage–employment relationship

Moving to the aggregate level, the real product wage–employment relationship is the horizontal summation of the individual enterprise relationship.
The relationship in Figure 19.1 is regarded as relating to a representative enterprise, and that aggregation across enterprises does not raise any particular
problems. Figure 19.2 sketches the aggregate relationship between the real
wage and employment based on enterprise behaviour and price, output decisions, and again labelled the p-curve. An increase in the number of enterprises
will shift the p-curve to the right, whereas an increase in the capital stock of
the representative enterprise shifts the relationship up. In Figure 19.2, the shift
from A to B reflects an increase in the average capital stock per enterprise and
the shift from A to C an increase in the number of enterprises.

It can readily be seen that investment will lead to rightward and upward
shifts in the p-curve, and the mix of those shifts depends on the degree to
which the investment leads to a rise in the average capital stock (per enterprise) and the degree to which the investment involves an increase in the
number of enterprises. The distinction between average capital stock and
number of enterprises corresponds to a distinction between capacity-
replacing investment and capacity-enhancing investment: the former replaces
older with newer vintage and (usually) raises the capital–labour ratio while
the latter adds to capacity. This leads to the important perspective that it
may be possible through appropriate macroeconomic policies to generate
increases in the capital stock and its composition which can be represented
as a shift in the p-curve. A sufficient shift in the p-curve can lead to a
corresponding NAIRU, which is compatible with full employment: such
a possibility is illustrated in Figure 19.3, where as noted above the RWE
curve is based on wage determination considerations. The achievement of

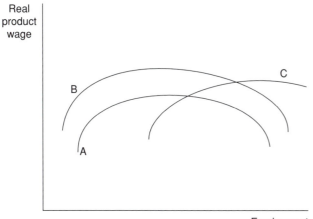

*Figure 19.2* Real product wage–employment relationships

full employment would still require the appropriate level of aggregate demand (so that enterprises would choose to operate at point A), recalling that each point on the real wage employment relationship corresponds to a specific level of aggregate demand. It is outside the scope of this chapter to discuss the determinants of the level of aggregate demand, and we confine ourselves here to making the point that there is no strong reason to think that the wages and profits generated at point A would lead to a level of expenditure which would purchase the output produced at A.

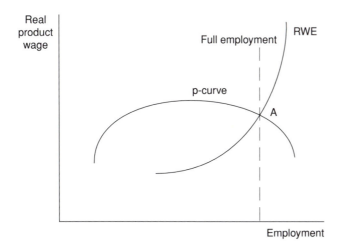

*Figure 19.3* Interaction of p-curve and RWE

In Figure 19.3, the slope of the p-curve around point A is clearly negative. However, a relationship which was positively sloped would not change
any significant conclusions, though it can be noted that if the real wage
employment relationship has a significant portion for which the p-curve is
horizontal, then moving toward full employment would require an increase
in the average capital stock.

In the approach adopted here, there would be unemployment in equilibrium if there is insufficient capacity for the enterprises to be willing to
employ the whole of the workforce at the real wage generated by the wage
equation at full employment. This can be illustrated in Figure 19.4, where
the NAIRU would be at point B, which falls short of full employment. Even
here, low levels of aggregate demand may prevent even point B being
reached, and a point such as E might be reached.

Any NAIRU which falls short of full employment is viewed in terms of
a lack of capacity (rather than being viewed in terms of, for example, labour
market imperfections). The notion that sufficient capacity can lift the NAIRU
to full employment does not, of course, mean that such capacity will be
forthcoming, and in particular high levels of unemployment will provide a
strong disincentive for such capacity to be built.

However, if investment increases capital intensity (represented by an
upward shift in the p-curve), then it is possible that the higher productivity
which thereby results leads to an upward shift in the RWE equation (based
on wage determination considerations). In terms of the two equations used
above, that is $(w-p) - T = G(L)$ and $(w-p) - (b-p) = H(L)$, this would
mean an increase in $T$ or in $(b-p)$. Clearly, if a 1 per cent rise in the p-
curve (as a result of increased capital stock) was associated with a 1 per

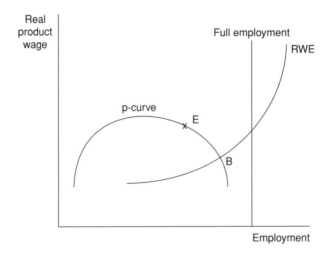

*Figure 19.4* Unemployment from inadequate capacity

cent rise in the target real wage (real benefit level) then the NAIRU would remain unchanged. This is, in effect, the case which Layard *et al.* (1991) examine, and to which they restrict their analysis. In such a case, it could be said that if the response of the wage equation to a shift in the real wage employment relationship arises from an increase in the aggregate capital stock, then workers (or at least those in employment) in association with employers are to that extent taking the increase in productivity in the form of higher wages rather than as an increase in employment.

It may be tempting to read Figure 19.4 as saying that a NAIRU below full employment is the result of the workers' demands for real wages (that is, the target real wage is too high) or the level of real unemployment benefits are too higher. But clearly what is relevant is the interaction of the two curves, and the figure could also be read as saying that the p-curve is too low as a result of enterprises' profit margins (and hence prices) being too high (and hence real product wage too low).

It would seem that through some apparently innocuous assumptions the models developed in the influential book by Layard *et al.* (1991) imposed conditions to the effect that any shift in the real wage employment relationship generated a corresponding shift in the wage equation, such that the equilibrium level of unemployment did not change (and the benefits of higher productivity fed through into real wages). Layard *et al.* use a Cobb–Douglas production function with constant returns to scale (and hence there is no significance to be given to the division of increases in the capital stock between the average per enterprise and the number of enterprises). In the Cobb–Douglas production function case, $w - p = ((e - 1)/e)\alpha . L^{\alpha - 1}K^{1-\alpha}$ and it can readily be calculated that the employment level will be constant if the proportionate rise in the real wage (imposed on the enterprise) is equal to the proportionate rise of output following a rise in the capital stock for a given level of employment. Any mechanism which imposes that condition (whether by a rise in the target real wage, the level of unemployment benefits or some other means) would lead to constant equilibrium level of employment (and hence a constant NAIRU). In the case of a CES production function, with the elasticity of substitution less than unity, then such a proportionate rise in the real wage would be compatible with a rise in employment.

In Layard *et al.* (1991), there are a number of reasons why the capital–labour ratio does not influence the equilibrium level of unemployment. In the union bargaining model deployed in their Chapter 2, they conclude that 'if the production function is Cobb–Douglas (not a bad assumption) and benefit replacement ratios are kept stable, then unemployment in the long run is independent of capital accumulation and technical progress. . . . If, however, the elasticity of substitution is less than one, capital accumulation (with no technical progress) raises the share of labour and reduces unemployment' (ibid.: 107). Rowthorn (1999) argues that the estimates of the elasticity of substitution between labour and capital are considerably below unity, and hence that a rising capital–labour ratio reduces the equilibrium level of unemployment.

In Layard *et al.* (1991, ch. 2), the mark-up of the wage over alternative income (a weighted average of wages elsewhere and the unemployment benefits) in a bilateral bargaining model does not depend on the capital–labour ratio, whereas Rowthorn (1998) shows that with a CES production function, that mark-up does depend on the capital–labour ratio. The equilibrium level of unemployment depends on the relationship between actual wage and the alternative wage. In the case of the Cobb–Douglas production function with a constant wage to benefit ratio, the level of equilibrium unemployment remains unchanged in the face of changes in the capital–labour ratio since the relationship between the wage-alternative wage and the level of unemployment remains unchanged. In the case of the CES production function, that relationship changes when the capital–labour ratio changes, permitting a change in the equilibrium level of unemployment (and specifically if the elasticity of substitution is below unity, the equilibrium level of unemployment falls when the capital–labour ratio rises).

These considerations would appear more relevant when investment takes the form of increasing the average capital stock per enterprise (equivalent to capacity-replacing investment) for then labour productivity would rise, whereas in the case of increasing number of enterprises (equivalent to capacity enhancing investment) the main effect is on capacity.

We would conclude from this discussion that when capital investment takes the form of increasing the average capital stock per enterprise, and where the elasticity of substitution is unity and the wage equation shifts up in line with the rise in output (and hence the labour share in national income remains a constant) then the NAIRU may become stuck below the full employment level, and it cannot be shifted through the expansion of the capital stock. But when the elasticity of substitution is below unity, or when the wage equation does not shift up in line with the rise in output, or when capital investment takes the form of more enterprises, then the NAIRU can be guided into compatibility with full employment through capital investment.

There are two conclusions from this analysis which are relevant for economic policy. The first is that, in general, an expansion of capacity would help to push back any inflation barrier. This point would be reinforced if spatial aspects were taken into account in that the spatial distribution of capacity has to match with the corresponding distribution of workers. Policies to create capacity become anti-inflation policies and in particular an industrial strategy which has capacity expansion as one of its objectives links with macroeconomic policy designed to constrain inflation.

The second is that when an economy has a capital stock (and the related p-curve) which cannot readily support the real wage claims being made, then the NAIRU will appear to be relatively high. The reduction in the NAIRU requires a sustained increase in the level of aggregate demand to stimulate investment (and also to underpin higher levels of employment).

According to the NAIRU approach, unemployment below the current NAIRU stimulates inflation, which often leads to policies that tend to abort the higher levels of demand. But unless the higher levels of demand are sustained, the lower NAIRU cannot be reached.

The usual discussion on the NAIRU provides a strong suggestion of the restoration of the classical dichotomy between the real side and the nominal sides of the economy. It is often specifically argued that the reduction of inflation (through control of the growth of the money supply) can be achieved without detriment to the real side of the economy, and that there is no long run-trade-off between inflation and unemployment. The discussion here suggests that the nature of any association between inflation and unemployment will be heavily dependent on the time path of unemployment and its effects on the level of the capital stock.

Finally, it can just be noted that capacity should be viewed as having other dimensions, including the skills of the workforce and the regional distribution of the capital stock. Insufficient capacity in either of these respects may be sufficient to prevent the achievement of full employment.[5]

## Balance of trade constraint[6]

While there is some debate over the degree to which and the period for which a country can run a trade deficit,[7] there is little doubt that there is some eventual limit. The importance of the balance of payments as a constraint to growth has been discussed extensively (see, for example, Thirlwall, 1979; McCombie and Thirlwall, 1997a, 1997b). The argument is that countries with high income elasticity of demand for imports and low income elasticity of demand for exports experience balance of payment difficulties which restrict governments in their attempt to expand aggregate demand. The equality of exports and imports would give $X(e,Y_w) = M(e,Y_d)$ where $e$ is the real exchange rate, $Y_w$ is world income and $Y_d$ is domestic income with exports negatively related to the real exchange rate and imports positively related. In growth terms, this gives $-\eta_X g_e + \eta_w g_w = \eta_M g_e + \eta_d g_d$ where $\eta$ refers to elasticities and $g$ to growth rate of the variable indicated by the relevant subscript. The domestic growth rate is then given by

$$g_d = (\eta_w g_w - (\eta_x + \eta_M)g_e) / \eta_d.$$

Clearly if the responsiveness of the demand for imports and exports to price changes is small or if the real exchange rate does not change to any significant degree, then domestic growth would be largely determined by world growth and the ratio of $\eta_w/\eta_d$ (which is often now termed 'Thirlwall's Law').

This analysis can be modified in a number of respects, and two are of some relevance. First, the exchange rate may continuously change to enable the domestic growth rate to diverge from $\eta_w g_w/\eta_d$, but there are some obvious limits to that. Second, it may be possible to run a substantial trade deficit for a significant period of time. But the borrowing required to cover the deficit implies a future stream of interest (or equivalent) payments. It can readily be shown that a trade deficit would lead to a foreign debt to domestic income ratio which increases over time without limit if the rate of interest on borrowing exceeds the domestic rate of growth, a condition which we would see as generally fulfilled (though the United States appears to have been something of an exception in recent years).

The focus on this trade constraint appears to be one on the conditions of demand. But there are obviously supply-side factors underlying the income elasticities of demand which feature so prominently in the above formula. It is here again evident that the factors limiting the performance of the economy lie with the conditions of production and not with the labour market. The role of industrial strategy at a general level is here perhaps self-evident, namely the creation and support of industries which supply or will be able to supply products for which there is a high income elasticity of demand in world markets. A successful industrial strategy in those terms would have considerable externalities in the sense that the growth of sectors which enable the growth of exports to rise thereby permits the faster growth of the economy.

## Conclusions

This chapter has sought to begin an exploration of the links between macroeconomic policy and industrial strategy. The debates over economic policy in recent years have often focused on the role of the labour market in the determination of macroeconomic performance: whether through attempts to reduce trade union power, reduce social security benefits, or to improve training and skill formation, the emphasis has been on the labour market. The perspective of the present chapter is rather different, and seeks to emphasise the role of the output and investment activities of enterprises. We have explored this aspect in some detail in connection with the inflation barrier, and have argued that such a barrier should be viewed in terms of a lack of capacity. We have briefly reviewed the balance of trade constraint on growth and employment. The overall implications of those two sets of analyses is that macroeconomic performance would be enhanced by appropriate industrial strategy, and that inappropriate macroeconomic policies will damage industrial performance. Policies designed to restrain inflation by lowering the level of aggregate demand will tend to depress investment and harm capacity. Improved industrial performance requires a climate conducive to investment and research and development, which in turn depends on, *inter alia*, high and stable levels of aggregate demand.

## Appendix

This appendix provides the formal algebra for the figures in the text. Lower-case letters are used to signify enterprise (plant) level and upper-case aggregates.

Suppose the typical enterprise has capital stock of $k$, and for that typical enterprise $q = f(l,k)$ where $f_1$ (the first partial derivative of $f$ with respect to $l$) $> 0$ and $f_{11}$ is seen as initially positive and then negative (so that the marginal productivity of labour initially increases with the amount of labour and then declines).

We can write $Q = nq = nf(l,k)$ where $n$ is number of enterprises (plants). The capacity of enterprise is denoted by $q^*$, and this is not to be thought of as physical capacity necessarily but some 'normal' level. Capacity utilisation is then defined as $u = q/q^*$, and the mark-up of price over marginal costs is taken to be a function of $u$. Then $w/p = b(u) f_1(l,k)$ where $b$ is the inverse of the mark-up of price over marginal labour costs and it is expected that $b'$ may be positive (that is, mark-up falls) for low values of $u$ but negative for relatively high values. Then $u = q/q^* = f(l,k)/q^*$ and $L = nl$ and hence $w/p = b(f(L/n,k)/q^* f_1(L/n,k)$.

An increase in $n$ would reduce $L/n$. At high levels of $L/n$ when $f_{11} < 0$ this would raise $f_1$, and reduce $f$ thereby raising the value of $b$. Hence real wage (at a given level of total employment) would rise for increase in $n$. However, at low levels of $L/n$, $f_{11} > 0$, and the effect on the real wage would depend on the net effect on the inverse of the mark-up $b$ and on $f_1$.

An increase in the average capital stock $k$ would lead to a rise in $f_1$, and it can be postulated that the effect of increased $k$ is that $q$ rises by the same proportion for all levels of employment, then $f(l,k)/q^*$ would not be affected. Then rise in $k$ would lead to higher real wage (for given employment).

The real wage equation given above suggests that the real wage can be viewed as a function of the rate of capacity utilisation, average employment per enterprise and the average capital stock (per enterprise).

## Notes

1  For a critique of the concept of the NAIRU, see Sawyer (1997a).
2  The approach outlined here is more fully developed in Sawyer (1997b).
3  See, for example, Sawyer (1982a, 1982b), for the theoretical aspects and Arestis (1986), Arestis and Skott (1993) and Arestis and Biefang-Frisancho Mariscal (1994) for further theoretical discussion and empirical estimation of the target real wage approach.
4  See, for example, Layard *et al.* (1991, ch. 2).
5  See Arestis and Biefang-Frisancho Mariscal (1997 and 1998) for some empirical support.
6  This section draws on Arestis (1997, ch. 3) where more details may be found.
7  Any trade deficit requires borrowing to finance it, whether in the form of short-term borrowing, long-term borrowing or inward investment, on which interest payments or profits have to be paid. The foreign debt to national income ratio (and hence the interest and other payments relative to national income) will spiral upwards for an initial trade deficit if the rate of interest exceeds the rate of growth of national income: in general we would expect that condition to apply (though there are exceptions and the USA for the past decade appears to have been one).

# References

Arestis, P. (1986), 'Wages and prices in the UK: the post Keynesian view', *Journal of Post Keynesian Economics*, vol. 8, no. 3, 339–358; reprinted in M.C. Sawyer (ed.), *Post-Keynesian Economics*, Cheltenham: Edward Elgar, 1988.

Arestis, P. (1997), *Money, Pricing, Distribution and Economic Integration*, London: Macmillan.

Arestis, P. and Biefang-Frisancho Mariscal, I. (1994), 'Wage determination in the UK: further empirical results using cointegration', *Applied Economics*, vol. 26, 417–424.

Arestis, P. and Biefang-Frisancho Mariscal, I. (1997), 'Conflict, effort and capital stock in UK wage determination', *Empirica*, vol. 24, no. 3, 179–193.

Arestis, P. and Biefang-Frisancho Mariscal, I. (1998), 'Capital shortages and asymmetric reactions as factors in UK long-term unemployment', *Structural Change and Economic Dynamics*, vol. 9, pp. 189–204.

Arestis, P. and Sawyer, M. (1997), 'Reasserting the role of Keynesian policies for the new millennium', Jerome Levy Economics Institute Working Paper and University of East London Working Paper.

Arestis, P. and Sawyer, M. (1998), 'Keynesian policies for the new millennium', *Economic Journal*, vol. 108, no. 1, 181–195.

Arestis, P. and Skott, P. (1993), 'Conflict, wage relativities and hysteresis in UK wage determination', *Journal of Post Keynesian Economics*, vol. 15, no. 3, 365–386.

Cowling, K. (1985), 'Economic obstacles to democracy', in R.C.O. Matthews (ed.), *Economy and Democracy*, London: Macmillan.

Cowling, K. (1987), 'An industrial strategy for Britain', *International Review of Applied Economics*, vol. 1, no. 1, 1–22.

Cowling, K. (1990), 'The strategic approach to economic and industrial policy', in K. Cowling and R. Sugden (eds), *A New Economic Policy for Britain*, Manchester: Manchester University Press.

Dixon, H. and Rankin, N. (1994), 'Imperfect competition and macroeconomics: a survey', *Oxford Economic Papers*, vol. 46, 171–199.

Frank, Robert and Cook, Philip (1995), *The Winner-Take-All Society*, New York: The Free Press.

Kaldor, N. (1970), 'The case for regional policies', *Scottish Journal of Political Economy*, vol. 17, no. 4, 337–348.

Kaldor, N. (1972), 'The irrelevance of equilibrium economics', *Economic Journal*, vol. 82, no. 4, 1237–1255.

Layard, R., Nickell, S. and Jackman, R. (1991), *Unemployment: Macroeconomic Performance and the Labour Market*, Oxford: Oxford University Press.

McCombie, J.S.L. and Thirlwall, A.P. (1997a), 'Economic growth and the balance-of-payments constraint revisited', in P. Arestis, G. Palma and M. Sawyer (eds), *Markets, Unemployment and Economic Policy: Essays in Honour of Geoff Harcourt, vol. 2*, London: Routledge.

McCombie, J.S.L. and Thirlwall, A.P. (1997b), 'The dynamic Harrod foreign trade multiplier and the demand-oriented approach to economic growth: an evaluation', *International Review of Applied Economics*, vol. 11, no. 1, 5–26.

Marris, R. (1972), 'Why economics needs a theory of the firm', *Economic Journal*, vol. 82, 321–352.

Myrdal, G. (1957), *Economic Theory and Underdeveloped Regions*, London: Duckworth.

Rowthorn, R.E. (1999), 'Unemployment, wage bargaining and capital–labour substitution', *Cambridge Journal of Economics*, forthcoming

Sawyer, M. (1982a), *Macroeconomics in Question*, Brighton: Harvester Press.

Sawyer, M. (1982b), 'Collective bargaining, oligopoly and macro economics', *Oxford Economic Papers*, vol. 34, 428–448.

Sawyer, M. (1995), *Unemployment, Imperfect Competition and Macroeconomics*, Aldershot: Edward Elgar.

Sawyer, M. (1997a), 'The NAIRU: a critical appraisal', Jerome Levy Economics Institute Working Paper.

Sawyer, M. (1997b), 'Aggregate demand, investment and the NAIRU', Jerome Levy Economics Institute Working Paper.

Shapiro, C. and Stiglitz, J. (1984), 'Equilibrium unemployment as a worker discipline device', *American Economic Review*, vol. 74, no. 3, 433–444.

Thirwall, A.P. (1979), 'The balance of payments constraint as an explanation of international growth rate differences', *Banca Nazionale del Lavoro Quarterly Review*, vol. 32, no. 128, 45–53.

# Index